Monatshefte Occasional Volume 15

Henry J. Schmidt (1943–1990)

Teaching German
in Twentieth-Century America

Edited by

David P. Benseler
Craig W. Nickisch
Cora Lee Nollendorfs

Published for *Monatshefte*
The University of Wisconsin Press

The University of Wisconsin Press
2537 Daniels Street
Madison, Wisconsin 53718

3 Henrietta Street
London WC2E 8LU, England

1   3   5   4   2

Printed in the United States of America

Library of Congress Cataloging-in-Publication Data
Teaching German in twentieth-century America / edited by
David P. Benseler, Craig W. Nickisch, Cora Lee Nollendorfs.
304 pp.   cm. —(Monatshefte occasional volumes ; no. 15)
Papers first presented at a conference entitled "Shaping forces
in American Germanics: teaching German in twentieth-century America"
at the University of Wisconsin—Madision in September 1996.
Includes bibliographical references and index.
ISBN 0-299-16830-1 (cloth:alk. paper)
1.   German philology—Study and teaching—United States—Congresses.
2.   German philology—Study and teaching—History—20th century—
Congresses.   I.   Benseler, David P.   II.   Nickisch, Craig W.
III.   Nollendorfs, Cora Lee, 1941-   IV.   Series.
PF3068.U6 T42   2001
438'.0071'073—dc21   00-008605

Professor Henry J. Schmidt (1943–1990) served the profession as a gifted Germanist, esteemed colleague, and fast friend. Henry's international reputation stemmed not only from his scholarship, but also from his professional service in a number of capacities entailing great responsibility. As a journal editor, he articulated his early interest in the history of teaching German in America and energized the endeavors leading to this volume and to many of the accomplishments in the field to date. We, and the entire profession, are deeply indebted to Henry as a person of great commitment and great vision. It is an honor for us to dedicate this volume to his memory.

Contents

Preface

Teaching German in twentieth-century America has been a highly problematic undertaking. The challenge it has posed is equaled perhaps only by the challenge posed by an attempt to write the profession's history. After all, American Germanics has become a field which reaches beyond and is influenced from beyond the walls of academe. Numerous aspects of German American cultural and political interaction during this time affected the discipline, its direction, its purpose, and its success. Unsettling events on the world scene have made the twentieth century, for better or for worse, "Germany's century," and the United States came into its own during the same period, partly as a reaction to Germany's undertakings. This resulted in fascinating and frustrating relationships between the two cultures which were reflected in the teaching of German in various American educational systems and settings — from the public and private schools to small liberal arts colleges and large and famous universities. It resulted also in a total redefining of the field: most Germanists no longer teach merely the long and venerable tradition of German "poets and thinkers," but focus on broader aspects of cultural transmission as their goal. This volume sets out to describe these developments.

Günter Grass, the 1999 Nobel Prize Winner for Literature, has observed that any history begins in the middle of things, moving in various directions, but especially backwards and forwards in time, from where it seemed to begin. Germanics in the twentieth century is an example of this, for it is in many ways a product of its past, and at the same time it has set the tone, or at least isolated some of the topics of significance for the coming century.

This volume may certainly claim to take a wide range of the kaleidoscopic topic under observation. Among the offerings here, one finds discussions of negative forces against which American Germanics had to struggle — the national xenophobia against German itself during the First World War, the effects of World War II, and the Holocaust. But other contributions present factors which breathed life and positive change into the field — including the fact that German states were in both the East and the West during the Cold War, the growing presence of women in the profession, the development of women's studies, the Jewish element, technology in support of research and teaching, and so on. As a whole, this collection of contributions seems historical in nature. We note but do not apologize for the fact that the authors are by trade or training neither historians nor detached observers. Rather they are active participants who have been deeply and personally involved in Germanics, scholars therefore whose roles and viewpoints themselves are crucial for an understanding of the field.

An initial foray into the history of Germanics in America—a field of inquiry still in its infancy—was made in an earlier volume of *Monatshefte*'s Occasional Volumes series, *Teaching German in America: Prolegomena to a History* (University of Wisconsin Press, 1988). One significant contribution of this volume is the bibliography of both primary material and relevant secondary material, which reflects the fact that further groundwork has been laid. But other contributions to our field have also been made. We point to the establishment of the Frances Ellis German Textbook Collection at the University of Wisconsin–Madison, whose bibliography was prepared in connection with the 1996 conference, other conferences and studies which have treated some of the facets of our profession's history, and database development such as that encompassing the doctoral dissertations in German, the *DAAD/Monatshefte Directory of German Studies Departments, Programs, and Faculties* (new edition, *Monatshefte/Max Kade Institute Directory of German Studies, 2001*), and the DAAD database of German Studies Syllabi.

We are comforted by the fact that an inquiry into the history of Germanics in America has become a matter of serious concern. However, a great deal of work still needs to be done. In Grass's construct many directions remain in which the writing of the histories of teaching Germanics in America has yet to move. Building on the beginning which has been made, we are now challenged to move forward.

DAVID P. BENSELER
CRAIG W. NICKISCH
CORA LEE NOLLENDORFS

Acknowledgments

The contents of this volume were first presented as papers at a conference entitled "Shaping Forces in American Germanics: Teaching German in Twentieth-Century America" at the University of Wisconsin–Madison in September 1996. The conference was made possible by the generous support of the Deutscher Akademischer Austauschdienst (DAAD), the Anonymous Fund of the University of Wisconsin–Madison, and the Humanistic Foundation at the University of Wisconsin–Madison, as well as Case Western Reserve University, the Department of German at the University of Wisconsin–Madison, the Office of Research at Idaho State University, the Max Kade Institute at the University of Wisconsin–Madison, and the Memorial Library at the University of Wisconsin–Madison.

The editors are grateful to *Monatshefte* for providing financial support which made the publication of this volume possible. And finally, they owe much to the kind patience of each author, as well as to the staff at the University of Wisconsin Press.

Acknowledgments

Teaching German in Twentieth-Century America

How to Read Our Professional Past:
A Modest Proposal

PETER UWE HOHENDAHL

Now that we have experienced the end of the twentieth century and, by the same token, the second millennium, it becomes especially attractive to link the assessment of the present situation in German studies to a broader appraisal of the discipline's achievements during the century. In this situation the search for the future becomes at the same time a search for the past. How did Germanics evolve during the twentieth century? Why did it prosper before 1914, and then find itself beset by problems during the 1920s, then prosper again during the 1950s and 1960s, and then meet difficulties again in the 1970s and 1980s? Confronted with these questions, I cannot resist retelling an old anecdote: When an Englishman, a Frenchman, an American, and a German were asked to write a study about elephants, the Englishman wrote a book entitled "Hunting Elephants in India," the Frenchman's manuscript bore the title "The Love-Life of Elephants," while the American submitted a study entitled "How to Produce Bigger and Better Elephants." The German, finally, wrote an analysis with the title "Versuch einer Einführung in das Leben der Elefanten in vier Bänden." The national stereotypes could not be defined in a more typical and apparent manner. Still, one may ask: what does this little story have to do with the history of German studies in America? The point becomes evident when we compare the response to the present crisis of Germanics both in this country and in Germany. Whereas in the United States most energy has been spent on solving the problems of the present with only occasional glances at historical roots, in Germany the historical assessment of the discipline has received considerably more attention. In fact, during the last decade *Wissenschaftsgeschichte* has blossomed as a separate sub-discipline within *Germanistik*. It is safe to say that at this point among the modern languages the history of the field of German literature and language has been researched and defined more thoroughly than any other.[1] But this astounding amount of research has had, it seems, not much of an impact on the theoretical and institutional advancement of the discipline in Germany. While our pragmatic search for "bigger and better elephants" has focused on the present and left the past to a few hobby historians, the German "Versuch einer Einführung" seems to have been very thorough but less interested in confronting the problems of the day, possibly because there is no general awareness of a crisis at all.[2]

Obviously, our more recent interest in the history of German studies in America has been closely related to the current struggle to keep our discipline alive and vital during a period of budget cuts and the ongoing process of restructuring in the American university. From the point of view of a discipline that no longer has a secure future, at least not in its traditional conception, the past may well take on the form of a ghost that haunts us—a history of missed opportunities, problematic turns, and dead ends. Hence I suspect that most of us, and in particular those who have just begun their careers and cannot find secure jobs, are not in a celebratory mood. Since we must come to realize that within the American university we find ourselves in a rather marginal position, the return to a past when the elephants were bigger and perhaps even better has possibly a nostalgic appeal but does not hold much of a promise for the future.

In spite of the present gloom and doom, I want to argue that we should take the history of our discipline more seriously, not as a collection of isolated facts nor as an edifying narrative, but rather as a map that might help us to orient ourselves in a time when familiar and stable parameters seem to disappear into thin air. My contention is that we do not yet have this map and that previous research has been too incidental, isolated, and haphazard to provide us with pertinent structural information.

Compared with the situation of the 1970s and early 1980s, German studies has made significant advancements in terms of theory and methodology.[3] Today the discipline is much closer to neighboring disciplines than a generation ago. Especially the younger generation has closed the gap between the discourse on German culture and the work that is coming out of English departments or culture studies programs. This change has been achieved mostly at the expense of traditional links to *Germanistik* in Germany that helped to shape the field after World War II.[4] The new emphasis on cultural studies, including film studies, feminism, gay and lesbian studies, and postcolonial studies, among others, has helped to structure research and teaching in the field. In terms of programmatic changes, the struggles of the 1980s for a new paradigm are beginning to pay off. If German studies gets a chance to apply its new tools, the field will be well positioned in the new century.

But that is the crux: we cannot take for granted that the discipline will be helped and encouraged by present university and college administrations. As part of the humanities, German departments have been targeted for downsizing or even elimination. And we all know that the most sophisticated reading of Celan's "Todesfuge" or the most daring reinterpretation of the German canon will not automatically change the minds of administrators looking for savings. From their point of view, small language departments are costly and not productive enough. In other words, quality and sophistication are not a guarantee for institutional success. When we turn for answers to the history of German studies in America, no immediate and obvious response comes to mind except the time-honored advice that the discipline has gone through tough times before and has survived in the face of worse odds.

While the history of German studies does not offer an immediate solution to our present problem, it might well help us to make projections, develop new models, and reassess our present commitments by stepping back and taking the long view. Although our present knowledge of this history is fragmented and incomplete, we can at least draw a provisional map with enough information and enough structure to provide directions for a more systematic and thorough project. I am convinced that such a project is needed; I am less certain, however, that we possess the money and the scholarly resources to carry it out, since we have no organization such as the Deutsche Forschungsgemeinschaft, which has funded the German efforts to explore the history of our discipline in a broad and systematic fashion. We cannot count on the survival of the National Endowment for the Humanities anymore, and even if that organization does survive in future administrations, it is not likely to provide the financial basis for such a major project.

Most important at this point, however, is an extensive discussion of what such a project should look like, about its goals and methods, its theoretical apparatus, and its institutional framework.[5] It seems to me that our efforts to illuminate our disciplinary history have relied somewhat uncritically on the assumption that this history is simply out there and that we can retrieve it simply by going to the archives and studying the facts. Once we introduce the notion that historical presentation relies on methods of construction and that historical narratives are based on rhetorical concepts just as any other form of narrative,[6] we become aware that the task that seemed to be a simple matter of archival research and scholarly rigor has both major epistemological and ideological ramifications. I am talking about the stakes of the project, its purpose, and its functions.

Before addressing these issues, I want to review the present state of research. Since the beginning of more systematic efforts in the 1980s, for instance, in the volume *Teaching German in America* (Benseler et al.), the outline of this history has more clearly emerged. One can distinguish, for example, between the early preprofessional phase of German instruction in the early and mid-nineteenth century,[7] and the institutionalization of Germanics as a professional scholarly discipline in the late nineteenth century (Spuler, "Genesis"; H. J. Schmidt, "Rhetoric") largely under the influence of the German model of *Philologie* (at a time when this model was seriously questioned in Germany itself; see Dainat). The climax of German studies occurred during the early twentieth century, certainly helped by the fact that a high percentage of high school students took German as their first foreign language and also aided by the expansive *Kulturpolitik* of the German Empire.[8] It was a phase in which the national mission that had been an essential part of German *Germanistik* since its inception was transferred to the United States as a special cultural mission of the discipline. In this mission the descendants of the millions of German immigrants played an important role. They were expected both to embody and to represent German idealism. As we know, this dream came to an abrupt end in 1917 when the United States entered the war on the side of the Entente. As the military conflict was systematically carried over into the realm of culture, the general hostility towards things German nearly snuffed out Germanics altogether. Even after the war the institutional setbacks were severe.[9] It is safe to argue that in certain ways German studies have never recovered all or even much of the lost ground.

The actual recovery during the late 1920s and early 1930s was challenged again by the impact of National Socialism after 1933. We are relatively well informed about the response of American *Germanistik* to the ideological onslaught coming from German academic institutions and their specifically fascist assumptions about the nature and quality of German literature and culture.[10] It is surprising, however, that the postwar years, that is, the rebuilding of German studies in the era of the New Criticism, have not received more attention — surprising because, by and large, it has been a success story (see Trommler, *Germanistik* 7–43). Between 1950 and 1965 the mission of American German departments seemed to be clear and unproblematic: based on the teaching of the German language, the task of the German department was to interpret the canon of German literature. It suffices to mention the names of Oskar Seidlin, Heinz Politzer, and possibly the early Egon Schwarz, to characterize the intellectual climate of those years. It is only through recent criticism that the era of the New Criticism, which was very much in synchrony with *werkimmanente Interpretation* in Germany, has come under closer scrutiny.[11] It has been criticized for its blindness towards noncanonical literature and modern mass culture, its bias towards male writers, and its uncritical dependence on a German model of scholarship.

Finally, when we come to the recent past, the 1970s and 1980s, the record becomes even more fragmented. The years of crisis after the fall of the language requirements at American universities seem to be still too much with us, too close for comfort. The assessments of this recent past can best be described as polemical in nature; these events are part of the current debate about the function and task of German studies in this country.

Looking at this record and the scholarship that has built it, it becomes apparent that the historians have, for the most part, dealt with the macro-level, that is, with the history of the discipline in the context of American political and cultural history or in the context of literary criticism in general, in other words, with the formation of theoretical and methodological positions. Some significant work on the institutional aspect of our history has been done, for instance, in the project on oral history, but on the whole this side of our history has not received the attention it deserves. Not even the history of a major professional organization, such as the American Association of Teachers of German (AATG), has been fully explored, not to mention the role of German within the Modern Language Association (MLA), although the archival material is available.[12] What is missing in general is the micro-level, for instance, the way individual departments functioned and changed their institutional practices within the context of the American university. What we obviously need is a kind of *Alltagsgeschichte* in order to reconstruct our past and thereby make sense of our present.

Still, the narrative of lived experiences is clearly not the whole story. Other important dimensions cannot be approached by way of autobiographical statements, interviews, and the like. The history of Germanics would be incomplete without the institutional dimension to which I have already referred. It is around professional organizations such as the AATG, the MLA, and the more recently established German Studies Association (GSA), that the self-understanding of the discipline has crystallized, in such areas, for instance, as its relation to neighboring fields (other languages and literatures in the case of the MLA, and more distant disciplines such as history and political science in the case of the GSA), but also its internal self-definition. The AATG has traditionally emphasized the German language and language instruction as the unquestionable core of the field; the GSA, already responding to the crisis of the 1970s, has focused its attention on problems of interdisciplinarity and cultural studies in the broadest sense. Another significant aspect of this more recent institutional history would be the history of Women in German, an organization that has helped to shape the academic debate on women's studies in this country through its regular meetings and its *WiG Yearbook.* To this list we would have to add more specialized author societies such as the Goethe, Lessing, Heine, and Brecht societies. The work of these organizations has reflected not only fluctuating currents in literary criticism but also in more general ways the changing conception of the German literary canon, an aspect that definitely deserves extensive discussion in the appraisal of German studies. Here we must also mention transformations in the structure of the curriculum, changes which tell us more about our actual practices in German departments than do programmatic statements.

As we can see, the institutional dimension and questions of methodology and theory are more intertwined than conventional conceptions of disciplinary history would have us believe. Still, for analytical purposes we have to conceptualize them as distinct sets of questions and problems. While the history of literary criticism and/or literary theory cannot be defined in strictly national terms, there is certainly room for an analysis of dominant theoretical positions and schools within Germanics, for instance, in comparison with the domain of English or the realm of German in Germany itself. The same would apply to German linguistics and the teaching of language, which have to be placed within the larger context of either a theoretical discipline such as linguistics or a group of modern European languages.

Another dimension that our provisional map should include is, of course, the politics of the discipline, the way German studies has articulated its ideological and professional commitments within the university and vis-à-vis the society at large. I have already mentioned a crucial turning point in the history of American Germanics: World War I is clearly a case where the larger political context called the entire profession into question. The broader question behind such struggles is the social function of the discipline. The recent call for the Americanization of German studies, that is, the claim that the field ought to be seen as distinct from *Germanistik* in Germany, again reflects a specific political notion of the field.

So far I have given a list of elements belonging to a potential map of our history, but not a properly defined and integrated project. My list has a certain random quality, just as there has been a certain random quality about the research done on the history of German studies. As a result, our present map is not only incomplete but also somewhat flat and distorted; it is too much determined by the idea that there must be a single narrative, beginning with the early attempts to provide language instruction and basic information about German literature, and leading up to the latest debate about the legitimacy of cultural studies. The time has come to develop a more sophisticated project that would allow us to look at the links among the various dimensions I mentioned before. But how could this be accomplished? What models and methodologies would be available for this task?

In a recent essay Nikolaus Wegmann made a passionate plea for a history of *Germanistik* from within, by which he means a history based on self-reflection in the tradition of advanced hermeneutics (including Paul de Man). He argues that the application of sociological models borrowed from social theorists such as Niklas Luhmann or Pierre Bourdieu misses the essential quality of self-reflection and thereby turns our history over to the objectifying approach of *Wissenschaftsgeschichte*. While I am sympathetic to the intent of this critique insofar as it wants to rescue this history from the danger of reified objectivism, I am less sympathetic to its potential results. The hermeneutic approach with its strong and almost exclusive emphasis on the literary text tends to isolate the history of the discipline. It leaves us with little awareness that *Germanistik* functions within larger academic institutions which have tended to impose their own agendas on the definition of the field.

With this criticism in mind, I want to introduce two models that have been tried and tested in other disciplines, namely, a version of systems theory in recent German *Wissenschaftsgeschichte* and the model of Bourdieu as applied in recent American studies of the history of English literature. As much as they differ from each other epistemologically, ideologically, and politically, they share a broader understanding of institutional and organizational problems within the profession. A look from the outside is helpful, or even essential, for a critical assessment of the discipline that transcends the dimensions of literary theory.

For the model of systems theory, access to the history of *Germanistik* is defined in terms of internal differentiation. This concept means that *Germanistik* is perceived from the very beginning as part of the philological disciplines, which again are seen as part of the historical disciplines. The historical fields, finally, belong to the system of science *(Wissenschaft)*. To formulate this relationship in more abstract terms: what this model borrows from Luhmann is an insistence on the fundamental difference between system and environment as well as the conception of internal differentiation *(Ausdifferenzierung)* within the system of science, which occurred several times during its development (1800–1880–1930). Distancing himself from the approach of the 1970s, Jürgen Fohrmann ("Von den deutschen Studien") claims that the new model is able to formulate a more comprehensive research project by clearly distinguishing four levels. They are: (1) the level of the social system; (2) the level of method and theory *(literaturwissenschaftliche Ar-*

beitsweisen); (3) methodological self-reflection; and (4) the question of mission and function (*Leistungsbezug der Literaturwissenschaft*). I leave aside the question of whether this program could not have been carried out by the socio-historical model that dominated the 1970s.[13] Instead, what interests me in this context is the question of how this new model translates into actual research projects (which are supposedly superior to older models). While the second and third levels are well-known aspects of the history of scientific disciplines, namely, the history of theories and methodologies, the actual improvement comes to the fore primarily at the level of the interaction between social system and the system of science (which does not follow a base-superstructure model), on the one hand, and at the level of function and mission, on the other. To put it more specifically, the approach of the 1970s, which foregrounded the problem of ideology, was too narrow in its definition of function.

Let me try to translate this abstract language into more comprehensible concrete research projects. I want to begin with questions of organization. When the discipline of Germanics constituted itself in the United States in the late nineteenth century (by and large following the model of German philology), it considered itself almost from the beginning as part of the MLA, that is, a larger organization that brought together under one roof the professionally active teachers of modern languages and literatures. Unlike *Germanistik,* which showed a strong national profile and even tried to transcend its traditional disciplinary boundaries in the so-called Deutschkunde-Bewegung,[14] Germanics, at least partly, foregrounded a common denominator, namely, the teaching of a foreign language and the study of medieval and modern literature. As a result, the discipline has defined its identity in comparison with neighboring modern languages and literatures such as English, French, and Spanish.[15] While Germanics also developed its own professional organizations, it has always seen itself as part of the MLA. The history of this relationship deserves our close attention. My sense is that it has undergone considerable fluctuations between 1887 and 1996.

It was certainly not accidental that Leo Spitzer, when addressing the situation of Germanics in 1945, proposed to reorganize the study and teaching of German literature within the larger framework of European literature (Spitzer). This programmatic call for a comparative approach from a leading scholar of French literature, who had been forced to leave Germany in 1933, emphasized one possible option for German literary studies in the United States. Under the organizational umbrella of the MLA, the study of the German literary tradition loses its specifically national bent, for example, the assumption that this tradition is unique as the articulation of the German spirit and, therefore, particularly valuable. I do not believe that German departments of the 1950s took Spitzer's advice very seriously since they were, as far as I can see, more interested in establishing a strong rapport with German *Germanistik* on the methodological basis of the New Criticism and *Werkimmanenz.* The rapprochement with the other languages in the MLA came much later under the guise of literary theory and/or cultural studies, a process that in the self-reflection of the discipline has taken the form of an "Americanization" of German studies, which emphatically underlines the difference between *Germanistik* in Germany and German studies in this country.[16]

By focusing on the question of organization we would learn a great deal about the changing identity of the discipline. However, the aspect of differentiation vis-à-vis other disciplines has to be complemented by an analysis of the process of differentiation within the German department. What has been the role of language instruction and how have medieval and modern literature/culture functioned as elements of the larger mission of the German department? Until 1970 language instruction was generally seen as the basis of the German program, a concept that was then seriously undermined by the partial or total abolition of the language requirement at the American university.[17] If one includes in our historical research project a concentrated effort to reconstruct the curricula of German departments from the early twentieth century to the present, in other words, a reconstruction of the knowledge that was taught at specific times, we would have a much richer understanding of the development of Germanics as a professional field.

I have stressed the intertwining of knowledge and organization without defining the mode of knowledge that is produced and disseminated by Germanists. In the late nineteenth century American Germanics could adopt the emphasis on a rigorous conceptual apparatus as a prerequisite for a professional discipline from the European and specifically the German discourse, especially in areas such as textual criticism (editions). However, it would apply much less to literary history and language pedagogy — the two fields that were to become the center of German studies in the United States in the first half of the twentieth century. These more amorphous fields offered special opportunities for American teachers and scholars: in the case of language instruction, *Germanistik* did not offer a usable paradigm, and in the case of literary history the task was different, insofar as American Germanists had to address an American audience for whom the German literary canon is not per se an unquestionable value. To put it differently, the national mission of literary history — so firmly established in Germany — could not be taken for granted in the American context.

This raises important questions about the knowledge that professional American Germanists developed and transmitted to their students. Is this knowledge identical to that produced in Germany or is it closer in kind to the knowledge produced by American specialists of French literature? A reconstruction of the curricula does not provide us with an answer, because a curriculum tells us about the objects to be taught but not the knowledge to be gained. We would have to analyze textbooks, literary histories, pedagogical handbooks, and the like, to understand and to characterize the specific kind of knowledge sanctioned by the discipline through its leading representatives. Among other things, one would have to look at programmatic statements about literary history, textual interpretation, and language pedagogy, in order to find out whether the organizational pattern which Germanics used to establish itself as part of the modern languages and literatures is also reflected in the paradigm of knowledge, that is to say, whether we find a comparative approach. Should this not be the case, one would have to explain why organization and knowledge follow different patterns.

An analysis of the specific knowledge that the field of Germanics produced finally leads to a broader question, a question that is once again very much on our agenda. What does the discipline contribute to the larger project of secondary and post-secondary education? This brings up the pressing problem of legitimation that ultimately cannot be answered by referring to the particular achievements of the discipline. The criteria for a persuasive and acceptable answer cannot be defined in terms of the discipline itself; rather, they are imposed from the outside, the system of education or the social system at large—a fact that our project must take into consideration. It means that the history of German studies cannot be written as an isolated phenomenon. As much as we like to think of our discipline as an autonomous field, we have to recognize that from the point of view of the social system it is expected to produce usable knowledge. Of course, this link has been interpreted in strikingly different ways, ranging from strictly utilitarian principles (for example, one has to know the culture of the business partner or the military enemy) to a concept of moral and aesthetic enrichment (in which, of course, the classical literary canon plays an important role). It seems to me that the present debate among social planners veers towards a pragmatic definition of the usefulness of the knowledge produced by language and literature departments.[18] It has to fit the needs of a postindustrial society increasingly determined by advanced electronic media, a society in which the meaning of work is being reconsidered and in which large parts of the labor force will have to be reorganized and retrained.[19] It is also evident that this pragmatic definition is at odds with much of what the discipline thinks about itself and what it teaches. Yet a history of German studies would have to analyze this kind of tension. How has the field dealt with superimposed definitions of useful knowledge and to what extent has it succeeded in providing its own definitions that have been accepted by the social system? Has it simply adapted the definition coming from the outside, or has it developed strategies of opposition and resistance? Has Germanics cooperated with the other modern languages, or has it preferred to stand by itself?

These are also the kind of questions that a student of Bourdieu would ask. Instead of taking the historical narrative for granted, Bourdieu's approach would treat the knowledge produced and disseminated by language and literature departments such as German as "cultural capital," that is, as a socially determined form of knowledge to be invested by social groups. As John Guillory has shown in a thoughtful analysis of the present canon debate, most of its contributors have misunderstood its stakes because they have confused the ideological concepts of that debate with the structural process that has informed the controversial discussion. Hence Guillory identifies the problem in the following manner: "In the case of the literary curriculum, I propose that the problem of what is called canon formation is best understood as a problem in the constitution and the distribution of cultural capital, or, more specifically, a problem of access to the means of literary production and consumption." He wants to shift the analysis from specific questions about inclusion and exclusion or problems of value to institutional issues. Not the canon is ultimately important but the structures of the school and the university, including the ideas they produce to develop a specific literary canon. For Guillory my distinction between internal and external aspects of knowledge, between scientific criteria, on the one hand, and social criteria, on the other, has to be read as class-specific. The moment of class difference and class antagonism, however, does not articulate itself at the level of canon formation; rather, it occurs at a deeper level, namely, at the level of the concept of literature, or culture. This is the reason why the repeated attempts to formulate an American version of the canon of German literature (the most recent attempt by Van Cleve and Willson) have failed to produce lasting results. They kept the concept of literature firmly in place and, therefore, shared with their imagined German opponents the foundational category that enabled the discussion in the first place (Guillory, chap. 1). But it is the category of literature that is at stake in a critical history of our discipline. Hence its historian will have to pay attention to the ways in which this ideological category preoccupied American Germanists during the twentieth century and especially after World War II, when German departments linked up with the pedagogy of the New Criticism.

It is generally acknowledged that New Criticism reformulated the canon of English literature in fundamental ways by setting up a new order of canonical works.[20] Yet not only the literary tradition was remodeled, the radical turn also included a new method of reading and thereby ultimately a different definition of literacy. Similar changes, I believe, occurred in Germanics. But the question of influence is not important in this context. Instead, what has to be explored is the notion of a new center of the discipline, namely, the idea that a specific approach (i.e., close reading) to a selected number of literary texts must be its basis and, therefore, inform all other efforts and projects as well. The consequences for language instruction are apparent: under the hegemony of New Criticism, language teaching becomes a vehicle to prepare students to do close readings of literary text.

The open question is whether there was indeed a consensus about the centrality of literature and literary sensibility in the field of German, as it seems to have existed in English departments during the 1950s and early 1960s (Guillory 137–38). For one thing, the continuing significance of language instruction in the German curriculum with its own methodological and pedagogical traditions may have had a modifying influence. Second, older traditions of literary criticism, among them the history of ideas, may have been more resistant in German than in English (see Viëtor, 1967). And, finally, the opposition between serious literature and mass culture, which underlies the project of the New Criticism, was probably less meaningful in German studies, where the negative Other of the 1950s was fascism and its culture.[21]

If we assume, at least tentatively, that during the two decades after World War II the theoretical and methodological discourse of German studies remained close to the development in English, then we have to explain why this constellation changed in the late 1960s. The key term for the analysis would be theory. From the point of view of French and English, German studies failed to participate in the theoretical turn. Deconstruction, for instance, did not become a major movement in German, and the impact of Foucauldian discourse analysis came rather late. From the point of view of the German tradition, however, the difference appears as a preference for a distinct theoretical configuration in which hermeneutics (Gadamer, Jauss, Iser) and critical theory as a part of Western Marxism (Adorno, Benjamin, Habermas) played a major role.[22] To put it differently, the difference was perceived as a competition or confrontation between theoretical schools (Jameson). Only in the late 1980s does the confrontation begin to break down and make way for the new paradigm of interdisciplinary cultural studies that was again shared with the American mainstream. Obviously, this brief outline of the theoretical discourse in German studies needs refinement, something I cannot do in this context. The crucial question, however, is the following: how do we explain the distance during the seventies and eighties and the rapprochement in the 1990s? What were the institutional forces that moved the discipline in certain directions at certain points?

Let me summarize my argument. During the last 15 years or so the efforts to provide us with a history of American German studies have clearly increased but, by and large, these ventures have been carried out through the isolated research of individual scholars who have done most of the spade work without much help from the profession. Given the growing pressure on the profession from the outside, a more integrated project is necessary, since a reasoned defense of German studies as well as a rational approach to the planning of our future will have to make use of a more complex conception of our past, a past related to, but not identical with that of *Germanistik*. I have suggested that we must shift our focus from a narrative based on events to an analysis of structural problems, particularly those at the micro-level. I see a number of distinct but related research projects that would supply us with a better map of our professional past. One of them would be a study of the German department, its organizational and institutional structure, which we tend to take for granted. A closely related project would focus on the development of curricula and textbooks. In both cases, of course, the professional environment has to be taken into account, that is, the position of the German department within the humanities, the faculty of arts and sciences, and the curricula of neighboring fields, respectively. This brings me to a third, so far largely neglected aspect: the position and role of Germanics within the American university. Again, this is a structural question that tends to elude us because we treat it as self-evident. Beyond this, my emphasis on the German department and the university as the primary sites of our activities does not acknowledge another very important element, that is, professional organizations as the locus for scholarly and pedagogical communications.

So far I have stressed institutional and organizational problems. This is not to say that more traditional questions, such as the history of methodology and theory, should be left out. On the contrary. But they might be treated in a different fashion—and here we can learn from the work of John Guillory. Instead of working out isolated narratives of these issues, the point would be to reconstruct discursive fields which then have to be connected with institutional and organizational questions.

Clearly, each of these research projects is large enough to keep a team of scholars busy for a number of years. And the more archival work they would do the more these projects might grow. At least this has been the experience of our German colleagues doing research on the history of *Germanistik* in Germany. But these problems are not yet our concerns. At this point, I believe, we have to make up our minds as to whether we want to continue to leave the history of our discipline to hobby historians and heroic *Einzelkämpfer* or whether we, as a professional group, are ready to commit energy and funds to a more integrated and systematic effort.

Notes

1 See Fohrmann, *Projekt;* Weimar, Fohrmann & Voßkamp; Hermand, *Kultur im Wiederaufbau.*
2 See also the self-critical volume by Danneberg & Vollhardt.
3 Sander; Reichmann, *Teaching;* Lohnes & Nollendorfs; see also Lützeler; Peck; Seeba; M. Jones; Lennox; Seyhan; Teraoka; Gilman; Adelson; Kaes; Taubneck; and Hohendahl.
4 For the war years see Hatfield and Merrick; for the recent developments see Hohendahl, "Germanisten in den Vereinigten Staaten."
5 For an assessment see Trommler, *Germanistik;* McCarthy & Schneider.
6 For the theoretical context see Hayden White; LaCapra.
7 See Zeydel, "Teaching of German to the Present," "Teaching of German through WWI"; Bottigheimer; T. Frank; König.
8 See vom Bruch; Kloosterhuis.
9 See Deihl; Moore; Luebke; C. L. Nollendorfs.
10 See Pentlin "Effect," "German Teachers' Reaction"; Salloch.
11 See Lentricchia; Jancovich.
12 See the years 1884–1926 of the *Proceedings of the Modern Language Association of America;* for 1884–1892 see *Proceedings of the Modern Language Association of America* (Baltimore: Furst); for the years 1893–1926 see "Proceedings of the Modern Language Association of America," Suppl. of the *Publications of the Modern Language Association of America* (1884–1921, Baltimore: Furst; 1922–present, Wisconsin: Banta).
13 See for example Kolbe, *Ansichten* and *Neue Ansichten;* Mecklenburg & Müller; Hohendahl, "Germanistik als Gegenstand."
14 See Peper; Hofstaetter.

15 For English see Graff.
16 A good example would be Weiner.
17 For a response see V. Nollendorfs, "German Studies"; Reichmann, "German Culture Studies"; Gittleman.
18 For a cultural assessment see Kramsch, *New Directions.*
19 Useem; Moulakis.
20 See Graff; Guillory, chap. 3.
21 Hermand; Horkheimer; Adorno; Grimm & Hermand.
22 See Holub, *Reception Theory;* Hohendahl, *Reappraisal.*

The Ideology of American Germanics:
An Aspect of Its History of Perennial Isolation

ARTHUR TILO ALT

Germanics in the United States has always had to contend with a nationalistic heritage, its Romantic legacy, and its *völkisch* distortions. Its golden age coincided with the period of maximum expansion and ideological assertiveness of the nineteenth-century nation-state in the Western world. In times of mutual tolerance between the United States and German lands, it could flourish in an atmosphere of friendly good will of each toward the other's culture. The seeds of good will and tolerance, however, could not grow in the contaminated soil of unenlightened self-interest and nationalism and quickly mutated into their opposite of hostility and isolation. Therefore, one saw the sharp decline in the popularity of German after the Revolutionary War, because of the Hessian and Hanoverian mercenaries, and again after the outbreak of the First World War. In order to develop the theme of this essay, it is necessary to sketch in certain historical data relating to the rise and decline of Germanics in the United States prior to and immediately following World War I.

The professors at the newly established German departments in America at the turn of the century were of different ethnic backgrounds, with those of German ancestry (who were bilingual) and German immigrants making up the majority. To focus briefly on the career of a "minority" Germanist of the time in order to highlight the attractiveness of the field to Anglo-Americans, let us consider the case of Marion Dexter Learned, dialectologist at the University of Pennsylvania. He hailed from Delaware. Not until his tenure at a private day school in Dover, Delaware, did he come into contact with the German language. It was the period of the founding of Johns Hopkins University and the initial influence of the German educational system on the American. Three teachers at the academy (day school) had either studied in Germany, were interested in Kant's philosophy, or spoke German at home (Bosse 399). This exposure provided the impetus for Learned to become interested in the Germans in Pennsylvania and the Pennsylvania Dutch dialect. After an orientation tour through Lancaster county, the home ground of the Amish, he decided to make German philology his life's work. He continued his Pennsylvania German dialect studies in the early 1880s at Johns Hopkins where he, along with like-minded fellow students, established a German club. In his courses German was the means of communication, and in order to prepare himself for a near total immersion in German, he roomed with a German family in Baltimore, Maryland. Later in his academic career, beginning in 1884, he attended the University of Leipzig. In an account of those years, he writes:

> Jetzt erntete ich die Früchte meines Fleißes, da ich von Anfang an jedes Wort verstehen und sämtliche Vorlesungen im Hörsaal belegen konnte. Und nun trank ich mit vollen Zügen aus dem Brunnen der Wissenschaft, nach dem ich so lange gedürstet. Ich geizte nicht mit dem Belegen der Vorlesungen . . . . Jetzt erst wurde mir die wahre Aufgabe der Wissenschaft klar und ich erkannte den eigentlichen Zweck und die einzige Methode im Studium von Literatur und Sprache, die den höchsten Ausdruck nationalen Lebens bilden. Der große Reichtum deutscher Kultur, der sich in deutscher Architektur, deutscher Kunst, deutscher Musik und im deutschen Drama offenbart, verbunden mit der Einfachheit deutschen Lebens, all das erregte Empfindungen in mir, die mich begeistert ausrufen ließen: "Es ist eine Lust zu leben." Das war meine Welt, das war mein Volk, das ich gewissermaßen wiedergefunden hatte nach jahrhundertlanger Trennung: und es ist wahrlich nicht zu verwundern, daß ich damals das wurde, was ich heute noch bin, nämlich ein Yankee-German. (Bosse 400)

The high point of this passage culminating in the Ulrich von Hutten quotation ("juvat vivere"), the rose-colored glasses through which he views the world of German culture and national life at the time, show a level of affinity with German life and thought which is probably necessary if one wishes to succeed in a field like a national philology that is not one's own.

Learned's enthusiasm contrasts sharply with certain negative attitudes and behaviors toward Germany and German cultural politics that were to emerge in the first decade of the twentieth century. They were fueled by a combination of factors, not the least of which was the absence of democratic institutions in Germany and German cultural politics based on ethnocentrism and an ideology of pan-Germanism. These circumstances, as we shall see, also led to the beginning of the isolation of Germanics. As early as 1903, in his inaugural speech on the occasion of the opening of the Germanic Museum in Cambridge, Massachusetts, Carl Schurz expressed his concern about emerging hostile attitudes: "To my mind there is nothing more abominable, nothing more hideous, nothing more criminal than the reckless goadiness of nation against nation for the purpose of disturbing their friendship and peaceful intercourse . . ." (Bosse 407). Schurz was alluding to the British press that had begun to vent its feelings of frustration and enmity toward Germany, and thereby contribute to a negative influence on the American image of Germany. Only ten years later, Americans were routinely referring to Germans as militarists and "Huns" — an allusion to the Kaiser's notorious speech in which he indicated that Germany might descend on its foes as had Attila the Hun on his. In the same year (1903) the Vereinigten Deutschen Gesellschaften der Stadt New York disseminated a pamphlet which urged that area schools should offer German language instruction not only for practical, commercial reasons, but also because German is the language of science and ". . . weil von allen europäischen Sprachen

Deutsch, die Mutter des Englischen, nach dem Englischen die verbreiteste ist und gegenwärtig von etwa 100 Millionen . . . geschrieben und gesprochen wird . . ." (Cronau 365). This pamphlet was intended as a protest against efforts to replace German with other subjects in the curricula of the city schools. Aside from the dubious but widespread view that German was "the mother of English" we should note that attempts were made by German immigrants as well as Germany itself to achieve bilingualism among ethnic Germans through bilingual instruction in the schools. As will be remembered, for a period during and after World War I, it was not permitted to use any language of instruction other than English in many of the nation's public schools (Gilbert 165).

Nevertheless, around 1908, one million out of a total of 15 million students at secondary schools in America were enrolled in German language courses. Three influential books on the subject of Germans in the United States in general and the issue of bilingualism in particular owe their existence to a contest which was launched in Chicago in 1904 under the aegis of the German Consul General. Georg von Bosse, a German clergyman in Philadelphia, Rudolf Cronau, and Albert Faust were the winners of the three prizes awarded by the contest. Bosse's and Cronau's monographs seek to promote good relations between the home in the old and the home in the new world. Both also acknowledge the right of the adopted country to demand that its new citizens be familiar with its language and culture. Nevertheless, the writers of both books view Germany as a homogeneous ethnic unit and urge that the pride of German Americans in their German heritage be strengthened and that Germany view America as a close relative like England. In addition, the second edition of Cronau's work, which appeared in 1924, attempts to put the blame for the war on Britain and to explain away the United States' involvement as the result of warmongering and propaganda. The work by Faust is the only one of the three written in English. Published in New York, it was intended primarily as a reference work on the subject of the German political, moral, social, and educational influences on the United States and has remained one of the standard works on the subject.

All hopeful developments in Germanics came to naught with the outbreak of the First World War. As is well known, the war was the most devastating blow to the study of foreign languages in the history of the United States, going far beyond a mere setback for German. Kuno Francke's 20 volumes of English translations of German literary works, which appeared in 1914, was to be the last important event in the history of Germanics in the United States. The German language which, for all intents and purposes, had enjoyed the status of a second unofficial language in the country, because it was a required subject in the country's schools, at this point became an outcast. Until America's entry into the war in 1917, it was normal for college students to enroll in advanced German courses, since they had already received instruction in the language prior to college. In 1890 there were more than 800 daily and weekly German-language newspapers in the country. In 1910 more than nine million Americans (11 percent of the population) spoke German as their mother tongue. German was far and away the leading foreign language in the country's schools (Sammons, "Die amerikanische Germanistik" 106). But there was a drop in student enrollments in German in all American public and private schools, from an all-time high of 28 percent in 1915 to an unprecedented, catastrophic low of 1.1 percent at the end of the war (Hugo Schmidt 3). The Germanic Museum had to close its doors in 1917 and did not reopen them until 1922. During the war many German Americans were arrested, telephones were tapped, and whoever spoke German was suspected of espionage. According to one account, excessive zeal by the military forced even the Amish to strip in midwinter and to put on the uniforms that were placed before them unless they wanted to freeze to death (Sammons, "Die amerikanische Germanistik" 107). The fact that their religious beliefs forbade military service did not matter. Germans and Germany were linked to Prussian militarism and barbarism as part of a new chapter in the book of American demonology.[1] America had, sadly, come full circle since John Quincy Adams's very positive reports about Prussia, written prior to his presidency, when he served as U.S. ambassador there, and about Baron von Steuben's lasting contributions to the training of Washington's army.

The year 1917 not only dealt a blow to Germanics but also caused the loss of a whole generation of Germanists. Only the exiles from Germany of the 1930s and the importation of Germanists from Germany in the 1950s and 1960s could plug the hole and bring Germanics up to the level of like disciplines in teaching and research (Sammons, "Die amerikanische Germanistik" 110).

Recovery from the events of 1917 began gradually, and German classes in secondary schools and colleges resumed; German enrollments had sustained a loss of nearly 96 percent (Sammons, "Die amerikanische Germanistik" 108)! The American Association of Teachers of German was not founded until 1927, however, even though the Association of Teachers of German in Pennsylvania had been established in 1898 with the ultimate intention of establishing a national union of teachers of German (Spuler, *Germanistik* 49). It was clear to the founders of the AATG that they had to convince their fellow citizens that it is not unpatriotic to learn and teach German as one of the more important languages of Western culture and that to produce ever more highly educated Americans is, after all, a higher form of patriotism. The disruptive force of the First World War is also evident from the original publication dates of the four most important and traditional scholarly journals in Germanics: the hopeful beginning made with the publication of the first "German issue" of *Modern Language Notes* (Johns Hopkins University Press) and *Monatshefte* (University of Wisconsin Press) in 1886 and 1899 respectively is not carried any further until 1925 and 1927, when the first issues of *Germanic Review* (Columbia University Press) and the *German Quarterly* (AATG) were published.[2]

Not only the vagaries of diplomatic history impinged on German, however. Because of its Romantic heritage, Germanics bore the burden of isolation from European Enlightenment or, if you please, the shunting aside or even betrayal of the unfinished Enlightenment project in Germany, which led to national unification without democratic representation in the new nation's political institutions. Hence, the fundamental character of the field, the volatility built into the concept of a nation state, and the "accident of history" forced Germanics into a state of periodic if not constant academic and public isolation. The penalty to be paid was severe: its proponents and practitioners were put on the defensive and, what is worse, ignored. It may be argued that a national philology and literature in an alien context—be it in the academy or in the school system generally—faces the threat of isolation and disinterest. However, German since the end of the First World War has been in a special bind that separated it from other major European languages.

America's policy regarding minorities and hence its attitude toward the teaching and tolerance of foreign languages has always hinged on its equivocation on the question of a public policy of assimilation versus the securing and safeguarding of minority rights. However, there never was any doubt about the thrust of Germany's cultural politics. Wilhelm II's ethnocentric and nationalistic policies found their outlet in the Allgemeiner Deutscher Sprachverein (founded in 1885) and its journal *Muttersprache* established in 1886. Issues of language and Weltanschauung—especially their extensions as racism, anti-Semitism, and ethnocentrism—finally came to a head in the policies of the Third Reich, when such prominent scholars as Friedrich Kluge, Alfred Götze, and Otto Behagel defended linguistic purism generally and in the case of Götze also racial purification of language in *Muttersprache* (Polenz 89ff.). The pan-Germanic ideas and ethnocentric policies of the pre–World War I era continued unabated, albeit underground. Thus, in addition to the Sprachverein and *Muttersprache,* the Deutsches Ausland-Institut [*sic*], which had been founded in 1917 to counteract British and French anti-German propaganda, continued to thrive in the 1920s. To be sure, it had by then become primarily a research institution of dialectology whose purpose was to study the practice and theory of German language and culture abroad. Certain notions, however, that were connected with the most important contingent of German ethnicity abroad, namely in the United States, had become firmly entrenched because of the nationalistic tenets of *Germanistik.* The essential unity of the Germans had already been defined metapolitically in the works of Gottfried Herder, Friedrich Schiller, and Johann Gottlieb Fichte in terms of "die reine deutsche Sprache, unvermischtes Deutsch" (Lämmert 25). The notion of the prophetic truth of a poetic work, the idea of the poet as genius, and the resultant cult of originality in the humanities during the 1920s (the pursuit of "Geisteswissenschaft" by *Germanistik*) are a part of the background of this ethnic essentialism underlying certain assumptions by the members of the Ausland-Institut. Jacob Grimm's definition of a Germanist "als ein[er], der sich deutscher Wissenschaft ergibt . . ." —and he calls it "eine schöne Benennung" —is a generous determination of the field but remains tied to the Romantic notion of poesy as the real source of the national spirit. His idea was inspired by the Romantic aesthetic of prose and poetry (*Dichtung*) as "aller Wissenschaften Wissenschaften," as was his specific conclusion: "ein echter deutscher Dichter könnte sich gefallen lassen, Germanist zu heißen ..." (Lämmert 26). Finally, this Herderian and Grimmian Romantic legacy of an all-encompassing Germanics, which included such diverse subjects as pre-Germanic evidence for historical linguistics, poetics, Germanic antiquity, and German literature, was to evolve toward a national ethic, according to Wilhelm Scherer. When these various areas of knowledge began to evolve into disciplines in their own right, the newly founded Germanistenverband (1912) demanded a program whereby German intellectual life with the help of an all-encompassing *Germanistik* could be firmly based on "völkische Grundlagen." This impulse then no longer represented a theoretical paradigm but a shift toward ideology, advocated openly (Lämmert 26f.).

The Romantic as well as *völkisch* background of Germanics just described made the discipline vulnerable to the blandishments of German fascism. It may also account for the fact that numerous obscure and some prominent Germanists supported the Third Reich in the mistaken belief that their hopes for the field and the nation coincided with the aims of national socialism (Polenz 90; Lämmert 23f.). This collaboration was made easy in part because after 1933 the concept of language as the unifying substance of nationhood could easily be blended with the concept of race and militarism. The Nazis, however, merely used the linguistic purists, as they had other nationalist circles, to help solidify their dictatorship.

> Die Wegbereiter wurden zu freiwilligen Mitläufern. Sie sahen nun die Stunde gekommen, in der ihre alten, von Generationen ererbten "vaterländischen" Ziele von der mächtigen rechtsradikalen Bewegung verwirklicht würden. Die stark irrationale Art des in der Geschichte zuspätgekommenen, noch nicht mit Demokratie verbundenen und deshalb unbefriedigten deutschen Nationalgefühls machte sie empfänglich für den Mythos vom "Dritten Reich," aber blind gegenüber den wahren Zielen und Methoden einer totalen Diktatur des Massenzeitalters. Man konnte sich damals in diesen Kreisen nicht vorstellen, daß die Reinigung der deutschen Sprache gar nicht zu den eigentlichen Absichten der Nationalsozialisten gehörte. Und doch war es so. Von ... Hitler und Goebbels ist niemals eine Aufforderung zur Sprachreinigung ergangen. (Polenz 97)

Something similar occurred regarding the Deutsches Ausland-Institut (DAI). The policies of imperial Germany regarding Germanness and bilingualism to promote continuing dual identity and thus loyalty to the fatherland were perpetuated by the DAI under the Nazis. It was officially designated as a private research organization, while in reality it served as an arm of Heinrich Himmler's Amt für Erneuerung des deutschen Volkstums, the "Auslandsorganisation" of the NSDAP and Joachim von Ribbentrop's foreign office. The DAI was to deliver scholarly studies that could serve as a basis of foreign policy, specifically with regard to the United States and its ethnic Germans. One aim of the institute was to create a strong sense of unity among German Americans and to promote the rights of ethnic groups such as the Germans. The unity of all ethnic Germans regardless of citizenship was one of the explicit planks of the Nazi party platform (Smith 24). Outside of its significance as an anthropological distinction, ethnicity has been a part of the vocabulary of nationalist ideologues and politicians to foster divided loyalties.[3]

All of this affected Germanics, because of its dependence on the mastery of German as a prerequisite for further study and research. Linguistic politics in the American context is a difficult subject. As is well known, World War II produced a much more rational response to the foreign language question than World War I, at least officially. Earlier in this period American Germanists expressed the opinion that language learning and literary criticism were not ideological and quite separate from any question of national allegiance. As will be remembered, there was indeed no interruption in the college curricula and in German research activities. The professional journals continued to appear throughout the war years, and the names of prominent American Germanists, including those of some refugees from Germany, are represented regularly in the issues between 1941 and 1945. There are clear signs that German faculty members adapted to the times and also sought to stem the threat of declining enrollments by offering courses in military German for American soldiers. For example, in the March 1942 issue of the *German Quarterly* Professor John Frederick of Northwestern University pleaded his case by warning not to repeat the mistakes of 1917 by turning one's back on the languages and cultures of the enemies (he avoids naming Germany, Italy, and Japan), and he urges that one should take comfort in such works as Goethe's *Faust,* a new translation of which had recently appeared. Besides, there were practical reasons as well to continue teaching German and Japanese: No one could predict America's future role in the reconstruction of the world, and a knowledge of foreign languages would be indispensable (Frederick 71f.).[4]

Just as Middlebury College in Vermont before World War I promoted a program of "total immersion" to learn a foreign language, so did the Army Language School in Monterey, California. In 1943 the Office of Censorship announced in an issue of *Monatshefte* that the U.S. Post Office needed censors "to read international mail written in those languages [German, Spanish, Italian, Japanese] . . ." (95). As mentioned above, the federal government initiated the Army Specialized Training Program (ASTP) in the context of which Germanists—among others—lectured to soldiers about German literature. As early as the beginning of 1944, the prominent German scholar Bayard Quincy Morgan of Stanford University published a six-point program concerning foreign language instruction after the war, entitled "After the War: A Blueprint for Action." The points were practical, intended to assure continuity and, above all, to promote foreign languages as something that matters but which can by no means be taken for granted.

This describes fairly well the state of affairs in Germanics in the United States since its inception, the initial enthusiasm, occasional chauvinism in connection with the Romantic-*völkisch* heritage, and imperial cultural politics notwithstanding. Whether justified or not, it would appear that German Germanists, reacting to the prevailing influence of indigenous Marxist criticism in Germany during the late 1960s and the 1970s, were eager to point to certain virtues that foreign Germanists are presumed to possess. Thus, Eberhard Lämmert at the Germanistentag held in Munich in 1966 urged that *Germanistik* be as unpretentious as its foreign counterpart. Friedrich Sengle in 1980, for example, praised American Germanics for being practical, factually accurate and free from pretentious jargon. Such positive reaction, however, does not alter the fact that American Germanists seek self-definition and have experienced serious crises concerning the role and significance of their field in a country that is at best indifferent to the cultural legacy of foreign countries, especially toward that of a former enemy. This put Germanics after the disaster of 1917, between the wars, immediately after the Second World War in a special bind regarding the nationwide rebuilding of the discipline (Spuler, *Germanistik* 11ff.).

After World War II there were almost immediate efforts at reestablishing ties between *Germanisitik* and Germanics. For example, Otto Springer (University of Pennsylvania), "used the few spare moments of a military assignment in Germany last summer [1945] to gather information concerning the fate of scholars, libraries, book-dealers, and publishers, and also concerning scholarly publications which appeared during the years 1940 to 1945 in Germany, all within the scope of Germanic philology . . . ." He reported the destruction of buildings and collections and also the rescue of valuable objects such as the interior furnishings of the gutted Goethe Haus and Goethe Museum in Frankfurt. The German professors he visited (mostly prominent members of the profession) had all been very productive during the war years. Many of them were again at work and not impeded by the postwar chaos in the country—including Alfred Götze in Giessen, who continued working on *Trübners Deutsches Wörterbuch* (Springer 177, 179). Of course, Springer's odyssey also implied considerable concern for the profession at home, since, obviously, American Germanists depended heavily on German source material (especially in the area of historical linguistics or "philology" as Springer calls it), despite impressive collections of Germanica at some prominent American university libraries.[5]

The February issue of *Monatshefte* (1946) contains a brief statement by Leo Baeck, formerly chief rabbi of Germany's Jewish congregations, that Germany should be encouraged to become a democracy and to excise the tumor of Nazism (114f.). The Holocaust continues to cast shadows over the field, and the negative legacy will, along with demographics and pressures of assimilation, keep the number of students in German small in comparison with other European languages, especially Spanish. The attacks on the "canon" of German literature, feminism, the elevation of minority cultures to equal status in the traditional Western cultural context, and declining enrollments have all conspired to transform the traditional concept of Germanics into a broad concept of German studies that regards the "aesthetic privileging" of a German text (as distinct from the traditional assumption of its fictionality as belles lettres) as merely one limited approach of several to it. Any claim about its structural integrity, that is, that it possesses an identifiable core, is rejected. Thus, theoretically at least, a work by Goethe has no more claim to importance than that by someone else. What is more important, however: with the advent of interdisciplinarity, German has emerged from the isolation in which it has found itself since 1917, as it now has the opportunity to reinvent itself as an interdisciplinary subject not unlike other foreign languages and the humanities in general. Its marginal status as a national literature outside of academe and vis-à-vis other major European languages and their literatures inside the academy may indeed have come to an end through its contextualization as a European language and culture (Sammons, "The Tragicall Historie" 32). There may be other questions that need to be raised concerning European languages generally (excepting Spanish perhaps) that have to do with identity and self-definition in an age of mass culture and ostensible egalitarianism. This time, however, to ask "what is German" or "ein Volk" and to be, say, an "oppositional critic" in the sense of Edward Said and the late Henry Schmidt may not only extricate Germanics from the gridlock of irrelevance but, at long last, also enable it to add its distinct register to a large chorus of voices.[6]

Notes

1 The official dissolution of the state of Prussia in 1947 was the fulfillment of a deep-scated American desire.
2 To this list must be added the early versions of *Monatshefte* dating back to 1870, *Americana Germanica* (1897), and *Journal of American Philology* (1897) (Spuler, *Germanistik* 49).
3 The DAI's specialist for America was the dialectologist Heinz Kloss, who was actively involved in promoting Nazi policies regarding ethnic Germans in the United States; see his books listed in the bibliography below (Arthur Smith 26, 39). At a meeting of German dialectologists at the University of Texas (Austin) in 1968, Kloss continued to promote bilingual instruction for the "needs of the state" which take precedence over the "interests of the individual" (Gilbert 177). It would appear that this is still the same ideology of Germanness or of divided loyalties, except that it no longer represents German government policy.
4 Professor Frederick at that time was "Professor of Modern Letters" at Northwestern University's School of Journalism.
5 Examples include the Yale University Library with its holdings of the archives of the Kurt Wolff Verlag, the Baroque collection of Faber du Faur, Harvard's Heine manuscripts, Hofmannsthal's literary estate as well as Beer-Hoffmann's, the Harold Jantz collection of Americana and Baroque literature at Duke University, and the Thomas Mann autographs at Princeton University, to name a few.
6 Jacob Grimm addressing the first congress of Germanists in Frankfurt in 1846 answered his own rhetorical question "was ist ein Volk?" by pointing to the fact that a nation is a

nation because it speaks the same language. Language as a distinguishing and unifying factor had already acquired a metapolitical significance in German lands that harked back to Herder and Fichte, who believed that "unvermischtes Deutsch" distinguishes a German from all other nationals (Lämmert 24f.). For a discussion of Germanics in the United States in recent years, see also Ziolkowski's "St. Hesse," 23.

Recovering the History of Germanics in the United States: An Exploration

FRANK TROMMLER

Stunned by the devastating military and ideological confrontations between the United States and Germany in two world wars, contemporaries have often wondered about the relatively steady course of German departments in American universities during the twentieth century. Insiders have seldom failed to respond with the objection that, on the contrary, the terrible events of 1917–18 and 1941–45 have cost the discipline of German (Germanics, Germanistics, *Germanistik*) dearly, both in terms of student interest and intellectual input in the academy. What has gone virtually unmentioned is a casualty of a different order: the loss of a sense of professional history with which traditions are evoked and present achievements and shortcomings are put into focus. To be sure, academics, accustomed to taking their discipline for granted, rarely inquire about the conditions under which their predecessors built institutional structures and conducted everyday business. Germanists, in particular, had special reasons to let the demons of the past rest. Yet whereas the balance sheet of Germanics in the upheavals of the twentieth century is open to debate, the lack of historical reflection allows some to infer a sense of security that is not only misleading, given the challenges to the discipline in recent years, but also unhelpful in determining the severity of the challenges. With the current interest in disciplinary histories—*Fach-* or *Wissenschaftsgeschichte*—a new, less filiopietistic and defensive look at the continuities before and after 1917 seems warranted.

The pre–World War I history was, of course, never completely forgotten. It was, however, usually transferred and connected to the mythology of the once-important Germans in America, a legendary age in which things German acquired a respected place in the Anglo-based American universe, until they were kicked out of it in the heat of nationalism during World War I. While the year 1917, in which the two countries engaged in war, loomed large as the moment of the fall from grace, to be regained with happier times never, little thought was given to the fact that the continuous presence of Germanics at universities in the twentieth century owed to these times at least as much as to the ever-renewed needs for knowledge of the other language and culture. In fact, one might say that the ascent of German as a discipline of scholarly study in America had been so strongly linked to the transformation of the college into a full-fledged research university, that the elimination of the discipline would have raised doubts about the scholarly mission of these institutions. While size and nature of German programs were always determined by changing educational needs, their academic legitimacy continued to derive from the concept of the multidisciplinary academy which had come into its own in the second half of the nineteenth century.

Writing the history of American Germanics means exploring these twists and turns of educational needs and institutional developments during the political climate changes in the twentieth century. The underlying academic continuity, however, can only be grasped through a thorough reflection on the conditions under which the professionalization of the discipline took place. The period between 1850 and 1900 not only holds the key to understanding the limited role of German studies for the American public—by documenting that it was not always so confined—but also to comprehending the importance of the philological orientation which extended much beyond German, encompassing the modern languages in their successful fight to replace the classical languages as the backbone of the liberal arts education. It was in this period that modern language teaching emancipated itself from the instructional confinements of Latin and Greek. At this time the definition of the discipline, in order to legitimize itself against the scientific assertions of classical philology, was formulated largely as that of a modern philology, embracing the claim that the study of language leads right into a culture's origins and development.

At the end of the twentieth century, when the teaching of foreign languages is less and less supported by the traditional liberal arts agenda according to which a foreign language belongs in well-rounded education, it might help to trace this agenda back to its origins and to illuminate the steps that led to the academic study of German. As the discussions dwell increasingly on matters of relevance and usefulness at the expense of the educational and scholarly rationale, arguments for foreign languages become part of a broader reflection of the university's mission. After 100 years of phenomenal growth, the American research university as an institution of educational, professional, and scientific advancement has obviously reached a plateau where its rationale has itself become open to debate. The fortune of German which was settled in the 1880s with the establishment of graduate studies in the major universities, is again linked to the changes in the self-definition of the academy. In these changes of the 1990s many features which contributed to growth are being dismissed. Foreign language study, once a symbol for the transformation of the old-fashioned, Latin- and religion-based college into an outward-looking, scientifically minded university, has lost its weight in the new transformations. In response, one needs to demonstrate that maintaining the dialogue with foreign cultures as an ingredient of education and not just as a matter of downloading information represents a vital contribution to the survival of the university as an institution of intellectual advancement.

Establishing German as an Academic Subject

Looking as a literary historian at the years between 1850 and 1900, one can easily discern the difference between the history of Germanics in America and *Germanistik* in Germany, Austria, and Switzerland. To be sure, there is a clearly delineated history of teaching German in schools, colleges, and universities, comparable to the history of *Deutschunterricht,* as outlined by Horst Joachim Frank in his pathfinding work on German-speaking countries (Frank; Benseler et al.). In fact, the history of German instruction in America has been one of the more popular topics of research; it might be mentioned that the two outstanding early works also carry a government imprimatur: Louis Viereck's *German Instruction in American Schools,* first published in 1900 (Viereck), and Charles Handschin's *The Teaching of Modern Languages in the United States,* which appeared in 1913 (Handschin). In contrast, there is only a gingerly treated history of the academic discipline, seen either through the lenses of local antiquarianism or those of World War I experiences. Its spirit is still encased in archives and libraries, ready to be rediscovered, though it will hardly result in voluminous narratives as in the case of the *Wissenschaftsgeschichte der Germanistik im 19. Jahrhundert* (Fohrmann & Voßkamp). Furthermore, one feature makes the history of the discipline in America not only different from that in German-speaking areas but also from its development in other countries like England, France, or Italy, where German was studied as a foreign language: the fact that German was brought in and used by the nation's second-largest immigrant group shaped America's communication with German-speaking countries as well as the public discourse within the United States on German language and culture.

Still another factor, probably the most important one, made the American development different. It concerns the different place and function of the university in German lands and in the United States during the nineteenth century. The German university, after its reform in Prussia, took center stage in the organization of knowledge and assumed an increasingly prestigious and publicly influential stature, whereas the American college and the small group of universities were clearly on the sidelines of the intellectual discourse. At a time when 10,000 American students decided to leave the country in order to study a variety of subjects at German universities and returned not just with a diploma, an M.A. or a Ph.D., but also with the cachet of having been at the center of professional learning and scientific progress, there was little doubt about the difference between the academic standing of the universities in the two countries (Herget; Jarausch). As long as the college, "controlled by the classicists and religionists,"[1] set the tone of academic pursuits, there was little room for academics to engage in debates of national issues that went beyond religion, education, and history (Marsden 99–112). Manifestations of public commitment with such far-reaching political symbolism as the protest of the "Göttingen Seven" in 1837, the "Germanistentag" of 1846, and the "Parliament of the Professors" in Frankfurt's Paulskirche in 1848–49 were not within the purview of the college professor. In the American democracy with its local constituencies, party orientation, and free press, the public agenda was set by other forces. Universities clearly did not function as *Vordenker* as they did in Germany (Langewiesche).

Given this difference, it makes little sense to treat the growing interest in the study of German or Germanics in the nineteenth century like the institutionalization of *Germanistik* in Germany. In this period, the part of German culture that Americans considered accessible for a broader audience was music, the part for the literary or intellectual minds was philosophy (Pochmann 257–323, 639–76). German literature played a lesser role and was considered less accessible and relevant than English and French literature, although Goethe, Schiller, Lessing, and a few other authors received increasing attention as relevant to modern education (Pochmann 327–47). Thus, the institutionalization of German which began to take shape after 1850 and even more fully after the Civil War, was primarily directed toward the instruction of the language, the study of its structure and, prominently in the 1880s and 1890s, philology. Its academic success which went beyond the enhancement of language and literature studies, was based on a combination of two intentions, first the desire of a growing clientèle to gain access, through German, to advanced knowledge and to the scientific debates of the time, and second the wish to transmit, through the study of philology, a deeper perception of the roots of culture and human behavior. In the words of Daniel C. Gilman, the founding president of Johns Hopkins University: "In the study of humanity and history, language is the master-key which unlocks all doors." Gilman reflected on the needs of the research university: "In these days, when so much that is new and important first appears in German or French, no system of education can be called liberal, as it has well been said, which does not include those tongues" (D. Gilman 173). Gilman made sure that the study of philology was represented at Johns Hopkins after its founding in 1876, as did other university presidents such as Henry P. Tappan at the University of Michigan and Andrew D. White at Cornell (Pochmann 310f.), who promoted the study of German and French as an insurance policy for the progressive spirit in newly established graduate programs.

Even at this stage, however, Germanics was not always the discipline which American students chose when they intended to engage in German thinking and writing. As mentioned before, they took philosophy, German philosophy, often in a combination with courses in literature, especially Goethe and the Romantics. This choice represented an unusual involvement with intellectual trends of the foreign culture. It enhanced the standing of the American university, as it demonstrated the fact that one did not have to go to Göttingen, Berlin, Heidelberg, or Leipzig in order to receive a full-fledged academic education in one of the crucial fields of the humanities. The flip side of this policy of academic self-empowerment revealed itself in the initial eagerness of departments to come close to the German "original." This was, more often than not, the rule for graduate programs in German after 1880, but it does not necessarily hold true for other programs in the newly established graduate schools. Gilman was careful in signaling that although Johns Hopkins took certain structures from the German research university (especially in medicine), it did not attempt to copy it. Johns Hopkins, Clark University, and the University of Chicago, the newly founded private research universities of this period, pursued different strategies in adopting the German combination of research and instruction (*Forschung und Lehre*).

This development characterized the later years of the period 1850–1900, and led, at the turn of the century, to a network of German departments with full-fledged programs in language, philology, and literature, representing an enormous increase in prestige compared with earlier decades. For many contemporaries, this increase in prestige constituted the real achievement in a society that valued practical work and business activities much higher than intellectual pursuits. Crucial was, of course, the hard-fought understanding that the university should become the conduit to the much heralded progress. Of further importance was the professionalization of what was considered academic work which, in the case of modern language teaching, helped elevate a lowly activity to a (somewhat) respected occupation. In his 1913 report on the teaching of modern languages, Charles Handschin found it "within the memory of men still living" that "the modern languages, once unwelcomed upstarts in the college curriculum, attained such a standing that the graduate schools began organizing the scientific study of these subjects on a parity with the other research studies leading to the doctor's degree" (Handschin 20). Handschin adds that the case of French was strongly advanced by the founding of L'Alliance Française in 1883, a national organization established for the purpose of extending the French language in the colonies of France and in foreign lands. A comparable push for German had earlier been the result of Germany's unification in 1871 and the increasing scientific and commercial ties with the emerging Empire. Competition between the different languages notwithstanding, this professionalization was a combined effort, culminating in the founding of the Modern Language Association, whose first charge was to offer vigorous competition to the classical-language offerings in higher education.

And then again, a study just of these transformations in academe would not account for the fact that for the longest time the relevant intellectual engagement with things German took shape outside of the universities. The most illustrious example of this are the Transcendentalists in the 1830s and 1840s. What Ralph Waldo Emerson, Margaret Fuller, Henry David Thoreau, Henry Wadsworth Longfellow, and others pursued in their engagement with German writers and philosophers, with Goethe, Schiller, and the Romantics, was not academic stocktaking but rather the creation of a genuinely American movement in the realm of letters inspired by the other culture. In this period the momentum of learning and discussing German lay with writers and dilettantes of the best caliber. Aside from personal encounters and written exchanges, the forum for this intellectual fermentation was the journal. The printed medium served as a kind of universal college, making the foreign culture accessible while creating an American culture.

The preponderance of the journal is well documented in two dissertations written at the University of Wisconsin under the guidance of Alexander R. Hohlfeld, Scott H. Goodnight's thesis of 1905, *German Literature in American Magazines prior to 1846,* and Martin H. Haertel's thesis of 1906, *German Literature in American Magazines 1846 to 1880.* The two Wisconsin Germanists took the year 1846 as a caesura between the enthusiastic cult of German letters, especially in New England, and a "normalization" of the literary interest of Americans in the middle of the century, followed by a period of decreased interest between 1854 and 1868 (Haertel 287–98). They identified a change in emphasis in American journals and magazines from general information about German life and culture before 1850 to a more focussed discussion of literature thereafter, and they excluded broader agenda from their studies.

A fascinating and not yet fully explored chapter concerns how in the period between 1850 and 1900 a different medium—different from the culturally oriented magazines—emerged as the main forum for the encounter with German life, culture, and politics: the fast-growing press of the Forty-Eighters, the politically active refugees from the failed Revolution of 1848–49. This daily, weekly, and monthly press had as its main audience the expanding communities of German Americans and was written mostly in German. Yet many of the political immigrants soon extended their public base in their struggle for freedom and social justice and moved into mainstream American publications and political networks, among them Carl Schurz, Franz Siegel, and Karl Heinzen, who became influential voices in the fights leading to Lincoln's presidency and the Civil War. Assuming "an important role in American politics" (Bergquist 139; Arndt), the strength of the German American press lay in its broad base among German Americans and their increasing involvement in the life of their new home country. However, the press remained a strong bridge to German-speaking countries and served as a catalyst for a critical approach to these once-so-distant lands that was different from the older approach when poets and thinkers or the unpolitical and mostly uneducated German immigrants had been the only links across the Atlantic.

While most historians of the German American press have been eager to show the extent of its involvement in American affairs—proving its integrative nature—the cultural and intellectual bridge-building has received much less attention. Between 1850 and 1890 several hundred newspapers and regular publications provided not only a sentimental reminder of the old country but also a discourse on contemporary Germany. This function became particularly relevant after Germany's unification, with repercussions in the non–German-speaking American public. When in 1853 the *New York Staatszeitung* remarked that the new immigrants "transplanted German science and enterprise" to America (Wittke, *Refugees* 314), it did not imply that thereafter these things were lost to Germany. The fact that the circulation of the paper surpassed the 50,000 mark in the 1870s also reflected the prestige of the newly founded *Reich,* at least among speakers of German, in the United States.

Historians have failed to use adequately the German American press as a source of information about developments in Germany. This perspective would have lessened their dependence on the idiosyncratic *Reichsideologie* with which Prussian advocates like Heinrich von Treitschke shaped the discourse even of their liberal opponents in Germany. One incident might illustrate what this outsider's view could mean for the overall view of Germany. When the German engineer Franz Reuleaux, in his famous letters from the Centennial Exhibition in Philadelphia in 1876, caused a scandal in the new *Reich* by pointing to the shoddy quality of German products, he referred to the German Americans as the most outspoken critics. Reuleaux explained:

> For years German-Americans have talked about the achievements which the reborn, strengthened Germany would bring to light; with pride they prophesied how their former fatherland would frequently surpass if not even outdo the other nations. And now none of that, rather the opposite, has happened, and therefore our embarrassed former friends have become our embittered adversaries and critics. Yet maybe they are indirectly our friends insofar as they publicly present to Germany the mirror which its friends in Europe so often tried to hold up in a small circle without being believed. (Reuleaux 4)

In view of such public attention and debate, one is hardly tempted to look for a more intensive engagement with contemporary Germany in the rather inward-looking colleges. In other words, for those who wanted to engage in a more substantive study of Germany and did not have the opportunity to visit the country or meet eyewitnesses of its recent developments, newspapers and other publications provided the classroom. It was a nonacademic kind of German studies which kept a strong presence after the institutionalization of graduate studies in the universities.

German as Part of the MLA Culture

It seems unwise, at this stage of historical inquiry, to separate the academic from the nonacademic study of German during the nineteenth century. There was seldom more than the occasional instructor or professor of German. Even when Amherst, Cornell, and Pennsylvania put more resources into this area of instruction in the 1870s, they did so largely in reaction to the initiatives of individuals like Bayard Taylor at Cornell, whose translation of *Faust* became the standard text in the late nineteenth century, John Genung at Amherst, or Oswald Seidensticker at Pennsylvania. A century earlier, between 1754 and 1775, William Cremer had made the study of German "highly popular" (Handschin 32) in the University of Pennsylvania, followed by Johann Friedrich Kunze from Halle, who conducted the study of classics in German, and Justus Heinrich Christian Helmuth, who was named professor of German and oriental languages in 1792 (Cheyney 132f.). When Karl Follen, appointed as professor of church history and ethics, instituted the teaching of German at Harvard College in 1825, it was understood as a breakthrough of sorts and may have left a legacy in academe of more significance that can be ascertained at this stage of research.

What can be documented, though, are the frustrations among German teachers and members of the German American communities concerning the shortcomings of the college. Karl Follen himself gave expression to these frustrations when he wrote the first memorandum for the founding of a German American university. Such an educational institution, comprising all branches of human knowledge under a democratic constitution, would serve, as he asserted, as the center for the Germans in their intellectual pursuits and as a crucial resource for America in its ambitious mission of becoming a model community for all mankind (Follen 74). Follen's memorandum was lost,[2] but similar programs were drafted in subsequent decades, based on pertinent criticism of the educational system. A German American congress of about forty delegates in Pittsburgh in 1837 called for a reform of the educational system and the founding of a German university, as did Forty-Eighters such as Friedrich Kapp and Karl Heinzen in the 1850s and 1860s. As captivating as the idea was for German American leaders and teachers, it did not lead to a consensus between the education-minded and the pioneer-minded members of the community. The "conflict between the enthusiastic guardianship of the traditions of abstract thinking and aesthetic culture and the necessary materialism and practical turn of economic beginning" was too hard to resolve; it showed, "if anything, the fluctuation, under the vicissitudes of peripheral existence, in the conception and appreciation of 'culture' " (Maurer 525). The only tangible result of the Pittsburgh meeting was the establishment of a teachers' seminary which, though not in its initial form, came into being as the National German-American Teachers' Seminary in Milwaukee in 1878. The concept of this seminary as the backbone of German instruction in America became one of the few rallying points of the scattered and heterogeneous groups of German Americans. Though an important center for conceptualizing and training pedagogy, it never exerted leadership in the academic study of German.

And yet, what did leadership mean in this endeavor? Was it exercised by those who had read Wilhelm Scherer's positivistic history of German literature and translated its findings into cursory histories in English? Or by those who had not been blessed by philology and Scherer's positivism and exercised their freedom of interpretation in a direct encounter with literary texts? Or those who wrote textbooks that capitalized on the institutional requirement of German language learning? The institutionalization of graduate studies in the 1880s was obviously important not just as a step towards professionalization of the field but also towards a division of identity between "American" life and "German" culture. The more German the departments appeared, the more authentic appeared their claim of contributing to American higher learning. An important reason for their orientation toward, even imitation of, departments of *Germanistik* in Germany was their intention to prevent American students from going abroad, giving them instead what they needed for advanced study of philology and literature on this side of the Atlantic. The features that later contributed to the isolation of German departments were, at this time, beneficial to the academy. Few professors, however, proceeded like Marion Dexter Learned at the University of Pennsylvania. He not only maintained a rigorous graduate program of philological and literary training in the German style but also legitimized the study of German American language and literature and an investigation of their contributions to the development of a genuinely American higher culture.

The rise of Germanics reflected clearly the delicate relationship between German scientific scholarship and the ambition of building the American research university. The philological orientation in which German had taken the lead helped transform French and English programs into academic disciplines. And yet, this development would hardly have been so successful, had it not been for the founding of the Modern Language Association (MLA) in 1883, which provided an action forum for the common interests with French and English programs. The MLA, initially strongly oriented toward pedagogy as the legitimizing common endeavor, provided a professional umbrella under which the confrontation of modern languages with the classical languages was mounted in public. Germanists like W. T. Hewett (Hewett) and Julius Goebel, a cofounder of the Modern Language Notes at Johns Hopkins, played leading roles in this confrontation, for which the battles between classicists and modern philologists in Germany provided much ammunition. The decisive impulse had come from the address, "The College Fetish," in which Charles Francis Adams attacked the usurpation of education by languages no longer spoken (Emerson ix–xiv). When times became rough for Germanists, especially during World War I and during the Nazi regime in Germany and World War II, the umbrella still provided a measure of professional protection and continuity for the study of language and literature. The MLA was not just a lobbying organization; with its journal, *Publications of the Modern Language Association,* and its annual conference, it offered more than a forum of internal exchange across the disciplines and institutions. It contributed to a cross-cultural academic identity between America and Europe.

The importance of the developments between the 1880s and World War I for the relatively steady course of Germanics in the twentieth century is strongly linked to its integration in the MLA culture of literary studies, something that is less easy to define 100 years later when European cultures have lost their privileged position and literary cross-references are being less and less understood. This MLA culture was still a reality in 1944, at the height of the war against Germany, when a professor of Germanics, the distinguished Luther scholar Robert Herndon Fife of Columbia University, served as president of the organization and presented at the annual conference a spirited keynote address on "Nationalism and Scholarship," better called an appraisal of America's intellectual debt to Europe. It was coupled with a friendly reminder that American scholars should find their own ways of asserting their prowess.

This MLA culture was, of course, a culture of elite literacy, a thinly veiled academic patriarchy whose funeral bell rang in the 1960s and 1970s, giving way to a more democratic concept of professional citizenship based on full participation of women and minorities. Any reference to the protective features of the older MLA culture cannot overlook the long-lasting marginalization of women on the university level, in contrast to their increasing integration on the school level. The German notion of the university professor's far-reaching authority reinforced existing concepts of male superiority in the academy. It confirmed the social conservatism regarding women's suffrage that prevailed among most German Americans and found expression in their press, even when their editors propagated liberal politics (Stuecher 19). At its core, the agenda of *Bildung,* which was to enrich the university curriculum with texts of German classical authors, contained little that transcended the submissive role of women as the guardians of cultural tradition in ethnic communities.

An important exception was Karl Heinzen, the Forty-Eighter, who lost many friends over his stern and unrelenting dictum that women were, and had to be recognized as, the equals of men in status, rights, privilege, and potential. In *Deutsche Schnellpost* and *Janus,* Heinzen complimented the few German women, like Mathilde Franziska Anneke, Mathilde F. Wendt, and Marie Blöde, who dared to challenge the special privileges of the German male (Wittke, *Against* 219f.). And yet, Therese Robinson reflected the prevailing attitudes when she had her German American heroine of the novel *The Exiles* rebuff an American matron's inquiry as to her opinion on a linguistic point with the words: "I have no opinion about it . . . we German women leave such learned investigations to our philologists." [3] These philologists, as was to be expected, did little to make the study of language and literature particularly appealing to women.[4]

The negative effects of gendering both the profession and the professionalism between university and school levels have taken their toll in the foreign languages as well as in the humanities in general. At the same time, it would be misleading to categorize the import of European notions of academic professionalism as antimodern. It clearly had features that helped break up the unquestioned authority of the "classicists and religionists" in the colleges, opening the profession to those who were building their identity on scientific advancement and disciplinary innovation. American students who experienced the stimulating exchange between professors, their students, and assistants in labs and seminars in Germany, became staunch supporters of German *Fachmenschentum* and increasingly scorned the dilettante as teacher. "There was a stern moral overtone to specialization," the sociologist Edward Shils has stated in his assessment of the growth of the American university. "It meant no trifling, no self-indulgence, getting on with the job. It was uncongenial to false pride and all-knowingness. Specialization was quite consistent with the secularized Protestant Puritanism of the quarter [*sic*] of the century which preceded the First World War" (Shils 186). In Shils's account, learning from Germany meant less accumulation of scientific information than acquiring an academic code of behavior that allowed younger scholars to advance because of their specialized work. This change in attitude met with strong resistance on the part of college teachers, but it was clearly an important step in the modernization of the university.[5]

Shils emphasizes that specialization in this period was still linked, in a reflection of German *Bildung,* to a broad grasp of philosophy and literature. Despite the praise of the specialist which was rampant in Germany, young Americans were in awe of the breadth of reading of German professors:

> William James' description of Dilthey in one of his letters home in 1867 spoke for the thousands who came after him. Many of the young Americans themselves had already read with omnivorous zeal before they went to Germany; they had already studied modern literature and classics as well as scientific subjects. In Germany they sometimes became intoxicated with reading, not just in their own subjects but over a wide range. The aftermath of religious doubt deepened their philosophical interests. In later years many of those who had studied in Germany retained their knowledge of German. (Shils 186)

Viewed through this lens, the ascent of German language proficiency—though often only reading proficiency—as a sign, even status symbol of a good education in the decades before World War I is hardly surprising. Advocating the replacement of Greek by German as the premier measure of higher education was widespread. William Cranston Lawton's article in the *Atlantic Monthly,* "A Substitute for Greek" (Lawton), received, of course, applause on the part of German teachers (Stern). One should not forget that this was the period of a general trend toward cultural hierarchies in the United States (Levine), where German musical culture was at the pinnacle of its success. After its founding in 1883, for example, the Metropolitan Opera in New York presented all operas in German, at least for a while.

Lawton, in his advocacy of German as the "chief instrument of utterance for the most advanced specialists in many fields of research" (Lawton 808), added that this predominance would wane. He estimated its duration as "three generations of the incoming century." One might detect in this admittedly vague time frame the approximate duration of the high standing of German in the academy: barely surviving the devastating blow of World War I, yet somewhat renewed with the influx of academic refugees from Hitler's Germany, and finally giving way after World War II.

A century after Lawton's prediction the tables have indeed turned. In German universities English is about to set the standards of academic literacy. The question is whether this change goes beyond the instrumentalization of the other idiom as postulated in the late nineteenth century. In order to give a pertinent answer, one would have to account for the transformation of the cultural elitism of that period to our culture of information, where accessibility itself reshapes the function of language.

Traditions of Germanics and German Studies

The fact that German literature, except for the period of the Transcendentalists, never caught on as much as English and French literature in the American public, puts a question mark behind the success story of German science and the related ascent of German in the academy. Looking at the most often used literary texts in American classrooms reveals a pattern that helps understand the limited appeal. When Henry Remak, the comparatist and Germanist, came to Indiana University as a refugee from Nazi Germany in the 1930s, the most often used (and commented) texts were Theodor Storm's *Immensee,* Friedrich Gerstäcker's *Germelshausen,* and Paul Heyse's *L'Arrabiata,* three staples from the nineteenth century. Of these Handschin already mentioned *Immensee* and *L'Arrabiata* as the most popular school texts in 1913 (Remak 176; Handschin 61f.). Remak underscores the traditionalism in the curriculum which also included Hermann Sudermann's *Frau Sorge* and *Fritzchen* with the remark: "For Hauptmann the time had not yet come in the classroom" (Remak 176). Although Hauptmann had been the topic of dissertations in departments before World War I, the curriculum in literature had maintained the taste for idyllic "storiettes," as Handschin called them, for a stale and isolated romanticism, "entirely lacking in the virility of modern Germany" (Handschin 61). Handschin's comments, directed toward high school instruction, seem to have applied also to the offerings in the college. This interpretation is corroborated by Remak's statement that in 1936 "Hebbel and Storm were the last German authors about whom one would dare offer a course" (Remak 176).

These random samples will have to be checked against more thorough statistical material which some departments or college libraries still have available. Whether graduate studies which encompassed a broader canon of literary works really transcended the spirit of idyllic withdrawal and classicist exemplification characteristic of school and college texts is open to debate.[6] The 750 dissertations on literature between 1873 and 1949 surveyed by Ralph Rosenberg in his 1955 study reflect the adherence to established names, themes, periods, and methods, from the Old High and Middle High German periods (*Nibelungenlied,* Gottfried, Wolfram, and Hartmann most frequently) to Humanism, Baroque, and the Enlightenment, with 15 dissertations on Lessing, 16 on Herder, 25 on Schiller, and 82 on Goethe (R. P. Rosenberg 39f.). The figures for later authors are Tieck (12), Heine (16), Kleist (12), Grillparzer (15), Hebbel (22), Wagner (10), Keller (12), Fontane (8), Storm (6), Hauptmann (22), Hofmannsthal (4), Schnitzler (5), George (2), Rilke (4). "Even though Thomas Mann (6) is the darling of the American intellectual," Rosenberg added, "and Americans by and large accept him as the lode star of German culture, he does not enjoy anywhere near the interest of the doctoral candidate as does Hauptmann. Hermann Hesse (1) and Kafka (0) are neglected figures also, even though the latter has been enjoying a popular American vogue at the present" (R. P. Rosenberg 40). This picture changed drastically, of course, in the 1960s and 1970s, when twentieth-century and contemporary authors began to dominate courses and dissertation topics.

A more unusual feature of the statistics which differs also from those in Germany during this period pertains to the large number of comparative topics, with interesting titles in Anglo-German and Franco-German literary relations. This orientation increased certainly during the two wars. At Wisconsin, Alexander Hohlfeld initiated the "Wisconsin Project on Anglo-German Literary Relations" during World War I, an exemplary and successful model of revamping the German program "as a combination of comparative literature studies, reception of German literature in America, and Anglo-German literary relations" (Hohlfeld, "Address" 197). The 1940s saw new initiatives toward rethinking the discipline in connection with comparative literature, most prominently formulated by Leo Spitzer against Karl Viëtor in 1945 (Trommler, *Germanistik* 23f.).

Only a few departments made an effort to encourage studies in German American literary relations as well as language and literature of the German Americans. At the University of Pennsylvania Oswald Seidensticker, son of a famous liberal of the Göttingen revolt of 1830, and Marion Dexter Learned made the department a center for such studies (with 13 dissertations in this field, according to Rosenberg); at Cornell A. B. Faust, who wrote the first dissertation about German American literature at Johns Hopkins in 1892—on the novelist Charles Sealsfield—pursued his studies for the pathfinding two-volume study, *The German Element in the United States with Special Reference to its Political, Moral, Social, and Educational Influence* (1909); Wisconsin with Hohlfeld and Harvard with Kuno Francke encouraged such studies. Overall, however, Germanists preferred to keep a distance from German American subjects, afraid to mix the hard-won academic distinction with the humdrum status of the ethnic community.

By tabulating the 750 dissertations in literature and 200 in philology as part of the 2,500 dissertations on social, political, philosophical, and aesthetic aspects of Germanic cultures, Rosenberg outlined a context that nowadays would be considered an ideal foundation for German Studies. It might be too early to draw broader conclusions, but it seems that few connections existed among these academic fields. As every discipline struggled for its legitimate place in the academy, developing its own ethos and sense of mastery—History as well as Philosophy, Sociology as well as Germanics—interdisciplinarity was not ranked highly or even identified as an academic concept. The pendulum still swung away from an institutionalized cross-disciplinary outlook that was perhaps the nonacademic practice in the nineteenth century.

The real challenge to the efforts of legitimizing Germanics lay somewhere else: in the increasing tension between the interpretation of Germanness in language and literature and that of sober philological and literary analysis as practiced in the other modern language fields. In the course of World War I this tension tore apart many departments, even many Germanists who tried to adhere to both positions since both positions provided a sense of righteousness, if not professional identity

(Schmidt, "Rhetoric"). While much attention has been directed toward the vogue of nationalism—for which the American nationalism, as the overriding phenomenon, still needs a broader analysis—not enough thought has been given to the links to what I have called the MLA culture, the explicitly textual or philological exploration of literature within the context of the assumed transatlantic culture. It was within the institutionalized communication of the Modern Language Association that Germanists developed their brand of sober literary exegesis which has characterized most of American Germanics since World War I, while seminar rooms in German universities were filling up with more flamboyant but foggy *Geistesgeschichte* and, later, with *völkische Literaturwissenschaft*. The scholarly achievements of Germanists like Walter Silz, Ernst Feise, Harold Jantz, Hermann Weigand, or Stuart Atkins—of which their sense of intellectual accountability is still the most important—are more closely linked to the achievements of their colleagues in English and French than to those of their colleagues in German universities.

This should help in the reflection of the place that German studies—nowadays: German Studies—has been promoted to occupy at a time when philology has lost its importance and literature is losing appeal both as an aesthetic creation and as a conduit to another culture. As the study of German culture increasingly integrates social, political, philosophical, and historical aspects in the reading of literature and, moreover, relegates academic mastery to interdisciplinary curricula, German Studies appears as a balancing, even saving tool for many departments. In view of the isolating tendencies which characterized academic disciplines since the late nineteenth century, it is hardly surprising to find out that German Studies in its twofold agenda of contextualizing literature and analyzing German-speaking countries in a multidisciplinary way has its own tradition. It originated in the beginning of the twentieth century as an initial response to the lack of engagement with the lively features of contemporary Germany. Handschin, again, provides an example with his demand that the student of German be given a sizable amount of "easy, diversified reading" and a textbook "containing real German anecdotes, written by Germans, about historic persons, places, and events as well as descriptions of the Germany of today, its forests, mountains, the love of its people for outdoor life; its customs, geography, people; its amusements, music festivals; its schools, churches, and government" (Handschin 62). Alas, such a reader did not exist (a fact which has its own historical reasons), and the hope was that an increase in direct contacts with Germans and Germany would help the understanding of the country. In this period when 23.8 percent of teachers of German were natives of Germany—while 11.4 percent of the teachers of French were natives of France (Handschin 50)—the direct encounter with Germany did indeed become more common through exchanges of professors and teachers as well as group and individual visits.[7] At Columbia, at a time when Harvard had the foremost department in Germanics, the Germanistic Society of America set a model for a broader, livelier approach to the study of German culture.[8] Kuno Francke's extended efforts toward establishing the Germanic Museum at Harvard were meant to provide a focus for the actual, physical experience of German art and culture.

Considering the speed with which the two countries were drifting apart in the period before World War I (Trommler, "Inventing"), one might overlook the innovative spirit of these ventures. They were designed to introduce, on an academic level, a variety of direct encounters with the foreign culture that helped contextualize the study of literature and language and, thus, make it more attractive. Nonetheless, when the Germanist Camillo von Klenze, in his 1915 address on the future of German culture in America, surveyed the success of these endeavors, he was rather critical. He asserted that the German departments had not done enough for the understanding of contemporary Germany. He criticized the German Americans for their failure to provide financial support to German departments which, consequently, did not attract enough graduate students (Klenze, *Zukunft*). In his critique, Klenze, a strong advocate of Germany's politics, also revealed, involuntarily, the vulnerable side of this kind of German Studies: its dependence on the political climate and the supply of teaching materials from Germany, which raised the suspicion that the academic study was a rather thinly veiled political promotion of the foreign country. In retrospect, one can now point to the period of National Socialism in Germany and understand the suspicion of this kind of "comprehensive" study of present-day Germany as justified. In challenging periods of international confrontation, therefore, language and literature instruction remained a more reliable core of departmental activities. While the appeal of German Studies has existed for a long time and can with some justification be viewed as part of a new strategy of reinvigorating the discipline, one must not overlook the more vulnerable side of this approach to Germany and its culture.

By invoking these features, this historical exploration has returned to the point of departure: that the loss of disciplinary memory needs to be overcome in order to arrive at a realistic assessment of available strategies for the survival of Germanics in the United States. The understanding of the time before 1917 might help in this assessment, not least because it opens up an unexpected and fascinating chapter of American life and history.

Notes

1   Cowley and Williams (139) point to Oxford and Cambridge, but the phrase is similarly applicable to the American college of the nineteenth century.
2   It resurfaced in the Geheimes Staatsarchiv Berlin. See "Vorbemerkung" des Herausgebers [Julius Goebel] (Follen 56).
3   Cited from Stuecher 21.

4   See, however, the overall positive assessment of the German impact on the education of women in the United States in Albisetti.

5   An excellent comparison of German and American academic codes and structures can be found in Liebersohn. For more about German support for "Impersonalism" see Cowley 148.

6   First assessments in Spuler, *Germanistik;* Benseler et al.

7   Handschin (58) mentions "a recently established interchange of secondary teachers between the U.S. and Prussia," organized by the Carnegie Foundation for the Advancement of Teaching.

8   The German historian Karl Lamprecht, who became influential with his innovative concept of cultural history, visited Columbia for an extended period of time. For a reaction see Kern.

The Roles of History and Public Policy in Shaping Germanics

THEODORE ZIOLKOWSKI

Dedicated to the memory of Victor Lange
(13 July 1908–29 June 1996)

In March 1897, Harvard University announced a fundraising campaign to establish a Germanic Museum for the study of "the most important monuments of Germanic civilization." Such an institution, the appeal concluded, would be "a worthy monument to the genius of a people which has had a large part in shaping the ideals of modern life and which has given to this country millions of devoted citizens" (Viereck 681). The proposal was greeted with widespread enthusiasm, although each constituency had its own interests in mind. The German ambassador to the United States, Baron von Holleben, was quick to appreciate its usefulness for shaping public opinion and in March 1899 delivered a luncheon speech in Cambridge to further what he termed "the noble object." "The creation of such an institution must needs be, to far wider circles, the source of an abundance of suggestions and intellectual impulses in the interest of the German language and German ideals" (Viereck 682). Von Holleben's conjecture turned out to be accurate: his visit to Harvard soon produced invitations—and propaganda opportunities—to several other leading universities, including Chicago, Johns Hopkins, and Columbia. On the same occasion Professor Kuno Francke confessed a more narrowly professional aim: "If we succeed in forming an institution that will bear the proper relation to teachers, there is no doubt but that in a few years Harvard will be the chief seat and central point of Germanic studies in America. That is what we have in mind" (Viereck 683). The trustee members of the visiting committee added another dimension: "Three of us . . . are of German extraction, and the others, as do all Anglo-Saxons, belong to the large Germanic race . . . . Through our race relationship the committee hopes to interest Americans in this project, and I hope that the German Americans of Boston will take a special interest in demonstrating the art and practical methods of the Fatherland to the American students of the most prominent universities" (Viereck 684).

Thanks to a gift from Kaiser Wilhelm II—in reciprocation for the honorary doctor of laws awarded in 1902 to Prince Heinrich of Prussia—of casts of German sculptural monuments from the Middle Ages and Renaissance, the museum was able to open in 1903. Other gifts — from the King of Saxony, the city of Nuremberg, a citizens committee in Berlin, and private donors in the United States — included reproductions of works of German goldsmiths and silversmiths from the fifteenth through the eighteenth century as well as 10,000 books on the history of German civilization. Support from the brewery magnate Adolphus Busch of St. Louis and his son-in-law, Hugo Reisinger of New York, made possible the construction of a building to house the collection, which was completed and dedicated in 1921.[1]

However, the luncheon speeches in 1899 had already adumbrated the three goals that the new institution was intended to meet: the political goal of cementing German American diplomatic relations; the academic goal of furthering German studies in what was supposed to become the leading department in the United States; and the cultural goal of sponsoring pride among German Americans and cementing their bonds to the Fatherland.

It is tempting for students of institutional iconography to look for symbolism in the history of the Busch-Reisinger Museum. Established at the turn of the century as a testimony to the stature of German culture in the United States, the museum has in the past two decades been almost wholly dismantled, its contents distributed across the Harvard campus, and the building itself modernized into a well-endowed Center for European Studies. It currently houses, in addition, the author of the most widely publicized anti-German work in recent memory: Daniel Goldhagen's *Hitler's Willing Executioners,* which has resurrected the long discredited notion of "collective guilt" to indict the Germans as a people. It is tempting to see in this transformation from temple to tribunal, in this subsumption of German within European, an image of our discipline. After all, we seem to have fallen on hard times. Since the much-heralded *Jahrhundertwende,* when every fourth high school student studied German,[2] when nine million German-speaking American citizens read 800 German-language newspapers, when college students flocked to Europe to acquire degrees from German universities, German enrollments in high schools have plummeted to under 3 percent, there are only three German-language daily newspapers in the country,[3] and Germany ranks sixth — after England, France, Spain, Italy, and Mexico — as the destination for U.S. students studying abroad (T. Davis).[4] As for the German American heritage, even in North Dakota, in towns named Bismarck, Berlin, and New Leipzig and where half the residents are descended from German immigrants, high school students of Spanish outnumber those learning German by six to one.[5]

But rather than succumbing to the fashionable sense of anxiety and crisis that has informed many of the recent colloquia and volumes on the history, the current state, and the future of our field, it is perhaps more productive to ask by what process we got from there to here: from a Germanics that regarded itself as an advocate of the glories of German culture — Kuno Francke's title was Professor of the History of German Culture, and he designated his well-known *Social History of German Literature* (1896) as "a study in the history of civilization" — to a German

Studies that sees as its principal responsibility the unmasking of hidden tendencies in that culture that led to Hitler, National Socialism, and the death camps, not to mention the repression of women, minorities, and homosexuals; from a conception of German that embraced according to Francke all political, social, intellectual, and artistic phenomena of German history (2) to a German Studies that foregrounds theory, film, popular culture, and *Exilforschung*. In response to the collective soul-searching of our discipline, the past two decades have produced a stream of books and articles dealing with aspects and stages of that development. But when I read those often valuable contributions I feel uncomfortable because the picture of our profession that emerges does not coincide with the field as I have known it for the past 45 years. There is often another way of looking at the same material. This essay examines four problems that have produced a distorted view of our field and its history: the prevailing image of a fin-de-siècle Golden Age of German studies; the effects of the two world wars; the perspective that sees German studies as essentially an *Emigrantendisziplin* and ignores the uniquely American contribution to the field; and the narrowly national viewpoint that tends to regard our field in isolation from neighboring fields.

How Golden Was the Golden Age?

The facts of the nineteenth-century American Germanophilia are too familiar to be rehearsed here in detail. The infatuation of the New England Transcendentalists with German idealism, and in particular Goethe, is legendary (Braun; Walz; Spuler, *Germanistik*). Americans welcomed the creation of the new German state in 1870–71 with enthusiasm for a variety of reasons: Prussia had supported the Union during the Civil War; the unification of Germany was viewed as analogous to the unification of the United States following the Civil War (indeed, Americans often compared the Civil War to the Prussian wars of 1864, 1866, and 1870–71); post–Civil War Americans were impressed by the liberal ideas of such Forty-Eighters as Carl Schurz, who were active abolitionists and advocates of social reform; and the two countries, having come late to industrialization, were both rapidly emerging as powerful economic states in the late nineteenth century (Schieber ix, 3–37; Herbst 10). The founding of Johns Hopkins in 1876 signaled the broad adoption of the German system of higher education, and in particular the seminar method, as the model for American graduate schools (Berelson 6–16; Veysey 158–73). We know about the 9,000 students who flocked to Germany to obtain their doctorates in fields ranging from mining to medicine, from law, theology, and science to the humanities and social sciences.[6] Gustav Mahler is simply one among a distinguished cohort of conductors who advanced the esteem of German music in the United States (Rippley, *German-Americans* 129–43).

But by 1900 the midcentury enchantment was rapidly diminishing if not already vanished. The stream of students heading for Germany slowed dramatically following a peak of 517 in 1895–96 (Veysey 130); moreover, after 1870 the proportions had shifted significantly as students of science, law, and theology began to stay at home in the rapidly improving American institutions, leaving Germany to a growing number of social scientists and humanists. This latter increase was due in no small measure to the fact that many German provincial universities had become notorious as diploma mills where unqualified American students could obtain a Ph.D. more quickly and much more cheaply than in the United States (Herbst 9; Veysey 13–31). One student wrote in 1894 to Wisconsin's Richard T. Ely, who had taken his Ph.D. in economics at Heidelberg in the late 1870s: "Halle is the place where many Americans go to take their degrees. Especially from Cornell and Penn. This is greatly due to the ease in which one can be obtained there by an American. I know of students who are coming up at the end of two semesters" (Veysey 131 n.26). By the turn of the century, even students in humanities and the social sciences were disenchanted with German idealism and historicism and attracted by the exciting new social and economic approaches being developed at American graduate schools. As the historian David Kinley wrote from Berlin in 1901: "I think far less of Germans, German education and German educational institutions than I did six months ago! . . . I wonder why American students come here to study in any lines except such as Germanic philology, Roman jurisprudence, German history, art, and other subjects in which the material can be found only here" (Herbst 5). In 1900 the Association of American Universities was established in large measure in an effort to stop the invasion of these cheap German degrees into our institutions of higher learning, as emerges from the letter of invitation sent by the presidents of Harvard, Columbia, Johns Hopkins, Chicago, and California to 14 leading universities: "European [read: German] Universities should be discouraged from conferring the degree of doctor of philosophy on American students who are not prepared to take the degree from our own best Universities, and from granting degrees to Americans on lower terms than to their native students" (Slate 4). Irving Babbitt at Harvard provided just one voice in a chorus lamenting "the uncritical adoption of German methods" as "one of the chief obstacles to a humanistic revival" (136). "One can scarcely contemplate the German theses, as they pour by hundreds into a large library, without a sort of intellectual nausea. American scholarship should propose to itself some higher end than simply to add a tributary to the stream" (134). A few years later his former Harvard colleague George Santayana—anticipating by seventy years the argument of Allan Bloom's *The Closing of the American Mind*—launched a vicious attack against what he perceived as the "moral disease" of "egotism" that had corrupted German philosophy (170).

The public enthusiasm for German literature had died out along with Ticknor, Longfellow, Emerson, Margaret Fuller, and such midcentury Germanophiles as Bayard Taylor. At the 1904 World's Fair in St. Louis the planning committee ambitiously assigned one of the largest auditoriums to the session on German Literature, at which the star performers imported from Europe for the occasion were none other than Jakob Minor and August Sauer: on the appointed morning no one showed up in the vast hall except a photographer from the local newspapers and a few dozen curious spectators who wandered in and out during the orations of the infuriated luminaries (Francke, *Deutsche Arbeit* 40). Even the still growing numbers of high school students of German had little meaning for the profession of Germanics because of the total lack of communication between the two: in the years when plans for the Germanic Museum at Harvard were proceeding, Marion Dexter Learned of the University of Pennsylvania observed that "The organization of German American teachers known as Nationaler Deutschamerikanischer Lehrerbund has not received hitherto the cooperation of academic teachers of German which it deserves and invites" and that college and university professors of German were often ignorant of the character and existence of German organizations and efforts in this country (Learned, "Lehrerbund" 10). The situation was not much better at the universities, where German was often required only for students registered for a science curriculum. Francke believed that the creation of a Germanic Museum was an urgent necessity if his field was to assert itself in the face of "the overwhelming influence of English and French" (Francke, *Deutsche Arbeit* 41). "In the thirteen years of my tenure at Harvard," he wrote, "and despite all personal goodwill, I had always felt, and ever more clearly, how fundamentally alien were my surroundings to everything that moved me most deeply. German literature, and even its greatest representatives, remained something inwardly strange to the average New Englander; he knew absolutely nothing about German art; and German politics appeared more or less suspicious in his eyes." Fifteen years later, as editor-in-chief of *The German Classics,* Francke noted in his preface: "It is surprising how little the English-speaking world knows of German literature of the nineteenth century." A little Goethe and Schiller, Fichte by way of Emerson and Hoffmann as a source for Poe, the reverberations of Uhland and Heine in Longfellow — "these brief statements include nearly all the names which to the cultivated Englishman and American of today stand for German literature" (vii). Despite the prominence of German conductors and musicians in American musical life, H. L. Mencken scathingly characterized the German Americans of the early twentieth century as culturally ignorant with little interest in anything higher than such social organizations as Schlaraffia, the Turnvereine, and Liederkränze, and certainly without literary pretensions (486–95).[7] This view is confirmed by Francke's complaint that German Americans had no interest in supporting the construction of any such *Nationalheiligtum* as the Germanic Museum (Francke, *Deutsche Arbeit* 54). It is also generally the case that the thousands of Americans who studied in Germany in the course of the nineteenth century did not routinely bring home any particular appreciation of German literary culture.[8]

By the turn of the century, finally, the public regard for Germany had been considerably eroded by a series of incidents regarded as manifestations of German imperialism and trade expansionism (Schieber): notably, confrontation of German and U.S. commercial interests in Samoa in the 1870s and 1880s; the German military adventures in China in the 1890s; German interference with U.S. activities in the Philippines during the Spanish-American War; German ventures in the Caribbean and Latin America around the turn of the century in a perceived violation of the Monroe Doctrine; German tariffs against American goods, including prohibitions of American fruits and meat products in the late 1890s; and the threat of war over Morocco in the early years of the twentieth century.

Against this background we can perhaps hear a note of defensive concern, if not despair, in the proud speeches delivered at Harvard in 1899. In any case, the creation of the Germanic Museum can hardly be regarded as a glorious culmination: it represented, rather, the attempt to establish a bulwark against the rising tide of anti-German sentiment in the United States; against the decline of interest in German culture, especially its literature; against the criticism in American universities of German higher education; and against the polarization of professional Germanics and German American activities, notably high school language instruction. It was, in sum, a conspicuous early example of the alienation that has been characteristic of our profession almost since its inception. In fact, Francke initiated the litany of complaints regarding the neglect of Germanics in Germany that has been a constant refrain for the entire century (Francke, *Deutsche Arbeit* 74; Zeydel, "Tätigkeit"; Reichart).

If we hope to understand the effect of history and public policy on Germanics in the United States, we need to define clearly the baseline against which change should be measured. If we continually set it too high, in some Never-Never-Land where all the children sang German songs, and all the students happily discussed German literature and philosophy, and all the citizens venerated Wagner at the opera and Schiller in the theater, then we are inevitably doomed to disappointment.

How Disruptive Was the First World War?

We must look at the history of our discipline in this sober light. The first major crisis that interrupted the development of Germanics in this country was, by all accounts, the First World War, the effects of which have been analyzed in several studies.[9] We have been informed about the decimation of the German-language press, which fell from 488 newspapers in 1910 to only 152 in 1920. We know about the anti-German hysteria that virtually eliminated German from schools: while German was studied as late as 1915 by almost 25 percent of U. S. public high school students, by 1922 that figure had plummeted to less than 1 percent (0.6 percent). We are appalled by such horrors as the book-burnings and the prohibition of German spoken in public and even the scattered lynchings of German Americans. Kurt Vonnegut, descendant of a "Hoosier German" family, recalls in his autobiography, *Palm Sunday* (21), that "the anti-Germanism in this country during the First World War so shamed and dismayed my parents that they resolved to raise me without acquainting me with the language or the literature or the music or the oral family histories which my ancestors had loved" (Reichmann & Reichmann 289). Clearly these circumstances had an impact on Germanics as a discipline: Kuno Francke chose early retirement in 1917; Ewald Boucke, dismissed from the University of

Michigan, returned to Germany and continued his career at Heidelberg; Boucke's most brilliant protegé, Hermann J. Weigand, who received his Ph.D. in 1916, found his own instructorship eliminated, and was reduced to working briefly in a ship-yard until he obtained a job with the Curtis Publishing Company in Philadelphia. These three examples are representative, not exceptional.

Yet the long-term impact on Germanics was not nearly so severe as is often assumed. We have already seen that the field as an academic subject was marginal as early as the turn of the century. German American popular culture was rampant, to be sure; but it is a fundamental mistake to identify academic Germanics with German Americana. So the academic baseline interrupted by World War I was not nearly so high as is often assumed. By 1919, Weigand recalled, returning veterans had flocked back to the campuses in such numbers that he was hired practically from one day to the next at the University of Pennsylvania to teach German lan-guage and literature (Schmidt, "Interview" 33). At the University of Wisconsin German enrollment recovered rapidly, from a low of 180 in 1918 to more than 1,000 in 1923 and almost 1,600 in 1927 (C. L. Nollendorfs, "The First" 188). At Prince-ton the German faculty fell from eight to three between 1915 and 1919; but by 1925 it had recovered to six full-time members (Bottigheimer 91). The major transfor-mation that took place at college level was a new emphasis on language instruction now that the secondary school base had been eroded: according to Zeydel's esti-mates, 60 percent of German students at the college level were now beginners (Zeydel, "Die germanistische Tätigkeit" 240). But the faculty positions were still there, and the undergraduate enrollments quickly recovered. Moreover, graduate work in the field intensified. While only 99 dissertations on German literature had been written in the United States between 1900 and World War I, some 137 were submitted in the years between 1914 and 1930 (R. P. Rosenberg 37). (In Germanic philology the corresponding figures are 23 and 33.) In sum, as devastating as the First World War was to German American culture, to German classes in secondary schools, and to public interest in Germany, its impact on Germanics as an academic discipline was not nearly so great as has often been represented. College enroll-ments were rapidly restored; graduate study continued at a more accelerated rate than previously; and American scholarship was making rapid progress. Edwin Zey-del's report evaluates the dissertations written after the war as clearly the equal in quality to German dissertations, and American Germanists, though constrained by the heavy demands of language instruction, were producing works that demanded recognition abroad (243).

The Emergence of Germanics

While generally knowledgeable and incisive in his judgment, Zeydel reveals one conspicuous blind spot in his evalution: he accuses American Germanists of being clumsy and tentative (*unbeholfen und tastend*) in their methodology. Although they vaguely realize, he says, that "so etwas wie ein Umsturz in der deutschen Literaturwissenschaft vor sich geht," nevertheless "[es] mangelt ihr zuweilen an der erforderlichen Schulung und an philosophisch-wissenschaftlicher Vertiefung, um in jeder Hinsicht begreifen und folgen zu können" (242). At this early stage in his career Zeydel (born 1893) still believed—a view he later outgrew—that Germanics should strive to become a *Germanistik im Ausland.* Zeydel makes the (in my opinion incorrect) observation that the preceding generation of American Germanists had been precluded from distinction by a deficient preliminary education. But if we look at the lives of those prominent early Germanists, born in the 1850s and 1860s—Marion Dexter Learned, Henry Wood, William Henry Carpenter, Henry Cohn, Arthur H. Palmer, Gustav Gruener, Horatio S. White, Calvin Thomas, James T. Hatfield, A. B. Faust, Starr Willard Cutting, and others[10]—they were in fact all exceptionally well educated: the common denominator that precluded them from creative originality was the fact, rather, that they all obtained their advanced training at German universities. As a result, "American" Germanics in the decades before 1914 had for the most part a very German face: the Americans as well as the Germans, such as Francke and Jagemann at Harvard, Hohlfeld at Wisconsin, or Julius Goebel at Stanford, all shared scholarly values acquired in Germany. (The notable exception was Calvin Thomas: his books on Goethe and Schiller as well as his *History of German Literature* were conspicuously addressed to an American public.) Inasmuch as one of these values was the superiority of German culture and the responsibility of German scholars abroad to act as advocates for that culture, American professors of Germanics were often caught, like Kuno Francke and Alexander Hohlfeld, in a *crise de conscience* between their cultural loyalty to Germany and their political loyalty to the United States.

It was the generation of long-lived American Germanists born in the 1890s and the first decade of the new century that first produced a recognizably American version of Germanics. Hermann Weigand (1892–1985), Edwin H. Zeydel (1893–1973), Walter Silz (1894–1980), Harold Jantz (1907–1987), and their contemporaries were concerned with literature that happened to be in German rather than German values as expressed in literature. Their goal, in short, was literary criticism and not glorification of the *Reich.* Coming from German American families, they often had a near-native command of the language. But they were trained almost exclusively in this country, having often been prevented by the war from contact with Germany. (Weigand made his first trip to Germany in 1922 at age 30.) Zeydel initially failed to appreciate this characteristically American scholarship because it had no ambition to submit itself to developments in German literary scholarship. Weigand's work, for instance, was conditioned by his exposure in graduate school to the theories of Freud, and the detective-like analysis for which he became famous is closely akin to the interpretive method that was becoming known in English studies as the New Criticism—all this at a time when German *Germanistik* was dominated by *Geistesgeschichte.* Similarly Silz's publications were characterized, as the editors of his *Festschrift* put it, by "painstaking attention to the text; dispassionate evaluation of evidence; a refreshing freedom from cant; a lean and muscular scholarly prose [as well as] a certain Yankee pragmatism, a reluctance on the part of the scholar to lose himself in abstractions and to becloud the lucidity of his arguments" (Crosby & Schoolfield xvii). The specifically American perspective that governs almost all of Jantz's work—in German American literary relations, in the classical background of German literature, in his studies of the Baroque—is once again characteristically the standpoint of an outsider looking from a critical distance at the object of his contemplation. And Zeydel's view of his mission as a cultural mediator is evident in the many translations and editions of neglected literary classics that he produced in the course of a long career. All but one of these representative American-born scholars were trained by German scholars—Boucke, Francke, Hohlfeld (Zeydel studied with Calvin Thomas at Columbia)—but they found a uniquely American path to their scholarship, a path that veered dramatically away from the traveled roads of German academic discourse. In sum, World War I undermined German American culture in the United States; but not only did it not severely curtail the academic discipline of Germanics; it even created, by breaking the close and intellectually restrictive contacts with Germany, the circumstances under which a characteristically American Germanics could begin to emerge, a method of German studies as distinct from *Germanistik* as was the discipline as practiced in France and England.

The point is worth stressing because the image of German studies in the United States has all too often been shaped by a German point of view—a point of view that tends to ignore what is written in English for the American public (e.g. Koepke, "Germanistik"). The German contribution is of course enormously important—from Kuno Francke's generation down to the young Germans who came to this country as graduate students and junior faculty in the 1960s and 1970s. But it is a one-sided point of view because it tends to ignore the English-language side of the equation. This accounts for the perception, even among some American Germanists, of what Jeffrey Sammons has called the "invisibility" of our profession ("Considerations"). To the extent that we—Germans and Americans alike—write in German for German audiences, we are invisible not only to the United States at large but also to our colleagues on our own campuses (43). And to the extent that we have largely left the public management of German literature to non-Germanists—and this has been the case since the days of Ticknor, Emerson, Margaret Fuller, and Longfellow down to the recent round of Thomas Mann biographies—we consign ourselves to intellectual irrelevance in this country. But that is not the whole story. A significant number of American Germanists—and also a small group of exceptionally capable German colleagues—have made it their task to communicate with the non-Germanist world in public English. (I exclude here the many recent works written in an obscure Theorese that bears little resemblance to English as spoken by normal Americans.) The line begins with Kuno Francke's *Social Forces in German Literature* (1896) and Calvin Thomas's *History of German Literature* (1909) and extends by way of such seminal works as Weigand's study of *Der Zauberberg* (1933), Silz's *Early German Romanticism* (1929), Werner Friederich's and

Oskar Seidlin's *History of German Literature* (1948), and Henry Hatfield's *Thomas Mann* (1951), down to Victor Lange's *Classical Age of German Literature* (1982) and Jeffrey Sammons's studies of Heine. It is representative of this trend that of the 23 presidents of the Modern Language Association elected from among our Germanist colleagues from Calvin Thomas (1896) to Sander Gilman (1995), all but six have been American-born while the others—from Francke and Hohlfeld to Peter Demetz—have established their reputations with books in English and are thus known to a larger public than the tight little world of Germanics. Our invisibility is therefore a highly relative matter.[11]

The Effects of the Nazi Years

Our understanding of the period 1933 to 1945 has benefited recently from several careful source studies. But their results are limited, for two reasons, in their usefulness for our purposes. First, they are concerned less with Germanics as a discipline of literary scholarship and more with the political attitudes of German scholars in this country vis-à-vis the Third Reich. As a result, they do not take into account the activities of scholars who preferred to make no political statements but to work quietly as individuals.[12] Second, their focus on publications in specific journals— for example, the *German Quarterly* and *Monatshefte*—means that they ignore not only important book publications and scholars who published in other journals, but also the 276 doctoral dissertations on German literature written from 1931 to 1940 (R. P. Rosenberg 37).

The Second World War interrupted the smooth emergence of an American Germanics. Many scholars at the beginning of their careers, both American and German, spent time in the military: Stuart Atkins, Henry Hatfield, Herbert Penzl, Herman Salinger, and Oskar Seidlin are representative.[13] At colleges and universities, meanwhile, many professors of German found themselves engaged in the national defense effort through the Army Specialized Training Program, which from the end of 1942 brought military personnel to campuses for training in German and other critical languages. The United States, having grown more sophisticated since World War I, recognized the need for personnel with a good command of German, Japanese, and other languages.

It was not only the Americans whose careers were thus interrupted. Many German scholars who came to the United States as refugees were unable to find positions that enabled them to have any impact on the field: Melitta Gerhard, who taught German to soldiers in St. Louis and then to high school students in Milwaukee before finding positions in small colleges with no graduate programs, is typical for a group that included Richard Alewyn, Bernhard Blume, Wolfgang Liepe, Werner Richter, Martin Sommerfeld, and others. Alewyn, Liepe, and Richter, who returned to Germany soon after the war, cannot be said to have had any impact on U.S. Germanics. Blume, of course, went on to influential positions at Ohio State, Harvard, and the University of California at San Diego. Paradoxically, one of the few Germanists who moved immediately into a major chair was Karl Viëtor, whose nationalistic (not to say Nazi) past precluded him from advancing the cause of Germanics in America.

It has perhaps not been sufficiently emphasized how the study of German literature in this country was opened up and enriched during and after World War II by a number of refugees whose nonacademic backgrounds would probably have disqualified them from *Habilitation* or university chairs in German universities: Bernhard Blume, famous in the 1920s along with Brecht and Bronnen as one of the Three B's of the German theater; Curt von Faber du Faur, who came from a background as a bookdealer and collector in Germany to establish the study of Baroque literature in the United States; Erich Kahler, an intellectual historian associated with the George Circle; and many others. It is impossible to estimate the impression made by Thomas Mann on the hundreds of Princeton students who heard him lecture on *Werther, Faust,* and other topics. Anyone who first encountered Stefan George's poetry through his disciple Ernst Morwitz, a lawyer who ended up teaching German at the University of North Carolina and who moved around the campus in garb and mannerisms reminiscent of the Master, intoning the poems in George's cadences — such students can never erase George from their personal canon of modern German poetry.

The Postwar Recovery

In his 1943 presidential address to the Modern Language Association, Robert Herndon Fife of Columbia University spoke of the need to establish an independent American literary scholarship that would be at once cosmopolitan and freed from all taints of German nationalism. In a survey of "Studies of German Literature in the United States 1939–1946" Henry Hatfield and Joan Merrick pointed out that "the study of German in the United States had traditionally been bound to the *Reich* by closer ties than would seem to be the case in Great Britain or France" (353–54). But they go on to point out that "The emotional tie to the 'fatherland,' particularly strong among some of those who studied in Germany before the first world war, is not likely to be shared by many of those who had personal experience of the second conflict." This turned out to be an accurate forecast. I am not referring to the cluster of articles at war's end by Werner Richter, Karl Viëtor, and Leo Spitzer calling for a more American literary scholarship (see Daemmrich). Apart from the hubris of writing their exhortation to American scholars in German, all three advocated a traditional *Geistesgeschichte* modified by close attention to the texts. In any case, Richter returned to Germany; Viëtor died (in 1950) before he could carry out his program; and Spitzer devoted his effort mainly to the Romance languages.

The real development of an American *Germanistik* was carried out by scholars like Atkins, Hatfield, Jantz, Silz, and Weigand, who were now able to continue the kind of scholarship they had initiated between the wars, and by their students. This group has been well characterized by Blake Lee Spahr, who after being decorated for his military service as navigator in a B-17 over Germany went to Yale to study Baroque literature with Faber du Faur.

> The year 1944 was a significant one, for it marked the return to graduate studies of the first generation of post–World War II students, a generation . . . which was distinguished—if for nothing else—as a more mature, or at least an older, a more seriously motivated, if somewhat cynically oriented graduate contingent . . . . Their interest was not the romantically predicated and judgementally devoid predilection which one often found in the students of that day. On the contrary they were prepared to look askance at any mentor who dished up prepared pap as well as his opposite number who demanded unreasonable mastication of undigestable critical fare. (195)

Spahr was speaking specifically of his immediate colleagues—an influential group that came to be known within the field as the Yale Mafia—but his characterization applied equally well to most graduate programs in the country during those years. These skeptical young scholars, many of them fresh from years in military intelligence and denazification programs in Germany, were not remotely interested in the vague theories of *Geistesgeschichte* or in the romanticized image of Germany still cultivated in German American social groups. Coming to graduate school on the G.I. Bill, they wanted the knowledge of a no-nonsense history and the skills of an incisive textual analysis that would help them to understand the culture with which they had so recently been hostilely engaged—and they found mentors in the generation of Germanists who had assiduously been devising Germanics here; but also in German refugees like von Faber, Blume, Erich Heller, Victor Lange, Heinrich Henel, Oskar Seidlin, and Heinz Politzer. What characterized this generation of German scholars, in contrast to most earlier ones and many subsequent ones, was their recognition of the obligation to mediate, to introduce and explain German culture to the postwar American public, and their cultivation of an accessible and often brilliant English style, which expressed itself in essays for wide-circulation journals as often as in scholarly monographs.

If the G.I. Bill and the millions of returning veterans enabled this new generation of American Germanists to mature quietly, it was the Russian Sputnik and the National Defense Education Act of 1958 that enabled the discipline to expand on the foundations of this postwar development. The three public occasions that most dramatically symbolized the coming of age and public recognition of Germanics were the Goethe commemorations at Aspen in 1949, the 1966 Princeton meeting of the Gruppe 47 followed by a symposium involving major figures from the American literary scene, and the 1970 Princeton meeting of the International Association of Germanists (IVG) during Victor Lange's presidency. For a brief time German studies had the attention of the American literary public: basking in the glamour surrounding figures like Günter Grass and Uwe Johnson and reported in the national press, Germanics—its authors and its professors—enjoyed the publicity that normally attended only English studies and, occasionally, French cultural affairs. Enrollments in German courses nationally reached an all-time high for the postwar era. During that same period the infatuation of American youth with the works of Hermann Hesse brought thousands of students into German courses, at least in translation (Ziolkowski, "Saint Hesse"). The Golden Age seemed at last to have arrived.

Years of Disenchantment

Then came 1968. The universities surrendered their authority to the students, who began to dismantle all requirements, including language requirements. The results showed up almost immediately. By 1970 German enrollments nationally had fallen from an alltime high of 216,000 to just over 200,000, initiating a decline that continued until 1986. This is the situation that John Van Cleve and A. Leslie Willson had in mind when they began their recent book on the crisis in our field with the statement that our profession "is sliding silently toward oblivion" (vii). They base their conclusion on the analysis of statistics showing that enrollments in college German courses fell by 44 percent between 1968 and 1986. But if we look at a larger frame—say, from 1960 to 1990—the picture appears quite different: in that scenario German lost only 9 percent and has been slowly recovering toward the norm since 1986 (Brod & Huber). The peak enrollments in 1968 were a fluke, an exception created by the rapidly expanding colleges and universities of the 1960s, when total enrollment more than doubled—from under four million to more than eight million—in one decade. However, the unusual expanding academic economy of the 1960s is taken as the norm by many people in our field—both the colleagues who flocked to this country from Germany to fill the sudden need for trained German teachers after Sputnik and the large generation of American Germanists who were drawn into the field by the promise of job opportunities. As we revert to the norm that prevailed until 1960, the generations of the 1960s and early 1970s often perceive it as a decline. I argue in contrast that it is simply a readjustment to the normal baseline. (If that is the case, then the ninety Ph.D.s in Germanics awarded in 1996[14] is still much too large in proportion to the number of students needing to be taught, in comparison to the average of 45 awarded from 1960 through 1965.)

At this point comparison is useful, for the statistics recording our decline also record a decline of almost 30 percent in French enrollments since 1968 and in Greek and Latin of 15 percent and 20 percent respectively. We should not take the satisfaction of *Schadenfreude* in the fact that our colleagues are suffering as much as we. Rather, I would suggest that we are all suffering from the same phenomenon: the multicultural turn away from a Eurocentric culture. The huge increase in Spanish enrollments (up 46 percent from 1968 to 1990) does not signal any great interest in Cervantes or Ortega y Gasset; talk to our colleagues in peninsular Spanish! The facts can be attributed almost wholly to an American public policy that has focused on Latin America and the Pacific Basin, with increases of almost 300 percent in Chinese and almost 1,000 percent in Japanese. Similarly the increases in Russian enrollments (10 percent from 1968 to 1990) are probably related to immigration policies that have brought an influx of Russian families to the United States in recent years.

What this suggests is the need for long-range comparative studies of ethnic groups. It would be interesting to know whether there is any pattern in the desires of immigrant groups to keep up with their native languages and cultures. The first wave of German immigrants to the United States, who were generally less well educated and congregated in tightly knit German-speaking communities in Milwaukee, St. Louis, and Texas, managed to retain German as a cultural possession for several generations, much as appears to be the case among Cubans in Miami, Puerto Ricans in New York, Koreans in New Jersey, and Mexican Americans in the Southwest. But the more highly educated German-speaking émigrés of the twentieth century succeeded much more rapidly in assimilating into the English-speaking community; their children often speak no German. To what extent does assimilation depend upon education? How long will Spanish continue to be a dominant factor in immigrant communities in this country? Are there any patterns?

Another issue worth exploring would be the effect of comparative literature upon our field. Increasingly we have surrendered certain key figures—Hölderlin, Kafka, Nietzsche, even Rilke—to colleagues in comparative literature who often, despite their familiarity with the language, lack the profound familiarity with the larger cultural context and therefore deal with the literary figures in intertextual isolation. Indeed, one cannot always count on the linguistic command: as influential a figure as Paul de Man was capable of gaffes in German that totally discredited his reading, say, of Kleist's *Über das Marionettentheater*.[15] This criticism does not apply to older comparatists—for example, René Wellek and such of his students as Ralph Freedman and Peter Demetz, who are thoroughly grounded in the national literature that constitutes their home base.

Finally, the sometimes frantic turn away from—dare we use the word?—the canon of German literary culture to film, theory, and to texts newly foregrounded by women's studies, ethnic studies, and Jewish studies has been paralleled in other fields as well, notably English and French (Ziolkowski, "Der Text"). It would be useful to see these developments in a comparative context in order to understand what is characteristically American about these turns in literary scholarship.

Cooperation among disciplines is becoming increasingly urgent in the face of the common problems forced upon us all by national policy decisions. According to a report issued in 1996 by the National Association of Scholars, the foreign language requirement, in force as recently as 1964 at 96 percent of American colleges and universities, was in effect at only 64 percent of those same institutions (*New York Times,* 20 March 1996, B9). At more and more universities, notably America's third largest university system, the City University of New York, student diversity and fiscal crises have produced a conspicuous shift away from the liberal arts and toward vocational programs (*New York Times,* 8 April 1996, A15). At the same time, the presidents of the American Association of Universities—the same body that in

1900 was formed to counteract the cheapening of the doctorate in German universities!—have proclaimed a new emphasis on undergraduate education, which has already at many institutions resulted in a reallocation of funds away from graduate programs and drastic cutbacks in graduate enrollments at universities from Stanford to Princeton. In the face of problems like these, our hairsplitting disputes about the niceties of literary theory bear a startling resemblance to Nero's tuning of his lyre above the conflagration of Rome.

It will be evident to many that the foregoing remarks have exploited precisely the sources cited by Henry Schmidt in his suggestive piece on "Rationales and Sources for a History of German Studies in the United States": journals, literary histories, newspapers, memoirs, and university archives. Moreover, I have used the approaches cited by Egon Schwarz in his brief piece on "Methodological Approaches," which appeared in the same issue of *Monatshefte* as Schmidt's: genetic, ideological, and comparative. Those are of course inevitably the sources and methods of any historical study. If we had time in our ever expanding curricula and if we had the means to require our students to do anything at all, then we might argue that a basic prerequisite for the degree in any field of study should be the history of its discipline (Ziolkowski, "Polysyllabification" 81–82). For history puts every discipline back into the broader human and social contexts that produced and shaped it. History can teach every student respect for the achievements of the past and appreciation for the social role of each discipline or profession. It can instill a sense of humility by reminding students how quickly the cutting edge can become a blunt instrument, fit only to be relegated to the museum. As we deal with Goldhagen's indictment of Germany, along with the revisions of Romanticism and Nietzsche and Weimar culture, it will pay to remember Kuno Francke's idealization of German culture. We do not need to share that idealization to understand that German culture did not cause the Holocaust; it simply did not prevent it—another matter altogether. We have rounded the circle and returned under the name of German Studies to Francke's vision of German culture and civilization. What has been lost in the process is nothing less than German literature itself.

Notes

1 Rippley, *German-Americans* 56–58. For a first-hand account see Francke, *Deutsche Arbeit* 41–47.
2 See Draper 8, Table I. Foreign Language Enrollments in Public High Schools 1890–1990. In fact, the proportion in 1900 was only 14 percent, but it rose by 1915 to over 24 percent.
3 Rippley, *German-Americans* 166. Rippley notes that by 1975 there were altogether only 44 German-language publications in the United States, including scholarly journals and fraternal newsletters.

4   Of 49,000 students who went to Western Europe in 1993–94, only 3,500 went to Germany.

5   *New York Times,* 2 March 1996, 6. This piece generated a lively exchange on the internet, which has been duplicated and circulated by Professor Ruth Reichmann of Indiana University/Purdue University–Indianapolis.

6   Herbst 1 n.1. I am persuaded by Herbst's justification of his figure, which is more conservative than the figure of 10,000, which is frequently cited.

7   It is symptomatic that Rippley, in his otherwise conclusive study of *The German-Americans,* makes no mention of literature or German studies.

8   Herbst, ix, observes that "although the German-trained American students of history and social science often referred to their German 'masters' of the historical school, they did so only rarely to the great proponents of the historical thought in literature and philosophy."

9   Zeydel, "The Teaching of German"; Sammons, "Die amerikanische Germanistik"; Schmidt, "The Rhetoric of Survival"; Trommler & McVeigh, II; and Kirschbaum.

10 See the biographical note in Viereck, *German Instruction in American Schools,* esp. 695–703.

11 My view differs from that of Schmidt, "Wissenschaft als Ware," who perceives our field as "ein von Emigranten beherrschtes Fach."

12 E.g., Hermann J. Weigand, who made a point of taking no political stance in his scholarship, but who was instrumental in helping German scholars (notably Paul Oskar Kristeller) find sanctuary in the United States.

13 The *PMLA* personalia for 1944 indicates by a flag-symbol the members currently serving in the armed services.

14 My estimate is based on the list of accepted dissertations published in *Monatshefte* 88 (1996): 379–82.

15 See my review of de Man's *The Rhetoric of Romanticism* in "Uses and Abuses," 278–79.

World War I as a Shaping Force in American Germanics

CLIFFORD ALBRECHT BERND

In Germany, as modern reception aesthetics reminds us, interpretations of literature have differed greatly depending upon whether an interpreter's critical assumptions and persuasions were influenced by the political climate of 1870, 1914, 1933,
1945, or the 1990s. An awareness of the particular historicity of the interpreter has
become as important for determining a literary text's evolving meaning as the historical conditions surrounding the life of the text's author. No interpreter of literature can ever overcome the intruding perspective of his or her own time and place,
no matter how hard he or she may try; any attempt to rehabilitate the conditions
of an alien past is a futile undertaking. What we reproduce, Hans-Georg Gadamer
has said, can never be the original, but only a version of the original codetermined
by the vision of our own historical circumstances (Gadamer 159, 280).

How, then, have the interpretations of German literature by American Germanists been influenced by their places in history? In order to answer this question, a
great deal of spade work must be done. As Valters Nollendorfs has properly stated,
we have yet to acquire "a sufficient data-base" ("Practical Approaches" 266). Still,
even now we can be absolutely certain that at no point in the history of German
letters in the United States did the interpretative act become more entangled in the
web of American political forces than in the years immediately following America's declaration of war on Germany on 6 April 1917. Curiously, however, as Cora
Lee Nollendorfs has observed, "this era and the activities of the leading Germanists of the time have scarcely been investigated" ("The First" 176). In the following
we seek to show how the critical act of interpreting German literature after 1917 in
America was conditioned by a harrowing set of wartime vicissitudes visited upon
the American German professor at the time.

The Assault on the German Language

Before the year 1917 could come to a close, the German language came under attack. From the Atlantic to the Pacific it was viciously assailed. The *New York Times,*
which by then had assumed "the character of a national newspaper more nearly
than any other in America" (E. Davis 338), had set the tone for what quickly developed into a national tidal wave of hatred for German. The readers of the Sunday issue on 2 December 1917 could read in heavy black letters that German "Is

a Barbarous Tongue, Which Is Lacking in Cultural Worth and of No Commercial Importance" (Dunlap).

As assaults on the German language were repeated everywhere in the nation's press, school children and college students in ever larger numbers boycotted the study of German. Less than four months after the *New York Times* had launched the anti-German language campaign, the *Literary Digest* published a lengthy set of statistics showing how drastically the formal study of German had declined in the various states of the union as well as in its major cities (30 March 1918, 29).

Soon organized efforts were made to ban the study of German in public schools with the end of the school year in June 1918. The California High School Principals' Convention, for instance, voted in favor of such a recommendation at its meeting in April 1918 (California State Board 129). Acting quickly, the California State Board of Education then formally suspended the study of German in the high schools, stating that "it does not seem either logical or patriotic . . . to continue instruction in a language that disseminates the ideals of autocracy, brutality and hatred" (13–14).

At the invitation of the U.S. Secretary of the Interior, Franklin K. Lane, a council of state governors and their representatives convened in the nation's capitol on 3 April 1918 to discuss "Americanization as a War Measure." Banning the language of the enemy in schools loomed heavily among the topics discussed. The governor of Oklahoma, Robert L. Williams, boasted that he had successfully "appealed to the Lutheran ministers to stop it [the teaching of German] in the parochial schools" of his state ("Americanization" 56). The governor of Idaho, Moses Alexander, was haughtier. Not willing to wait to see whether the courts would uphold the constitutionality of outlawing the teaching of German, he informed his fellow governors that "Idaho had solved, law or no law, one question that we discussed today. German is not taught in the State of Idaho, probably will never be, even after the war is over" (55). The most searing denunciation of German instruction came from Senator Lafayette Young, representing the State of Iowa: "I believe that 90 per cent of all the men and women who teach the German language are traitors and out of sympathy with our Government" (35).

Since the war with Germany was over seven months later, one might think there would no longer be a patriotic reason to clamor for the suspension of German instruction. Just the opposite, however, happened. After the armistice was declared, the assault on the German language assumed even greater intensity.

This intensification was due largely to a vicious campaign of hatred waged by the governor of Ohio, James Middleton Cox. During the war his patriotism had burned fiercely (Bagby 74). He had urged that a firing squad for suspected German traitors be organized in Ohio (Hubbart 401). The record he acquired as a particularly militant prowar governor found such favor with his constituents that in November 1918 he was reelected for a third term, an honor previously conferred on only one Ohio governor, Rutherford B. Hayes. Since the national prominence Hayes had gained as a result of that election quickly helped him to become President of the United States, it was inevitable that Cox, too, should immediately be considered a candidate for the presidential office. Ohio, it must be remembered, had sent more favorite sons to the White House after the Civil War than any other state; successful politicians from Ohio were always prime contenders for the presidency. During the war against Germany, Cox's public office as well as his ownership of many newspapers had given his violently anti-German statements national publicity. Now that the war was over, he naturally did not wish his position on the central stage of American patriotism to vanish, especially since it was precisely this intense patriotism that had given him the notoriety he needed to be returned three times to the Ohio State House and then to become a candidate for the highest public office in the land. With the eyes of voters all across the country turned upon him, he began to stoke the fires of a new, postbellum anti-German hysteria in Ohio for all they were worth (Roseboom & Weisenburger 342).

Cox was competing, after all, with another prominent contender for the presidency in the next national election of 1920, James W. Gerard. This former American ambassador to Germany, soon after his return to the United States in 1917, also actively sought the nomination for President by taking advantage of the superpatriotic sentiments of an America at war with everything German. Gerard's "long-simmering interest in becoming a candidate for President of the United States" (Gerard, *My First* 291), his firsthand knowledge of Germany in wartime, and his excellent financial resources all combined to give him the opportunity to stump the nation with a message of hatred for Germany (266). His anti-German books, *My Four Years in Germany* and *Face to Face with Kaiserism,* moreover, were fast climbing to the top of national bestseller lists. The more Gerard's trailblazing campaign against Germany and his concomitant campaign to be President assumed ever-widening national dimensions, the more naturally voters all over America took notice of the verbal war against everything German that was being waged at the same time by his political rival Cox.

Cox's postbellum campaign against Germany began in earnest when, in an address to the Ohio State Assembly on 13 January 1919, he fanatically cried out: "Every germ of Prussian poison must be squeezed out of the organic law of Ohio" (Mercer 26). On 20 February 1919, he urged the Assembly to ban German instruction in Ohio's schools, stating that, even though the war had ended, "the Prussian spirit of intrigue [is] not dead in America" (Mercer 38). Unrelentingly, Cox continued to fuel the fires of hatred. He insisted that "the children of Ohio" had to be "protected from the possibility of poison from the German virus"; "the teaching of German to the tender youth of the state," he added, "is a menace to the ideals of this republic" (Mercer 37). In Ohio's Lutheran churches, Cox demanded, readings in German were to be banned: "If any man in Ohio wants his child indoctrinated with Prussian creeds, let our safeguards be such that he must go elsewhere for it" (Mercer 38). On 1 April 1919 the maddened governor went so far as to call the State Assembly into a Special Session for the express purpose of enacting far-reaching laws to prohibit German. In his address he indulged in the extreme statement that "the teaching of German . . . is not only a distinct menace to Americanism, but it is part of a conspiracy formed long ago by the German government in Berlin" (Mercer 71). The prominence Cox continued to acquire in his bid for America's highest political office only let such frenzied attacks on the German language echo in print from one newspaper to the other all across the nation. Of course, the closer the presidential conventions of 1920 came, the more Cox's statements received widening coverage in America's press (Bagby 76). By 21 July 1920 the governor's statements about the dangers of German propaganda, conveyed via the medium of its language, must have gained such extensive press coverage that Cleveland's German language newspaper *Wächter und Anzeiger* felt obliged to call him a "Deutschenfresser erster Classe" (Wittke, "Ohio's German" 474). An Indiana publication, in a statement much quoted in the press of the nation, had this to say about Cox: "The new standard bearer of the so called Democratic Party has revealed himself already as a fanatic Germanophobe" (quoted in *Cincinnati Freie Presse,* 1 Nov. 1920).

The Assault on German Literature and the German Book

With the national publicity given to the attacks on the German language, a hostility quickly arose for anything written or published in German, especially works of German literature. Once more, the most prominent national forum, the *New York Times,* became a leading force in spreading this anti-German sentiment. In the 2 December 1917 issue readers everywhere in the nation were informed that

> . . . a knowledge of German introduces the student to no literature worthy of the
> name. The two or three authors whose names are suggested by the expression
> "German literature" are important because they are the best German affords, pre-
> cisely as certain Mexican authors may be important. Compared with English, Ital-
> ian, French, and Russian literature, German literature is practically nonexistent.
> (Dunlap 9)

Four months later (7 April 1918) the *New York Times* ran a further derogatory editorial entitled "The German Book, The Enemy." In it the American public was told

> The German book is the most active agent in spreading the mental disease with
> which the whole German nation is gangrened . . . . The German book is respon-
> sible for the lowering of the moral level of humanity. Any book whatsoever, from
> the innocent-looking schoolbook to the pretentious treatise on philosophy . . .
> anything, in short, that comes to us from a German printing press—is open to
> suspicion. The German microbe is hiding somewhere between its covers . . . .
> The plague is with us here in America, in our circulating libraries, schools and

colleges, and it behooves us to use strong prophylactic means to guard against its
ravages. (E2)

With the national attention drawn to the disease of German books, the next step in
the hate campaign against the printed German word followed only too logically.
Hysteria took the form of a fanatical cleanliness, the germ patrol overwhelmed
cooler heads, and all editions of German literature that could be quickly grabbed off
bookshelves were thrown indiscriminately into patriotic bonfires. Ohio, as could
hardly be otherwise because of its militant anti-German governor, apparently led
the nation. The headline on the front page of the *Cleveland News* (5 April 1918)
carried in heavy typeface the words "City to Burn Hun Poison." Citizens were
urged to bring works of German literature and anything suggestive of German
propaganda to a central location where the books would be collected and then
burned in a huge bonfire. A report about this grotesque German book-burning cere-
mony appeared the same day in the *New York Times* (24) and quickly prompted
many other cities to imitate Cleveland's example.

The Assault on the Professor of German

First the German language; then everything ever written in German, including all
works of German literature, came under the sledgehammer of an appallingly mis-
guided American patriotism. Next came the worst of all: the professor of German
literature in the United States became the stock villain in this drama of wartime
hysteria. He was branded as the deluded, if not subversive, agent of an abhorrent
"Kaiserism."

This thesis was argued particularly doggedly by James W. Gerard, Cox's rival
in the race for nomination for President in 1920. In his book *Face to Face with
Kaiserism* Gerard had engaged in a campaign of professorial witch-hunting, naming individual Germanists as examples of "Kaiserism in America" (Gerard, *Face*
282–88).

Ohio's Governor Cox, not wishing to lose the nomination to Gerard, tried, of
course, to outdo his political rival in patriotism and targeted many more professors
of German in the nation for their "resolute desire to combat Americanism" in the
college classroom (Mercer 75). They, he argued, were the prime instruments of
"the Prussian spirit of intrigue" in America (Mercer 38). In view of the Ohio governor's frenzied hostility to professors of German it could come as no surprise that
it was a professor at Ohio State University, Ludwig Lewisohn, who should become
what may well have been the most persecuted Germanist in America. Lewisohn
had grown up in Berlin, and that made him an easy target for witch-hunters searching for agents of "Prussian intrigue" on university campuses. To make matters
worse, Lewisohn had the misfortune of living but a short distance from Governor
Cox's official residence in Columbus. It was almost as if a personal emissary of the
Kaiser were spreading the gospel of Prussianism right in the governor's backyard!

In his autobiographical chronicle, *Up Stream,* Lewisohn gives us a gripping account of what happened. It all began when he wrote, in the war year 1916, a book on modern German literature and claimed that Nietzsche (a native Prussian who had the added misfortune of having been named after a King of Prussia) "was indisputably one of the great masters of prose" (*Up Stream* 214). The book fell into the hands of an Ohio real estate broker, a zealous patriot who quickly dispatched a letter to Governor Cox protesting what he believed to be pro-Prussian attitudes unfitting for a professor whose salary was being paid by the taxpayers of Ohio. It did not take long before Lewisohn was summoned to the office of the district attorney. "Well, professor, I thought we'd better have a talk," the district attorney said when Lewisohn entered the office. "What have you against me?," the German professor asked. "Didn't you say . . . ?," the district attorney thundered back (217). The interrogation went on for over an hour. Ruthlessly, Lewisohn tells us, the district attorney "roared me down" (218). "I tried to reach his reason," Lewisohn reports, but the Ohio civil servant "didn't want that to happen" (218). The session ended with the interrogator shaking his head gloomily and saying: "he would see . . ." (218). Lewisohn did not wait to find out what action the district attorney would take. He resigned from his teaching post and left Ohio.

It was, of course, not only in Ohio that professors of German were cruelly subjected to such unbelievable personal humiliation. In Ohio things may have been more extreme than elsewhere, but the witch-hunting of the professor of German, engineered by Cox and Gerard, occurred essentially all across the nation. Albert B. Faust, the American-born and American-educated chairman of the German Department at Cornell, gave perhaps the most concise account of the harrowing plight of the embattled German professor in American universities at the time: "Professors were dismissed from their chairs for having been what was called 'pro-German,' others were coldly tolerated or isolated. In all walks of life the same tyranny prevailed . . . we were invited to spit at the effigy of the Kaiser" (Faust, "Teaching" 2). Never before and never afterwards have the teaching members of our discipline had to contend with such vicious, virulent, and chauvinistic attacks.

Julius Goebel's Call for a New Study of Literature

From this brief narrative one might infer that Germany's literary heritage had been singled out to disappear into the realm of oblivion in the United States. Surprisingly, however, this did not happen. Professors of German survived the onslaught. Despite the Damoclean sword of political unpopularity hanging over their heads, they neither exhausted themselves in pointless rejoinder nor succumbed to the temptation to abandon the teaching of an unwanted literature. Instead, they began to concentrate their energies on revitalizing the academic interpretation of German literature in the United States. These scholars, finding inspiration in their time of trial, not only arrested the mediocrity in their profession—typified by the numerous editions of textbooks with stereotyped introductions, footnotes, and glossaries,

which had been the main scholarly contribution of pre–World War I Germanics—
but they also ushered in a new era of sensitive literary criticism that was to raise
the standards of German studies in America to heights never known earlier.

Laying the foundation for this renewal was a proposal by Julius Goebel in late
1918. He had been a prominent spokesman for German studies in the United States,
having taught at Johns Hopkins, Stanford, and Harvard before becoming head of
the huge German Department at the University of Illinois and also the managing
editor of the *Journal of English and Germanic Philology*. During the war years he enjoyed an advantage most of his fellow American Germanists did not possess: he had
never been a champion of Wilhelminian values. Indeed, in 1909, he had expressed
in writing his opposition to the falsehoods of Wilhelm II's empire (Goebel, *Hebbelprobleme* 445). His anti-Prussian sentiments doubtless had developed early when
his father, a senator in the Free City of Frankfurt/Main, could not bring himself
to swear allegiance to a Hohenzollern monarch when Frankfurt was swallowed up
in the Wilhelminian empire after the close of the Austro-Prussian War; he elected
instead to emigrate to the United States (Kimball 531).

Untarnished by the stigma of the pro-Kaiser sentiment which had paralyzed
the activities of so many of his colleagues when anti-German feeling was at fever
pitch, and never willing to languish in public inactivity (O'Connor 441), Goebel
was quick to indicate how the beleaguered professor of German could regain the
confidence of the American academic community. He appealed to his colleagues
to make "literature" the center of German studies and he urged them, specifically,
to turn to hermeneutics or the art of interpreting. This shift in focus was as radical
as it was new, for prior to Goebel's call, few, if any, American teachers of German had ever used or heard of the term "hermeneutics." Their daily pedagogical
and patriotic concerns had given them little opportunity to think about the art of
interpreting literature or the problem of literary methodology. Goebel asked for a
change in attitude and schooling that would overcome the strain of pedantry then
current in the profession:

> One of the essential functions of . . . the teacher of literature consists in the proper
> understanding . . . of literary productions and of conveying to others the insight
> thus gained. Yet little or nothing is being done at present for a systematic train-
> ing in the exercise of this important function. At best the future interpreters of
> literature, whether teachers or commentators, will follow for better or worse the
> example of their teachers who in all probability themselves had reflected little, if
> at all, on the fundamental principles of their hermeneutic methods, but had fol-
> lowed certain trends of the times and thus developed a more or less successful
> dilettantism which could easily be imitated. (Goebel, "Notes" 602)

Goebel's clarion call to his colleagues to stake out new interpretative turf was just
what they needed in their hour of peril. For by encouraging a new study of literature that was more consciously "literary," he could redirect the energies of his col-

leagues away from the political sphere where they were most vulnerable. Here the profession could redeem itself and regain respectability. Goebel's advice was soon acted upon. Younger colleagues began to turn their attention to the more proper interpretation of German poetry, prose, and drama as "literature" rather than as manifestations of a German national culture.

Thomas M. Campbell's Study of Hebbel

The first of a new set of exciting literary studies conditioned by the vicissitudes of the American German professor in World War I addressed itself to the trage- dies of Friedrich Hebbel. The author, Thomas Moody Campbell, would become so famous that he was elected president of the Modern Language Association of America. His book appeared in 1919, only one year after Goebel had issued his call for a new study of literature as "literature," and it expounds an interpretation of Hebbel that was suggested by Goebel himself (Goebel, *Hebbelprobleme* 445). Departing decisively from the idealistic Hebbel hero-worship so characteristic of prewar German scholarship, Campbell clearly rejects the notion that Hebbel was preeminently a philosophical thinker whose every utterance, fictional as well as nonfictional, should be understood in the light of an illustration of metaphysics (Wiehr 291). Instead, Campbell invites his readers to study Hebbel's plays as works of art and, specifically, to analyze them with him, one by one, as haunting trage- dies in which individual characters are trapped, though no fault of their own, in the crises of their day and age. "The fate of [Hebbel's] persons was rather the product of their times than of their own action" (Campbell 234). The result of this "critical relation between individual and society" (228) is that life "from the standpoint of the individual" (118) appears "gloomy and hopeless in the extreme" (118).

Campbell's detailed analyses of the plight of characters as victims of the world in which they live, as victims in the dramatic interplay with other characters whose fates are likewise determined by the circumstances of their time and place, con- stituted literary criticism of a high order in the discipline of German letters in the United States for 1919. Yet Campbell might not have read so sensitively if the trauma of the American German professor at the time had not conditioned him to be especially receptive to Hebbel's recurrent portrayals of human beings victim- ized by historical events over which they have no control. The parallel between the tragic experience of Hebbel's characters and that of American professors of German in 1917 and 1918 was, I suspect, all too suggestive for Campbell.

Walter Silz's Study of Kleist

Other new "literary" studies by American Germanists that followed also reflected the shattering experiences endured by the members of the profession at the time. Particularly notable is a book on Heinrich von Kleist, written in 1922 by Walter

Silz, who, like Campbell, would go on to an illustrious career in German letters in this country.

Silz had been more than coincidentally affected by the nightmare that befell American teachers of German at the time. His German immigrant parents had settled in Cleveland, Ohio, the city that gained national attention in April 1918 for starting the national expression of outrage by the public burning of German books. The *Cleveland Press* reported (8 April 1918, 4) the very day the book-burning occurred that federal agents had seized the correspondence of Walter Silz's father, Max A. Silz, who had been secretary of the German School Association of Cleveland. Thereafter, life became a personal catastrophe for Max Silz. He was interrogated, forced to repudiate statements he had made earlier, publicly accused of anti-Americanism and of spying for the Kaiser, which the federal agents all too readily assumed because he was, after all, a native of Berlin and, to make matters worse, even a former Prussian cavalry soldier who once had sworn allegiance to his Kaiser. As a consequence of such unrelenting public and official harassment Max Silz lost his manufacturing business, the means to support himself and his family, and was compelled to return to Germany when the war ended.

It requires little imagination to recognize how much all this must have stirred the son, Walter, who was at that time studying to become a teacher of German; it cannot be surprising that of all the German writers to whom Silz's sensibilities were awakened, Kleist should stand out as first and foremost. The sudden eruption of the bewildering violence that rocked the German American community of Cleveland, as well as his parents' lives, sharpened Silz's vision for Kleist's shocking image of an unstable world in which no well-ordered life could rest secure.

Silz is particularly persuasive when he discusses *Die Familie Schroffenstein, Robert Guiskard* and *Amphitryon*. These plays, he demonstrates, most acutely "exhibit the conflict with other powers . . . . There is undeniably a pathetic appeal in the suffering of [the characters in these plays], baffled and destroyed by forces which they neither understand nor are fit to cope with" (Silz, *H. V. Kleist* 1–2). But Silz convinces also in his interpretations of Kleist's other productions. *Das Käthchen von Heilbronn,* he shows, "is a consummate indictment of the disordered and unhappy state of the world in which we live" (57). If we accept Silz's close readings of the texts, we realize again and again how much we are helpless victims, prey to the caprice of powers outside our control; how much we are molded, as *Die Familie Schroffenstein* in exemplary fashion informs us, by the forces of misunderstanding, error, and ignorance, which we can neither grasp nor influence.

Silz argues, as he makes especially clear in his interpretation of *Amphitryon,* against the majority of Kleist critics who came before him (33). The insights he offers are as innovative as they are disquieting. Undoubtedly it took the anti-German hysteria of Governor Cox's Ohio to open the eyes of this young German American from Cleveland in a way that would hardly have been possible in a more peaceful time and place.

Harvey Waterman Hewett-Thayer's Study of Fontane

For another American Germanist at the time, Harvey Waterman Hewett-Thayer, it was the world of Fontane's novels that seemed to acquire a particularly telling significance. In a remarkable book written when the profession was still suffering as a result of the wave of anti-German terror, Hewett-Thayer took as his theme the *Modern German Novel*. Although he treats more than one novelist, the pivotal figure in his account is clearly the father of the modern German novel: Fontane. All other authors portrayed in the book pale in comparison with the innovative genius he ascribes to Fontane. As with the books by Campbell and Silz, this important study, too, acquires its scholarly vitality when viewed as an American Germanist's response to the personal shock which the members of his profession experienced during and immediately after the war.

Hewett-Thayer had been exposed at an early age to German culture and manners. Unusually fortunate circumstances of birth, upbringing, education, and family connections had made it possible for him to travel extensively in Germany as a young man and to engage in prolonged and sympathetic study of German institutions and literature. His uncommon mastery of the whole range of German life and letters led to his appointment in 1905 to a newly established preceptorship in German at Princeton. Hewett-Thayer had barely established himself as an enthusiastic torchbearer of German literature in one of the most important American citadels for the humanities, however, when the anti-German feeling precipitated by World War I began to rear its ugly head at Princeton—perhaps more so than at other universities because Woodrow Wilson's famous dictum of 1896, "Princeton in the Nation's Service," had taken on a heightened meaning after half the class of 1918 had enlisted in military service and was now seen on campus in uniform (Oberdorfer 112–19). Suddenly, the flame of Hewett-Thayer's spirit was darkened when he saw himself pitted against an entire university mobilized in the service of a nation at war with everything German. Was all he had dreamed and worked for now to be extinguished?

Hewett-Thayer turned in this difficult time to Fontane's novels. In them he discovered, particularly perceptively, what happens when an individual finds his inclinations and aspirations strangled by a constricting web of surrounding antagonistic forces. More and more, this Princeton instructor must have seen his own predicament mirrored in the fortunes of Fontane's characters. This impelled him to investigate the intricacies of Fontane's novels with an intensity that was at that time astonishing, for up to then Fontane had been virtually unknown in America. The study Hewett-Thayer produced became one of the most significant contributions to early Fontane criticism. Again, however, it must have been the harrowing professional situation—this time that of a lonely German professor in a university community actively engaged in a war with Germany—that gave Hewett-Thayer the perspective required to discover the world of Fontane's novels and, in particular, to observe how the individual characters are "ruffled by the winds" of their time and place (28). With one story after another Hewett-Thayer makes this point absorbingly and clearly, but nowhere perhaps better than when he interprets Fontane's supreme masterpiece, *Effi Briest*. Pivotal for the proper understanding of this novel, the pioneering Fontane critic claims, is the fact that "Effi is enveloped in the drab dreariness of un-enlivened routine" characteristic of her unfriendly local society of town and countryside (37). The prison of the environment, the young Princeton scholar tells us, leads to a "fatalistic interpretation of life" that proves to be as incomprehensible as it is shattering for the individual (64).

Literary studies of such a high critical caliber as those of Hewett-Thayer, Silz, or Campbell were unknown in Germanics in America prior to World War I. The theses these books advanced would probably not have taken the shape they did if the critical act of interpreting had not been conditioned by the wartime terror to which these professors had been exposed. The war had thrown the study of German in the United States into a state of deliquium, but out of the smoldering embers of the war the interpretation of German literature received a phoenix-like rebirth, freeing it of the shackles of pedantry and a vulnerable patriotism, and ushering in a bright new dawn of creativity.

Three Stages of a Precarious Relationship: German Culture and Germanics in America, 1940–1995

JOST HERMAND — TRANSLATED BY MELISSA SUNDELL

As in the *Germanistik* of all non-German-speaking countries, language teaching traditionally occupied and occupies still the preeminent position in American departments of German Language and Literature. It was and is the broad basis, the foundation, upon which rests that extremely fragile superstructure in which the teaching of literature takes place, where a relatively small elite of German majors, M.A., and Ph.D. candidates are transformed from "eager youngsters" into "promising scholars," hoping to snare poorly paid but relatively unalienated college or university jobs with their "marketable dissertations." Literature, for the majority of these American German departments, has long meant, at least until the 1950s, the same works which made up the prevailing canon in *Germanistik;* namely, works from the Middle High German classical period, the Age of Goethe, Romanticism, Bourgeois Realism, and a number of selected authors from around 1900. If a few troublemakers tried to revolt against this canon, there was generally a bitter struggle concerning the long-established reading lists, which seldom led to any change. After all, the majority of literary experts teaching in this country understood their primary role to be the transmission of those works which had been considered canonical up to the First World War, and these experts defended themselves against the invasion of all tendencies which might have called this canon into question. Despite many a committee meeting and reform discussion, then, things remained unchanged throughout the Weimar Republic. Not even the time of the Third Reich brought about a break in this respect. Apart from a few exceptions, American Germanists of these years sought to justify their positions through a preservation of the conventional pride in the so-called masterpieces of German literature, instead of getting involved in any critical discourse which might have called into question the foundation of their existence.[1]

Not even the wave of German and Austrian émigrés, who had been fleeing to the United States since the middle of the 1930s, altered the situation to any extent. To be sure, this group was quite critically, even wrathfully disposed toward German politics, and once in the States professed allegiance to all democratic opinions and institutions which would enable assimilation and integration. Yet these newcomers held the established masterpieces of German literature in as high a regard

69

as their generally conservative-minded American colleagues throughout the following years. In only one point did this group feel differently. Though it likewise honored the canon of so-called masterpieces of German literature recognized in the States, which it merely broadened to include a few German Jewish authors such as Hofmannsthal, Schnitzler, Werfel, Kafka, and Broch, it could not come to terms with American "culturelessness." When among themselves, representatives of this group found that, though there were many "nice" people in America, these people simply had no classical culture—everything in this country was either still too immature, or already overcommercialized. Therefore a rigid dichotomy became fixed in their minds: Germany = catastrophic politics, but the highest culture; the United States = democratic politics, but near-complete culturelessness. This is why many, even after becoming citizens of the "new world," chose to continue to live intellectually in the "house of German literature and culture."

This position, however, in no way made them outsiders on American campuses. As the so-called New Criticism, which also drew a sharp line between politics, history, and society on the one hand and great, autonomous literature and culture on the other, developed into the predominant literary-critical methodology, they recognized its close congruence to their own outlook. René Wellek and Austin Warren's *Theory of Literature,* published originally in 1942 and brought out again in many further editions in the 1950s, seemed to coordinate perfectly with their views. Both émigrés and American scholars, withdrawing from the "ugly" spheres of economic depression, World War II, and the culturelessness of the media industry, declared themselves against the consideration of all so-called "extrinsic values" in the examination of literature, and concerned themselves almost solely with the so-called "intrinsic values," from which the true formal quality of all great literary works was constituted.

Admittedly, a number of *geistesgeschichtliche,* philosophical, and even political aspects continued to have an influence on many of the writings by literary scholars exiled from central Europe, including those penned by Bernhard Blume, Dorrit Cohn, Peter Demetz, Melitta Gerhard, Erich Heller, Peter Heller, Wolfgang Paulsen, Heinz Politzer, Henry H. H. Remak, Oskar Seidlin, Walter Sokel, Werner Vordtriede, among others. These aspects were, however, mostly of a "conservative" nature, at any rate as the term was understood at that time. Moreover, they rapidly gave way in this group during the course of the 1950s to a formal-analytic way of looking at things, which was designated in the Germany of the same period, with reference to Emil Staiger and Wolfgang Kayser, as *werkimmanent.*[2] In any case, whether *geistesgeschichtlich,* philosophically, or formal-analytically oriented, what all of these émigré Germanists shared was their constant esteem of great, internally harmonious works of art. These masterworks seemed to them, in a world wholly given over to the barbarisms of politics and the culture industry, to be guarantors of true humanity, from which they could take heart in moments of bad temper, sorrow, and despair, and which served as testimony of true "culture"; that is, of that which is imperishable and generates lasting values of the highest quality.

The representatives of the second wave of Germanists coming over from Germany to the United States, who generally arrived here in the course of the late fifties and middle to late sixties, in the wake of the Sputnik shock and the subsequent expansion of universities, had by contrast a much different attitude toward German literature and German culture in general. In this group belong Ehrhard Bahr, Barbara Becker-Cantarino, Klaus L. Berghahn, Robert Cohen, Reinhold Grimm, Peter Walter Hinderer, Peter Uwe Hohendahl, Andreas Huyssen, Anton Kaes, Gerhard Knapp, Herbert Knust, Edgar Lohner, Paul Michael Lützeler, Siegfried Mews, Heinz Osterle, Klaus Peter, Jochen Schulte-Sasse, Ernst Schürer, Dieter Sevin, Alexander Stephan, Frank Trommler, Hans-Rudolf Vaget, Hans Wagener, and many others. I do not want to lump them together indiscriminately, but they did have several things in common. They were not as strongly fixated as the representatives of the exile generation or the older American Germanists, such as Stuart Atkins, Henry Hatfield, Alexander Hohlfeld, Harold Jantz, Herman Salinger, Walter Silz, Jack Stein, Hermann Weigand and others, on the great masterpieces of German literature from Goethe to Thomas Mann and Franz Kafka, but rather were not afraid, as sympathizers with the social view of literature developing in West Germany in the sixties in opposition to the *werkimmanent* method, of including even works with so-called "extrinsic" elements. What interested them—trying to come to terms with the fascist past—was not so much the formal aesthetic, or uplifting aspects, but rather the social, ideological, and therefore politically oriented function of literature. Like many West German scholars who came into their own around 1968, they dismissed all ideas of aesthetic autonomy and developed an apparatus for ideological criticism with which they approached both the masterpieces honored as exemplary by exponents of New Criticism and the works of so-called trivial literature despised by these same New Critics as undifferentiated trash. Because their sights were set on a more detailed knowledge of political and social literary development, everything written was literature to them, no matter how "high" or "low" the works had previously been judged. That they extended their ideologically critical inquiry even to concepts like the Age of Goethe or Romanticism, as at the 1970 Wisconsin Workshop "Die Klassik-Legende," left many older representatives of German high culture, like Oskar Seidlin, profoundly embittered.[3]

Yet the members of this group also had a conception of literature as high culture, perhaps even a political program for cultural reform. They did not wish to completely demolish or wholly dismiss the older canon, but simply to read it against the grain, in good Habermasian fashion. Their sympathies lay thus not with literary greats such as Klopstock, Goethe, Novalis, Brentano, Eichendorff, Mörike, Hebbel, Grillparzer, Conrad Ferdinand Meyer, Stefan George, Rilke, Hofmannsthal, Kafka, or Broch, the favorites of the preceding exile generation, but rather with Lessing, Heine, Hauptmann, Heinrich Mann, the left Expressionists, Ernst Toller, Lion Feuchtwanger, Bertolt Brecht, Anna Seghers, and Arnold Zweig, and so on—in short, with those authors who had done what they could within Germany or in exile for a left liberal or socialist turn of events, against all restorative and reactionary tendencies. But this group strove for more than that. Its members were also the first to discuss the works of left-oriented German Jewish exiled politicians, sociologists, historians, philosophers, and psychoanalysts such as Theodor W. Adorno, Walter Benjamin, Ernst Bloch, Magnus Hirschfeld, Max Horkheimer, Karl Korsch, Siegfried Kracauer, Georg Lukács, Herbert Marcuse, and Wilhelm Reich, whose writings had, whether from inner conviction or due to the political pressure of the McCarthy era, been consistently avoided by the older, even Jewish, Germanists loyal to the humanism of the Goethean Age. In this way, a group of politically engaged scholars was formed within Germanics between 1967–68 and 1975, composed of newly established West German and younger American Germanists, such as David Bathrick, Russell Berman, Jack Zipes, Robert Holub, Sara Lennox, Helen Fehervary, and others, calling itself the "New Left." This new point of view found its best expression in *New German Critique,* a journal founded in Madison in 1973, which concerned itself with the materialist and leftist, rather than the idealist traditions of Germany.[4]

This had the following consequences for the adherents of this concept of culture. On the one hand, they were much more interested than earlier Germanists in all forms of culture which, in use or purpose, were politically disruptive. On the other hand, they held fast, in time-honored leftist tradition, to ideas of high culture propagated by German enlighteners, left liberals, and socialists, who, since the eighteenth century, had not been interested in the elimination of high culture, but rather in the continuing cultural education of the underprivileged classes, aiming toward the creation of the "one, great, cultured nation." Their leftist counterattack against the established cult of German Classicism and Romanticism thus displayed no vandalistic characteristics. It rather sought simply to emphasize the other, more progressive line of German literature and to relate it, through a critical or dialectical appropriation, to the problems of their own situation.[5] For this group, high literature was thus nothing exalted, eternal, or existential, but, like all forms of culture, something embedded in the dialectical stream of time, which stood and stands under the same compulsions as all other intellectual and cultural manifestations of a given epoch. Within the context of this group, the decisive criterium in the assessment of works of art was thus their potential to foster critical thinking and to support all avant-garde movements that are ultimately directed toward a different and better future.

All cultural products with progressive leanings were thus interpreted as part of those modernizing thrusts toward enlightenment and liberalism which attempt to evade earlier hierarchal pressures, patriarchal molds, and ideological restorations, that is, try to put themselves at the service of a prograde liberalization, democratization, or even socialization. Although their concept of culture thereby forfeited some of the older "aura" with which conservative Germanists had surrounded it, it was in no way, despite all emphasis on political and sociological factors, reduced by this process. At most, emphasis shifted to different intellectual and artistic standards. While the older *Bildungsbürger* saw the importance of a given work of art first and foremost in its inner harmony and formal-aesthetic perfection (and only secondarily in its basic humanistic orientation), this new group stressed above all the historical decision-making powers of the authors in question; that is, their ability to have made the ideologically correct choice within the context of the dialectically complex situation of their own time. Along these lines, they favored authors who had written as realistically and clearly as possible, in a way understandable to a wide spectrum of social classes. This is why this group rejected both the elevated classicism of the "Art period," already attacked by Heinrich Heine in 1835, as well as the aesthetic snobbery of some schools of modernist-elitist literature after 1900.

Criteria were thus established which could be applied not only to the history of German culture, but to the development of other cultures as well, giving them more relevance to the prevailing conditions in the United States. As a result, an intense but short-lived symbiosis of German and American Germanists developed within this camp in the early seventies. Some of the younger Americans, on the basis of their own rebellious outlook, became enthusiastic about the antifascist-minded leftists and left liberals of the late 1920s and early 1930s, seeing their "Weimar" not in Goethe and Schiller, but in the culture of the Weimar Republic. On the other hand, some of the West German immigrants—while remaining oriented toward the German situation, having indeed been called to America in the first place as experts of this situation—became more and more caught up in ideological and methodological questions of an interactive reception, which contributed to their gradual "Americanization." Thus this group's concept of culture remained a relatively demanding and discriminating one, containing all of the important works of the enlightening, Jacobin, humanist, realist, left liberal, and socialist traditions. Though its adherents no longer approached these works with the same reverential manner reserved by representatives of the older, culturally conservative group for the canonical works of Classicism and Romanticism, they did grant these works, as cultural-political vehicles of democratization, an important function with regard to society as a whole. Only two things, then, had changed with respect to the great and important accomplishments of German literature: a paradigm shift from conservative to progressive authors, and a change in function from literature as possession of the few, the elect, and the chosen to the aspiration that even high literature might one day belong to all. Some even went so far as to see literature as the most important tool for the creation of a great and cultured nation, if not for humanity as a whole.

So much—in typological simplification—on the central concepts of culture as they were discussed by Germanics between 1945 and 1980, whose leading representatives can be divided into three distinctly different groups: (1) the more conservatively oriented older Americans and exile Germanists; (2) their conservatively or traditionally oriented students such as Jeffrey Sammons and Theodore Ziolkowski; and (3) the West German new arrivals of the late fifties and sixties and their sympathizers within the American "New Left." The situation of the last 15 years has,

by contrast, become considerably less clear. If one can determine central guidelines concerning the value placed on German culture at all anymore, they would
most likely be the following: the exile Germanists generally stepped down during
this period, and the succeeding West German group has, meanwhile, also gotten on
in years. The majority of the new impulses in regard to culture studies these days
comes from younger or middle-aged Americans such as Leslie Adelson, Sander
Gilman, Nancy Kaiser, Alice Kuzniar, Biddy Martin, Jeffrey Peck, Marc Silber-
man, James Steakley, Geoffrey Waite, Marc Weiner, David Wellbery, and others,
who, though in part students of the West German liberals, are often, in the wake of
the increasing internationalization of literary studies, much more familiar with the
latest French, Italian, and American theoretical formulations than their teachers,
who had made their careers within the context of German ideas.

Former German-influenced concepts of culture, whether conservative or left
liberal in nature, have therefore retreated further and further into the background.
Though there are still German departments, or single professors of German, who
continue to value a detailed knowledge of the earlier canons of conservative or liberal masterpieces, they are hardly able to produce compelling reasons for demanding such knowledge of their students any longer. After all, the national, social, and
political preconditions for these works are gradually disappearing. There is hardly
anyone among current professors who is still proud of his or her own nation, hardly
anyone who is still eager for positivistic knowledge in the old, bourgeois sense,
and hardly anyone who still endeavors to be a respected representative of higher
culture, or a left liberal changer of the world. This leads us to the final question:
does that which once had value, in a conservative or in a progressive sense, as a
culture worthy of preserving or striving for, have any function at all any longer?

As I see it, a tendency to simply shrug off the earlier concept of culture as
a tiresome burden is momentarily the dominant trend, not only in the realm of
Germanics but in most areas of the humanities. Ironically enough, this generally
occurs under the aegis of a paradigm shift from a more narrowly understood literary studies to a more broadly conceived culture studies or culture theory. In this
way, a conglomeration of highly disparate types of texts or other aesthetically recast
forms of representation has often taken the place of the older literary canon. These
texts are supposed to stand in for something which is also designated "culture,"
but which has little or nothing in common with the concepts of culture espoused by
earlier Germanists on the right or the left. In reality, there is little reflected in this
contemporary understanding of "culture" which is normative, whether in an aesthetic, national, moral, political, or socially critical sense. What is understood under
the concept of culture today is usually something much more diffuse, something
which has dissolved into myriad different subcultures appealing to group-specific
or individualistic interests rather than to society as a whole.

Those positively disposed to this process like to represent it as an increasing democratization, dehierarchization, depatriarchalization, de-ideologization, and so
on; that is, as a process which leads to the condition of a multicultural society. This

new society, according to ideas of political correctness strictly observed, no longer engages in any sort of religious, ethnic, gender, political, or cultural discrimination against anyone, but rather tolerates, even encourages, every individual peculiarity, in order to bring about a society of individually empowered people. For many of the representatives of this camp, this has led to a decidedly decentralizing way of viewing their objects of study, bolstered philosophically by the poststructuralist tendencies and their deconstruction of older concepts of totality or so-called master discourses imported from France into the humanities at American universities. This trend reinforced the idea of a cultural conglomeration in the area of culture theory, which for the last 10 or 15 years has been included under the heading "postmodern"—a term as casual as it is suggestive.[6] That many things within this camp are muddled wildly together, indeed are often represented as consciously disparate or contradictory so that no new paradigm or totality is evoked, should not blind us to the fact that these trends aiming at the fracturing or the radical destruction of older concepts of culture and society also display recognizable commonalities, which can most certainly be reduced to a common denominator through ideological criticism.[7]

Let me try to do that in regard to the concept of culture in contemporary Germanics. For many of the younger representatives of this discipline, whose training took place within an already denationalized, dehistoricized, and de-ideologized context, "culture" does sometimes still include the—increasingly functionless— canon of German literary works. At the same time, however, and with greater emphasis, they direct their attention to all forms of cultural representation of certain gender-specific, minority-oriented, or supposedly subjective problems, preferably to the mass-media mediation of such problems—that is, their treatment in radio, film, and television. Especially for those who see themselves as helplessly isolated or group-specific beings within a globalizing multicultural society, "culture" is no longer that which is bound up with national concerns or the interests of society as a whole, but rather as that which in highly industrialized, affluent countries with high rates of immigration like the United States has begun to develop into a cultural conglomeration of transethnic groups or individuals. Younger American Germanists therefore like to take the relatively advanced state of social plurality in the United States as their sole standard, criticizing the enduringly and strongly national color of German culture as a symptom of a lack of pluralistic tolerance. In view of the catastrophic development of Germany in the first half of the twentieth century; that is, given the two world wars instigated by Germany, fascism, and the massacre of Jews, leftists, Slavs, gays, Gypsies, the mentally retarded, and others bound up with it, much of this criticism is justified, and should by all means be continued, in all sharpness. However, this criticism also runs the risk of interpreting everything in German history and therefore German culture in light of later developments, à la Daniel J. Goldhagen, thus, through a complete denigration of their objects of study, pulling the rug from under American German departments.

To explain: I am against every strict separation of culture from politics. Art has no intrinsic development, it does not constantly reproduce itself from within, in that it repeatedly enters into new intertextual intersections, as some champions of postmodernity claim. Rather, art is largely dependent upon the functional use made of it by its surrounding society and that society's different social classes, without which it never would have come into being in the first place. And these different classes always had highly different cultural intentions, to put it bluntly. For this reason, art in all class societies was always polarized into at least two feuding camps. German politics and culture was no exception; there was always a white line and a black line, an enlightening, humanistic, left liberal, and socialist one against a conservative, ultraromantic, nationalistic, and finally fascist one. To try to mix undifferentiatedly all manifestations of German culture into the same brown sauce and portray it as an expression of a *Sonderweg* necessarily leading to Auschwitz, would not just be ahistorical; it would be downright blind. After all, almost all of the best representatives of German culture, among them outsiders such as Jews, have stood behind the white line. And who would deny that they, too, have made an important contribution to German culture?

It is essential in my view to hold fast to this distinction in the future as well, if the study of German culture in the United States is to have any point at all. Every constructive relationship to the history, art, and culture of another nation is in the end contingent upon critique and dialectical appropriation. When one criticizes, one should always define the perspective from which this criticism comes. Whoever proceeds purely negatively in this respect, and represents only the "German misere," will necessarily do damage to our discipline. The positive which German culture has produced, especially in areas such as theory and music, but also in literature, should be duly stressed alongside the critique. And this cannot happen without a detailed knowledge of German history. German culture was, until late in the twentieth century, more or less oriented toward a nation-state, and therefore cannot be overgeneralized into anthropological terms, deconstructed into identitylessness, or diluted into a purely aesthetic construct. It reveals its manifold richness only through a dialectical approach to its unusually conflict-laden course, which, in addition to problematic and detestable products, has also brought forth things numbering among the "highest and holiest" accomplishments of humankind, as the German Jew Heinrich Heine expressed it.[8]

If we want to give this discipline a new relevance in the United States, we should proceed, then, more decisively than before against the following two tendencies, which currently work against a productive study of German culture in this country. These tendencies, though they developed independently of one another, have nearly the same consequences. They are (1) the tendency to examine hypercritically just about everything in German history and culture since the eighteenth century, be it left or right, white or black, according to exaggeratedly politically correct needs, with the sole purpose of finding patriarchal, antidemocratic, militaristic, aggressive, homophobic, antisemitic, or protofascist tendencies; in short, to characterize everything as a trend leading to Hitler or Auschwitz; and (2) the tendency, by contrast, to propagate a pluralistic-postmodern way of thinking which no longer exhibits any political, social, or cultural goals at all, leading to a situation in which even representatives of the humanities and of culture studies have resignedly accepted the dominant system of an elitist and a popular culture existing side by side. They help themselves from the high-culture delicatessen in the gourmet corner of the current aesthetic supermarket, while the rest of the population is conditioned to content itself in the bargain basement with cheap products from the market-oriented culture industry.[9]

In this way, a highly contradictory situation has arisen within Germanics. On the one hand, a critical investigation of the last three centuries of German culture is undertaken, which pretends to great social relevance, but in which even the good accomplishments of this culture often enough end up in problematic proximity to the dangerous, even murderous consequences of chauvinistic politics in Germany. In a countermove, on the other hand, a tendency toward internationalism and multiculturalism is praised, which, however, fabricated within the contemporary culture and consciousness industry, often has equally unfortunate consequences. This industry is, as we know, to a large extent dominated by multinational corporations whose main goal is mass cultural standardization and leveling, so that they may rake in the largest possible profit from the society they have brought into line. To fight these two trends—the totally negative view of German culture or the disobliging aesthetization of German culture—will be difficult. One cannot counter the false ideologies and values of the past solely with a thoroughgoing renunciation of all ideology and values or a postmodern flight into pluralistic indecision. One can stand up to evil only with good, to the false only with the true—even in the field of culture. Evasive maneuvers into ideological detachment, subjective grumbling, or aesthetic elitism do not help here at all.

In the future, then, we should view the last 300 years of German culture not merely as a protofascist assembly grounds, nor merely as a field of that negative dialectic Adorno and Horkheimer so often discussed. Investigated in these two ways, it would be, except as material from which to cull negative examples, relatively irrelevant. We should rather try to rescue from it, as, for example, Franz Mehring did, the "positive" of each respective form of cultural consciousness, and to arrange it within that "white line" which still today confers upon portions of German culture, old and new, their high intellectual and aesthetic status. Otherwise we will be nothing more than gravediggers of our discipline—and surely few among us want that.

Notes

1   See the first three chapters of Gisela Hoecherl-Alden's dissertation.
2   For an historical analysis of this method and its international ramifications see Hermand, *Geschichte der Germanistik* 123–32.

3 The proceedings of this conference appeared in Grimm & Hermand, *Die Klassik-Legende*. A much debated reaction to these and similar activities provided "Politics in Poetry: The Search for a Radical German Tradition" (*Times Literary Supplement*, 30 April 1971). In this respect see also Trommler's introduction to *Germanistik in den USA*, 34. How deepseated the resentment against this trend among conservatively oriented American Germanists was, is still evident in some remarks Jeffrey L. Sammons made in his 1987 article "Germanistik im Niemandsland" in the same book. Sammons stated (109): "Die Literatursoziologe interessiert in [den USA] niemanden" and " 'Politisierung' ist bei uns kein positiver Begriff in den Geisteswissenschaften."

4 For a more detailed treatment of this development see my "Madison, Wisconsin 1959–1973" and Bathrick's "On Leaving Exile."

5 A good survey of the various types of reappropriation of this heritage in West Germany from an American perspective is offered in Bersier et al., "Reappropriation of the Democratic Bourgeois Heritage."

6 For the most concrete discussion of this phenomenon see Jameson, *Postmodernism* and Huyssen, "Postmoderne."

7 See the left liberal critique of the concept "postmodernism" by Bullock and Holub in *Postmodern Pluralism and Concepts of Plurality*. For a Jewish critique of the concept "postmodernism," see Gilman's "Why and How I Study German." Gilman stated (201): "For me this is not the age of 'postmodernism,' it is the post-Holocaust age."

8 The best example for this view is to be found in Heine's *Romantische Schule*. See Heine's *Sämtliche Schriften*, 3, p. 379.

9 Similar perspectives can be found in my statement: "Some Thoughts on the Question: What is Still 'Political' in German Culture Studies."

German History, Jewish History, German Jewish Studies: Old Wine in New Bottles?

David Brenner and Michael Berkowitz

We are in the midst of a self-conscious burgeoning of German Jewish Studies. North American Germanics has not been immune to this trend; to some extent it helped give birth to it. In the area of research, one need only turn to the current offerings of the publishing houses of the University of Nebraska, Indiana, Johns Hopkins, California, Princeton, Yale, Wayne State, and others.[1] A cursory glance at the DAAD-sponsored online archive of German Studies syllabi reveals a similar eruption in pedagogy. Scholarly works now abound on German Jewish refugee academics, artists, and intellectuals in the United States and elsewhere. In his wildest dreams—or nightmares—Walter Benjamin never could have imagined the ongoing mechanical reproduction of his own icon and the commodification of his publications. Even trade bookstores feature biographies of Hannah Arendt, Paul Celan, Franz Kafka, Rosa Luxemburg, and Theodor W. Adorno—just to name a few. Not surprisingly, the Frankfurt School continues to be an attractive subject in studies of intellectual migration; both the Germanness and the Jewishness of these individuals have received due attention. And thanks to Sander Gilman, Karen Remmler, Jack Zipes, Anson Rabinbach, Jeffrey Peck, and John Borneman, the postwar Jewish presence in both Eastern and Western Germany is no longer being repressed. Clearly, there is a growing interest in German Judaica, much of it generated in the field of North American Germanics, broadly defined. This is a tendency which bears "cultural" as well as "social capital," in the words of Pierre Bourdieu, and which is for the most part a felicitous development.

In order to shed critical light on this phenomenon, we begin by asking: *Nu*, so what's new? Has this not been an ongoing trend for some decades? We will therefore glance at a few of the forebears of this crop of scholarship. Second, we inquire: in what direction does this seem to be heading, and why? Third, we will briefly discuss some works representative of the finer fruits of this endeavor. And last, we will show how the convergence of German and Jewish Studies may be used in order to decode the symbolic world of fin-de-siècle Central European Jewry.

Were not some notable minds accomplishing the same sort of fusion of matters German and Jewish in the 1950s, 1960s, and 1970s? We believe it impossible to disconnect our learned perspectives on German Jewish culture, and the process of its decimation in the Holocaust, from the interpretations of Gershom Scholem, Hannah Arendt, Peter Gay, Fritz Stern, and George Mosse. By grouping these distinctive scholars together we do not intend to diminish the differences between them, but rather to stress that they comprise something of a "loose field" of intellectual inquiry, again borrowing from the thought of Bourdieu. Although all of them focused on anti-Semitism in looking at the relationships between Germans and Jews, attention also was paid to the possibility of a German Jewish symbiosis, which generated a number of responses. Yet even if we accept Gershom Scholem's indictment of the so-called "German Jewish dialogue" as a one-way street—with non-Jewish Germans offering little or nothing in return for the Jewish embrace of *Deutschtum,* we may see this as at least opening the door for further investigation. Already in the 1960s George Mosse wrote on the Prague circle of Zionists, whose attraction to certain German cultural ideas did not lead them to declare their fealty to the world of *Deutschtum.* Instead they were inspired to create a national movement of their own out of a humanistic and open-ended reading of German nationality. As Mosse has shown in his current studies of B'rith Shalom, the mostly German Jewish circle which advocated a binational Jewish/Arab state in Palestine as an alternative to the normative "majoritarian" Zionism, a great deal of work remains to be done on this fascinating subculture.

At the risk of doing a disservice to several significant scholars who bridged the chasm between German history and Jewish history, we will mention but three: Steven Lowenstein has produced a number of articles on the emergence of the Haskalah, or Jewish Enlightenment, in Central Europe, as well as a superb study of the transplanted Orthodox German Jewish community in Washington Heights, *Frankfurt on the Hudson,* and in 1994, a detailed analysis of Jewish Berlin in the days of Moses Mendelssohn. Another synthesis of German and Jewish history, now available in English translation, is Mordechai Breuer's *Jewish Orthodoxy in Germany.* The very existence, not to mention vibrancy of this community, helps to debunk the myth that German Jews fell into one of two camps: either hyper-assimilationist, on the one hand, or the minuscule group of Zionists, on the other. In the literary-historical field, Evelyn Beck, in her work on *Kafka and the Yiddish Theater,* one was of the first scholars to mine the rich intersection of cultural traditions which help account for Kafka's power and illuminate an integral part of his historical moment. All of these scholars, before it came into vogue, evinced a remarkable fluency in the realms of German Jewry, East European Jewries, and the general German milieu.

By no means, however, do we wish to suggest that the orientation of Mosse and the other scholars remained fixed. Clearly, Mosse's views have been influenced by insights of colleagues such as Jost Hermand, Marion Kaplan, Sander Gilman, and David Sorkin. Nevertheless, it is possible to distinguish some characteristics which separate the previous vintage of scholars from those who came of age after the Second World War. Since the 1980s, German Jewry from the early nineteenth century onward has been recognized as a palpable "sub-culture," a historical formation given its most convincing articulation in the work of David Sorkin. Sorkin has steered or colored the interpretation of scholars across the generations with his exposition of the seminal creed of *Bildung* among German Jews. Sander Gilman, in his monumental *Jewish Self-Hatred,* called attention to the interplay and construction of languages and literatures in the making of, and also the challenge to, Jewish identity. In his most recent book *Kafka, The Jewish Patient* Gilman asserts that "Kafka's Jewish experience is caught in the web of words that surrounded his life—words in Yiddish, in German, in Czech, and in Hebrew" (Gilman, *Kafka* 230). He explores "Kafka's self-construction in fiction, letters and diaries to show how some of his most important identities—a man, a sufferer from illness, a Jew—relate to his fear of becoming exactly what the world says he must become" (Gilman, *Kafka* 10). This work is particularly strong in interpreting the "messages" to which Kafka was exposed, such as the disturbing cartoons of the Dreyfus Affair. In the realm of Jewish Studies, Gilman's imaginative integration of medical knowledge, material culture, and visual sources is beyond comparison.

Thinking of German Studies without German Jewish Studies is difficult. While the danger is still present that it can all be reduced to Holocaust-related phenomena (see the discussion below), a younger generation of scholars—at greater historical distance from their *émigré Doktoreltern*—is pointing out that German culture was not only a seedbed for Jew-hatred. German culture, particularly the traditions related to *Bildung,* Young Germany, and German liberalism formed an important part of German Jewish identity—not only for the so-called "assimilationists," but for Zionists, and even the German Orthodox community. German culture, underscoring Schiller, Goethe, Kant, and Thomas Mann—but also Moses Mendelssohn, Heinrich Heine and Emil Ludwig—helps explain who the German Jews were, why they thought what they thought and did as they did.

Furthermore, these scholars—including Mark Gelber, Michael Brenner, David Myers, John Efron, Keith Pickus, and Jeffrey Grossman—are also conversant in Yiddish and Hebrew and more attuned to Jews *qua* Jews than the earlier crowd. Brenner's *The Renaissance of Jewish Culture in Weimar Germany* may be seen as the pinnacle of the scholarly recognition of the cultural space inhabited and nourished by the Jews of that era. In its investigation of adult education (the Lehrhaus Movement), the popularization of Jewish history and German Jewish literature, music and the visual arts, and Hebrew and Yiddish, Brenner's work constitutes a substantial revision of existing historical assessments of German Jewry. Brenner convincingly shows that Germany's Jews—even if they identified with neither the Zionist nor Orthodox communities—were not nearly as un-Jewish or a-Jewish as has been intimated in the work of Peter Gay and Jehuda Reinharz. Furthermore, the harsh lines drawn between so-called assimilationists and nationalists did not necessarily reflect the reality of Weimar Jewry, where such distinctions were becoming ever more blurred. Brenner's book will be especially helpful for those who teach courses on the Holocaust who wish to gain a sense of the vitality of German Jewish life before the rise of Hitler. The work of Brenner's *Namensvetter* David complements this thesis with an interpretation of a secular, but nevertheless distinctively Jewish cultural space that was being carved out since the late nineteenth century. In the marketing of an ethnic identity, German *and* Jewish culture—in both its "high" and "low" manifestations—were inextricably bound.

One of the great strengths of this newer scholarly community, and a legacy of its tie to Mosse in particular, is its theoretically self-conscious engagement with the world of images. The work of Steven Aschheim on East European Jews in Germany, Marc Weiner on Wagner, James Young on Holocaust memorials (discussed below), and Michael Steinberg on Aby Warburg and the Salzburg festivals, offer ample testimony to this current. After the appearance of Steven Aschheim's *Brothers and Strangers* it appears increasingly disingenuous to refer to German Jewry without noting the important presence of, and tensions resulting from the influx of Polish and Russian Jews into their midst. Weiner, in a work that is unsettling to those who prefer to regard Wagner's anti-Semitism as irrelevant or exaggerated in the post-Nazi world, has shown that the composer knew full well what he was doing with regard to the Jews, and much of his audience understood as well.

But as opposed to examining images primarily for decoding the anti-Semitic onslaught against the Jews, the newer research is more concerned with the Jews' mediation of their own perceptions, fears, and aspirations. It is not surprising that Michael Steinberg's perceptive essay on Aby Warburg correlates Warburg's analysis of group photographs of American Indians, with the pictures of Polish Jews which were included in Warburg's personal archive. "Despite his German posture," Steinberg writes, "Warburg's sympathy was for the subjected, for the Pueblo Indian whose imagery, culture, and commerce were being replaced by those—literally, in the images he stressed—of Uncle Sam. Surely the parallel of the wandering American Indian minority and its 'primitive' traditions (remembering that Warburg used the quotation marks) to that of the Jews in Imperial Germany occurred to him. The American Indians and the German Jews faced similar predicaments of assimilation and orthodoxy" (Steinberg 104). What is more, Warburg was literate in things Jewish; he could also read Hebrew.

Our own work further illustrates this trend. Michael Berkowitz has studied in great detail the iconography of the Zionist leadership, especially of Theodor Herzl. Although it is also important to discuss these images vis-à-vis anti-Semitic portrayals of Jews—Herzl is invariably depicted as beautiful but manly—and Herzl's role as an arbiter of German culture in the Viennese *Neue Freie Presse,* they are specifically Jewish mediations. Indeed, Herzl with his prophet's beard is always recognizably Jewish, and E. M. Lilien's famous photos of him were used repeatedly in montage against backgrounds mixing "old" and "new" Jewish motifs. One of numerous examples is a promotion for a Herzl stamp, where the neologism at the top, "Jewish National Fund," is juxtaposed with the biblical Hebrew, "If I forget thee O Jerusalem let my right hand forget its cunning." Such peculiarly Jewish reinventions of tradition were featured in postcards and other materials from each successive Zionist Congress and were frequently captioned with well-known quotations from scripture and liturgy: "Behold: I will take the children from amongst the nations and bring them to their land" or "Let our eyes witness your loving return to Zion." Another example is a postcard with a farmer and what appears to be an earth goddess cites the *birkat ha-mazon* (the grace after meals) "Those who sow in tears will reap in joy."

David Brenner's research on *Ost und West: Illustrierte Monatsschrift für modernes Judentum* (Berlin: 1901–23) shows how the magazine's programmatic "note of Jewishness" (*jüdische Note*) was enshrined visually in the its brown-yellow front cover. Designed by the Jewish Jugendstil artist Lilien in collaboration with the journal's editor, the drawing depicts an impressive female figure who fills the entire left side of the tableau (physically "West"). Though she wears a Renaissance-style blouse, her bottom half is draped in a garment interspersed with Stars of David — the dominant motif of the graphic.[2] A Star of David also adorns her hair; the bejeweled head-covering in the back evokes Jewish tradition. In a state of inspiration, she gazes into a small treelike root. Whereas the root blossoms on the upper right side of the tableau (physically "East"), it expands to encircle the lower left side of the page (physically "West") in thorns.

While this outgrowth appears to recapitulate Jewish history, rendering Western Jewish life as a bitter diaspora, one might interpret the entire image differently. If the robust Jewish female on the left signifies Eastern Jewishness, as suggested by "Ost" in the title directly above her, the small plant against the dark background on the right may symbolize the embryonic state of Jewish nationalism in the West. In this, as in other cases, the editor of *Ost und West* showed a preference for multivalence over lucidity when attempting to market the idea of pan-Jewishness.

This female cover figure became a staple of Zionist iconography in the early days of the movement, a Jewish counterpart to Germania, Marianne, and Britannia. Most images of her disappeared after a few years, however. By contrast, the magazine's masthead never changed in 23 years of publication. Like the cover, it was also drawn by Lilien and also outlines the historical transition from traditional to enlightened Jewish identity. On the masthead, the word "West" begins at the exact center of the phrase "Ost und West," indicating who the journal's target audience was. Whereas the letter "O" in "Ost" is covered with a flourish that resembles a yarmulke, the head covering of observant Jews, the "W" in "West" is crowned by a mustache shape, symbolizing the Westernization of the traditional Jewish beard. In addition, the "W" looks imprisoned, even though the bars enclosing it are part of a Star of David. This and other distinctions between Western and Eastern Jewish identity in *Ost und West*'s iconography recall Ahad Ha'am's dictum regarding European Jews: they were free, but enslaved.

The study of how Jews visualized themselves is suggestive for interrogating theoretical ideas about how religious identities become secularized. And it problematizes the complex relationship of images, and the mediation of those images, to identity formation. Furthermore, the ways Jews in German-speaking lands saw themselves, and the ongoing significance of their self–re-creation, merits inclusion in the contemporary discourses of the history of art and photography—as well as the history of anti-Semitism and racism.

What we learn, say, from David Myer's study of the often eccentric scholars of the "Jerusalem School" is not just what made them unique, but how their reinvention of the Jewish past was so similar to reinventions of national histories by historians of other emerging nations. At the same time, such scholarship belongs to a newer tendency in Jewish Studies: to see beyond the belief in Jewish uniqueness toward an understanding of Jewish culture as one moment in human culture and to situate the Jews in their larger cultural environment as children of their age. Parallel to placing "immanent" and "internal" histories of Jewish populations into their larger sociopolitical contexts, an academic normalcy has set in.

A sign of this "normalization" is the opening of the field of Judaics to non-Jews—and particularly non-Jews in Germany. On the one hand, one might worry about the postwar practice of Jewish Studies without Jews.[3] On the other hand, the discourse of apologetics introduced with the *Wissenschaft des Judentums* is refreshingly absent in post-1945 Germany despite the "unscholarly" factors at work, such as the enormous burden of guilt and expiation. But freed of the burden of public relations typical of American Jewish studies programs, the *Bundesdeutsche* are doing superb work. Most impressive of the institutes are those in Leipzig, just getting off the ground, and Reinhard Rürup's virtual *Dissertationsfabrik* at the Technical University in Berlin. A Fulbright German Studies seminar in summer of 1996 brought U.S. professors on a tour of these bastions of *Judaistik*. As one participant, a historian of anti-Semitism, wrote:

> These institutes are very demanding of their students. I was continually impressed. They seem to operate on the (unspoken) proposition that Jewish culture and history are subjects we study like any others, no matter the emotional baggage they carry. "We expect you to use your critical intelligence, not to waste your or our time . . . acting as prosecuting attorneys for the Jewish people . . . or atoning for the murderous deeds of your fathers and grandfathers. Our objective is the truth, the only justifiable reason to study anything." (Levy 1)

This deliberate process of normalization also gives the lie to the cliché of anti-Semitism—or even philosemitism—without Jews. What seemed unlikely after the Holocaust has arisen out of the ashes—and with dynamism to boot. Thomas Nolden's book on contemporary German Jewish literature is part, if not the pinnacle, of the scholarly recognition of the cultural space inhabited by Jews in post-Shoah Germany and Austria. In excellent analyses of prose and poetry penned by the so-called *Nachgeborene* of the second and third generations, Nolden and other German-born non-Jews are contributing to the continuing revision of existing historical assessments of Jews in the Federal Republic, the former German Democratic Republic, and Austria.

On the whole, this area of inquiry is balanced and vigilant in problematizing both binary oppositions and inherited taboos.[4] By wisely eschewing constructs like "minority literature" and "literature of the margins," it has delivered sensitive and sensible readings of works by Rafael Seligmann, Maxim Biller, Robert Schindel, Robert Menasse, Matthias Hermann, Chaim Noll, Barbara Honigmann, Katja Behrens, Esther Dischereit, Ronnith Neumann, and many other "angry" and not-so-angry young men and women. Their generational and aesthetic negotiations are productively navigated with the aid of leading American and French theorists ranging from James E. Young, Lawrence Langer, Ruth Klüger, and Eric Santner to Alain Finkielkraut, Jean-François Lyotard, and Deleuze and Guattari.

The students of *jüngere deutsche Literatur* are as interested in discerning poetic strategies—in particular, how to narrate the Holocaust—as in mapping identity formations. Instead of reading "identification" as performance (*pace* Judith Butler), Nolden employs a "concentric" model according to which the writers in question approach but never fully access the foundations of authoritative *Judentum*. But whereas the "Shoah" or even "Israel" may be focal points of contemporary Jews' self-understanding, it is one thing to outline their necessary remoteness from classic Jewish civilization and quite another to chronicle imaginative attempts to redeem and recover them. Hence the weakest moments in Nolden's "con-centrations" concern the sphere of Jewish "religion" (Nolden 77). No doubt this territory is overburdened and overdetermined. For a heuristics of tradition and change, origin and mimesis, may serve as well as Eric Hobsbawm's "reinvented traditions" or (more recently) Yael Zerubavel's "recovered roots." And most of all: you don't have to be a non-Jew to get Judaism wrong.[5]

With its multivalence, its self-referential "anaesthetics" (Nolden), and the way it ingests previous intertexts, the new German Jewish literature seems ideally suited to Bakhtinian polyphony. It may be most brilliantly illustrated in Schindel's novel *Gebürtig* (1992). And the performative penchant for black humor and the grotesque found in Seligmann, George Tabori, Edgar Hilsenrath, and Peter Sichrovsky moves in the experimental direction of Art Spiegelman's *Maus* (now on CD-ROM) and Agnieszka Holland's feature *Hitlerjunge Salomon* (1990; *Europa, Europa*), thus giving the lie to the "impermissibility" of art after Auschwitz.

But while Nolden is careful to differentiate Theodor W. Adorno's various pronouncements on this subject, he and others may still be too beholden to active/ passive dichotomies involving the so-called "culture industry." For in newer readings of the Frankfurt School, film is no longer the "most problematic" medium. Miriam Bratú Hansen, in an excellent essay comparing *Schindler's List* and Claude Lanzmann's *Shoah* (1985), favors an institutional, discursive approach that seeks to rehabilitate Spielberg's film for scions of the Frankfurt School. Hansen's is one of several recent approaches to memory and the Holocaust that draw on the pioneering writings of sociologist Maurice Halbwachs. Just ten years prior to his murder in Buchenwald, Halbwachs argued persuasively that it is primarily through membership in religious, national, or class groups that people are able to acquire and then recall their memories at all. Both the reasons for memory and the forms memory takes are thus socially constructed and continually renegotiated. Yael Zerubavel, in her pathbreaking research on memory culture in Israel, notes that the "constant need to mediate between the past and the present . . . ultimately accounts for the continuing vitality of collective memory" ("Death of Memory" 92).

This newer research on commemoration also challenges essentializing views of the Holocaust and is characteristic of a newer generation of scholars at further remove from the catastrophe (Kansteiner). Christopher Browning's history of one of the *Einsatzgruppen* sent to massacre Jewish civilians in Eastern Europe exemplifies such a "contextualist" approach. Instead of demonizing the Shoah as an extreme aberration—as Daniel Goldhagen appears to do in his book on the same *Einsatzgruppe*—Browning situates it within the course of modern European history. He also draws on social psychology, as do others who cross disciplinary boundaries. James Young calls on fellow literary critics to "re-historicize" the Holocaust (*Writing* 5), while folklorist Toby Blum-Dobkin insists that we interview survivors with "the same scholarly criteria we used to interview witnesses to other historical events" (50).

Work being done today on the representation of the Holocaust—not to speak of matters German Jewish—will have to account for the "future-shock" proliferation in the use of video, CD-ROM, and newer media. One leading voice warning of the devolution of collective memory has been the French historian Pierre Nora, for whom modern life's "sites of memory" (*lieux de mémoire*) are denatured, industrialized, corporate, and ritualized. Rather than embodying memory, monuments may displace it altogether. James Young writes: "To the extent that we encourage monuments to do our memory-work for us, we become that much more forgetful . . . . In effect, the initial impulse to memorialize events like the Holocaust may actually spring from an opposite and equal desire to forget them" (*Art* 8–9).

While this argument may have an internal logic, it is neither inevitable nor flawless. In fact, the discourse on "monumentalization" belies an unfamiliarity with newer media and their possibilities for contesting traditional commemorations. In contrast to blocks of granite, steel, or concrete—products of a particular chronotope—the architecture of "virtual" sites of memory is being constructed differently. For a cinematic commemoration like *Schindler's List,* when made available for repeated re-viewings, becomes a part of everyday life at "home." No memorial practice in some distant locale, videoplayback almost always takes place in a domestic setting. Reproducible mediations of the Holocaust in video format (and now on the internet and World Wide Web) can be stopped and studied at one's convenience on the family television or PC-monitor. This nearly "Brechtian" capability may well fulfill Halbwachs's thesis that "people . . . need to establish distance in order to preserve a collective memory" (196).

Many will not agree that *Deutschtum* and *Judentum* are inextricably defined by the Holocaust. Nor will they concur that our understanding of the Shoah shapes the very identities and self-definitions of both. Nevertheless, the near-explosion of postmodern historiography, collective memory, and commemoration research will—for the foreseeable future—have to refer to things German Jewish. At the same time, German culture's centrality to the Holocaust and Jewish death should not deter us from understanding its place in Jewish life. To quote from Steven Aschheim's critical assessment of Goldhagen's book:

> The enduring outrage and ongoing fascination, the scandal and the riddle, consists precisely in seeking to understand the penetration of the barbarous within the familiarly cultured, the transgression of basic taboo within the framework of advance civilizations . . . . In matters as dense and complex as these humility is of the essence: closure and certainty are probably unachievable. (64)

The *Wissenschaftswein* of our title—no matter how new its bottle may appear— must continue to ferment. The refining task of scholarship, and of a *Wissenschaft des Judentums,* is surely to call into question rather than reinforce stereotypical thinking and to encourage balanced and complex historical judgment on all sides. Thus the discipline of Jewish Germanics—encompassing a broad span of theoretical schools, methodological approaches, and objects of study—is not merely the legacy of so-called "Yekkes" who evaded the reach of Nazi Germany and remade their lives in Palestine, the United States, Great Britain, Latin America, and elsewhere. Although it may still be too early for a self-conscious *Wissenschaftsgeschichte* devoted to German Judaics, a steady flow of books and essays is attempting to (re)define the field, and "German Jewish Studies"—whether we choose to hyphenate it or not—will likely play an important role in shaping public and personal memory of things German in the years to come.

Notes

1 See, for instance, Gilman and Zipes' massive *Yale Companion.*
2 The later signet of the Jüdischer Verlag, the publishing house of the Zionist movement founded by Buber, Feiwel, Weizmann, and Lilien, appears in the background. Also designed by Lilien, it depicts a Star of David superimposed on a smaller menorah.
3 Gershom Scholem once observed bitterly, "es sei eine Ironie der Geschichte, daßausgerechnet, nachdem das deutsche Judentum praktisch zerstört wurde, das Studium der Judaistik—wofür jüdische Wissenschaftler ein Jahrhundert lang vergebens gekämpft hatten—an deutschen Universitäten eingerichtet wurde" (M. Brenner, *Nach dem Holocaust* 216)
4 For an excellent example by an American Jewish academic, see Leslie Adelson, whose work is also notable in attempting to unsettle the category of gender. On gender and sexuality, see also Boyarin.
5 Hermann and Noll come close to reenacting rabbinic Judaism and the "liturgy of de-

struction" (Roskies) that have marked the "people of the book" for two millennia. In their renewed striving to become Jewishly-literate, these authors and others are strikingly similar to their American Jewish colleagues. After all, the custom of talking back to God and to one's parents—not to speak of the self-defensive irreverence of Biller's "Auschwitz sehen und sterben" (*Wenn ich einmal*)—is a form of mocking defiance (see the modern term *davke*) most notably celebrated by Philip Roth, who is strangely elided in this study. Roth's insistence on multiple narratives in his most recent novels is echoed in contemporary Jewish German writing.

Toward an American Germanics?
Feminism as a Force for Change

SARA FRIEDRICHSMEYER AND PATRICIA HERMINGHOUSE

As the academic profession in the United States has changed over the past few decades, various terms have been advanced to describe the processes at work. Within
our discipline, scholars have identified the concurrent "graying of the professoriate" and the "feminization of the profession" as functioning in different ways
to transform the makeup of our ranks. The much-remarked "feminization of the
profession" that Valters Nollendorfs documented in 1994 is sometimes associated
with a decline in salary, prestige, and job security in our field, especially when
the phenomenon is understood to mean merely the swelling numbers of women
studying and teaching in the field (V. Nollendorfs, "Out of Germanistik" 6–8). But
because many of these women have been feminists, their increasing numbers can
be linked to more positive effects as well: the inclusion of women writers in the
curriculum, for example, or the transformation of the canon, the increased range of
sophisticated theoretical approaches to our subject matter, and the reexamination
of traditional literary definitions, periodizations, and genres.[1] This increase in the
number of feminist scholars and teachers has also contributed in unforeseen ways
to the development of a distinctly American form of Germanics.[2]

The ways in which feminist Germanists in this country have helped to shape the
discipline reflect the historical and institutional evolution of the American feminist movement, itself an outgrowth of the antiwar and civil rights movements of
the 1960s. Both were rooted in the desire for change, in the challenge to an established order. Within German departments a generation of women emerged in the
1970s who began to indict ingrained practices and habits of mind that had resulted
in their widespread exclusion from the realms of male academic privilege. Some
of the few senior women scholars in the profession at that time joined with their
younger colleagues and graduate students in calling attention to the near absence
of women in tenure-track jobs and administrative suites, in editorial positions and
offices of professional organizations. They also raised scholarly concerns about
how this situation affected what literature was being researched and taught, whose
works were admitted into the canon, and indeed which voices were even heard in
classes and seminars. Although they were convinced that it would be possible to
open the field to new influences through a combination of scholarly initiatives and
political involvement (Martin), the feminists of the early 1970s did not frame their
goal in terms of an American instead of a German *Germanistik*. Nonetheless, many

of the achievements of the movement, both institutional and intellectual, have led in that direction, transforming the discipline in the process.

Within *Germanistik,* the earliest feminist impulses were felt in the archaeology of literature, leading to discoveries of texts by and about women that had not been included in the purview of the field. From the belated unearthing of women who had written in the Middle Ages to the exhilarating discovery of contemporary literature being produced by women, feminist research began to flourish as women gained access, however limited, to academic citizenship.

In many German departments in the United States, the intersection of the feminist movement of the 1970s with the suddenly increased interest in the GDR that followed in the wake of *Ostpolitik* further served to establish a distinctive American research agenda. The impression of the GDR as a place where women were granted legal rights, not only to jobs, but also to training and advancement, and where the state seemed to recognize the needs of both children and parents, including access to abortion, struck a chord with the discontent of feminist Germanists. That women writers there were increasingly prominent in the literary scene also seemed at the time to underscore the concrete potential of the GDR system. With the exception of research that Germanists in this country had already begun on the biographies and writings of exiles from Nazi Germany, it was the first time that the American context of our professional identities was not a disadvantage: the fact that we were *not* employed in the Federal Republic actually facilitated access to writers and institutions in the GDR. In addition, the sheer lack of knowledge about the "other Germany" at the time was an important incentive for the sort of interdisciplinary communication and cooperation that had not been typical of mainstream Germanics.

It was, in fact, at the first American conference on GDR literature that the idea for what was initially known as *Women in Germanistik* was conceived by a group of women faculty and students who once again found themselves quite literally excluded from the seats of power: seated on the floor for lack of chairs while male colleagues dined in proper style at tables, a dozen women resolved in the spring of 1974 to undertake for women in German departments what had already begun to happen in English programs since the establishment of the MLA Commission on the Status of Women in the Profession in 1969 and which it continued with the Women's Caucus of the Modern Languages a year later.[3] Following an organizational meeting at the 1974 Midwest Modern Language Association (MMLA), the first *Newsletter of the Coalition of Women in Germanistik* appeared in December 1974. Published through 1981 by a collective at the University of Wisconsin, its triumphant—or was it defiant?—opening sentence asserted: "We exist." By February, however, the second *Newsletter,* reflecting the recognition that "language matters" in the attempt to reach colleagues outside of college and university German departments, announced a change of name to "a more neutral, all-inclusive term": "We are no longer *Women in Germanistik* but *Women in German.*" Because of concerns "that the term . . . might scare away potential members" (Clausen 2), the group opted at the time to retain its identification as "women" rather than feminists, a choice that male colleagues who present papers in WiG panels, publish in the *Yearbook,* or pay their membership dues have lived with gracefully for more than two decades. The first of WiG's by now traditional panels and sessions at the major professional conferences in the field took place at the 1975 annual meeting of the American Association of Teachers of German (AATG) with a session on "Women and *Germanistik.* " It was in fact one of the men at WiG's first organizational meeting at the 1974 MMLA who contributed to a discussion of the hostility with which most editors seemed to receive feminist articles by suggesting that we approach *Die Unterrichtspraxis.* The editor, Gerhard Weiss, responded immediately by announcing that the first 1976 issue would include a "Focus on Women and *Germanistik"*: seven articles on a range of topics, including literary scholarship, *Landeskunde,* and pedagogy.

The first WiG conference in 1976 announced a focus that has remained fundamental to the organization: "Feminism and German Studies: An Interdisciplinary Perspective." By 1977 WiG was recognized as an affiliate organization of the MLA and had a membership of several hundred, a tradition of annual meetings and panels at other professional meetings, and a substantial quarterly *Newsletter.*[4] By 1985 the organization had its own scholarly organ as well, the *Women in German Yearbook,* which moved to the University of Nebraska Press as a fully refereed publication in 1991.

The changes that have been brought about in the last two decades affect not only the content, but also the form of WiG's professional activities. Over the years, for example, WiG has developed certain modes of organization and communication based on a spirit of cooperation and collaboration that has always been more typical of American feminism than of mainstream *Germanistik.* The WiG *Newsletter,* the widely read internet WiG-List, and our inclusion of all ranks of the profession in WiG activities exemplify this spirit. By pairing more experienced members with newcomers to the profession in a range of undertakings, WiG makes a conscious effort to promote the professional growth and development of those upon whom the future of the discipline depends. The most recent development in support of this end has been the establishment of an endowment fund in memory of deceased WiG members that will support the award of an annual prize for the best recently completed dissertation in the area of feminist studies in German literature and culture.

Reflected in panels at professional meetings, the annual WiG conference, and publications, this operational style is, in fact, one of the most deeply held principles of the organization. Typical, too—and perhaps indicative of where many female members of the profession have traditionally been heavily invested—has been a more open concern with pedagogical matters than is characteristic of much of the field. For example, early projects of the fledgling organization addressed sexism in instructional materials, and, through the years, critiques of gender bias in language textbooks have yielded noteworthy results with some publishers. Several collections of model course syllabi have also been published. Finally, the annual WiG conference usually includes a focus on feminist pedagogy, as does one of the WiG-sponsored sessions at the AATG annual meeting.

A look at the record of the last few decades will further demonstrate the extent to which feminist Germanists in the United States have shaped the profession in ways that further differentiated them from *Germanistik*. Following the literary archaeology that began in the 1970s, for example, much attention was devoted to aesthetic and theoretical questions as feminist scholars began to recognize that the old tools of the trade as practiced by *Germanistik,* the tools with which we had been trained, were inadequate to fundamental changes in the practice of our discipline, at least in the United States. Attempting to transcend the nineteenth-century tactic of simply appending a chapter on the "ladies" to histories of German literature, feminist scholars struggled to establish intellectual contacts with other disciplines, especially through Women's Studies programs, where the initial impetus for equality had begun to modulate, sometimes painfully, into an acknowledgment of difference and, ultimately, an insistence on the value of diversity in curricula, research agendas, and human organizations.

By the beginning of the 1980s, feminists in many fields had begun to recognize that, in the attempt to secure equality for "women," the dualistic opposition of male patriarchy to female victimization had effectively blinded many of us to our own failure to address asymmetrical relations *among* women. At WiG conferences, lesbian and Jewish colleagues began to call attention to the marginalization of their particular categories within the undifferentiated concept of "women." Drawn into the academic context of Women's Studies programs, which tend to be more transgressive of disciplinary and national boundaries, feminist Germanists also encountered a broader spectrum of ethnic, racial, sexual, and national identifications. These further challenged false universalizations about the category "woman" as well as assumptions underlying the unexamined ethnocentrism of our identification with "things German." [5] Although similar developments had not yet taken place on any scale in Germany, where disciplinary boundaries tend to be less porous, contacts were initiated with feminist members of the profession there who were also interested in effecting change.

Perhaps because of this formative experience in Women's Studies, feminist Germanists have tended to be among the first to draw attention to ethnic and androcentric biases in most constructions of "Germanness." The increased urgency with which questions of "belonging," of nationalism and national identity, are being raised in unified Germany coincides with the issues of identity politics and racism that surfaced somewhat earlier in Feminist Studies on this side of the Atlantic. These intersections are beginning to be reflected in redefinitions of our disciplinary boundaries, as surely as they challenge the nineteenth-century notion of a national literature.

The heated discussions of multiculturalism, racism, colonialism, and essentialism that have shaped feminist and gender studies in the United States in recent years have, of course, intensified uneasiness about treating "German" as a category, that—at least until 1989—was rarely thought to be mutable or multivalenced beyond the East–West dichotomy. Like the masculine–feminine polarities that feminist theory began to abandon after the 1970s, the East–West dichotomy has been displaced in much recent feminist research by attempts to register the complexities of culture in Germany: Afro-Germans, ethnic Germans, asylum seekers, lesbians and gays, Roma and Sinti are finally disrupting tidy older representations of a culturally homogeneous society. And WiG has been very much involved in this development. WiG members in the past have invited Turkish-born writers to the annual conference, and again in 1996 they invited writers whose literature challenges traditional assumptions about the definitions of German literature: Libuše Moníková, who grew up in what was Czechoslovakia, and Herta Müller, who grew up in Romania.

The disproportionate representation of women among scholars dealing with these topics in publications and at professional gatherings, not only at WiG but at the MLA and GSA annual meetings as well, is not explained by any essentially feminine multicultural genes—or greater moral endowment. In most cases it derives from the formative experiences of feminist studies, where these issues have been in the forefront of recent research and theory and where the margins and borderlands are increasingly proving themselves to be the most fruitful locations for cultural insights. Being Germanists in the United States, then, has played a role; perspectives are always different when one is outside the center.

As feminist scholarship has broadened its focus from "women's issues" to more general questions of the construction of gender as it is inflected by issues of race, class, and national identity, it has become more closely identified with cultural studies. The emergence of a "cultural studies" approach, with its insistence on closer attention to the question of how its practitioners situate themselves vis-á-vis their object of study, has in turn benefitted from the concerns of feminist scholars. In fact, in his assessment of "The Formations of Cultural Studies," Lawrence Grossberg, one of the major theorists of the field, went so far as to assert that "it is fair to say that there is no cultural studies that is not 'post-feminist,' not in the sense of having moved beyond it, but rather in the sense of having opened itself to the radical critique and implications of feminist theory and politics" (Grossberg 26).

Although many of the initiatives and interests just described have had the effect of differentiating feminist Germanists from the general practice of *Germanistik* in Germany, this effect was not part of a conscious plan. In fact, only in retrospect have feminist Germanists in the United States become aware of the pivotal role of some of their activities in the development of an American approach to the discipline. Other more recent steps, however, have been taken with a deliberately articulated goal of broadening our contacts with English-speaking colleagues in various fields. Included here is certainly the 1995 WiG Conference, organized as a response to members' desires to transcend the borders of *Germanistik* by forging links with feminist scholars from cognate disciplines in this country. Historian

Atina Grossmann, sociologist Myra Marx Ferrée, and political theorist Joan Cocks
were invited to the conference to provide an overview of the important trends and
directions in current feminist scholarship in their own fields. They were also asked
to comment, again from the perspectives of their own fields, on a film that conference participants viewed together, *Beruf Neo-Nazi*. Although the presentations and
the ensuing discussions deepened convictions about the complexity of scholarly
work across disciplines, participants viewed this effort to understand other disciplinary positions as a valuable step in the process of overcoming isolation within
their own fields and institutions.[6]

   One more development, this also of recent vintage, has steered feminist Germanists in the United States away from *Germanistik* as traditionally practiced in
Germany and towards a redefinition of the field that takes into account the increasing need for contact with scholars in other disciplines. At its 1994 meeting, members of the editorial board of the *Women in German Yearbook* resolved to publish
all subsequent articles in English, a decision reaffirmed at both the 1995 and 1996
annual meetings. The original decision was prompted by a general desire to be part
of academic deliberations in this country. The intent was not to eliminate contributions from colleagues here or in other countries who preferred to write in German,
but simply to pave the way for their articles to appear in English translation. It was
not a decision casually made, and it was not viewed as irrevocable. There were,
however, powerful arguments for an all-English volume. Feminist Germanists in
the United States have for many years been making their own contacts with feminist colleagues in other fields in this country; yet while we have been incorporating
the results of their work into our own, the reverse was not happening. While our
disciplinary journals routinely published reviews of their studies, our yearbook
was not being reviewed in journals with English-speaking readers. The policy was
adopted, then, largely as part of an attempt to bring scholarship in our field into the
American mainstream.

   The 1995 volume was the first published after this policy took effect, and thus
it is too early to tell whether or not it will have the desired outcome. The editors of
the *Yearbook* will, however, be paying close attention to any results associated with
this strategy, asking continually if it really helps to overcome the insularity of our
discipline, if it really helps those in other academic fields to gain access to ongoing
developments in our own. Already it is clear that the publisher, the University of
Nebraska Press, has adjusted its advertising strategy because of this policy to include large ads in English-language publications such as *The Women's Review of
Books*.

   Although we cannot yet measure any external results, we have noticed some
internal effects that bear comment. Having now submitted two all-English volumes—and having worked through numerous translations, some of which we have
in the end decided not to publish—we acknowledge that the policy has cost the
editors, the translators, the anonymous readers, and even the authors themselves
much additional time and energy. Other considerations have also surfaced, many

of them related to the old dilemma of how to reward translators. The organization has no budget to pay them, and we are reluctant to ask contributors who write in German to hire their own translators. So until now we have relied on translators who volunteer their time and skills, knowing that they will not receive financial recompense—and knowing as well that they sometimes will have to do without adequate acknowledgment. We have not yet found a fair way to give them credit for their work. A line in a vita claiming a translation seems hardly adequate.

There are also problems beyond the actual translation process and evaluation, problems inherent in the very notion of translation. When early in 1996 the editors of the *Yearbook* put out on the internet WiG-List a call for translators, the call put us in contact with many qualified and willing volunteers. It also had another, unexpected result: a sometimes intense debate about the legitimacy of translation itself, not of entire works of literature, but of articles and of passages buttressing arguments in those articles. Soon the debate encompassed even translations as they affect our classroom and our institutions as well. Clearly it is an issue that evokes strong responses. Some advantages are certain: a chance to reach beyond the small numbers of scholars and students in German departments and thus bring developments in our field to a much wider audience. Ultimately, an all-English volume enables us to be part of a larger academic discussion than would otherwise be possible.

But there are concomitant disadvantages to publishing only in English, and as yet there is no consensus on their magnitude. We have asked ourselves, for example, if this policy could be seen as one more concession to the dominance of the English language, if we are in fact furthering another form of cultural imperialism? Is this policy part of a trend suggesting foreign languages need no longer be learned? Does it thus undermine what we are trying to do as foreign language teachers, that is, interest others in learning German? And could it in any way provide fodder to administrations intent on eliminating or "rightsizing" foreign language departments? Does it ignore those cultural spaces that refuse expression through translation? And does it ignore the language base of culture, the "otherness" of other cultures, by attempting to incorporate everything into the home culture and pretending that we live in a comfortable essentially English-speaking world?

We grant that the all-English policy has many ramifications, most of which we cannot yet know. Nevertheless, although we acknowledge that this decision might be seen in some corners as diminishing the uniqueness of foreign language expression, we believe the benefits outweigh the disadvantages, at least for the present. For those who do work that transcends the borders of traditional *Germanistik,* audiences outside the immediate profession are not merely desirable, but mandatory. From our present vantage point it therefore seems we have the alternative of waiting until they all learn German, or making some compromises.

We want to emphasize that the recent—conscious—moves to a more American kind of Germanics should not be seen as anti-German or anti-German literature and culture; on the contrary, our actions and decisions have been based on a desire to make developments in the field more widely accessible and valued. And we are not the first to recognize this potential. Our decision to publish in English in fact connects us with earlier generations of Germanists, including Kuno Francke, Walter Silz, Stuart Atkins, Henry Hatfield, and others, all scholars who viewed themselves as mediators between German culture and an American audience and who consequently favored English. There is a strong tradition of English-language publishing among Germanists in the United Kingdom too. Paradoxically, this publication pattern changed in the United States with the arrival of the exile generation of scholars; whereas one might have expected them to reject an overly close identification with all things German, they instead exerted considerable effort to re-create the forms and style of *Germanistik* here. Thus, from a historical perspective, it was the exile generation that broke with an existing American tradition to which a different generation now seeks to connect.[7]

Perhaps it is also worth pointing out that, rather than alienating us from *Germanistik,* the directions we are pursuing have led to some successful attempts to establish more direct links with the few scholars in Germany who are also working in the broad fields of feminist, gender, and cultural studies, areas defined and still dominated by Anglo-American scholars. The alliances that have been forged over the years culminated, for example, in the 1995 "WiG in Germany" summer conference organized by our colleagues in Potsdam and Berlin. Another sign of strengthening relations is that WiG conferences have begun to attract more German scholars. Further, we have increased the number of scholars from Germany on our editorial board, and we are happy to report that the number of submissions from colleagues abroad actually seems to increase each year, in part, as they have stated, because of the wider audiences for their work.

In view of the developments we have outlined, we conclude that feminist scholars in our discipline and WiG members in particular have thus helped to provide our discipline in this country with an identity in some ways distinct from German *Germanistik*. The field seems gradually to be moving in the direction of an "American Germanics" and WiG has played an important role in this evolution. But are we contributing to, indeed are we among the leaders in, the process of the "Americanization" of the profession? If by that is meant an unthinking embrace of all things American, then the answer is an unqualified no. If, however, the term reflects the desire to be more intimately tied to academic institutions and discussions in this country where most of us live, study, and teach, then—at least for the present—we answer affirmatively. We also suggest that, as members of Women in German pursue the goal of opening the borders of our field to the larger debates that are shaping the study of literatures and cultures in the United States today, the organization remains a force not only for change, but even for survival.

Notes

1 See, for example, Lennox's "Some Proposals" and "Feminist Scholarship." A brief summary of these developments is available in Clausen and Friedrichsmeyer.

2 Portions of these comments were published in our editorial postscript, "Towards an 'American Germanics'?" in *Women in German Yearbook: Feminist Studies in German Literature and Culture,* vol. 12, ed. Sara Friedrichsmeyer and Patricia Herminghouse (Lincoln: University of Nebraska Press, 1996). Reprinted here by permission of the University of Nebraska Press.

3 In 1978 Women in Spanish and Portuguese, now known as *Feministas Unidas,* and Women in French were established as standing committees by the Women's Caucus of the MLA and encouraged to emulate the success of Women in German. Some of this history can be gleaned from *Concerns: Newsletter of the Women's Caucus of the Modern Languages.*

4 All of the documents of this early history are preserved in the Women in German Archives at the Wisconsin Historical Society.

5 For a summary of these developments see Lennox's "Feminismus und German Studies."

6 A revised version of their presentations and an introduction by Sara Lennox, one of the conference organizers, forms a focus section for the 1996 *Women in German Yearbook.*

7 We thank Theodore Ziolkowski for elaborating this point during the discussion following the presentation of this paper.

Feminist Professionalism: A Brief, Critical History of the Coalition of Women in German

MARGARETMARY DALEY

During the course of its history, American Germanics has seen many dramatic changes. Though the language was taught as early as 1702 by Pastorious in Philadelphia (Zeydel, "Teaching" 19), the literature was not formally studied in American universities until much later. It was not until 1877 that German literature courses were introduced at Princeton University (Bottigheimer 86), a situation typical for many peer institutions. Perhaps the most fundamental change that has taken place in Germanics in this century has been the growing influence of women scholars. Though individual women taught and studied German more than a century ago, it was not until 1974 that a professional organization was formed, specifically addressed to the needs of women scholars of German. Only in the past two or three decades have a significant number of women advanced to positions of prestige and respect in American German departments. I do not wish to be overly sanguine about the ascendence of women scholars. Writing in 1991, Wiesenhahn points out that only 30 percent of permanent appointments in contrast to 69 percent of temporary ones went to women applicants (28). Nevertheless, looking at any cross-section of recent scholarship, it would be hard to deny that women scholars have arrived, and that because of them, the study of writing about and by women has become a central concern in contemporary scholarship (Finney 39).

This study provides a brief history of the Coalition of Women in German (WiG), the major feminist organization for American Germanists. WiG was formed in 1974 by a group of women Germanists who were disaffected with the professional organizations of the day and felt a need for an organization that would provide support for them as women scholars and serve as a forum for feminist research. While the early organization was small and had relatively little influence, over three decades WiG has grown to become an important shaping force in American Germanics. While becoming somewhat more like a conventional scholarly organization, WiG has, at the same time, preserved many of its original methods and inspirations and has demonstrated remarkable versatility, continuing to meet the needs of women scholars and participating in a major transformation of the profession as women scholars have risen to positions of influence and authority in the academy.

WiG's beginnings date back to 1974, a time when many American universities had had nearly a century to cultivate and establish Germanics as a profession. WiG, however, set out self-consciously to defy and undo many established conventions of academic universities and professional scholarly organizations. At that time, there were few tenured women professors in the United States, and feminism was viewed by many academics as a marginal and nonscholarly discourse. In the view of WiG founders, academic custom and professionalism were symptoms of an intellectual culture that thwarted the aims of feminist scholars. University and college departments, however, were generally unable or unwilling to address women's concerns and in effect excluded and restricted women's contributions to Germanics. These were the conditions under which the idea for WiG was born.

The plan to form a group for feminist Germanists was conceived by a group of about two dozen women who met in April of 1974 at a conference on the German Democratic Republic held at Washington University in St. Louis. They were concerned about the almost complete lack of attention given at the conference to women's literature and scholarship. A number of women scholars were present, but, for the most part, they were graduate students and junior faculty, and they had little say in the conference proceedings. Concern over this situation led to a discussion of potential courses of action among the women at the conference.[1] Looking back on the conference just a few years later, Goodman and Sanders summarized the many issues that were raised: "Women attending a conference on the GDR at Washington University in 1974 discussed their needs and resolved to share information of interest to all those concerned with the status of women in the profession—information on language and literary texts, on women's courses, on classroom experience, on speakers and resource materials" (Goodman & Sanders 1). The informal discussion eventually led to the coming together of WiG as a professional collective: a feminist coalition to discuss the status of women in the profession, with emphasis on Germanics at all ranks, not just among tenured university faculty, and also to support and develop research in Germanics from a feminist perspective. Deemed essential at that time were four projects: (1) a newsletter; (2) panels at professional conferences including the Modern Language Association (MLA); (3) a conference for women in German; (4) several collective projects such as feminist reviews of German textbooks.

The first major accomplishment of WiG was the publication of a newsletter, initiated at the end of the first year, 1974. For two years the newsletter was the essence of the organization, and it continues to be published to this day. The initial collective of Germanists who produced the newsletter was based at the University of Wisconsin–Madison and consisted of one professor and a group of graduate students: Professor Evelyn T. Beck, Angelika Bammer, Kay Goodman, Nancy Vedder Schultz, and Christa Stutius. The newsletter, which was originally titled "News from Women in Germanistik" and which appeared three to four times a year, linked together women all over the United States; the earliest preserved list of interested people, from 1974, names about 30 women representing all the geographic regions of the United States.[2] After only two years, the number of subscribers had grown to 200, and a network of scholars had been created. The increasing number of subscribers and the amount of effort needed to coordinate the

annual meetings were significant enough by 1978 to merit the formation of an official steering committee consisting of five members.[3] During the 1978–79 academic
year, friction between the newsletter collective and the steering committee arose
over organization, decision-making, and finances, and this resulted in a number of
contentious letters asking for changes in the organizational structure. Friction increased to such an extent that leaders offered to resign; however, within the year the
difficulties were settled, and the office of treasurer was created (in 1979) to over-
see the finances of all components of WiG. Since 1975 a subscription fee for the
newsletter had been collected. However, beginning in 1979 this was changed to a
membership/subscription fee under the management of neither the steering committee nor the newsletter collective but rather the treasurer. By 1983 WiG counted
350 paid members, and the 1995 directory lists more than 630 members.

Because WiG has never restricted its members on the basis of gender, a few
men have joined the organization, and some attended the annual conferences as
long ago as 1978. As early as the third newsletter, from May of 1975, WiG plainly
stated that its mission was feminist, but its membership was open: "In response
to several inquiries, we wish to make it clear that the newsletter invites all interested men sympathetic to our aims to take part in our effort" (*WiG Newsletter* 3:
1). Some conference programs from the late 1970s show that a women-only session was stipulated at some meetings. Current format no longer requires men to
absent themselves from any conference activity, and the WiG steering committee
maintains that it does not exclude male members.

The current WiG continues to define its internal organization in much the same
terms as the early organization, declaring the offices of president and secretary
to be pro forma and staffing them because of requirements for tax-exempt status
(Clausen, "Women in German" 4). Nonetheless, the growth of the organization
has necessitated major changes from the original structure, which deliberately had
no power hierarchy; WiG now has nine people in its organizational leadership and
additional volunteer staffs for conferences, newsletters, and yearbooks.

The early WiG came into existence in the politically charged atmosphere of
grassroots activism that prevailed on American campuses in the 1970s, and an
understanding of this beginning is essential for understanding the group. Rather
than a professional organization, it was a formalized network, a support group that
held "retreats," not conferences, and engaged in confrontational activities such as
compiling lists of German textbooks that were unacceptably sexist, or calling for a
boycott of the 1978 American Association of Teachers of German (AATG) meeting in Chicago because Illinois had failed to ratify the Equal Rights Amendment to
the Constitution.[4] Most members of WiG felt that it connected their personal and
professional lives; it prepared them emotionally and practically for the difficulties
facing female scholars in the late 1970s and the early 1980s. In the view of both
Clausen and Lennox, WiG generated a temporary but concrete utopia.

> It is our space, a place where, for a few days, we can begin to come closer to real-
> izing our visions. . . . The "utopian" aspect of the conferences will, again, mean

> different things to different women. For me, it means a supportive and stimulating environment where I feel stronger, more confident, even more "intelligent" than at other times. Women taking each other seriously, caring about each other, being ready to change if something isn't working, and the often mentioned attention to process are all part of the "utopia." (Clausen, "The Coalition" 15)

WiG held its first meeting approximately a year and a half after the initial discussions led to the newsletter, and it continues to meet annually at its own conference, independent of larger organizations, while still maintaining strong professional alliances with other scholarly organizations. In this respect it is more independent than some peer organizations, for example, Women in French. WiG-sponsored sessions at other conferences, most notably at the MLA's convention but also at meetings of the AATG, the Association of College Teachers of Foreign Languages (ACTFL), and the German Studies Association (GSA), differ from other sessions because of their topics. In the early years there was some controversy over whether participating in other professional organizations entailed a compromise of WiG's principles. An anonymous letter in the WiG archive called for discussion of this issue in 1977: "More and more I feel that this is something which we in Women in German *must* discuss: how do we go about creating in practice a real, human, feminist support system for each other?" (21 January 1977) Currently the session format conforms to the requirements of the various associations, but WiG-sponsored sessions do insist on pairing an experienced member with an unexperienced member, affirming a need for supportive mentoring of newer members of the profession during and beyond graduate school.

The annual WiG meeting remains the most important forum for maintaining this alternative vision and for finding a continuity in the organization. The unorthodox features of the early WiG evolved over the first several years of the organization's existence and can be traced in the correspondence in the archive and in the newsletters. The first WiG conference was held in the fall of 1976. It took place in September in Oxford, Ohio, and bore the title of "Feminism and German Studies: An Interdisciplinary Perspective." In 1976 and again in 1977 the WiG meetings had a recognizably conventional format. Each included a day of scholarly presentations, but the meetings also departed self-consciously from the formal atmosphere of other organizations. The vocabulary of the 1976 letter sent to registrants makes the departure clear; it speaks of "sisterhood" and hopes that the feminist scholars will "get to know each other," "share ideas," engage in a "truly collaborative effort" (Gebhardt & Lennox). The conference was devoted to feminist pedagogy and feminist literary criticism. Participants at these early meetings spoke of sweeping feminist revisions and attention to humanizing the profession (Lennox, *WiG Newsletter* 6: 4).

As with other professional organizations, the meeting site moves to different locations in the United States in order to accommodate the geographical spread of its membership. But, unlike many organizations, WiG members make a conscious effort to provide an alternative kind of professional meeting. One area of concern is a supportive atmosphere; to this end, the conference has been held at nontraditional venues such as a convent in Oregon and the grounds of a Jewish summer camp in Massachusetts. WiG conference attendees emphasize active and productive forms over passive listening to traditional scholarly papers. The newsletter of 1 November 1977 expresses this preference clearly: "We have held traditional conferences for two years now . . . [b]ut for many, the best part of the conference has always been the atmosphere and the more informal discussions" (*WiG Newsletter* 13: 1). Therefore, a workshop or *Arbeitsgruppen* format was adopted to make all conference attendees active, and collective work was encouraged at all levels — organizing, presenting, and responding. The tendency of conference attendees to use conventional models for their presentations must have been strong, as this message was repeated just two years later: "We would like to remind all prospective contributors that the format of the 1979 WiG conference calls for prepared discussion topics instead of finished scholarly papers which are read to an audience" (*WiG Newsletter* 18: 7). In the 1980 the organization held a longer conference and a mix of workshops, film screenings, and fiction readings, along with a few sessions with "finished scholarly papers." While early WiG meetings drew an average of about 30 attendees, conference participation grew to 70 in 1982, and in 1996 it exceeded 100.[5]

Consistent with its egalitarian ethos, WiG has always worked to keep conference registration fees to a bare minimum. In 1979, the fourth annual WiG meeting announced a registration fee of $35, which included not only registration fees but lodging and all meals for the three days of the conference. The WiG conference continues to include lodging and meals as a means of facilitating the supportive, feminist atmosphere that weaves together professional and private concerns. While the cost for an employed member attending the meeting rose in 1986 to $132, students and unemployed members were only required to pay half that amount. Currently, the conference registration regularly offers up to 30 different fees, scaled not just according to the number of nights but also according to the number of roommates, the option of day attendance with meals but no overnight accommodations, and the participant's level of employment.

Today, the annual WiG meeting maintains its workshop emphasis, and the conference is thriving. A new site is chosen every three years by the steering committee, while the program and meeting are organized by a collective, often involving students in the locality of the conference.[6] To keep the decision-making process democratic, it is not mandated that the collective's coordinators be members of the steering committee; instead, the burden is put on the steering committee to "make arrangements to ensure that there is adequate communication between [itself] and the site/program coordinators" (*WiG Newsletter* 71: 7). The conference program's format has evolved. The meetings now stretch from Thursday evening to Sunday morning; during this time some two or three panels with a traditional format convene, while several other sessions are held in the unconventional format that evolved at WiG meetings in the 1980s. In addition to workshops, these alternative sessions include contemporary women writers giving readings from their fiction, film screenings, "speak outs" or opportunities for participants to engage in spontaneously and open dialogue, and discussions on contemporary issues such as unification, racism, or, most commonly, self-scrutiny of WiG as a feminist organization.[7] As proof of WiG's philosophical insistence on integrating the personal and professional, breaks are intentionally scheduled in scholarly activities to allow for group recreational activities. Contemporary authors, scholars, or film makers from German-speaking countries have been invited, since 1980, not only to present but also to participate in all aspects of the meeting (Clausen, "Women" 2).

The original desire for the conferences to be models of consensus has not disappeared but only been modified over the years as the number of attendees grew. When the conferences were smaller, the topics for the next year were discussed and agreed upon through consensus. However, these planning sessions grew too long for the conference slot; now, as a time-saving measure, the program and topics are written out beforehand and accepted, adjusted, or rejected in response to suggestions of those attending the business meeting of the annual conference. While organizers continue to insist that WiG "has no president, no executive committee, etc.," yet the organization currently recognizes a steering committee and internal organization of power (Clausen, "The Coalition" 15). Some would argue that WiG's emphasis on consensual decision-making has helped it to overcome conflicts that might have otherwise been divisive. Constant growth is making WiG increasingly resemble ordinary, committee-driven professional organizations; nonetheless, rather than overlooking potentially divisive issues, WiG has consistently thematized them in the yearbook, in the newsletters, at the annual meetings, and most recently via the electronic list.

The importance of WiG as an organization in a broader context than its own annual conferences is confirmed by the sessions sponsored by WiG for annual conferences and meetings of other professional organizations. As early as 1977, WiG became an allied organization of the MLA in order to guarantee its participation at national conferences. Nevertheless, WiG conceived of its affiliation with the MLA and other organizations as simultaneously with and against them, striving to change such organizations via the presence of its feminist programs (Clausen, "The Coalition" 9). WiG sessions appearing at the AATG meeting (held together with the ACTFL) and at the GSA annual meeting are well-attended.

Other WiG publications include two volumes of feminist reviews of teaching materials (1984 and 1991) and a 1983 collection of syllabi. These collaborative projects were small desktop publications—another sign of WiG's radical feminist origins—radical not only in content but also in form. The reason WiG has not continued to produce reviews of teaching materials and course syllabi is perhaps because of the success of those efforts. In the 1990s textbooks no longer contain the level of gender insensitivities prevalent two decades ago, and most major German departments now have significant course offerings on women authors and feminist criticism.

The current reputation of WiG depends partially and inextricably on the prestige of its yearbook, because the yearbook is at present its major avenue of scholarly publishing and exposure among the majority of Germanists. Although a newsletter has appeared for more than 20 years, the group waited until it had survived 10 years of debate, growth, and change to begin publishing a scholarly journal. The first yearbook appeared in 1985 and was half the size of the current 1995 volume. The volumes depict an evolution of adapting to changes in both feminism and Germanics. A consistent policy maintained in all of WiG's 11 yearbooks is the practice of having two editors collaborate as equals; the editors contend that such collaboration is specifically feminist (Cafferty & Clausen).

The 1995 yearbook contains twice as many contributions as that of 1985; furthermore, it publishes predominantly the work of prestigious scholars. Thirteen of 16 authors of the 1995 articles are tenured. The present editors explain that their policy of anonymous review makes possible a range of authors, including graduate students and independent scholars (Friedrichsmeyer & Herminghouse, "Generational" 226). Nonetheless, about four-fifths of the authors in the most recent three volumes have tenure or similar professional status. The prestige of the yearbook depends on the recognition of its contributors in the profession overall, not merely within the smaller community of WiG members. In passing years, the founders who initially proclaimed a radical stance toward Germanics have come into positions of leadership and power in the profession. In a sense, WiG is confronted by a double bind. Either it purports to have achieved some of its goals and abandons its initial radical stance, or it must articulate the feminism of its cultural and political agenda in terms of contemporary power relations (Clausen & Friedrichsmeyer). A minor irony arises out of WiG's ability to endure into its third decade by adaptation. The organization that worked in the 1970s to break down the barrier between members' personal and professional lives continues today to run a column of personal announcements. However, in the 1990s the majority of these announcements concern awards of tenure, promotion, and other public measures of professional advancement. By accepting some standards of prestige and professional scholarship, the organization may reinforce some of the very power structures it has professed to critique. But many feminist readers enjoy WiG's current prominence and applaud the conventional successes of its members.

Two additional WiG activities, which arguably fall under the subject heading of publication, demonstrate that WiG is keeping pace with innovations in scholarly dialogue. WiG sponsors both a website and an electronic list. The electronic list called WiG-L is a virtual bulletin board, representing the most diverse cross-section served by any component of the WiG organization. As an e-mail list, WiG-L neither includes every member of WiG nor is it limited to members only. Like most electronic lists, it accepts anyone who can access the internet. Topics addressed by the WiG-L run the gamut from Afro-Germans seeking to meet other Afro-Germans, to German scholars verifying the accuracy of footnotes, to WiG members debating current issues such as the poor job market facing graduate students.

The second innovation confirming WiG's current vitality is its website. The website makes available—to dues-paying members and internet "browsers" alike —several important sources of information about WiG: the mission statement, the address of the WiG-List as well as the personal electronic mailing addresses and a picture book of some members, the conference program, information on the next yearbook, and links to other pertinent websites. Having a page on the World Wide Web serves WiG in its international outreach and helps to publicize the organization's activities.

WiG has been emulated by professionals in other national languages and literatures. The Spanish language Feministas Unitas has been active both at the MLA and its own annual conference, but it does not currently publish a journal. Women in French was founded some five years after WiG. Although WiF has published a journal since 1993 and reports tripled submissions in the 1995 journal, feminists in French have neither found a university press to publish their journal nor do they hold an annual conference; WiF holds its meetings concomitantly with the MLA. Further evidence of the success of WiG comes from the literary feminists in Germany who chose to participate in the predominately U. S. organization. WiG's members include many German feminists active in Europe. Especially in the last five years, the American-based WiG seems to offer Germans something they seek and do not find at home. German women no doubt wish to learn from American women who have had far more success in professional advancement than have women in Germany's more tradition-bound university system.

Numerous signs indicate that WiG is a professionally mature institution, having a measurable impact on Germanics in the United States. Mainstream scholarship is now addressing many concerns that were once the exclusive province of WiG. This convergence between WiG and the rest of the profession is most evident in the importance of feminism in much of contemporary, scholarly discourse. Bledsoe's 1991 volume *Rethinking Germanistik* contains no fewer than four articles specifically dealing with issues pertinent to American feminist Germanists, ranging from two discussions of the feminization of the profession to a feminist reading of the canon (Wiesenhahn, Finney, Kuhn, and Case). Finney's article in that volume cites a 1985 WiG article by Blackwell, in which she calls for "the inclusion of women writers in departmental reading lists around the country" (35), and then Finney states that "several German departments have modified their reading lists for the master's and doctoral examinations in light of new perspectives on women writers" (87). In addition, Blackwell has updated her canon study with her 1993 MLA talk, "Deconstructing the Canon: A Ten-year Comparison" (Clausen & Friedrichsmeyer 267), in which she points to a marked increase in the number of German women writers included not only in study lists but also in undergraduate curricula. The sustained growth of both the number of members in WiG and of the size and sophistication of the *Women in German Yearbook* confirms that the feminism cultivated by WiG has become one of the forces shaping American Germanics today.[8] The program of the 1996 conference on "Shaping Forces in American Germanics in the Twentieth Century" supports this claim strongly, in that four presentations primarily concerned the importance of feminism in the profession, and several more presentations involved women in German indirectly. Today WiG continues to be a forum for the most recent and innovative trends in feminist scholarship including cultural and queer studies.[9]

That WiG is now recognized as a successful, significant, and necessary force in Germanics speaks to the wide recognition and general acknowledgment of the principles that WiG asserted in its mission statement. In 1986, the editor of the *German Quarterly* felt compelled to respond to WiG directly in one of its newsletter to explain why he had "to send to the printer, as has happened a few times lately, a virtually all-male issue" and to balance that with his own tabulations of the next year's issues, one of which will "most likely have six articles by women and none by men" (*WiG Newsletter* 40: 3). Exactly 10 years later, the WiG newsletter revisits this issue; it cites statistics showing that women, who outnumber men in earning doctorates in German, now make up about 40 percent of faculty in the United States and Canada, yet in a worldwide bibliography dwindle to a mere 20 percent of authors of published books and articles on Germanics (*WiG Newsletter* 71: 28).[10] Thus, despite a history of more than 20 years of active existence and efforts on behalf of female scholarship, it is clear that WiG has not achieved all of its goals and will continue to map out areas for future development. WiG is a professional organization that maintains its *pro femina* perspective and that develops a constructive critique of the shape of Germanics today in part by supplementing the field with a feminist viewpoint and more radically by redrawing the field in order to include unexplored terrain both in scholarship and in the nonscholarly but nonetheless academic areas of concern for feminists.

Notes

1 Herminhouse, letter dated 3 Dec. 1991. WiG Archive, State Historical Society of Wisconsin, Madison.
2 Handwritten document, WiG Archive, State Historical Society of Wisconsin, Madison. The document, consisting of four pages of names and addresses gathered at the St. Louis, Missouri, conference shows that WiG had a broad geographic range from its inception. The locations range from California to New York and Maine to Georgia. Another list (circa 1974–75) adds 15 new subscribers, seven from the Midwest and the eight others representing a broad geographic range.
3 "Summary of WiG Business and Planning Meeting, Sunday, 24 September 1978," a document in the WiG Archive, reports steering committee members from Madison, Wisconsin; Valparaiso, Indiana; Eugene, Oregon; Amherst, Massachusetts; and Fuller-

ton, California. The number of steering committee members was later increased to six.

4   Russian and Stephan, letter of 28 November 1978, WiG Archive, State Historical Society of Wisconsin, Madison; see also "A Sample Resolution," which the steering committee sent to NOW, 10 December 1978.

5   112 preconference registrants are listed in the 1996 program, *Coalition of Women in German: Twentieth Annual Conference,* 31 October–3 November 1996, St. Augustine, Florida.

6   In a published report to the MLA, Clausen lists the seven sites and organizing collectives from 1976 to 1996: Oxford, Ohio; Racine, Wisconsin; Boston and Great Barrington, Massachusetts; Portland, Oregon; the area of Minneapolis, Minnesota; and St. Augustine, Florida.

7   Titles of such open sessions those without formal presentation of written research reveal the proclivity for self-scrutiny: "Who are we at WiG: National, Cultural, and Personal Identities," in 1991; "Homogeneity/Heterogeneity in WiG," in 1993; and in 1994 "WiG after (almost) 20 years: Where did we come from? Where are we headed?"

8   See also, as indirect evidence, V. Nollendorfs, "Out of Germanistik."

9   Kuzniar, while bemoaning the dearth of cultural and queer studies among Germanists, mentions the strength and support of Women in German for these fields of criticism (126).

10 For more detailed statistics, see V. Nollendorfs, "Out of Germanistik" (6–8).

Female Immigrant Intellectuals in Germanics: From Invisibility to "Women in German"

GISELA HOECHERL-ALDEN

The most cursory glance into the history of American Germanics reveals that although women published innovative articles, books, and textbooks, just like their male colleagues, they receive scant mention in the histories of the profession or in the chronicles of the colleges and universities in the United States where they taught.[1] This fact prompted Ellen Nagy to analyze the roles of women within Germanics. For the period from 1850 to 1950, she concluded that women were not only subordinate members of the profession, their activities undervalued or ignored by their male colleagues, even though they held permanent, full-time faculty positions and actively participated in professional organizations such as the MLA and the AATG; she noted also that although the percentage of doctorates in Germanics awarded to women over the years had increased, the percentage of female faculty, regardless of institutional type, remained less than half the percentage of doctoral recipients. Because teaching loads of academics in the lower ranks are heavier than those of senior colleagues, Nagy (*Women in Germanics* 23–38) concludes it is not surprising that women published less than their male counterparts.

A large number of the female Germanists, though by far not all, were either immigrants who had left Wilhelminian and Weimar Germany or exiles who had fled Fascism. In fact, three of the four women Nagy focused on in her dissertation belong to this group: Lilian Stroebe, Melitta Gerhard, and Helen Adolf. Yet even though a growing number of books and articles on the wave of Central European refugees from Nazi Germany and their contribution to American intellectual life have begun to include case histories of academic women, most studies of intellectual migration — if they mention Germanics at all — usually have its most famous proponents stand in for the well over 120 German-speaking refugees who became active in American Germanics within the first decade after they left Central Europe in the 1930s.[2] Apart from Austrian-born Marianne Thalmann, who taught at Wellesley, Melitta Gerhard is the only other *émigrée* ever mentioned. She is not remembered because she was well known to Germanists on the conference circuit — which she was not — but because Bernhard Blume names her in his memoirs.[3]

Many female immigrants from pre- and post–World War I Germany as well as the older Hitler refugees had belonged to a generation of intellectual pioneers of the Central European universities. In Germany, for example, women's legitimate access to higher education was only a little over two decades old when Hitler

108

came to power. Until female students were legally admitted to German universities in 1908 and received the legal right to an academic career in 1919 (with their *Habilitationsrecht,* granted one year after they obtained suffrage), they could only attend lectures or write a doctoral dissertation with the explicit permission of both the Ministry of Education in their respective states and the professor conducting a given course or willing to direct their dissertation (Soden 25). Yet even after 1919, some professors continued to bar women from their lectures and seminars (Hermand, *Geschichte* 83). The obstacles women who wanted to embark on an academic career had to overcome were so enormous that only two female full professors (*ordentliche Professorinnen*) taught at German universities in 1933, and neither of them was a Germanist.[4] Overall, at the time of Hitler's ascent to power, only 54 academic women were teaching at the university level, and, of these, only 24 held the German equivalents of assistant, associate, or full professorships. The remaining 30, including the few Germanists, were lecturers or teaching fellows. These numbers are all the more astounding when we note that 10,595 women had received their doctorates from German universities between 1908 and 1933 (Soden 25). Thus, the difficulty of obtaining adequate positions in German academe had spawned a veritable exodus of highly qualified academic women to the United States in the first decades of the twentieth century, where a tradition of women's colleges and of women teaching at colleges and universities was already well established.[5] Among these immigrants were Germanists who were to affect substantially the development of American Germanics.

One of the most enterprising female Germanists of the pre–World War I era and the following two decades was Lilian Luise Stroebe. Born in 1875, she studied German and English philology in London, Lausanne, and Heidelberg, where, in 1904, she received one of the first doctorates that university ever conferred upon a woman. After a fruitless job search in Germany, she emigrated to the United States one year later, accepting an offer from Vassar College. In the course of her career as an American Germanist, she was also the president of the New England chapter of the AATG, became an accomplished textbook author, and regularly contributed articles on etymological, linguistic, literary, and pedagogical subjects to scholarly journals (S. Freeman 20–29). Upon her retirement in 1944 after 40 years as an active scholar, Middlebury College awarded Lilian Stroebe the honorary degree of Doctor of Pedagogy in recognition of her most important contribution to American Germanics: the founding of the German Summer School at Middlebury. Not only had Stroebe's inability to tolerate the status quo prompted her to act in the first place, but her innovative pedagogical approach was largely responsible for the subsequent development of all Middlebury Language Schools, which became the model for many successive summer language schools and institutes throughout the country.

However, in terms of her career, timing had been unfortunate. The first German Summer School at Middlebury was conducted in 1915, after the beginning of World War I in Europe. Though highly successful for three consecutive summers, it had to be discontinued after 1917, because of vocal anti-German protests. That Lilian Stroebe was able to survive the surge of anti-German hysteria which swept the country and to hold on to her position at Vassar more or less unscathed, seems largely due to her focus on subject matter and her careful diplomatic and apolitical stance—an attitude similar to Julius Goebel's at the University of Illinois. Unlike many of their German-born colleagues, both Germanists refrained from overly zealous and patriotic pro-German utterances upon the United States' entry into World War I.

A case in contrast was that of Agathe Lasch, who came from a devout and poor Jewish family and had struggled hard as a student in Germany to find a major professor. Even after her dissertation had been published and she had also passed her teaching examinations, she was unable to secure suitable employment in Germany. She emigrated to the United States and found a position at Bryn Mawr in 1912. When wartime came, however, she spoke out patriotically against anti-German activities on her college campus and was subsequently forced to step down. Returning to Germany proved her only option if she wanted to continue her research and simultaneously support herself by teaching. In 1919, she was able to resume her career as a Germanist at the newly founded University of Hamburg, where she remained until escalating anti-Semitism cost her her job after the Nazi takeover. Unable or unwilling to attempt emigration again, Agathe Lasch became a victim of the Holocaust in 1942.[6] Her ground-breaking research in Low German linguistics, however, begun with her dissertation in 1909 and continued at Bryn Mawr and Hamburg, is still the most important philological work on this subject today and was reprinted as recently as 1979.

Even though—technically speaking—Agathe Lasch was part of American Germanics only briefly, her career is typical of the fairly large group of female German-speaking academics who were only able to find positions outside of Germany which were commensurate with their qualifications. Talented women with German doctorates, like Anna Jacobson, who joined the Hunter College faculty in 1924, and Ruth Hofrichter, who became Lilian Stroebe's junior colleague at Vassar College in 1930, continued to emigrate to the United States during the Weimar period. However, it seems that the initial "window of opportunity" that had presented itself to Lilian Stroebe was no longer open to women after World War I. Professor Stroebe's concept of a summer language school had proven immensely successful as the high enrollments in the still-functional French and Italian Summer Language Schools at Middlebury continued to reveal. Yet in 1928, when the profession had recovered sufficiently to consider reviving the German Summer School, it was not reopened under her directorship but under that of Ernst Feise, who had lost his job at the University of Wisconsin in 1917 and spent the next 10 years in Mexico, until he became a faculty member at Johns Hopkins University (S. Freeman 106).

As early as 1933, American Germanists were not only well aware of the virulent anti-Semitism in Germany but also of the harassment academic women had to endure; *Monatshefte* ("Umschau" 242) commented on the fact that the Nazis had begun restricting female enrollment numbers drastically.[7] At this time, the more or less voluntary immigrants from Wilhelminian and Weimar Germany who lived in America were joined by female refugees from Nazism. Some of them, like Marianne Thalmann, had already made a name for themselves with impressive publication records and years of university teaching experience. Thalmann had just been promoted to full professor at the University of Vienna when she received notice of her dismissal. Wellesley College offered her a job and an immigrant visa.[8]

Equally accomplished, but less fortunate than their Austrian colleague, were Melitta Gerhard, the daughter of exiled writer Adele Gerhard, and Edda Tille-Hankamer, the wife of the Goethe expert Paul Hankamer.[9] In 1933, they lost their respective positions at the universities of Kiel and Cologne.[10] Unlike Marianne Thalmann, they had to lead the lives of itinerant academics for their first 10 or so years in exile. While Melitta Gerhard was—for the most part at least—fortunate enough to teach at the college level, where she had access to libraries and continued to publish on Schiller and his contemporaries, Edda Tille-Hankamer had to turn her back on her linguistic studies while moving from one junior high and high school teaching job to the next, until she was able to secure a position at the University of Tennessee in Knoxville after 1945.[11] Judging from the recollections of her former colleagues and students, it seems that Melitta Gerhard, while continuing to be a prolific scholar publishing primarily in German, was reputedly quite unsuccessful as an undergraduate teacher.[12] On the other hand, Edda Tille-Hankamer, who had to abandon her academic publishing career, was an immensely stimulating teacher gifted in mediating the German language, literature, and culture to American undergraduates.[13] Also the medievalist Helen Adolf saw her academic career at the University of Vienna cut short by surging anti-Semitism. After her arrival in the United States, she first learned Spanish and subsequently taught at various high schools throughout the country before she was able to find a permanent home in the German department at Pennsylvania State University in 1945, where she became one of the few female Germanists of the exile generation to be honored with a *Festschrift* by her graduate students and colleagues (Buehne 3).

Since World War II—in contrast to World War I—saw a sharp increase in the need for competent teachers of the German language, and—as the Austrian writer-turned-Germanist Elisabeth Freundlich remarked in her memoirs—many men were missing from the universities and colleges, it was possible for women to find positions in academe (Freundlich 129–31). As reflected in *Monatshefte* (36 [1944]: 48–56), the country's language departments distinguished very clearly between their regular faculty and those listed as instructors for a military program. However, some of the highly educated refugee women and men were able to establish themselves permanently as American Germanists by working for these Army Specialized Training Programs. Among them were the former law student Marianne Bonwit (University of California, Berkeley) and former Romance philologist Liselotte Dieckmann (Washington University, St. Louis). Another whom the absence of men propelled into an academic position was Hedda Korsch, the wife of Bertolt Brecht's friend, fellow communist, and university professor Karl Korsch. Hedda Korsch was able to support herself and her husband with her position in German at Wheaton College. Others included Hilde Dorothy Cohn, the former writer who held a doctorate from Heidelberg and became professor emerita at Swarthmore College, and Lore Foltin, who held a doctorate in law from Prague and found a home in the German department at the University of Pittsburgh. While Foltin's literary specialty was Franz Werfel, her primary contribution to the university lay in her dedication to undergraduate education. Her devotion is commemorated to this day with the "Foltin Award for Excellence," which is granted to an outstanding undergraduate student each year with funds from an endowment that her colleagues established upon her death.[14]

Just how deeply this influx of women must have affected the profession is still palpable over 30 years later: when Stephen Freeman described at length and with obvious sympathy and understanding how Werner Neuse, the head of Middlebury's German department, was forced to admit more female students than ever before, he commends Neuse for exercising "judicious caution" in his admission policies regarding women. Since Neuse was considering female applicants "from the better women's colleges," one can only surmise that he and Freeman were similarly prejudiced concerning women's abilities to perform academically (S. Freeman 117).

In fact, if one of the yardsticks for measuring professional success and visibility are *Festschriften*, the acquisition of honorary degrees, and other awards, male colleagues outshone their equally accomplished female colleagues. This would lend credence to Nagy's conclusion that female academics' work was traditionally undervalued or even ignored in comparison with that of their male colleagues. During the 1930s, 1940s, and 1950s, most female Germanists worked on the same topics as their male colleagues, publishing articles on canonical works. Just like male Germanists, they had demonstrated their unflagging support for the American war effort by working for the ASTP and related programs. Nagy (*Women in Germanics* 195) demonstrates that they were equally active in the AATG and MLA, although they were rarely elected to the highest offices before 1950.

Thomas Mann, whom the exiled writer-turned-Germanist Ludwig Marcuse had somewhat sarcastically (Radkau 118) referred to as "the emperor of all emigrants," played a central role among writers and academics alike. He was not only object of their study but also maintained lively personal contacts with both American and exiled Germanists—male and female.[15] Anna Jacobson, for example, like Hermann Weigand of Yale University, had worked extensively on Thomas Mann during the 1930s and 1940s. Thus, when the German program at Hunter College was in danger of being eliminated in 1938, she solicited a spirited defense from Mann, which she not only published in the Hunter College Bulletin but also circulated among several other East Coast colleges. Yet in 1941—his lively correspondence with his "dear biographer" Anna Jacobson notwithstanding—Thomas Mann

(E. Mann, *Briefe 1937–1947* 409) significantly contributed to the notion of invisibility of women in the profession when he addressed only the male American German teachers in *The German Quarterly* and congratulated them on valiantly fighting to uphold the values of German culture and literature in such adverse times.[16]

As diverse as they were individually, both female immigrant Germanists and their American-born female colleagues shared their "invisibility." This invisibility is illustrated by the fact the fact that—unlike most of their male American and European-born colleagues—the women were not asked to join in the West German reeducation task forces after the war. American Germanists like A. E. Zucker from the University of Maryland or Frank Banta and Robert Ittner from Indiana University were as much part of denazification and reeducation efforts as were immigrants like Otto Springer (University of Pennsylvania) and illustrious refugee Germanists like Richard Alewyn. While Alewyn, Wolfgang Liepe, and Werner Richter reemigrated as soon as the British and American military governments allowed them to take up positions at German universities, in 1962, Marianne Thalmann became the only female Germanist to return permanently to Europe; she did so not to pursue her interrupted career but to retire to Munich at the age of 74, long after she had become professor emerita at Wellesley College. Though her portrait now hangs in the Vienna National Library to honor her merit as an Austrian Germanist, her former position there was never proffered to her.[17] There are no readily available records of any immigrant women returning from the United States to take up positions at universities in German-speaking countries. Melitta Gerhard did return to Germany in 1955, after she became professor emerita at Wittenberg College, but only to accompany her mother to Cologne. Following her mother's death a year later, she returned to the United States and settled in Cambridge, Massachusetts, where she resumed her research activities (Dane 225).

Though very few of the male refugees actually did reemigrate, many of them, like Bernhard Blume, Erich Heller, Oskar Seidlin, Henry Remak, and Hans Sperber, were frequently invited back to German universities. Most of them returned for brief or longer periods of time as guests, and their visits enabled them to develop a professional network on both sides of the Atlantic. Since the women did not have that option, they were at a disadvantage when it came to forging professional ties with the countries whose literature, language, and culture they were teaching and studying.[18] Solely their own personal sense of enterprise led them to establish contacts with postwar Europe, as exemplified by Eva Wunderlich's correspondence with Gertrud von le Fort, which is now in the Deutsches Literaturarchiv in Marbach. Wunderlich, the sister of the exiled social scientist Frieda Wunderlich, had received her doctorate from Halle in 1925 and had been a high school teacher in Berlin before her exile. To the extent she could, she came to the aid of needy fellow refugees, both financially and spiritually.[19] Her scholarly publications dealt mainly with German spiritual literature from the Baroque to the twentieth century, which she wanted to promote for an American academic public. She became a truly American Germanist, dedicated to teaching undergraduates at her institution, Upsala College in New Jersey, and she was active in the New Jersey chapter of the AATG.[20]

That these women were even able to establish themselves at American colleges and universities is largely because men were absent. Throughout the 1930s and 1940s enrollment figures for women in American universities had been growing steadily, as had the number of doctorates. However, at the beginning of the 1950s they decreased sharply (Solomon 172–88). Thus, for example, Harvard had opened its doors to the female students of Radcliffe in 1943. Yet a decade later women were still not being offered teaching fellowships and lectureships at Harvard (Conway 44–46). The Ivy League and major state and private universities remained unofficially closed to the majority of the immigrant female Germanists. By 1949, Marianne Bonwit, Liselotte Dieckmann, and Helen Adolf had been joined by only one more female Germanist at a prestigious state university: by Lida Kirchberger at the University of Wisconsin.

The war had made the women's integration into American academe not only possible, but essential. By the end of the war, however, colleges and universities found themselves once again supporting the age-old argument that women should be educated to be housewives and mothers, not professionals—especially since men now needed their positions. As early as 1947, as a direct result of the newly passed G.I. Bill, female enrollments were restricted drastically, and, in order for women's colleges like Vassar to generate enough tuition, they encouraged men to enroll (Solomon 186–91). What Elisabeth Freundlich had still seen as an opportunity for women in the 1940s, ceased to be one for a younger generation of female Germanists in the postwar years marked by blatant prejudice against academic women (Klüger 230). In addition, the political climate created by the McCarthy era, which was hostile to all foreign-born intellectuals, dealt an especially hard blow to female intellectual immigrants.[21]

After the end of World War II, refugees continued to arrive in the United States: women who had survived the war in Nazi concentration camps and who were to earn doctorates here and become academics (Ruth Klüger and Susan Cerynak-Spatz) or who had weathered the war years in Japanese exile (Dorothea Dauer and Elisabeth Mayer). Together with them, immigrants who had come to the United States as teenagers or young girls concluded their studies and began embarking on careers in American Germanics (Dorrit Cohn, Eva Schiffer, Gisela Stein, Ansi Gutmann, Evelyn Torton Beck, Lieselotte Gumpel, and Luise Helen Bronner—to name a few). For Klüger and Cerynak-Spatz their routes to Germanics were circuitous. They did not take up their graduate educations until after they had divorced their husbands and were raising their children alone. In fact, Klüger thanks fellow émigré Heinz Politzer for offering a "divorced librarian and mother of two small children" financial support to pursue her graduate studies at the University of California, Berkeley in the early 1960s (Klüger 199). Both Klüger's and Cernyak-Spatz's forced expulsion from the culture of their childhood and the subsequent horror of the concentration camps made it impossible for them to return to Europe permanently. De-nationalized German language and literature was the only identity left to them, since—as they themselves have stated—they never felt completely at home in the United States.[22] In an uneasy alliance with their multiple identities, they chose to mediate German language, literature, and culture for themselves and others, in addition to educating younger generations about the Holocaust.[23] In doing this, they added a uniquely American dimension to Germanics which has since been taken up by other scholars.[24]

The so-called "Sputnik shock" (1958) at the height of the Cold War precipitated the National Defense Education Act. The fear of not only a technologically, but intellectually, superior Soviet Union eventually helped convince President Eisenhower to supply the country's universities and colleges with thirty million dollars earmarked to globalize foreign language curricula and improve teacher training. Thus, between the late 1950s and early 1970s, West German literature and language experts, male and female, gained access to American academe, who were to become internationally renowned and highly visible in the profession: Klaus Jonas (1957),[25] Jost Hermand (1958), Peter Uwe Hohendahl (1965), Reinhold Grimm (1967), Wulf Koepke (1968), and Frank Trommler (1970). Martha Mierendorff (1970) and Ingeborg Glier (1973) were two of the first academic women to come from West Germany after the war.

It was not until the 1970s, in the wake of the women's movement, that female Germanists organized professionally as a group and moved more toward center-stage. One of the cofounders of the coalition of "Women in German," Evelyn Torton Beck, who as a child had been forced to leave her native Austria, gives existential reasons for taking this step ("The Search" 48–53): she became active in organizing the coalition first and foremost because she is a woman, and thus wanted to counteract women's outsider status not only in German literature, literary history, textbooks, and within Germanics, but also because she is Jewish, and hence doubly outcast.

Nevertheless, as late as 1982, an obituary described Melitta Gerhard as an "austere," "militant," "difficult," "persevering," and "persistent" personality—a character quite in contrast to her "dainty" physical appearance.[26] The very real resistance she had met with when fighting for the right to write a dissertation in Berlin in 1918, however, was—in this same obituary—harmlessly described as "shaking of heads" and "frowning." Seen in historical perspective, Gerhard graduated at a time when one of the Germanists in Berlin was still barring women from his classes, ignoring their legal rights. In addition, one should note that men's physical attributes are not mentioned or compared to their intellectual capabilities in obituaries published in scholarly journals.

On the whole, women's invisibility in Germanics is diminishing gradually. They remained in the background in part because most of them found positions at smaller colleges and universities, which needed them to teach more and publish less. How they shaped the opinions of scores of undergraduates is hardly measurable and only becomes evident in personal interviews with students who remember them. However, in many cases, these women have impressive literary or linguistic publication records[27] despite their teaching loads and in addition to their obvious pedagogical excellence—as attested to by their students and former colleagues.[28] In some cases, their frustration with the male-dominated discipline of Germanics led them to turn their backs on traditional literary or linguistic scholarship and invest their energies in second-language acquisition and applied linguistics. While these activities excluded them even more from the more traditional and male-dominated Germanics conferences and thus from the possibilities of professional networking,[29] they opened up a whole new area of study and were soon joined by others. Scholars like Renate Schulz, Janet Swaffar, and Claire Kramsch—to name just a few—wield an influence that has yet to be measured. Across the country, the results of their research on language acquisition is being used to train future professionals in the field of German.

Melitta Gerhard and Marianne Thalmann remained exiles, and some of the postwar immigrants like Ingeborg Glier and Katharina Mommsen never really overcame their expatriate status to become part of American Germanics, but instead kept in mind a mainly German-speaking audience for their scholarly work. However, one could argue that—regardless of their age differences—Helen Adolf, Liselotte Dieckmann, Edda Tille-Hankamer, Eva Wunderlich, Ruth Klüger, Lore Foltin and others became American Germanists in the sense that they contributed to the profession not only overseas but in the United States—either through excellence in undergraduate and graduate teaching, via bilingual publications, or through their involvement in professional organizations such as the AATG or MLA. For example, Liselotte Dieckmann, once elected to office within the MLA, became instrumental in securing leaves of absence for academic women with children.[30]

Undoubtedly, professionalization has made female Germanists more visible and enticed them to become more vocal. Since the 1970s, there has been a marked increase in the numbers of female professors. This fact led Valters Nollendorfs to conclude in 1994 that a certain "feminization" of the profession has occurred, which—among other results—means a "much more public and open profession and a movement away from one that is dominated by a group of male expatriate high priests." Nevertheless, Nollendorfs concedes that, even though the number of women among doctorates has exceeded that of men since 1975, women continue to have a disproportionately high number of temporary positions.[31] In 1988, female academics as a whole still perceived of themselves as "outsiders in the sacred grove,"[32] and as recently as 1992, a highly visible and internationally renowned Germanist like Ruth Klüger showed awareness of women's marginality in academe when she addressed her memoirs to a female readership, ironically remarking that men never read anything written by a woman anyway—academic or otherwise (Klüger 81).[33]

Yet by 1971, the concept of culture as put forth by an older generation of Germanists—by Americans and immigrants, male and female alike—had been profoundly challenged by their own disciples.[34] To the younger group of intellectual émigrés who considered themselves cosmopolitan intellectuals living between two cultures and who were not able to find a geographical home, teaching their own culture and language became instrumental to understanding their identity — as speakers of German and as Jews,[35] and with this approach, they have influenced their students, who, in turn, have come to investigate their own identities.[36] As feminist scholarship, applied linguistics, research on outsiders in German literature and culture, and interdisciplinary research have become mainstream, female Germanists helped to change permanently the face of American Germanics. For example, although Solomon Liptzin had already presented German Jewish authors as Germany's Stepchildren in 1944, it was Austrian-born Evelyn Torton Beck who broke the traditional mold of reading Franz Kafka's work as that of the quintessential modernist, when she placed Kafka into the Jewish tradition with her study of Kafka and the Yiddish Theater in 1971. Throughout her career Beck,[37] and many of her colleagues — foreign-born and Americans alike — continue to uncover outsiders of the literary canon who have previously been invisible within institutionalized Germanics.

Notes

1   In general, the histories of American colleges and universities tend to depict women's roles in the overall developments of their institutions only where the development of co-education is concerned and the development of womens' colleges. Usually, the women mentioned here are administrators, scientists, or members of English departments. The notable exceptions among women in Germanics are Marianne Thalmann, although she is mentioned only in passing (Glasscock 107), and Lilian Stroebe (S. Freeman 20–29).

2   Hoecherl-Alden 607–41. This is a conservative estimate based on the research done for my dissertation.

3   Blume 238. Blume's remark that she is among the most important refugee Germanists is quoted indiscriminately by Hermann 359, Weber, "Alewyn" 243, and Zelle 132.

4   The biologist Margarethe von Wrangell and Mathilde Vaerting, Professor of Pedagogy. See Förder-Hoff 64.

5   Anna Jacobson and Ruth Hofrichter — to name just two — finally left Germany to pursue an academic career in the United States. Their abbreviated vitas in *Who's Who in American Jewry* (1939) suggest that they moved from one high school job to the next before securing positions at Hunter College and Vassar respectively. Conversely, those women with doctorates who stayed in Germany because they were married and were raising children, such as Bertha Badt-Strauss, who wrote on Annette von Droste-Hülshoff and Rahel Varnhagen, had to forfeit academic careers and were often not able to find teaching positions after going into American exile. See Hahn 152–65.

6   Regarding Agathe Lasch's biography, see Maas 447–52.

7   See also Wunderlich, "Deutsch-Mann" 94–105.

8   Thalmann, who was to become professor emerita at Wellesley, was later commemo-
    rated as an actively publishing scholar whose speciality was Romanticism. Glasscock
    107.

9   Before Marianne Thalmann took the position, Wellesley had hired Melitta Gerhard.
    The "Emergency Committee in Aid of Displaced German Scholars" had secured the
    position at the respected women's college. However, after only one academic year, in
    June 1935, Gerhard returned to Berlin because she wanted to stay in Europe. After sev-
    eral unsuccessful attempts to find work in Italy or Switzerland, she accepted an offer in
    1938 from Rockford College, Illinois, and returned to the United States. See Dane 224.

10 At this point it should be noted that their German university positions did not secure
    Gerhard's or Tille-Hankamer's financial independence. In both positions, remunera-
    tion was dependent on the number of student enrollments in any given semester. Tille-
    Hankamer was married to a full professor, and therefore had few, if any, financial
    worries. Dane points out that, while Gerhard commuted from Berlin to Kiel and simul-
    taneously taught at a school in Berlin, she continued to receive financial support from
    her parents. Dane 222.

11 In 1976, her publisher, Franke, honored her with a *Festschrift* containing a collection
    of her essays spanning 30 years of literary scholarship. Gerhard, *Auf dem Wege*.

12 I would like to thank both my Ph.D. advisor Jost Hermand and Clifford Bernd who
    shared their personal recollections of Melitta Gerhard with me. In July 1994 Hermand
    recalled that Melitta Gerhard seemed very proud of the fact that she had personally met
    Stefan George, and he remembers her as very national-conservative. As Bernd told me
    in Madison, Wisconsin, in September 1996, Gerhard "was spectacularly unsuccessful
    as an undergraduate teacher." It seems that Gerhard's outlook was akin to that of many
    male German professors who associated themselves with the "George circle," even
    after their arrival in American exile. This group, on the whole, was elitist and con-
    servative and was only suited for Ivy League institutions. Regarding the pedagogical
    ideas of some members of this group, see Weber 137–65; concerning their difficulties
    with adapting to life in the United States, see Hoecherl-Alden 91–105; Gerhard's own
    outlook is described in Dane 223–24.

13 I would like to thank A. Tilo Alt, an alumnus of the University of Tennessee, for sharing
    his recollections of his teacher Edda Tille-Hankamer in Madison, Wisconsin, Septem-
    ber 1996.

14 I thank my colleague Dee Ashliman for sharing his recollec tions of Lore Foltin and
    the origin of the award with me.

15 See Thomas Mann, *Briefe 1889–1936*, ed. Erika Mann (Frankfurt/M.: Fischer, 1961);
    and *Briefe 1937–1947*, ed. Erika Mann (Frankfurt/M.: Fischer, 1963).

16 "Dieser Aufruf gibt mir die Möglichkeit den Männern Sympathie und Achtung zu be-
    zeugen, die in diesem Lande—unter Umständen, die ihrer Arbeit nicht günstig sein
    mögen—die Sprache lehren." Mann, "An die Deutschlehrer" 67.

17 Glasscock mentions that Thalmann's portrait is now in the National Library of Vienna,
    but she does not refer to her reemigration.

18 See Gabriele Kreis's interviews with Hedda Korsch in *Frauen im Exil* and Eva Wunder-
    lich's correspondence in the Deutsches Literaturarchiv in Marbach: Eva Wunderlich
    to Gertrud von le Fort, Union, New Jersey, 19 April 1953 (Marbach, 74.843/12).

19 Her correspondence reveals that she invited Kurt Pinthus to her college as a paid guest speaker (letters of Wunderlich to Pinthus, 10 May 1950 [Marbach, 71.3746/3 and 4]), and continues to worry about his well-being in New York (Wunderlich to Pinthus, 27 July 1951 [Marbach, 71.3746/5]).

20 In fact, as Clifford Bernd recalled, Wunderlich's high energy level and dedication to teaching kept the New Jersey chapter of the AATG afloat. "She was the AATG," he told me in Madison, Wisconsin, September 1996.

21 In 1952, for example, arguments along the lines that intellectual women were "unnatural" and hence susceptible to the pitfalls of Communism were brought forth in rationalizing Luella Raab Mundel's dismissal as the head of the art department at Fairmont College in West Virginia (McCormick 30–39, 58–60).

22 For Klüger, see her autobiography; for Cernyak-Spatz, see the essay on her personal life, Cernyak-Spatz 103–10.

23 Ruth Klüger's memoires as well as her work on the editorial board of the Simon Wiesenthal Center bear witness to this fact, as does Susan Cernyak-Spatz's anthology *German Holocaust Literature* (1985).

24 Most notably, by fellow émigré Germanists Richard Plant in *The Pink Triangle: The Nazi War Against Homosexuals* (1986), Alfred Hoezl's teaching and interdisciplinary research interests in Holocaust literature, and Carl Steiner's work on Jurek Becker and the Holocaust; as well as the more recent and more personally motivated discussions instigated by Sander Gilman (e.g., "Why and How I Study German" *German Quarterly* [1989] and *Jews in Today's German Culture* [1995]), and others.

25 The year in brackets does not refer to the date they received their doctorates, but to the year they took up employment at an American university.

26 Spaethling 630–31. Robert Spaethling contrasts Melitta Gerhard's physical appearanc to her mental characteristics: "Sie ging genügsam und unverdrossen ihres Weges, eine zierliche Gestalt, mit strengen, streitbaren Augen, die gern und unbequem examinierten."

27 For a list of Adolf's, Gerhard's and Stroebe's publications, see Nagy (*Women in Germanics* 141–52). Liselotte Dieckmann's publications are referred to in the appendix of Hohendahl et al., *Essays.* For other female Germanists, comprehensive bibliogrpahies have not yet been compiled.

28 I have already quoted some former students and colleagues. One way to measure pedagogical influences would be to analyze college textbooks these women authored or co-authored. Lore Foltin, for example, collaborated with Hubert Heinen in the publication of an anthology for undergraduates, *Paths to German Poetry.*

29 I thank Janet Swaffar for pointing out to me in September 1996 that she turned to pedagogy and the field of applied linguistics precisely because she was not invited to give papers at traditional literature conferences, even though the research she did for her doctorate was in literary analysis and interpretation.

30 Liselotte Dieckmann, who had arrived in American exile with her husband in 1938, had raised her children alone after her divorce, while simultaneously teaching at Washington University. I thank Patricia Herminghouse for pointing out Dieckmann's involvement in issues of professional women's rights and needs during her tenure with the MLA.

31 V. Nollendorfs, "Present Trends" 53. "Expatriate high priests" refers to Van Cleve and Willson's monograph critical of Germanics.

32   Aisenberg & Harrington makes no special reference to female Germanists.
33   "Wer rechnet schon mit männlichen Lesern? Die lesen nur von andern Männern Geschriebenes."
34   See the collection of essays from the Second Wisconsin Workshop entitled *Die Klassik Legende* (1971), David Bathrick's 1975 MLA presentation, which was printed under the title "On Leaving Exile: American Germanistik in its Social Context," printed in *German Studies in the United States: Assessment and Outlook* (1976), and Schmidt's provocative article on oppositional criticism.
35   These reasons are cited by both male and female refugees, for example, in the the autobiographies of Egon Schwarz and Lilian Fuerst.
36   See here especially Suchoff's article.
37   See Beck, *Nice Jewish Girls*.

Representations of Women in the AATG, 1850–1950

ELLEN MANNING NAGY

Women have been actively involved in Germanics nearly from the beginnings of the discipline in this country. They have made their impact by designing and teaching courses, by their scholarship as reflected in the books, textbooks, and scholarly essays they have authored, and by being actively involved in professional associations. While each of those activities and signs of professional involvement can be measured to some extent, this essay concentrates on women's membership and involvement in professional organizations.

Concerns of the profession and suggestions for advancing it are often best reflected in the articles published in an association's journals as well as in the types of papers presented at annual meetings and scholarly symposia. In addition to disseminating scholarship, an individual may advance professional and personal goals by functioning as an elected officer, by working as a committee member, and/or by becoming involved in local organizational chapters.

This study investigates and evaluates women's historical involvement in one professional organization, the American Association of Teachers of German (AATG), from its founding in 1926 through 1950. The concluding date takes us to the eve of the impact of the women's movement and the changes the profession has witnessed since then. A close examination of the roles of women in the AATG until 1950 shows their low academic status and their preclusion from top offices—an indication of both a lack of awareness of, and lack of recognition for, women's professional abilities and contributions.

A drop in women's academic employment during the late 1940s and 1950s, as well as the general changes in American higher education and society beginning in the 1960s, changed the course of women's academic history. However, although modern Germanics is becoming increasingly feminized, that is, more female graduate students complete doctorates now, and more women are employed in the profession than in previous decades, the proportion of women represented in the professional organizations has changed little.

Women's involvement in the AATG is a natural choice for examination because the organization focuses exclusively on teaching and research concerns in German language, literature, and culture. The organization consistently addresses both pedagogical as well as literary issues. An examination of women's involvement in the organization provides significant insights into their commitment to and their range of interests in Germanics.

121

In order to assess women's participation in and contribution to the AATG, available data were compiled and evaluated on membership, officer nominations and election results, conference presenters and discussion leaders, and committee assignments and activities. A thorough examination of annual meeting reports, constitutions and revisions thereof, membership listings, local AATG chapter reports, and editorials and letters published in the *German Quarterly* (*GQ*), the official publication of the AATG (*By-laws,* V, 1, 1931), provides much of the information analyzed here.

The history of the AATG has been documented in several studies: von Klenze's "The American Association of Teachers of German," Liptzin's "Early History of the A.A.T.G. (1926–31)," Zeydel's "The Teaching of German in the United States from Colonial Times to the Present," and Weiss's "From New York to Philadelphia: Issues and Concerns of the American Association of Teachers of German between 1926 and 1970." Each confirms that World War I and its aftermath greatly affected the teaching of and enrollment in German in American schools and colleges. Zeydel comments: "The propaganda, which had concentrated upon the German emperor, his army and submarines . . . turned immediately, now that we were at war, against the language, its literature as a whole, and in some cases even against its teachers" (360). That this propaganda destroyed the earlier, positive image of German is evidenced in the dramatic drop in German language enrollment. Zeydel writes:

> Between 1917 and 1919 the teaching of German became practically nonexistent in the public and private high schools, 315,884 (28%) of whose students had still been studying it in 1915. By 1922, four years after the end of the war, the high schools had less than 14,000 students of German, or little more than one-half of one per cent of the high school enrollment of 2,500,000. (361–62)

The AATG was established in 1926 primarily to improve the status of German in American schools. German enrollment never really recovered; in 1949, German high school enrollment was less than one percent (0.8 percent) of the total school enrollment in the United States (Zeydel 368).

The process of restoring German to the American school curriculum increased the demand for a strong organization of teachers who could advance the study of German and offer one another professional support. The first step in improving the position of German in American schools and colleges, according to Camillo von Klenze, was the "formation of an organization embracing all teachers of German in every part of the country" (3). The founding of the AATG in 1926 was, therefore, intended "to spread the knowledge of German in this country by increasing the efficiency of the teaching of German" (Klenze 4). Yet other factors encouraging the establishment of the AATG included the relative success of the American Association of Teachers of Spanish (established 1917) in advancing the growth of interest in Spanish, and the concurrent founding (1926) of an American Association of Teachers of French (AATF).

The idea of a new German teachers' organization was met with skepticism. Some individuals felt that German teachers could voice problems and discuss issues at the Germanic section of the MLA. Furthermore, the *Modern Language Journal,* in which articles on German language teaching could be published, already existed. It was, however, argued that the MLA had never encouraged the membership of high school teachers, so the concept of a German teachers' organization for secondary and college instructors was new. In addition, it was proposed that the new organization be formed initially from local groups which would be sponsored by a national or central chapter. Once enough local chapters had been established, the recruiting functions of these groups could then be taken over by the national organization.

In 1926 two organizations, Der Verein deutscher Lehrer von New York, exclusively male, and The New York Chapter of High School Teachers, predominantly female, established the AATG, or more specifically the Metropolitan Chapter. The following year four additional chapters were established—Finger Lakes, Western New York, Central New York, and Hudson Valley. The founding members of the Metropolitan chapter felt that as the situation in Germany had changed, pedagogical methods and textbooks needed to be reviewed and materials published that were more attuned to the current needs of American students (Klenze 5). The first officers elected, Camillo von Klenze (president), Sol Liptzin (secretary), and H. A. Buschek (treasurer) were authorized to initiate further development of the organization.

That the initial AATG was comprised of two groups—male and female—invites comment. Some would believe that gender bias is apparent from the segregation of men and women in the early organization. This notion has some merit, since the percentage of college professors was noticeably higher in the early years of the AATG and there were proportionally more men employed in colleges and universities. There is, however, no evidence to indicate the number of males and females in the original AATG organization. The membership then could possibly have been equally divided between men and women. Women presumably constituted half of the initial founding group of teachers, yet none was elected to a senior officer post, that is, president or secretary of the new association, a void which lasted until 1949.

By 1932, only five years after the founding of the AATG, it was a well-established national organization. As others had before, Robert H. Fife, who was then president, endorsed a review of the present curriculum and methodology and acknowledged that "we (German teachers) have got to consider what is best to meet present American conditions and experiment until we shall have arrived at a methodology that will be adopted to them" (Fife, "Members" 53).

The goal of the association in the early years was primarily pedagogical; members were invited to evaluate and devise syllabus materials that would be useful in developing a new methodology. This project entailed the selection and rating of vocabulary, idiom, and syntax materials, as well as the publication of experiments and time-saving methods to use these new resources. These topics were regularly addressed at the annual meetings and in articles published in *GQ*. "The welding of the various chapters into an efficient organization would best be accomplished by means of a journal, since no organization of this kind can flourish without a medium of discussion" (Liptzin 22). The founding of the *GQ* in 1928 fulfilled this need.

Papers read at the early annual meetings, like the articles appearing in the *GQ*, focused primarily on pedagogical topics. In fact, one of the principal purposes of the AATG, via papers presented at annual meetings, was to "help those teachers who find acquaintance with recent currents difficult, to become energetically alive to the new problems and the new possibilities" (Klenze 5).

Ordinarily only four or five papers were read and discussed at each annual meeting. Between 1931 (the first annual meeting) and 1949, a total of only four women—Jane Goodloe (Goucher College) in 1936, Carola Geiger (DePaul University) in 1945, Elfriede Ackerman (Von Steuben High School, Chicago) in 1947, and Elise Heyse Dummer (Elmhurst College) in 1948—presented papers at annual meetings. This is fewer than in the current programs, where half of the presenters are female. While these four women represent only 2 to 6 percent of the total number of presenters, the number of women leading symposia or discussions was greater—approximately 45 percent of all symposia and discussion leaders (Elfriede Ackerman [1933, 1934], Lydia Meyer [1933], Lilian Stroebe [1935], Emma Ceremak [1938], and Marjorie Lawson [1939]). This apparent discrepancy between scholarship and organization tends to suggest a certain irony: the AATG asks women to furnish leadership and organizational skills at AATG meetings, but seems to overlook their scholarship by effectively silencing them, since they were not presenting their own scholarship, but acting primarily as hostesses. This unfortunate situation was doubtless not due to a conscious containment of women, but nevertheless, it does not alter the fact that women were not presenting their research.

Assigning women to administrative positions at annual meetings effectively blocks the presentation of their scholarship; it may also imply a feeling that they had nothing of importance to contribute to the intellectual development of the profession. Women were not widely accepted within the professional network. A report from the 1902 MLA annual meeting states: "In the evening the gentlemen of the Association were entertained by the Local Committee at the Graduates' Club. The ladies were received, at the residence of Professor A. S. Cook, by the wives of the University Instructors in Modern Languages." Although this practice later changed due to protests led by Henriette von Klenze, how could a female Germanist ever hope to gain professional acceptance and recognition when she was also overlooked in the informal professional arena? Based on practices which continue even today, I find it likely that those women who were publishing were also submitting papers to be read at annual meetings. The average percentage of articles authored by women between 1926 and 1949 is approximately 10; therefore, the number of papers presented by women at the annual meetings was minimal.

The high level of pedagogical concern is also reflected in various AATG activities. Such activities show a concern for quality teaching and materials, as well as involvement in improving the status of German in the United States, and include, for example, the development of a minimum standard vocabulary list, the establishment of a national service bureau, involvement in curriculum planning, and teacher training. Several of these activities enjoyed relative success, notably the standard vocabulary list and the service bureau.[1] Other activities, however, remained in committees with discussions continued in articles and editorials. Women's involvement in any of these endeavors, as is any one individual's, is difficult to ascertain. The names of committee members have evidently not been preserved, since the AATG's national office does not have records of this nature.

The German Service Bureau grew out of the Interscholastic Federation of German Clubs (1927), which was established as a result of the revived postwar interest in teaching German. The Service Bureau, established at the University of Wisconsin, acted as a central clearinghouse for available teaching and cultural materials. The bureau was frequently used by all German teachers who needed good quality, current teaching materials.

With the advent of World War II, the Interscholastic Federation of German Clubs was suspended and with it the Service Bureau, since materials were difficult to acquire during the war. Stella Hinz worked as the bureau's secretary and librarian from its establishment until her death in 1938. Hinz began working at the University of Wisconsin in 1922 as an assistant in the German department. She received her Ph.D. in 1925 from the same institution, doing her work with Alexander R. Hohlfeld. Her career was spent training and providing adequate supplemental teaching materials to individuals (Ernst 332–33). Through the "Service Bureau Notes," which appeared regularly in *Monatshefte,* Hinz suggested "Realien" and periodicals, supplied addresses of publishers, encouraged individuals to send in notes on successful methods and ideas, and generally tried to solve problems connected with the teaching of German. Although Hinz was the impetus behind the bureau, establishing, organizing, and supplying materials to teachers, she has rarely been recognized beyond the University of Wisconsin for her accomplishments.

Although AATG membership increased steadily between 1926 and 1950, a constant problem was its relatively small representation of college and high school teachers in terms of number of members compared to the number of Germanists and German teachers in the profession. Since membership in the AATG is not mandatory for any German teacher and is open to anyone interested in German language, culture, and literature, it is impossible to determine what percentage of members were employed as German teachers or what percentage of German teachers were AATG members. In a letter to Nagy, Zimmer-Loew noted that the *GQ* published its first list of AATG members in 1950, but the AATG office kept no records of individual memberships earlier than 1978. Neither the number of female members between 1926 and 1949 nor the total membership can be determined.

While its configuration has changed over the years, the AATG is today directed by an executive council consisting of a president, two vice presidents, a secretary (elected by ballot at the annual meeting), the managing editor and business manager of the *GQ* (appointed by the executive council), the executive director (nonvoting) and six additional elected members. The executive council also confirms the editor's appointments to the editorial board of the *GQ*. Because the policy making body of the AATG is its executive council and the association's business is conducted by elected officers and committees, it becomes significant to examine AATG nominations and elections (AATG Constitution, IV, 3). It is reasonable to assume that those nominated and elected as officers and council members are respected members of the profession.

The original AATG constitution and bylaws were unanimously accepted at the annual meeting in 1931. Subsequent changes in 1934, 1938, and 1941 primarily affected the administration of the organization, such as terms of office and executive appointments. These changes to the constitution remained in effect until 1969. In 1969 the changes to the constitution eliminated the third vice-presidential position, and stipulated that one of the two other vice-presidential positions must go to a primary or secondary school teacher, but the six executive council member positions no longer needed to be equally divided between secondary and university teachers (*GQ* 42: 622–28).

In 1934 a committee headed by Lilian Stroebe proposed that in order to advocate better representation for women as well as improve consideration of regional distribution and representation of high school and college teachers in balloting and elections, an amendment be added to Section IV, Paragraph 3 to read: "In making up the ballot, due consideration shall be given, so far as possible, to the representation of the several regions, to the representation of teachers from the several schools and colleges, and to the representation of the women members of the Association" (*GQ* 7: 127–28). Obviously the committee members felt that the association was not sufficiently representing all members fairly. That such a committee even existed—albeit temporarily—indicates that, while women were not a negligible group in the AATG, they were not receiving the recognition they felt they deserved. In addition, the proposal recommended that "(i)n order to insure the success of this plan . . . the ballot (shall) pit women against women, high school teachers against high school teachers and college teachers against college teachers" (*GQ* 7: 127). The attempt to balance AATG officers is due to the less than desirable participation of women and high school teachers from authority, that is, leadership positions as evidenced by the activity of Stroebe's committee. Consequently, beginning in 1938 those nominated for executive council positions were divided into a high school group or a college/university group, and those nominated for other offices were academic equals. To illustrate, four individuals were nominated for two available executive council positions. Generally the nominations included both high school and college teachers, but there was no guarantee that both would later be represented on the council. In 1938 nominations for executive council members were divided into a college and a high school group. One individual was then elected from each group, thus ensuring council representation for both high school and college teachers.

It is difficult to determine from available data whether the issue of providing better representation for women continued to be a concern after 1938. In fact, by 1957, because of "inconsistencies and inaccuracies," changes were proposed to the constitution which resulted in dropping Article 3, which mandated due representation of women on the election ballot. Changes to the constitution were recommended by the Committee for the Revision of the Constitution of the AATG, an all-male committee, consisting of C. R. Goedsche, Werner Neuse, H. H. J. Peisel, and Alfred Senn, who was then president of the AATG. The constitutional changes were voted on and approved at the 1957 annual meeting. Yet, in surveying election results from 1939 to 1949, it becomes clear that the committee's resolution was not a panacea. Women still were not elected as president or secretary, and only two women were elected as first vice president, one in 1938 and one in 1942. Not until 36 years later, in 1978, was another women elected to that position.

Lists of those nominated as officers and members of the executive council are not universally available. For example, between 1927 and 1932 none was published, and nominations after 1946 were not published in *GQ,* but mailed separately to AATG members (*GQ,* "Decennial Index" 3). Consequently the conclusions reached here are based only on the nominations published in *GQ* between 1934 and 1944. The ballot was assembled by a five-member nominating committee appointed by the president. Normally, two of the five committee members were women. Women comprised at least one-third of the ballot each year and in 1939 were as much as 50 percent. Election results for the same years indicate that women held approximately one-third of the offices (tables 1–3).

Women's success in elections, particularly after 1938, was essentially guaranteed, since the constitution required that women oppose women on the ballot. One obvious flaw in the system is that the constitution does not guarantee the type of position to which women might be elected. One can conclude that women were adequately represented in the AATG (40 percent of the nominating committee; 33 percent of the ballot), but they were not nominated for the presidency. Even the position of executive director had not been held by a woman prior to 1986 when the executive council selected Helene Zimmer-Loew, who still holds the office.

Between 1927 and 1950 AATG members elected 19 presidents, but none was a woman. Not until 1949, when Emma Birkmaier (University of Minnesota) was elected, did a woman serve as secretary of the association. Another female secretary was not elected until 1981 (Ingeborg Hinderscheidt, Purdue). Between 1927 and 1950 the majority of female officers held vice-presidential positions, but they made up only 37 percent of even these offices. The list of AATG elected officers (tables 1–3) shows a lack of female representation in top positions. The majority (approximately 75 percent) of officers elected were college and university profes-

Table 1. Elected Officers—President and First Vice President, 1927–1950, of the American Assocation of Teachers of German

	President		First Vice President	
1927	Camillo von Klenze	University of Munich	E. W. Bagster-Collins	Columbia University
1928–1931	E. W. Bagster-Collins	Columbia University	Adolf Busse	Hunter College
1932	Robert Herndon Fife	Columbia University	Max Griebsch	University of Wisconsin
1933	A. R. Hohlfeld	University of Wisconsin	Erwin Mohme	University of Southern California
1934	John A. Walz	Harvard University	Frederick Betz	George Washington H.S., New York
1935	Albert W. Aron	University of Illinois	J. B. E. Jones	DeWitt Clinton H.S., New York
1936	Theodore Huebener	Asst. Dir. MFL, Board of Ed., New York	F. W. Meisnest	University of Washington
1937	Frank H. Reinsch	University of California, Los Angeles	Christian F. Hamff	Emory University
1938	Edward F. Hauch	Hamilton College	Thelma Bryant	Thomas Jefferson H.S., Virginia
1939–1940[a]	Ernst Feise	Johns Hopkins University	Alfred Kalmer	Louisville Male H.S., Kentucky
1941	John O. Hess	Ohio University	Lawrence M. Price	University of California, Berkeley
1942	George Danton	Union College	A. E. Zucker	University of Maryland
1943–1944[b]	George Baerg	DePauw University	Otto K. Liedke	Hamilton College
1945	Richard Jente	University of North Carolina, Chapel Hill	Victor Lange	Cornell University
1946	John C. Blankenagel	Ohio Wesleyan University	Harold von Hofe	University of California, Los Angeles
1947	Curtis C. D. Vail	University Washington	Alfred Senn	University of Pennsylvania
1948	Charles M. Purin	University of Wisconsin	B. Q. Morgan	Stanford University
1949	Ernst Jockers	University of Pennsylvania	Günther Keil	Hunter College
1950	Günter Keil	Hunter College	Walter A. Reichart	University of Michigan

[a] In 1940 all officers were reelected due to a modification in the Constitution changing their terms of office from one to two years.
[b] The executive committee postponed elections in 1943 since only thirty ballots were sent in, not enough to hold an election (*GQ* 16 [1943]: 43).

Table 2. Elected Officers—Second and Third Vice President, 1927–1950, of the American Assocation of Teachers of German

Year	Second Vice President		Third Vice President	
1927	Adolfe Busse	Hunter College	Katherine Kümmerle	Walton H.S., New York
1928–1931	Katharine Kümmerle	Walton H.S., New York	NONE	
1932	William R. Price	Ed. Department, New York	Katherine Kümmerle	Walton H.S., New York
1933	F. A. H. Leuchs	New Utrecht H.S., Brooklyn	Jane Goodloe	Goucher College
1934	Charles M. Purin	University of Wisconsin	Ernest O. Eckelmann	University Washington
1935	Emily White	Central H.S., Washington D.C.	Oscar C. Burkhard	University Minnesota
1936	Lydia L. Meyer	West Allis H.S., Wisconsin	Christian F. Hamff	Emory University
1937	Helen Ott	Albany H.S.	Claire S. Schradieck	University Maryland
1938	Sister M. Coronata Schardt	Rosary College	Henry Safford King	Reed College
1939–1940	Lilia Garms	East H.S., Aurora, Illinois	Dorothy Johns	University H.S., Los Angeles
1941	Anna Meyer	Central H.S., Binghamton, New York	Arnold Ortmann	Lafayette J.H.S., Baltimore
1942	Jacob Hieble	Michigan State University	Henrietta Way	Fairfax H.S., Los Angeles
1943	Gustave O. Arlt	University of California, Los Angeles	Annemarie M. Sauerlander	University of Buffalo
1944	Emma Birkmaier	University of Minnesota		
1945	Ruth Hofrichter	Vassar College	Albter Van Eerden	Princeton University
1946	Hubert J. Meessen	Indiana University	Ella Liskey	Central H.S., Minneapolis
1947	Elfriede Ackermann	Von Steuben H.S., Chicago	Sister Catherine Teresa Rapp	Nazareth College
1948	Emma Birkmaier	University Minnesota	Werner Neuse	Middlebury College
1949	Florence Anderson	Davenport H.S.	Louis DeVries	Iowa State College
1950	Walter A. Reichart	University of Michigan	Frederick Klemm	Union College

Table 3. Elected Officers—Secretary, 1927–1950, of the American Association of Teachers of German

	Secretary	
1927–1931	Sol Liptzin	City College of New York
1932	Albert W. Aron	University Illinois
1933	F. W. J. Heuser	Columbia University
1934	Hermann B. Almstedt	University Missouri
1935–1937	Edward F. Hauch	Hamilton College
1938–1945	Charles M. Purin	University Wisconsin
1946–1948	Paul Radenhausen	Brooklyn Technical H.S.
1949–1955	Emma Birkmaier	University Minnesota

sors. However, most women nominated and elected were secondary school teachers (approximately 64 percent). Conversely, the men holding AATG offices were almost exclusively college and university faculty (approximately 90 percent).

The situation for women at the local chapter level was not dramatically different. Listings for chapter officers began to be routinely published in *GQ* in 1937. Prior to 1937, local chapters may have submitted information regarding their meetings, but information on elected officials was sporadic. An analysis of local chapter officers between 1937 and 1949 shows that women were averaging 46 percent of all officers. In local chapters women were mostly elected to secretarial and/or treasurer positions—56 and 40 percent respectively. Only 30 percent of presidential positions and 39 percent of the vice-presidential offices were held by women. As on the national level, most women elected to local chapter offices were secondary school teachers (81 percent), whereas the men were routinely college or university faculty.

The information clearly indicates that the vast majority (93 percent) of individuals directing the AATG on the national and local levels consisted of male college professors. Weiss (4) notes that the membership ratio of college teachers to secondary school teachers was two to one in 1950. The evidence shows that women were left out of the top executive positions in the AATG. From 1926 to 1950, the configuration of AATG officers never changed. From the start, male college professors consistently held the high leadership positions in the organization. Although women were actively involved from the beginning—the New York Chapter of High School Teachers, whose membership was mainly female, is estimated at half the initial AATG membership—they were relegated to subordinate positions. In 1950, the organization had approximately 950 members, and 40 percent were women.[2] Women were routinely members of the nominating committee, but women did not hold a percentage of offices (between 1927 and 1949 the percentage of female officers was almost 30 percent) commensurate with their membership, nor were they elected to the presidential or secretarial positions.

In the early decades of the twentieth century, it would have been unlikely for the membership of the AATG to elect a woman to a position simply to avoid charges of sexual discrimination. Perceived merit and, more likely, politics were the primary factors in getting elected. In general, in the early decades of the twentieth century, women in American higher education were professionally hindered by prevailing male attitudes. Even with adequate training (gained in foreign universities), women were not widely accepted on college and university faculties in the United States. Men on college faculties and in administrative positions were reluctant to hire and promote women for fear that being associated with women would raise doubts about their own professional status (Rosenberg, "Limits" 125). In a major study on academic employment, Caplow and McGee write: "Women tend to be discriminated against in the academic profession, not because they have low prestige but because they are outside the prestige system entirely . . ." (111). Carolyn Heilbrun notes in an anecdote that depicts the mood of many men in academic departments, ". . . Charles Everett [Columbia], . . . remarked on the receipt of an application from a woman professor: 'We don't want a woman in Hamilton Hall, do we?' And the application was promptly lost" (409).

The membership did not seem to recognize the female members as leaders, and women were excluded from the fraternity of male college professors that controlled the executive positions of the AATG. These findings suggest a strong tendency toward sexual bias within the ranks of elected officials of the organization; and they reflect biases resulting from the "men's club" politics of the organization. Women who were full-time contributors to the profession were often denied the informal signs of belonging and recognition. Male Germanists did not accept women as professional equals. This prejudice is indicated by the unequal representation of women and high school teachers among the officers of the AATG, by the few papers read by women at annual meetings, and by the disproportionate number of papers published in the association's journal.

Historically women were not welcome in academe. In general, women's relative lack of success in higher education in the early decades of the twentieth century is due, in part, to generally held social attitudes that a woman's place was in the home. William H. Chafe writes; "The distribution of sexual roles made it impossible to do both (marriage and job), because, in order to achieve success in a man's world, they (women) had to accept failure in a woman's world" (101–2). College and university teaching was at odds with societal expectations of women, that is, women did not need to prepare themselves to support a family.[3] The entrance of women into academe threatened the established male foundation. The response of male academics, and possibly many women as well, was to strengthen and reaffirm their principles by keeping women away from leadership positions where they could change and renew the profession.[4] Too often in the past, academic employment operated with closed faculty selection, an "old-boy network," where positions were filled by individuals who knew someone in or who had prior professional contact with the hiring department. The purpose of this type of internal hiring was to maintain the prestige of the department as well as the status quo.[5] As Geraldine Clifford points out:

> The formal criteria of competence in teaching and research might qualify women; the informal criteria of "collegiality" and "fitting in" could exclude them ... "old-boy networks" are believed by their members to protect institutions from taking overly large risks and making mistakes that will reflect badly on an institution's prestige or, where it has little prestige, cause embarrassment if a faculty member must be "let go." ("Introduction," 7–8)

In an article on the profession, Carolyn Heilbrun remarks about the professoriate in general, stating that women entering into an academic career

> ... paid the price of being not as other women, of forbidding themselves to explore the ramifications of their gender. They paid the price of a loneliness difficult either to imagine or describe: I can scarcely, in these days of professional female friendships, even remember that isolation. And we took that isolation wholly for granted: that was the worst of it. (408)

Changes within the profession—in the curriculum and in approaches to literature and methodology—would have shattered the status quo. As noted above, men were reluctant to hire and promote women, fearing that their professional status would diminish via association with women. In addition, women "had to fulfill increasingly more stringent professional expectations, expectations fashioned mostly by men, who had wives ready to assume all the other responsibilities of their lives" (Rosenberg, "Limits" 126). It seems that because a significant number of highly qualified women were involved in Germanics, male Germanists, up until 1950 at least, felt the profession was in danger of becoming feminized and, thus, devalued.[6]

It becomes apparent that the leading members of the AATG, not unlike members of virtually any such organization or institution, developed and perpetuated a professional "inner circle" which controlled the organization. John Creswell notes that, according to a mathematical distribution of performance rates, for every 100 authors who produce a single paper, there are 25 who produce two, 11 with three, and so on. Consequently, approximately only 6 percent of an academic community is producing 50 percent of the papers (240). In Germanics a small number of scholars publishes more than once in professional journals in any year. Thus the impact of these few scholars on the profession is great. Likewise, the number of individuals elected to several AATG offices over a number of years and who are frequently journal editors is small. In fact, the individuals who publish frequently are more often than not AATG officers and journal editors. These individuals make up the profession's "inner circle." Quite simply, the AATG was and is governed by a handful of scholars. Nominations are made by a nominating committee whose members are appointed by the president, normally with the advice of the executive council; likewise, the editor of *GQ* is appointed by the president, also subject to the advice and consent of the executive council. These scholars judge others by their own standard of achievement. Although this "inner circle" did not entirely exclude women, one had to be a well-published scholar to have a chance at being elected to a leadership position. For the nearly 40-year period from 1926 until 1972, when Margaret McKenzie was elected president, it seems one also had to be male.

Many women published consistently and were elected to leadership positions in other organizations (National Federation of Modern Language Teachers, Central States Modern Language Association, and local AATG chapters), yet never received the same recognition from the AATG membership as their male counterparts. For example, Lilian Stroebe was a frequent contributor to *GQ,* was a member of the executive committee, and was elected honorary member of the organization in 1953, yet she rarely read papers at annual meetings and was never considered for a top executive office. Stroebe was, however, greatly involved in her local chapter. She writes "particularly important for us [members of the Vassar faculty] are the meetings of the Hudson River Section of the American Association of Teachers of German. All members of the department have given generously of their time and energy to make the meetings a valuable occasion for school and college teachers to come together and discuss their problems" (12). Perhaps she felt her professional obligation was to those she worked with daily. Other women include, for example, Emma Birkmaier, who taught high school German, French, and Spanish and was AATG secretary from 1949 to 1955, vice president of the National Federation of Modern Language Teachers Associations (1952–54), and president of the Central States Modern Language Association from 1954 to 1958; Ruth Hofrichter, who was chair of the Department of Modern Languages at Midland College (1922–25) and later professor and chair of the Vassar German department; Bertha Reed Coffman, president of the Simmons College chapter of the AAUP, secretary and later chair of the Anglo-Germanics section of the MLA (1933, 1934); Hanna Hafkesbrink, chair of the German department at Connecticut College (1936–67); Else Fleissner, chair of the MLA committee on the development of German culture and tests for teachers (1956–59); and Anna Jacobson, chair of the German department at Hunter College from 1947 to 1956.

The absence of women from the "inner circle" of a profession has prompted many disciplines to investigate the status of their female members. There have been no studies on the status of women in Germanics, although females in other foreign languages have been included in investigations of women who publish in *PMLA.*[7] The committee to revise the AATG constitution, led by Lilian Stroebe in 1934, specifically called women's status in the organization into question, although few long-term effects were noticed. Since the early 1970s, feminist research in Germanics has expanded. The development and growth of Women's Studies departments and programs has encouraged women to take a more active role in their education and professions. The broader focus of German, as demonstrated by a trend to establish "German Studies" as a discipline and to expand Women's Studies, has had an impact on Women's Studies in German.

Dissatisfaction with the AATG and the professional configuration in general led women in Germanics to form their own organization, the history of which is addressed elsewhere in this volume. The AATG has never officially denied membership or elected offices to women members; however, until relatively recently, women were consistently overlooked for the highest association offices and editorships. Furthermore, without the establishment of Women in German (WiG), women Germanists, many of whom are also AATG members, would not have had a professional outlet for their concerns. These concerns include, for example, feminist critiques of textbooks and other teaching materials and of literary works. The existence and growth of WiG imply the that the AATG has not addressed women's issues adequately, even though the proportion of women in the profession has grown steadily and continues to do so today.

Notes

1　See Weiss, "New York to Philadelphia" 215–27.
2　*The German Quarterly* published a membership directory in the 1950 volume.
3　See, for example, Howes, *American Women* 99; Epstein, *Woman's Place* 23.
4　See for example, Hummer; Clifford, "Women's Liberation" 165–82; Rosalind Rosenberg, "The Limits of Access" 107–29.
5　Caplow & McGee 111. See also Clifford, "Introduction" 7–8.
6　See, for example, Nollendorfs & Arness 330; Heilbrun 408–13.
7　See, for example, Hartman, Morlock, Perkins & Tinsley 124–36.

American Germanists and the Holocaust, 1933–1945: The Legacy

SUSAN LEE PENTLIN

In the twentieth century, German teachers have found themselves caught between the desire to promote language study, the demands of academic responsibility, and the American tradition of a neutral or nonpolitical classroom. Most, but not all, have hesitated to confront the Nazi years and have often resisted the Holocaust, both as a classroom subject and as an area of professional concern. Both the Holocaust and the Third Reich have thus posed special problems in education for German teachers. The implication is not that their difficulties were unavoidable or inherent in German study. While other teaching professions may not deal with the Holocaust any differently, the question is whether German teachers bear a special responsibility in Holocaust education, simply because of the association of the German language and culture with the Final Solution.

The German teaching profession in America felt insecure and cautious after the experiences of World War I. Victor Lange explained that this behavior on the part of American German teachers was based on firmly held beliefs. He commented, after looking at early issues of *Monatshefte:*

> We shall be struck by the curious mixture in almost every issue, of labored pedantry and the unquestioned assumption that the teaching of German should be motivated by a passionate and unswerving attachment to the values—political, philosophical and literary—that were then held in Germany . . . and, most emphatically, the example which this sum of superior aspiration offered for the missionary work of American teachers of German. (Lange, "Thoughts" 11)

As a result of World War I, the profession learned to hush its nationalist tone in teaching, realizing that jingoism would no longer be tolerated. However, teachers of German did not abandon their faith that "these studies offer nearly absolute models of thought, behavior and artistry which American students could be urged to emulate" (Lange, "Thoughts" 13). Native-born teachers as well as those not of German ancestry continued to believe in German academic ideals and in the tradition of German idealism as a social and cultural model.

Enrollments in German were, in fact, just beginning to stabilize when Hitler assumed power. In 1933 teachers were still defensive about their field and were frightened that their professional careers as well as the success of their discipline might be jeopardized again. As a whole, teachers reacted by leaving politics out of the classroom and by ignoring the contemporary German scene almost totally in the 1930s and 1940s. H. G. Doyle remarked in an article in the *Modern Language Journal:* "the parallel with 1917–1918 is unmistakable." He thus cautioned:

> We must all "watch our step." The future of our subject is largely in our own hands. My counsel is the counsel of prudence. I believe it is farsighted. I think it should be followed now. We have but one real job—to preserve the modern foreign languages in American education. To justify their retention we must prove that they deserve to be retained. (92)

Following his and others' counsel, the majority of the teachers sought to remain neutral, not to attract attention, and to hope for peace. The profession worked to draw clear distinctions between German study in America and Hitler. They argued energetically that the study of a language is not an endorsement of the politics of a country where that language is spoken and that people can admire and study the literature and culture of a country without condoning its current political system.

However, as a result, German teachers failed to take a stand against the dictatorial acts, racial policies, and open atrocities of the Nazi state. At Northwestern University, Werner Leopold argued that the only recourse was to ignore politics and stay judgment. He wrote in a 1935 issue of *Monatshefte:*

> As matters stand at present [i.e., in Germany], the wisest course to my mind is to postpone judgment on the unsettled political situation in Germany and meanwhile abstain from classroom utterances concerning it. The truth can more easily be established about matters of a somewhat remote past, and we should stop teaching before we come to the point where the establishment of truth seems no longer assured. We shall have to revise that attitude sometime. The changes in institutions and mental attitudes wrought by the new system in Germany are so deep and revolutionary that we cannot long shut our eyes to them. But everything is still in such a state of flux that I believe we should suspend revision of our teaching and our textbooks until time will reveal the stability of the changes. (Leopold, "Reise" 300)

He also relates that when he was writing a beginning reader, a colleague advised him to omit mention of Hitler's becoming chancellor. While Leopold found this "too over-scrupulous" (Leopold, "Realia" 24), others did in fact pursue this policy and continued to picture an "ideal" or tourist Germany in their classes and in language textbooks. This Germany was, of course, more imagination than truth and certainly did not match the brutality and repression of the new Nazi state. Marshall Evans's and Robert Röseler's reader *Das Rheinland* (1934) had ignored even the geographical realities of the New Reich. Photographs in this and other texts showed the beauty of German forests, peasants, and the new Autobahn, but not the swastika flags flying over the Reich.

In 1937, Eugene Jackson and W. D. Pearson published a text, *High Points in German: Two Years.* They also tried to straddle the fence and to deal with Hitler's

Germany in a purely neutral, academic way, thereby avoiding taking sides. They summarized the two viewpoints, writing:

> In short, they [i.e., the friends of the Nazi dictatorship] believe that the present regime represents the highest aspirations of the German people and will lead it to prosperity and happiness . . . they [i.e., opponents of the Nazi regime] declare that the racial policies of the Nazis, which manifest themselves primarily in relentless persecution of the Jews, represent a throwback to barbarous practices of the Middle Ages. (86–87)

Other teachers argued that the heritage of German idealism must not be forgotten and tried to find positive features in the new German state, while ignoring reports of book burnings, actions against Jews and other minorities, and the suppression of basic freedoms in the Reich. They spent their energies resisting the truth. After a 1938 tour of Germany, B. Q. Morgan at Stanford reported in a letter to colleagues:

> The German people are sound, and the greatest hope for the future resides in the youth that is now growing into maturity, and that is beginning to voice an insistent demand for all those ideals that we have long associated with German character at its best. I am not a prophet, and I can't say how things will work out in detail; but of the final outcome I no longer have any doubt. ("Dear Folks")

An editorial appeared in the *New York Times* in 1939 ("Two Germanys"), advocating that Americans look beyond the Nazis and preserve the greatness of German culture, and counseling teachers of German to do the same:

> The fact that the present Chancellor wrote *Mein Kampf* in German need not close our eyes and ears to the beautiful power of a Goethe or to forbid us the sweetly simple sadness of a Theodor Storm's *Immensee*.
> . . . Wise teachers of the language, alertly aloof from political issues, will be doing the service in the interim period of keeping fresh our memory. We ourselves would be the losers if we forgot. A spirit of justice requires that all of us keep the two Germanys distinct in our minds and judgments. ("Two Germanys")

Some teachers were not only optimistic in professional journals. Gerhard Baerg published a cultural reader (1938) which shows a painful lack of perception about the new Germany and a continuing resistance to the truth about Hitler's Germany. He wrote:

> Hitlers Verstreben geht dahin, alle Deutschen zu einem einheitlichen Volk zusammenzuschließen und das Reich in jeder Hinsicht unabhängig von andern Ländern zu machen. Seitdem er Reichskanzler ist, hat er der politischen Zersplitterung ein Ende gemacht, hat wohl fast allen Erwerbslosen Arbeit verschafft und hat besonders der Jugend neue Hoffnung und neue Begeisterung für Deutschland gegeben. (97)

Paul Curt's textbook on German history for language students (1939) is an example of a text which even extolled the new German leader in a small paragraph devoted to the events of the previous year: "Die Arbeitslosigkeit hat er beseitigt, die Wirtschaft geordnet, die Armee aufgebaut, die Grenzen befestigt, Österreich und das Sudentenland in das Reich einverleibt. Voll Hoffnung schaut das deutsche Volk in die Zukunft" (93).

Even after 1940, preserving German culture and securing the future of German studies in the United States had the highest priority. In 1941 Guy Vowles of Davidson College wrote to his colleagues, warning: "In sum, then we must not be so shortsighted as to cut ourselves off from the culture of a great and able people even though we feel that today under false leadership they are a menace to our way of life" (850).

German teachers continued to echo the attitudes of their colleagues in Germany and of many German exiles in America. Certainly, Thomas Mann's 1941 letter to American German teachers would have encouraged this nonactivist attitude. In his remarks, he also failed to recognize the evil of Hitler and his followers:

> Die deutsche Sprache ist die Trägerin und Vermittlerin großer und keiner Zukunft entbehrlicher Traditionswerte, ein herrliches Instrument, eine Orgel, auf der einige der reichsten Fugen und emportragendsten Melodien der Menschheit erklungen sind und auch in der Wirrnis dieser Zeit fortfahren zu erklingen. Was ändert Hitler daran? Zuletzt ist dieser Mensch nur ein Werkzeug, dessen der Weltwille sich zu Erreichung von Zwecken und Zielen bedient, die ganz außerhalb seines Armen Bewußtseins liegen. ("An die Deutschlehrer" 67–68)

Teachers recognized the dangers in Nazism, but continued to hold firmly to a belief in the intrinsic value of German culture.

There are only a few reports of German teachers who openly propagandized for Hitler or advocated a Nazi view of life in their classroom instruction in America. Perhaps the most notorious propagandist in the American classroom before 1939 was Otto Koischwitz, a professor at New York. Lucy Dawidowicz, a historian of the Holocaust, recalled an incident when she was a student:

> That conflict between Jew and Nazi was enacted on our very doorstep, as it were, in the corridors of Hunter College. Dr. Ernst Riess, German Jew and professor of Latin, confronted Dr. Otto Koischwitz, Nazi sympathizer and professor of German. We watched at a distance in open-mouthed dismay. The elderly Riess vehemently protested Koischwitz's anti-Semitism and his defense of Germany. Koischwitz became abusive. We were afraid he would strike the older man. (Dawidowicz 17)

A colleague, S. Etta Schreiber, also recalled: "Dr. Koischwitz was an ardent admirer of Nazi Germany."

There has also been recent attention to the case of a German professor Lienhard Bergel, who charged he was dismissed at Rutgers University because of his anti-Nazi position. He also alleged that his chair Friedrich Hauptmann was a Nazi sympathizer. In 1985 his case was reopened. Although the faculty panel did not reverse the earlier dismissal, they did conclude that there was some truth to the allegation that Hauptmann had used his classroom "to preach Nazi doctrines and to disseminate propaganda" (Oshinsky 115).

Koischwitz took a leave of absence from Hunter in 1939 and was soon his voice was heard as "Dr. Anders" and "O.K." over German shortwave broadcasts from Berlin to North America. In 1943 he was indicted for treason, but did not come to trial, due to his reported death in 1944 (Pentlin, "Reaction" 244). Hauptmann left for Germany in 1940. He joined the Nazi party in 1941 and worked for the Deutsche Akademie in Slovakia during the war years. After the war, Hauptmann was apparently not allowed to return to the United States (Oshinsky 119).

Of course, some teachers felt the profession must involve German students more actively in an attempt to assess the policies of the new Germany. They advocated German language study for the insight it could contribute to an understanding of contemporary events. As early as 1939, Gilbert Kettelkamp stood virtually alone in encouraging the adaptation of headline news to classroom language teaching. He addressed the issue of academic responsibility in *School and Society,* pointing out that

> As teachers of foreign language, few of us are anxious to dwell on the tragedy surrounding many of the localities when the cultural life of the past has been so rich and yet it is questionable, if we are fair to our pupils and to ourselves, that we should deliberately avoid mention of the foreign names that are directly associated with this culture. (661)

Eugene Jackson called the profession's attention to the role German teachers could play in "combatting the myth of racial superiority" and in preventing racist groups from exploiting American ethnic and racial hatreds (69).

Yet we have little evidence that such advice was heeded in many classrooms. There is likewise no real record of individual professional leaders who took an open, public stand against the racial policies and treatment of minorities in Hitler's Reich. To be sure, the American Association of Teachers of German (AATG) had passed four resolutions to that effect in 1939. But its statement was very mild and avoided any tone of protest. It stated that:

> I. We [i.e., German teachers] believe that there are traditional and enduring values in German culture which we, as teachers of German, should help to preserve. II. We pledge ourselves to maintain and defend the ideals of tolerance, humanities, and individual freedom and III. We sympathize with the oppresssed minorities in Germany. IV. We believe in defending and promoting those principles of American democracy which make for peace and understanding. (Feise 221)

Thus while pro-Nazi writers like Ina Seidel, Wilhelm Schäfer, and Hans Grimm appeared frequently in German readers published in the 1930s, there was no mention of the Nürenberg laws, boycotts against Jews, or concentration camps.

Joseph Alexis and William Pfeiler published a cultural reader in 1938. Their book is a rare example of a text which analyzes the rise of Hitler and at least mentions the crimes of the Nazi state. A young American in Germany speaks with a German teacher who praises the new Germany. The American concludes the conversation by cautiously remarking:

> Ich weiß nicht, ob ich Ihnen beistimmen kann. Natürlich ist es Sache des deutschen Volkes zu bestimmen, was für eine Regierung es haben will, aber als Amerikaner finde ich, daß es in Deutschland manches gibt, worüber ich mein Urteil zurückhalten möchte. Ihr Kirchenkampf, Ihre Rassenphilosophie und Ihre Behandlung der Presse und der freien Meinung werden in amerikanischen Zeitungen viel besprochen. (48)

After Pearl Harbor, German teachers threw themselves fully behind the American war effort. The earlier optimistic attempts to justify German actions and remain optimistic were abandoned. But, if anything, even less attention was paid to a consideration of the policies and activities of Nazi Germany in the classroom, at least as far as reflections in professional articles and contemporary textbooks would indicate. The profession helped in the fight against Hitler but still resisted dealing with the issue of Germany's politics and policies. Ignoring political realities, teachers focused only on the cultural values of German idealism and the high points of German cultural achievements which could continue to be appreciated and emulated.

While the German language teaching profession rose to the call of American patriotism, it had no history of concern for the atrocities of Germany against minorities to build Holocaust education on. In the postwar years, German programs in America persisted in following European cultural models and the traditions of *Germanistik* at German universities. Not until the 1970s did the Holocaust begin to appear in American German programs, the same time period in which Holocaust education began in West German schools following the NBC "Holocaust" series aired in 1978. Henry Geitz had commented two years earlier about the American teaching of German: "I suspect that the thirties in particular would be a topic most German teachers would stay away from (Letter to author)." Even in the 1980s a German teacher who was interested in Holocaust studies struck many as unusual, if not in fact an anomaly, a contradiction in terms.

Still, the belief that German teachers are representatives of German ideals and German traditions has not disappeared. Many educators still feel it is best to put the past behind and to emphasize the positive aspects of German culture. Jane Vogel Fischman, in a recent survey on teaching Holocaust literature, notes that, of course, some teachers may also be sincerely concerned about the need for Holocaust study, but they feel inadequate to the task, since they received little preparation in graduate school or when studying abroad (456).

One of the first tentative forward steps taken in the profession came as early as 1968, when a forum was held in Munich on "Nationalism in German Study and German Literature." Elizabeth Wilkinson, a British professor of German, told colleagues in the closing session of the meeting that "the gain of this last week for me personally is that I for the first time have been able . . . to speak freely and openly with colleagues of my generation as well as with younger colleagues." She preceded her remarks with a mention of her own reticence at discussing the war years (362). In the conference proceedings, Benno von Wiese expressed hope that the volume would: "perhaps . . . contribute to the efforts at self-criticism of German studies in Germany which began in Munich and that it [would] further and intensify these efforts" ("Dear Folks" 5).

One of the first encouragements to support an open, honest approach toward the Nazi past in American German classes came at a 1972 German Studies Conference at Indiana University. At the conference on "Teaching Postwar Germany in America" Gerhard Weiss told colleagues:

> It is time that this Neuschwanstein view of Germany be finally laid to rest, and we owe it to our students that they get an accurate, clear, and, as far as is possible, an unbiased view of Germany as it really is. . . . Students need facts. They must know something about the topography of a country, a bit about its history, its political structures, the current socio-economic problems. They should be aware of the German education system, and the shadow that the Third Reich still casts upon Germany. ("Teaching" 145)

At the same time Wulf Koepke pointed to the link between German and American views of German studies and to the nonpolitical tradition of German studies in American education. He began his presentation by remarking that

> Our profession has done little so far to explain the facts and consequences of the separation of Germany to our American students. We are still hesitant about teaching more than language and literature, and when we introduce German culture we are tempted to stress its noncontroversial features, such as classical music, Gothic cathedrals, or the "romantic Germany." We are in fact hampered by American and German taboos. ("Reader" 151)

In the last 20 years, as the past has grown more distant, the postwar generation has joined the profession, feminist scholarship has influenced the profession (Lorenz 9), and younger Germans have felt compelled to address their country's guilt (Dührkop; Heyl). German teachers in America have exhibited a growing receptivity and readiness to discussing the Nazi past. The awareness of the need to evaluate Germany's past has come both to younger teachers and to those for whom the Holocaust years are memory, and there has been a noticeable increase in papers on Holocaust literature or teaching about the Third Reich and Nazi culture on the programs of professional meetings and the agendas of conferences and forums. A Fulbright Seminar in Bonn and other postgraduate educational opportunities such as the NEH seminars have recently included the Third Reich and modern German society within the context of its past. Of the 43 respondents in a recent survey of German literature teachers, 20 were teaching Holocaust literature in their departmental courses (Fischman 464). To be sure, this does not mean that the profession as a whole has become receptive to the Holocaust. Many in the profession still prefer to discuss the German resistance rather than German guilt, and only a few German teachers have become involved in developing new course offerings about life in the Third Reich, Holocaust literature written in German, German exile literature, and the Holocaust experience.

Those of us who teach the Holocaust are still viewed from many sides with suspicion. Because I taught a course "Nazi Germany and the Holocaust" in 1979 and again in 1993 in my department and one on "The Holocaust in Memory" annually since 1985 in the honors program, and because I have appeared in recent years on several panels which dealt with Holocaust education, I am frequently asked what good might come from stirring up old memories. German-born teachers on several occasions have questioned why I am interested in this part of the past and have hastened to assure me of their own "innocence."

Charles Weber's revisionist book on the Holocaust is another indication of problems which still haunt the profession. The winter 1984 issue of the *German Quarterly,* carried an astonishing advertisement for Weber's book, *The "Holocaust": 120 Questions and Answers.* In the copy, Weber identified himself as a "long-time member of the AATG who has taught German and German area studies on the university level for 32 years." At the bottom of the page there was a note about subscription prices for the revisionist *Journal of Historical Review (JHR)* (*German Quarterly,* Advertisement xv). The *JHR* is published in Torrance, California, by the Institute for Historical Review (IHR), a revisionist group which calls the Holocaust a hoax.

The *German Quarterly* advertisement describes the book as follows:

> This short, propaedeutic book tackles one of the most difficult problems with which American teachers of German . . . have had to deal since 1945. It undertakes a rational, objective assessment of the controversy which has been raging among historians during the past decade concerning the allegations of extensive Jewish mortality during the Second World War.

Furthermore, the ad recommended the book for classroom use. Ironically, a note also appeared on the same page, asking readers to mention the *German Quarterly* when writing advertisers (Advertisement xv).

This advertisement elicited immediate shock and protest in the German teaching profession and among the editorial board of the journal. German teachers were clearly alarmed that such an advertisement was published. The spring 1984 issue of the *German Quarterly* published statements indicating that neither the *GQ* staff, nor the editorial readers, nor the AATG office had seen the ad before it appeared. The editor Henry Schmidt and his staff added: "Moral considerations require, in our opinion, that such advertising be unequivocally condemned" (Schmidt, "Policy" 361) .

A letter to the editor from Ruth Angress at Princeton was also included. She emphasized that "the Institute for Historical Review . . . is in the business of issuing propaganda tracts exclusively concerned with white-washing the Nazis of their crimes." She added that she wanted to question "how an advertisement for anti-Semitic literature got past him," referring to Robert Govier, who was then executive director and business manager of the AATG. She concluded that the profession should be entitled to an explanation and to "a statement disassociating us [i.e., the AATG membership] as an organization of scholars and teachers from efforts to subvert our professional tasks" (Angress 362).

Govier added a postscript explaining that the AATG did not endorse Weber's book (Govier 362). He later sent a letter to the members who had protested the advertisement, writing: "Again I iterate that there is no excuse for my inadvertent acceptance of the ad" (Letter to inquirers). In December 1984 he sent a memorandum to all AATG members at the direction of the executive committee, apprising members that the Council had unanimously passed a resolution on 16 November in Chicago, which stated that the group "Categorically repudiates and condemns the dissemination of material that is anti-Semitic or that can be construed as an apology for Nazism." They also announced measures to avert a reoccurrence and to protect the membership mailing list ("Dear AATG Member").

The mailing list had become an added concern when AATG members began in the winter of 1985 to receive mailings of hate literature from the Institute for Historical Review and from GANPAC [the German-American National Political Action Committee], a group related to the revisionists ("IHR has Links"). Members protested to the AATG offices again, but they were not assuaged by Govier's reply that "I share your concern as regards GANPAC and the viewpoint the people involved represent . . . . The AATG has cooperated in no way with GANPAC and will not do so" (Letter to author).

Unfortunately, not all members of the profession were ready to take a responsible, public position and to involve themselves in controversy. I received a postcard from GANPAC at my university address in June. The card explained that the purpose of this group is "to regenerate pride in the heritage of German Americans, to build a political power base and to fight against the constant defamation of all things German" and pointed out that "this includes setting the record straight on World War II. Jews were not gassed by the Nazis . . . the numbers and reports of predetermined extermination are greatly exaggerated by professional liars" ("Dear Friend"). A short time before, one of my students had brought from home a GANPAC revisionist publication about the fire bombing of Dresden. It referred to the Holocaust as "long discredited WW2 propaganda" (Dresden 1945).

At this point, I also wrote to the president of the Society for German-American Studies (SGAS), an interdisciplinary professional organization, to which I belonged. I wrote to bring GANPAC to the organization's attention and to ask that the Society consider taking a public stand against this propaganda literature. My request seemed to me a particularly appropriate course of action, since GANPAC uses the term "German-American" in its name and its literature. I was dismayed to receive a prompt response from the SGAS president, stating in words similar to the articles in the 1930s and 1940s that, in his view

> These materials are clearly abhorrent, but this is not a matter for the Society to address, since we are not a political organization, but rather a German-American Studies Society. Such matters would more appropriately be addressed by a civic organization concerned with involvement in political affairs. Finally, I can understand your concern, but as one who has been involved in German American affairs for many years I can say that I have enough faith in the intelligence of German Americans to feel that such materials would be recognized for what they are, and be quickly discredited. (Tolzmann)

My student, however, had explained that her father belongs to the organization primarily because he is a German American. GANPAC does claim in its literature to be a political action committee representing America's largest minority, the German Americans (J. Thomas 2).

Regrettably, there was still resistance to the Holocaust among German teachers and, in the profession, to taking a political position. The AATG did take an initial, positive step. However, as the present Executive Director of the AATG admitted later, "AATG has not recently dealt with the topic of Holocaust education as an organization" (September 1987). Few German texts which deal adequately with Germany's recent past are available for teachers who want to include Holocaust study in their courses.

The profession is still dealing with its legacy and misperceptions of the role German teachers must take in assessing Germany's historical past. An interest in the Holocaust can still have academic repercussions. In 1988, before I presented a paper at the Scholars' Conference on the Holocaust at Oxford, I received a personal letter from Charles Weber in which he demanded an apology (27 June 1988). Following my return from the conference, Hans Schmidt of GANPAC wrote to question me as a scholar, sending a copy of the letter to the president of my university. Fortunately, the president was understanding when I explained who Hans Schmidt is, but it could have caused me difficulties (7 July 1988).

I have also had two recent experiences at Central Missouri State University which offer insight into how others perceive the profession and students of German. In 1993, a group appeared on campus calling itself "The Champions of Reason." The group published a newsletter "The Voice of Reason." Articles in it are representative of the racism that drove the Nazi state and, in the wake of campus riots after the Rodney King verdict, they fueled racial tensions (J. Thomas 2).

Two of the leaders were students of German. They began "recruiting" in German classes. The editor of the newsletter was an older graduate student named Dennis Nix who allegedly has ties to the National Alliance. In the early 1970s, he wore a swastika (J. Thomas 2). It is not clear how the students of German became involved, but it certainly seems possible that he sought them out, assuming that

German students might be open to his beliefs. Other faculty members were reluctant to speak out and were particularly surprised that I ("a German teacher") thought this was the right thing to do.

In 1995, I proposed a course on the Holocaust for the German curriculum. My department had opposed this for years, but had finally understood why I felt it was necessary. However, at the Arts and Sciences Curriculum Committee one faculty member protested vehemently. He said that he could not understand how such a course would be offered "in a German department of all places." He also objected to the subject being taught in the German language. I explained that the subject was necessary and of interest to my students. He then said that Germans should be allowed to forget. I tried to explain that many Germans today do not want to forget. While the proposal did gain approval that day, several weeks later it was turned down by the University Committee. Its members also could not understand a Holocaust course in the German curriculum (University Committee).

Certainly changes are occurring. There is reason to think that the German teaching profession is starting to question its reliance on German academic traditions and on German culture as a model. There are also indications that some in the profession are ready to accept the challenge of the Third Reich and the Holocaust and that other academics are willing to consider this acceptance appropriate. I would like to suggest that German Studies in America will truly have "come of age" when German teachers can independently judge Germany's past and openly take on the academic responsibility, as scholars of German language and culture, of providing Holocaust education for this and future generations of American students. Other academicians and professionals must also be willing to let them take a leadership role in Holocaust education.

Having an academic group confront the Third Reich, speak out against hate, and educate American students on the consequences of a racial state may, in fact, preserve and enrich German studies in the next century. The National Archive building in Washington bears the inscription: "The past is prologue." Only by trying to understand the past of our profession as well as the German past can we hope to escape from "the shadow of Auschwitz" as our profession enters the twenty-first century.

"An Indigenous and Not an Exotic Plant": Toward a History of Germanics at Penn

JOHN A. MCCARTHY

It is commonly argued that Germanics in America was an essentially uncritical recipient of the German model of the profession well into the second half of the twentieth century (Koepke 1989: 46–50). Unfortunately, the actual heterogeneity of the emerging profession in Germany and its equally heterogenous reception in America is too little reflected in renditions of the discipline. The discipline was defining itself on both sides of the Atlantic during its first 100 years (1816–1916). This study is an attempt to provide a more differentiated view of that monolithic perception, adding details and archival information in the manner of Uwe Meves and Holger Dainat in their close and discriminating investigations into the professionalization of Germanics in Germany up to 1913–14 (Meves; Dainat).

My main focus is on the shaping of Germanics in the late nineteenth and early twentieth century at the University of Pennsylvania (colloquially dubbed "Penn"). The early phase of Germanics in the United States at Penn represents an Americanized version of *Germanistik* which proved decisive in its critical approach, its thematic preferences, and its admiring yet not uncritical reception of *Germanistik* even during the so-called "period of contentment from 1900 to 1915" (Rippley 1985: 221). The purpose of American Germanists in this early phase was first and foremost to integrate Germanics into the American academic mainstream; they did that long before the outbreak of hostilities between Germany and the United States. Thus I call into question the view that Germanics before 1917 had totally identified with the traditional image of Germany and the German mandarins as the appropriate model (Schmidt 1985: 205; Koepke 1989: 49). Given the richness of the archival material available at Penn, the disciplinary developments there after 1917 can only be hinted at here. It is a fascinating and complex phenomenon deserving of a full dress rehearsal. A detailed account of those later developments is necessary to test the accuracy of the thesis that Germanics from 1900 to 1967 sought to establish its disciplinary legitimacy through a fundamental alignment with *Germanistik,* avoided conflict by choosing "safe" texts, and practiced New Criticism as the dominant critical methodology in splendid isolation (cf. Trommler 1989: 13–14). This essay, then, is intended as a contribution to the institutional history of the profession of Germanics. I have chosen to focus on the very fertile early phase of Germanics in this country, especially in the very early part of the twentieth century because I believe the evidence demonstrates that Germanics then had the function more of a *Leuchtturm* than as an *Elfenbeinturm*.[1] A full and accurate view of the "shaping forces" of Germanics from an institutional perspective can be achieved only by examining the discipline's development at several key universities and colleges (e.g., Chicago, Columbia, Cornell, Harvard, Johns Hopkins, Illinois, Indiana, Ohio State, Wisconsin, Yale). Documentation in support of the argument presented here could not be included because of length restrictions.

The history of Germanics at the University of Pennsylvania is long, central, instructive, and as yet virtually unexplored. As host to one of the oldest German programs in the nation, Penn represents fertile ground for plotting the historical contours, past challenges, and future prospects for our profession. Tracing the ebb and flow of the department's appeal, student enrollment, curricular offerings, German Studies component, outreach efforts, publishing strategies, and placement of its graduate students can afford greater insight into the continuities and discontinuities in the history of Germanics in the United States. Last but not least, it can also serve to establish a historical framework for our current efforts to "authenticate" the Americanization of our profession (Trommler 1989: 239, 255).

The University of Pennsylvania, founded in 1740, first offered German in 1754, hired its first professor of German in 1857, and awarded its first Ph.D. in German in 1891. Numerous notable Germanists have graced its faculty from the appointment of the Göttingen-trained Oswald Seidensticker (1825–1893) in 1867 and include such "academic mandarins" (Ringer 1969) as Marion Dexter Learned (1857–1916), Daniel B. Shumway (1868–1939), Alfred Senn (1899–1978), Ernst Jockers (1887–1957), Adolf Klarmann (1904–1976), Otto Springer (1905–1991), André von Gronicka (1912–), Horst Daemmrich (1932–) and Frank Trommler (1939–). Additionally, Klaus Weimar, Hermann Weigand, and Albert R. Schmitt began their academic careers there, while George Schoolfield and W. Detlev Schumann also once served on the faculty.

The precipitous decline in enrollment in German across the Unites States in the wake of World War I represents a clear interruption in the growth of Germanics in this country (Schmidt 1985: 211; Rippley 1985: 221). Although much of the lost momentum could be regained during the 1920s and 1930s following the Supreme Court's action in 1923 regarding state-level bans on teaching German, the renewed hostilities with Germany and the horror of the Holocaust caused another decline in the teaching of German taught in the schools and colleges. The elimination of foreign-language requirements at many colleges in the 1960s and 1970s represented yet another blow to rebuilding efforts. These developments are chronicled in Frank Trommler's two-volume tricentennial assessment, *America and the Germans,* as well as in his *Germanistik in den USA.* However, those dramatic downturns, especially that of 1917, should not blind us to the real struggles our colleagues experienced both before 1917 and after in their quest for disciplinary legitimacy. Their "rhetoric for survival," as Henry J. Schmidt labeled the phenomenon (1985), that is, their endeavors to persuade colleagues, students, administrators, educators, and the general public of the value of the German language and culture was itself an echo of eighteenth-century efforts to "save" the German language and heritage from extinction in the United States. (Roeber 1995). That "rhetoric of survival" has lost none of its urgency today. Despite the benefit of close ethnic ties to the fatherland, students in the late eighteenth and late nineteenth centuries were not clamoring to major in German or even to enroll in an occasional German class any more than they are in the late twentieth century. *Fin-de-siècle* America was not a golden age of German studies. The reasons for that reluctance were multiple. Although demographic shifts can partially explain the lack of interest in Germanics approaching the year 2000, some of the earlier reasons still obtain.

Part of that enrollment problem surely had to do with the split noted between the "soul" and the "stomach" Germans among those who had recently immigrated to America (Schmidt 1985: 205). Even among American intellectuals there was no real willingness to learn a modern foreign language, a fact attested to by the difficulties experienced even by the field of History, which felt constrained to justify its methodology and focus in an age clearly inclined to the natural sciences (Pennsylvania, *Bulletin* [1893]: 8). Remarkable in this context, however, is the phenomenal growth that the Wharton School of Management and Business experienced at Penn in the late nineteenth and early twentieth centuries, enrolling as many students as the College did. Because of these circumstances, the Philadelphia effort to establish Germanics as a visible discipline proved unusually successful.

Two early Germanists at Penn—the German-born and -trained Oswald Seidensticker and the American-born and -trained Marion Dexter Learned—achieved great distinction within and outside their institution. They are good examples of the rise of the mandarin mentality which held sway in academia between 1890 and 1933, although they are far from uncritical in their adoption of *Germanistik*. Their achievements were celebrated in distinctive ways. When Oswald Seidensticker, who had served the university as Professor of the German Language and Literature for 26 years (1867–93), died in 1893, the University of Pennsylvania was closed for the day to mark and honor his passing, so respected and beloved was he as teacher and colleague. Seidensticker's successor as chair, Marion Dexter Learned (1857–1916), was eulogized upon his death 20 years later in 1916 by a large group of distinguished citizens: a trustee of the university (Joseph G. Rosengarten), a former mayor of Philadelphia (Rudolph Blankenburg), and a former ambassador to Germany (David Jayne Hill), as well as by colleagues at Penn (Daniel B. Shumway), Cornell (A. B. Faust), and Johns Hopkins (Henry Wood).

Given space limitations I cannot hope to render a complete history of Germanics at Penn. It seems more appropriate to focus on the early developmental phase as a means to understanding what is happening in the profession today, 100 years later. To this end I seek: (1) to place the debate on the significance and role of Germanics in the larger context of the development of a university which accompanied the emergence of the discipline; (2) to trace briefly the development of German at Penn; and then (3) to focus on activities in the Department at the turn of the century. By limiting my purview to Germanics in the United States during the period 1882–1916, I seek to shed light on the opportunities for and challenges to our profession today. That period displays striking parallels to our own turn from the twentieth to the twenty-first century, for we are challenged by a similar anti-intellectualism to legitimize our work and to (re)constitute our professional ethos. The old adage that everything is new and nothing is new still obtains. It is always worthwhile for us to pause in our headlong rush into the future to reflect upon the past, for that past was once someone else's future. We can learn from their expectations, aspirations, and strategies for success, gain consolation from their trials and tribulations, and draw inspiration from their dedication and innovation. The opening and closing frames of my inquiry are determined by the establishment of the Graduate School of Arts and Science at Penn in 1882 and the death of Marion Dexter Learned in 1916.

German and the Idea of a University

The idea of a university formulated in 1881 by Daniel C. Gilman, the founder of Johns Hopkins University, sketches the debate on the nature of the university and its relationship to traditional college education, a debate the legacy of which endures today (witness Allan Bloom 1987). That debate and Gilman's positioning on it provide the framework for the specific work of Germanists at the undergraduate and graduate levels both in the late nineteenth and the late twentieth centuries. The graduate program in German at Penn was established in the early 1880s in conjunction with that debate. In fact, because of its institutional structure, which was less indebted to the British model, Penn was always better positioned to fill the role of a university than the colleges of Yale and Harvard, of Virginia, California, Vanderbilt, and Cornell (the institutions specifically cited by Gilman). On the other hand, newly founded universities such as Johns Hopkins, Stanford, and Chicago were more forward-looking in their organizational structure and concept of mission, as noted by Learned himself (Learned, "Germanistik" 10).

Gilman calls for an indigenous, *American* university, one *not* slavishly beholden to the much-lauded German model or any of the European variations.[2] Good ideas for higher education can be gleaned from many quarters, yet, Gilman emphatically asserts, "an indigenous and not an exotic plant will thrive best in our climate and on our soil" (1881: 356). These words still ring true as we seek to define the Americanization of Germanics. Moreover, the idea of the university is grounded on the belief that the college of humanities must be at its center, must serve as the foundation if any higher structure is going to have any chance of enduring. The early study of mathematics, "the foundation of science," and of language, "the foundation of the humanities," are a sine qua non for university study, that is, for graduate work in any discipline. Gilman concludes: "it is obvious that the growth of American universities is not to be promoted by the abandonment of colleges" (1881: 359). Thus, "universities must include or must rest upon colleges" (1881: 357).

In 1904 Alexander R. Hohlfeld, who had just moved a few years earlier from

Vanderbilt University to the University of Wisconsin to build up the German department in Madison, and who served as president of the MLA in 1914, chose as his lecture topic to honor several professors visiting from Germany: "The Influence of German University Ideals on American Higher Education" (Hohlfeld 1904: 242–51). He notes that the older American college system (e.g., Harvard, Yale, Princeton) was indebted to the English model, whereas the university system concept is indebted to the German model. Interesting here is Hohlfeld's suggestion that the English college model is archly conservative, interested solely in preserving the traditions of the past and inculcating that canonical knowledge into students in rote fashion.

By contrast the progressive German model values the independence of thought and method of the individual scholar, who has total freedom in the choice of topic and sweep of intellectual content. Only the latter, Hohlfeld concludes, is really qualified to train the teachers and scholars of the future (246). Nevertheless, like Gilman a generation earlier, he grants that the American character is essentially different from the German, although both nations are driven to seek the truth through rigorous scientific inquiry: "Der treibende Geist streng methodischer Wahrheitsforschung wird sicher in beiden der gleiche sein; daran ist nicht mehr zu zweifeln. Doch dieser Geist wird sich in beiden Ländern in verschiedenen Formen und Einrichtungen ausdrücken" (247). The latter formulation echoes Gilman's prognosis that American institutions of higher learning must be like "an indigenous and not an exotic plant" in order to thrive. Hohlfeld locates the difference in the Americans' eager quest to find practical applications for all kinds of theoretical knowledge. This connection between practicality and theoretical innovation will always remain stronger in American than in German universities, he concludes, citing specifically the "practical tasks and demands of life in American academia" (247; cf. Bledstein 1977). This clash between theory and practice, between college canons and the relativizing research conducted in graduate programs continues to mark academic life today and strongly suggests that American Germanics must be "an indigenous and not an exotic plant" if it is to have a chance for long-term survival.

Manifest here are the dual roles of the teacher-scholar which are to be separated from one another. Dedicated teaching and the disciplining of the mind find their proper place in undergraduate (college) settings, while open inquiry is primarily at home in graduate (university) programs (see D. Gilman 1969: 360). What we learn from Gilman's and Hohlfeld's commentaries on the peculiar character of American higher education, moreover, is that Henry Schmidt's emphasis on the presumed chauvinism of American Germanists in the period 1882–1917 is perhaps one sided, as is his strong, negatively tinged suggestion that the Americans necessarily see themselves as "high priests of culture, as builders of character, and as interpreters of ultimate moral values" in alleged blind adherence to the German Germanist's model (Schmidt 1985: 205). While that notion (seen disparagingly) certainly dominated the educational views of such eighteenth-century clergymen as Justus Heinrich Christian Helmuth, founder of the Mosheim Society (1789) and

German schools in Philadelphia, its transferral from pietistic missionaries in colonial America to academic mandarins 100 years later obscures the larger picture of an altered academic world confronted by the pressures of capitalism and nascent consumerism. This is where Learned comes into the picture.

In a lecture at Columbia University around 1900 entitled "Germanistik and schöne Litteratur in Amerika," Learned offers his view of the relationship between the history of Germanics and American culture, especially during the nineteenth century. He refers to that influence not just as "leitend" but also as "umbildend" ("Germanistik" 5) and notes specific affinities between German culture and American culture: (1) religious earnestness (but with the German brand marked by humane tolerance); (2) principles of freedom and equality which caused the German emigrants to protest the slave trade in 1688; (3) the German colonists like the Puritans valued public schooling ("Volkserziehung"); and (4) the German colonists promoted book culture in much more emphatic fashion than the Puritans did ("Germanistik" 6).

Having noted these similarities between German and "American" culture, Learned remarks that there have been two major periods of German cultural influence in America. The first begins around 1815 ("die man kurzweg die *deutsche* nennen darf") and is associated with such men as George Ticknor, Edward Everett, and George Bancroft, all of whom studied in Göttingen where Georg Friedrich Benecke, Jeremias David Reuß, Johann Gottfried Eichhorn, and Friedrich Bouterwek offered courses on literary history. Benecke was joined in 1829 by Jakob Grimm and in 1835 by Wilhelm Grimm (Meves 1994: 122, 201). In 1824 Karl Beck and Karl Follen arrived in America and began teaching at Harvard. With Follen's activities in Cambridge, Learned avers, "eine neue Epoche in der Geschichte der Germanistik in Amerika [beginnt]" (8), whereby "Germanics" is understood to include the teaching of language, as was the case in Germany at the time, too. In 1826 he published his *Deutsches Lesebuch für Anfänger,* Henry Edwin Dwight produced his widely read *Travels in the North of Germany in the Years 1825–26,* and Alexander Hill Everett promulgated German culture (esp. Schiller) in the pages of the *North American Review* (9). The impact that Follen had on Margaret Fuller and Ralph Waldo Emerson is well known and is referred to by Learned. He also notes Longfellow's indebtedness to the "Altmeister" Goethe (9). Not surprisingly, Learned concludes this section by stating: "In dieser Periode der deutschen Anregung in Neu-England haben wir die Anfänge der amerikanischen Germanistik zu suchen" (9).

Learned dates a second major phase of German influence with the end of the Civil War (1861–65). It is institutional in nature rather than bound to the efforts of literary figures such as Fuller, Emerson, Longfellow, Everett, or James Russell Lowell. After 1865, namely, a number of "real" ("wirklichen") universities were founded which saw the introduction of German instructional methods (most notably the "Seminar" and philological rigor): Johns Hopkins, Stanford, Chicago. Additionally, older colleges were reorganized into universities: Harvard, Yale, Columbia, Pennsylvania, Cornell. "Gerade diese neuen Universitäten," Learned writes, "sind die Hauptstützen der germanistischen Studien in Amerika" (10). Strides made in these institutions had led to recognition in academic circles abroad, but at home little note had been taken of the accomplishments of these early Germanists. The reason for the lack of public recognition, Learned opines, lies in the superficiality and myopia of "our authors" (11).

The Columbia lecture on "Germanistik and schöne Litteratur in Amerika" provides an explanation for Learned's lifelong efforts as teacher and scholar. From the outset he advocated the study of Germanics in the broadest sense of the term (despite the German *Germanistik* in his title) as a way of promoting an American culture worthy of inclusion with the great cultures of the world, past and present.[3] Of course, his project must be seen against the backdrop of the major deleterious tendencies of the late nineteenth century, tendencies which he himself lists as follows: (1) the materialistic spirit [i.e., consumerism, capitalism, pragmatism] which has led to the decline of interest in humanistic studies and the overvaluing of monetary gain; (2) the rise of the newspaper culture which values local news ("Lokalgeschichten") and sensationalism ("Sensationen") at the expense of noble sentiment, originality, and cultured insight; (3) an insatiable demand for "Novellen" ("Novellenwut") which overshadows all other literary forms; (4) the loss of high standards in literary criticism ("Oberflächlichkeit und Kleinmalerei unserer Schriftsteller" 11).

The above sketches the intellectual climate within which German Studies first succeeded in profiling itself in America *avant les lettres* as a scholarly field of inquiry. We do well to recall that this debate more or less coincides with the institutionalization of the discipline in Germany, where it reaches back to the early nineteenth century. However, not until the 1850s did *Germanistik* begin to flower fully in Germany. New appointments ("o. Professoren") were made in Heidelberg (1852), Erlangen (1852), Kiel (1854), Würzburg (1856), Göttingen (1856), München (1856), Rostock (1858), Leipzig (1858), and Königsberg (1859). The Wilhelmine era saw the establishment of a great number of new departments and a drastic rise in enrollment, quintupling between 1871 and 1914.[4] Between 1910 and 1932 the number of "Ordinarien" doubled again, rising from 87 to 196. With this background information in mind, we have a context for the institutional history which shaped the emergence of Germanics at Penn as "an indigenous" plant on American soil, despite its close ties to *Germanistik*.

The University of Pennsylvania: A Brief History

The University of Pennsylvania likes to trace its origins back to the "Charity School" established in 1740 at Fourth and Arch Streets in Philadelphia, which was subsequently absorbed into the "Academy" established by Benjamin Franklin and other leading lights of the day in the winter of 1749–50. Benjamin Franklin served as the first president of the Academy's Trustees and is thus considered the "father" of the university. However, not until 1755 was the Academy converted into a "College" with the power of conferring collegiate degrees. At the first commencement, held 17 May 1757, seven students received the B.A. More notably for our current query, the state legislature, which had confiscated all the rights and properties of the Trustees in 1789, passed an act in 1791 "amalgamating the old College with the new University" (Pennsylvania, *Bulletin* [1940–41]: 25). That legislative act amounted to the first duly constituted university in the United States. Since then the official corporate title has been the University of Pennsylvania. From the French Revolution to the Civil War, things remained essentially unchanged; the number of students graduated in the Arts and Sciences from year to year hovered around 25, the entrance age remained at 14 years, the required courses continued as before, and the Medical School enrolled two to three times as many students as the "Collegiate Department" and "Academical Department" combined.[5]

German was first offered to students in the early days of the Academy, when a Mr. Craemer was appointed in 1754 to teach French, Italian, and German. Following the Revolutionary War, pastor Johann Christoph Kunze, a graduate of Halle and founder of a Lutheran preparatory seminary in Philadelphia, was appointed Professor of German and Oriental Languages at the College and in 1780 was made Master of a special "German School" added to the earlier lower schools, where German-speaking boys could be prepared for the higher studies and where others could be taught German. All subjects in the curriculum were taught in German in this new school. Beginning in 1780 the German Society of Pennsylvania awarded a few fellowships upon the recommendation of their German-speaking pastors to help young students pursue their studies (Roeber 1995: 161). On 9 April 1792, the board of newly elected trustees of the University of Pennsylvania made appointments to the newly formed "Faculty in the Arts." Six professorships were filled: one each in natural philosophy, moral philosophy, Latin & Greek, mathematics, English and Belles Lettres [!], and one in the German & Oriental Languages. The Rev. Justus Heinrich Christian Helmuth, D.D., was named "Professor of the German and Oriental Languages" (Pennsylvania, *Charters* 1853: 36).

There then appears to be a gap in the coverage of German from the late eighteenth century to the early 1830s. While I have not yet found an adequate explanation for this absence, I should note that the Pennsylvania legislature shifted its support from the Latin school (where Kunze, then Helmuth, taught everything in German) to transforming Franklin Academy in Lancaster, Pennsylvania, into Franklin College (today: Franklin and Marshal College). In a report to the Fränkische Stiftungen in Halle dated 27 October 1789, Johann Christoph Kunze remarked that German would surely die out, for "the people here are completely English, the coming generation understands no German and no new Germans are arriving here" (Roeber 1995: 173). Helmuth's frantic efforts to encourage instruction in German through such projects as the Mosheim Society attest to even this avid believer's real fear that German morals and customs would be lost with the demise of the German language. Of interest in this regard are the several pamphlets extolling the virtues of knowing German penned by Helmuth in the late 1780s and the 1790s under such titles as "Colloquium of Two Friends Concerning the Blessings of a Good Education" and "Humble Suggestions of a Plan How Religious Schools Might be Established" (Roeber 1995: 163). Other German Americans such as Schmidt and Mühlenberg joined Helmuth and Kunze in identifying the "lack of vision among the Pennsylvania German laity as a primary cause" of the failure to attract more students to study German (Roeber 174). Strikingly, all this occurred at a time when fully one-third of Pennsylvania's population was of German heritage (Roeber 162).

The earliest college catalogues available in the University Archives date from the 1830s. The bulletin for 1834–35 lists one Hermann Bokum as Instructor of German.[6] However, from 1836 to 1850 no instructor of German is registered. From the 1830s onward the following notation was frequently printed in the "Course of Instruction" as well as in the running description: "French, Spanish, and German, may be pursued if required by parents" (Session 1834–35: 28). In 1846–47, the notation reads: "The modern languages are taught by approved instructors, at a moderate additional expense" (31). In the academic year 1852–53 that fee is listed as $10. For the 1863–64 session tuition is raised to $35 per term, but the fee for each professor in the Department of Modern Languages remains steady at $10 (Pennsylvania, *Catalogue* 27). Despite some gains, then, German was offered until the end of the Civil War primarily on an ad-hoc basis to those students who explicitly requested it.

In 1850–51 John C. Brunner is announced as "Teacher of German" (*Catalogue* 1850–51: 7). In a "Report of the Trustees of the University of Pennsylvania" published internally in July 1851, major changes in the structure of the University were announced due to the continued growth of the institution. On 11 May 1851, the following plan was adopted, which proved decisive for the development of Germanics: "There shall be Departments of Ancient Languages, of Mathematics, of Natural Philosophy and Chemistry, of Intellectual and Moral Philosophy, of English Literature, of Modern Languages, of Physiology and Natural History, and such others as may hereafter, from time to time be adopted" ("Report" 1851: 2). What that amounts to is the formation of Penn's first Department of Modern Foreign Languages. Courses in five of the above departments were required for the B.A. degree. The minimum age for admission was 16.[7]

Most notably, we find here the first mention of the creation of a chair for the German language with the notation: "This chair has not yet been filled" ("Report" 1851: 7). Also a professorship of Italian Language and Literature is mentioned for the first time.[8] By contrast, a chair for French was established early on. The Italian position was filled in 1852, but the German one remained open until 1857, when the Rev. Charles C. Schaeffer (no academic degrees indicated) was appointed the first "Professor of German Language" at Penn, albeit not as a member of the Faculty of the Arts (*Catalogue* 1857–58: 5, 7). Strikingly, his appointment occurred the same year that the Deutsches Seminar at Rostock was established. Nevertheless, it was not until the 1867–68 academic year that a professor of the German Language and Literature in the modern sense of the title was named: Oswald Seidensticker, Dr. Phil., Göttingen (*Catalogue* 1868: 5). His appointment at Penn coincided with the founding of the "Deutsches Seminar" at the University of Tübingen in 1867. Thus, we might view the establishment of the discipline of Germanics at Penn as echoing the rise of the field in Germany.

Enrollment and Curricular Statistics

In order to keep the development of the German program in perspective, it is useful to document some comparative statistics for the College at Penn during its first 150 years. The number of students enrolled in the college was, as mentioned, small, averaging throughout most of the nineteenth century between 115 and 150 students for all four years. By contrast, the Medical School regularly enrolled 450 students from 1830 to about 1890, when the numbers increased substantially.[9]

Statistics of Attendance, College Department, 1740–1891

Academic Year	Number of Students Enrolled
1740–81	161
1781–91	113
1791–1801	97
1801–11	82
1811–21	135
1821–31	141
1831–41	194[10]
1841–51	1,011
1851–61	1,162
1861–71	1,327
1871–81	2,569
1881–91	3,991

The numbers increased dramatically after the Civil War years, and there was even a gradual rebuilding of the strong student base from the South in the School of Medicine. A retrospective of the University (1740–1893) notes unprecedented growth at Pennsylvania between 1882–83 and 1892–93, when student enrollment more than doubled: from 984 to 2,066. In the same time frame, the faculty grew from 124 instructors to 255. Of these, there were 618 students and 88 faculty in the College Department in 1893, and 117 students and 42 instructors were active in the Department of Philosophy (Graduate School).[11] It is claimed, moreover, that by 1893 "the University attract[ed] its students from a wider area than any other American institution," drawing them from 44 States and Territories and 77 foreign countries (Pennsylvania, *History* 14). By the 1893–94 academic year, Penn had enrolled over

70,000 and graduated 14,900 students, had a physical plant then valued at 3.1 million dollars, an endowment of $1.6 million, could claim 110,000 bound volumes in its library, 24,000 of which were in classical literature (i.e., Greek, Latin) and another 24,000 in modern languages and criticism (*History* 10, 14).

The numbers of students from Germany studying at the University grew dramatically from 1851 to 1891; that is, from one in the decade 1841–51, to four in the years 1851–61, to three from 1861 to 1871, 10 from 1871 to 1881, and eventually to 45 from 1881 to 1891 (*Bulletin* 1.3 [1893]: 5; cf. Geitz 1995).

For most of the nineteenth century tuition remained at $25 per annum. Following the Civil War it increased to $35. Until the appointment of Oswald Seidensticker, students who opted to study a modern foreign language — Greek and Latin were required of all students — could expect to pay an additional fee of $10. But that fee structure changed radically near the end of the century. In the 1884–85 academic year, for instance, tuition amounted to $150 per annum (14); room and board were estimated at between $150 and $210; textbooks ranged from $10 to $50; clothing cost between $30 and $100; and extras ran anywhere from $25 to $100. Thus, the total cost to attend the year at Penn ranged between $245 and $660 in 1884–85 (*Catalogue* 1884–85: 15). The tuition at Penn in 1896–97, 12 years later, ranged from $160 to $200, and the total estimated cost reached from a low of $334.50 to a high of $500 depending upon the course of study, type of accommodations, meal plan, and the amount of pocket money desired. Textbooks cost from $10 to $50 (*Catalogue* 1896–97: 54). Tuition for the Graduate Program (i.e., the Department of Philosophy) in the academic year 1897–98 was $100 plus a $25 graduation fee.

Admission to the college was based on entrance examinations in three general areas: I. English, History, Mathematics; II. Foreign Languages (Greek, Latin, French, German); and III. Mathematics, Physics. High school diplomas were subject to review by a faculty committee. The entrance examinations were offered twice a year at locations throughout the East, Midwest, and in California. Noteworthy is the condition expressed in the 1886–87 *Catalogue* that no candidate will be accepted "whose work [in English] is notably defective in spelling, punctuation, idiom or division into paragraphs" (*Catalogue* 1886–87: 56). Much earlier, beginning with the *Catalogue* of the University of Pennsylvania for 1873–74, a general statement of the educational goals and expectations was published:

> The Department of Arts is designed mainly to give that comprehensive and liberal culture, and to secure that mental training and discipline which was until recent years the sole aim of the best known American colleges. The methods by which these objects are sought have been enlarged here by the adoption of a carefully arranged elective system, by the introduction of new subjects of study (notably the modern languages), and by giving greater prominence to certain old ones. (*Catalogue* 1873–74: 9)

The entrance requirements for German courses stipulated knowledge of "Collar and Eysenbach's *German Lessons* (Longer Course) or an equivalent." The candidate's knowledge of grammar was tested partly by translating a simple passage of English prose into German. A minimum of 200 pages of modern German prose was also required. The passages were to be drawn from three of five named authors: [Roderich] Benedix (1811–1873), Hauff, Heyse, [Wilhelm Heinrich] Riehl (1823–1897) and [Heinrich] Zschokke (1771–1848) (*Catalogue* 1886–87). With the Nobel prize winner Paul Heyse (1830–1914) and perhaps Wilhelm Hauff (1802–1827) as the only truly canonical figures, the selection of authors reveals a German Studies approach rather than a narrowly literary one. The emphasis is nationalistic and patriotric; the preferred genre is the Novelle and other prose. Worthy of note is the fact that the Wharton School and the Department of Biology required German as one of the foreign languages (*Catalogue* 1886–87: 59). All other programs note that French or German could be used to satisfy the entrance requirement. Beginning in 1898 the admission test for German throughout the university was standardized. The stipulation for German reads:

> A. Grammar. The declension of the articles, adjectives, pronouns, and such nouns as are readily classified; the common prepositions; the simple uses of the modal auxiliaries; the elementary rules of syntax and word order. The test will consist in part of direct grammatical questions, and in part of translation into German of simple sentences.
> B. Sight Translation. The ability to translate at sight a passage of easy prose containing no rare words. The passage set will be adapted to the proficiency of candidates who have read not less than two hundred pages of simple German. (*Catalogue* 1896–97: 66)

Moreover, a foreign language (whether Greek, Latin, French, or German) had to be studied as an "elective" for a minimum of three hours during each of the eight semesters spent at the university. German was paired with either Latin, French, or English. Juniors had to take a four-hour "elective" in "German Classics, Prose Composition, [or] History of German Literature," while seniors had to invest five hours in "Classical German Prose and Drama, History of German Literature, [or] German Composition" regardless of the combination with Latin, French, or English (*Catalogue* 1896–97: 69–70).

Examples of the readings to be expected at each level were given in the catalogue descriptions following the Civil War. For example, the catalogue for 1870–71 lists the following:

1st year: German not required.
2nd year: German "grammar, both practical and theoretical (Douai). Hauff's *Mährchen.*"
3rd year: "German (Elective with Latin or Italian). Grammar continued. German Phrases and Dialogues. Storm's *Immensee.* Schiller's *Poems.* Goethe's *Hermann und Dorothea.*"
4th year: "German (Elective with Greek or Spanish). History of the German

Language and Literature, with characteristic specimens for Reading."
(*Catalogue* 1870–71: 33)

The list is slightly varied in the catalogue for 1871–72:

1st year: German not required, but French was.
2nd year: "Plate's *German Studies.* Practical Exercises in Translation.
3rd year: (Elective with Greek or Spanish). Douai's Grammar. Hauff's *Mähr-chen.* Lessing's *Nathan.* (32)
4th year: History of German Language & Literature with characteristic speci-mens of reading."

There was little change in 1872–73:

1st year: as before
2nd year: as before
3rd year: "German (Elective with Greek). Plate's *German Studies.* Whitney's *German Grammar.* Schiller's *Maria Stuart.*"
4th year: "German (Elective with Greek). Schiller's *Poems;* Goethe's *Faust.* Synonyms." (*Catalogue* 1872–73: 35)

A dozen years later we find some of the same canonical authors: Lessing, Goethe, Schiller. The university *Catalogue* for 1884–85 gives examples of readings to be expected at each level:

Junior Class: "German.—Whitney's *German Grammar.* Schiller's *Maria Stuart.* Goethe's *Hermann und Dorothea.* Storm's *Immensee.*
Senior Class: "German.—Goethe's *Torquato Tasso.* Lessing's *Dramaturgie.* Reading at Sight. Schiller's *Poems.* Translations into German. His-tory of German Literature." (*Catalogue* 1884–85: 20)

The pattern which emerges is quite clear: throughout the post–Civil War years until the end of the century, very little changed in the expectations of students study-ing German at the undergraduate level. Compared to contemporary requirements, expectations seemed to be higher. However, there is a clear disjuncture between the entrance requirements and the actual course work once the student arrived at the University. While the former had a German Studies slant, the latter reveal a clear bias toward "canonical" literary studies at the undergraduate level. This bias is mirrored in Learned's lecture at Columbia University at century's end on "Ger-manistik und schöne Litteratur in Amerika."

Foundations of Graduate Study at Penn

Graduate studies in Germanics at Penn got off to a slow start. Although the Gradu-ate School of Arts and Science was founded in 1882, the first real advanced program is created under Marion Dexter Learned. Thus, no graduate program is listed for the 1884–85 academic year. Seidensticker's lectures on German literature, so we are informed by a special notation, are open to "persons of both sexes . . . without examination" (*Catalogue* 1884–85: 6).

According to the *Bulletin of the University of Pennsylvania* 1.1 for 1893, the rule of thumb in the "Department of Philosophy" (i.e., Graduate School) is a dual concentration. German is always combined with something else. A few examples can serve to illustrate this tendency. The Rev. Max Felix Dumstrey of Philadelphia (who attended Gymnasium in Berlin) combined a major in philosophy with European History and German Language and Literature (3). Dana Carleton Munro, also of Philadelphia, majored in European History with concentrations in Political Economy and German Language and Literature (3). The Rev. John Richelsen of Philadelphia, who had attended Latin School in Flensburg, Schleswig-Holstein, combined philosophy with experimental psychology and German. Isaac Joachim Schwatt, a native of Mitau in Kurland, Russia, had spent three-and-one-half years at the Polytechnic School in Riga and a year at Berlin University before coming to Penn to study mathematics, experimental psychology, and German language and literature. Of an additional 34 students listed (but not named) in the category "special student," none majored in German (*Bulletin* 1.1 [1893]: 4). At the time, the total enrollment in Arts and Science at Penn was a little more than 2,000 (*Bulletin* 1.2 [1893]: 4).

The first year in which the graduate program in German took on a clear profile was the 1897–98 academic year. The *University Catalogue* lists the fellowship recipients and the numbers of students taking German full and part time. Regular students numbered 103, while there were 52 special students (presumably part-time) and one postdoctoral fellowship: Charles Reed Miller, who held the Ph.D. in Germanics. He received a Senior Fellowship of the George Leib Harrison Foundation. Five such postdoctoral stipends were open (only) to men in any discipline who had taken the Ph.D. at Penn. It paid $800 per annum (*Bulletin* [1897–98]: 453). Martin Schütze was a first-year graduate student on a Full Fellowship from the George Leib Harrison Foundation. This fellowship rotated among graduate programs at Penn and carried a stipend of $500 per annum plus $100 for books. The fellowship was reserved for those who had already pursued graduate studies at "another reputable institution" and who had a good reading knowledge of French and German; the candidate had to be in the humanities or social sciences. No teaching was required. There were five such Full Fellowships. Schütze was an 1886 graduate of the Gymnasium at Güstrow, Mecklenburg-Schwerin, and had studied at the Universities of Freiburg and Rostock (*Bulletin* [1897–98]: 453, 188). Thomas Seltzer, a first-year student, had graduated with a baccalaureate from Pennsylvania in 1897. He held one of 14 scholarships open to men who had studied at Penn (again offered by the George Leib Harrison Foundation). The nonrenewable scholarship included tuition remission plus $100 for one year.

In addition to the postdoctoral candidates and the two graduate fellowship holders, five regular students and one special student pursued the M.A. in 1897–98. Of these one was a teaching assistant, the other an instructor in German:

Eleanor Anne Fyfe Andrews (Sheffield, Mass.). German & French, 2nd year.

George Griffiths Bartlett (A.B. Harvard, 1885). German, 3rd year.

Samuel B. Heckman (Union College, Ohio), H.B. (Earlham College, 1893), A.B. (Harvard, 1894); graduate student at Harvard, 1894–95; Instructor in English Literature and Modern Languages at Juniata College, Huntingdon, Penn., 1895–97. Germanics. 1st year (*Bulletin* [1897–98]: 389).

Cornelius William Prettyman (Salisbury MD). A.B. (Dickinson, 1891), graduate student at Johns Hopkins, 1895–96; Fellow and student assistant in German, Johns Hopkins, 1896–97. Assistant in German. Germanics, 1st year (*Bulletin* [1897–98]: 390).

Edward Charles Wesselhoeft (Philadelphia). Graduate of the Real-Schule (Johanneum) of Hamburg, Germany, 1877. Instructor in German, Pennsylvania, 1891 to date. Germanics, 1st year (*Bulletin* [1897–98]: 391).

Hannah Edna Sleeper (Philadelphia). Special student. Germanics 1st year (*Bulletin* [1897–98]: 94).

As can be seen, graduate students in German were eventually drawn from a wide geographical area and include a mix of recent arrivals from Germany as well as native talent. After the turn of the century graduate students in Germanics at Penn came from the Midwest and California as well as from Philadelphia and the East Coast. To be sure, there were times when large numbers of candidates hailed from the immediate area. In passing let it be noted that both Prettyman and Wesselhoeft were hired into the program that produced them and spent long and active careers at Penn. In the twentieth century, Adolf Klarmann (Ph.D. 1931), Adoph C. Gorr (Ph.D. 1934), and Heinz Moenkemeyer (Ph.D. 1951) are further examples of Penn hiring its own students. Of these three, Klarmann enjoyed national prominence from the mid-1950s to the mid-1970s. Moenkemeyer was recognized as a dix-huitiémist and Goethe scholar in the 1960s and 1970s. Gorr became a dominant personality in the local German American community.

The course of instruction for a graduate major during Seidensticker's tenure is instructive as a point of orientation for subsequent developments. It was divided into four general categories which reveal an emphasis on traditional philology ("Altphilologie") together with a German Studies thrust. An example follows, drawn from the *Bulletin* for 1893, augmented by later catalogues of the University of Pennsylvania.

Requirements for the Major:

A.   "Germanic Language and Literature"
    1.   "Gothic." This course dealt with phonology and grammar. The re-

quired textbook was Braune's Gothic Grammar; Selections from Ulfi-
las' *Translation of the Gospels and Epistles* were included. (Prof. O.
Seidensticker)

2. "Middle High German." The textbook was Paul's *Grammar* with selections from the *Nibelungenlied* and the lyric poets (Seidensticker) (6)

3. "History of German Literature." Textbook: Wilhelm Scherer's *History
of German Literature* and Müller's *Selections.*

B. "Philosophy"

1. "Philosophy of Kant" (Lecturer William Romaine Newbold)

Requirements for a Minor Subject:

A. European History: "The ability to make use of French and German works is
almost indispensable in advanced historical work" (*Catalogue* 1897–98: 10).

B. Experimental Psychology: "Such a general knowledge of the subject as may
be gained from Wilhelm Wundt's *Physiologische Psychologie* plus two other
works, in English."

C. German Philology and Literature:
1. "A thorough knowledge of German Grammar."
2. "Reading of German texts at sight."
3. "A good knowledge of the History of German literature."

D. Romance Philology and Literature: recommended text—Schwann, *Gramma-
tik des Altfranzösischen*

E. German texts also cited for Semitic Languages & Literatures, Mathematics
(*Catalogue* 1897–98: 10).

Seidensticker's curricular legacy at Penn proved enduring, holding sway throughout the twentieth century. Both Seidensticker and his more famous successor,
Marion Dexter Learned, were productive scholars in terms of the number of books
written. Learned, however, proved to be more active in the town-gown arena.

When Learned moved from Baltimore to Philadelphia in 1895, he introduced
significant changes to the graduate program at Penn. By 1897–98 a clear profile had
emerged, as is clear from the above survey. Learned is even credited with having
established the Penn department as the United States' premier German department
around the turn of the century.[12] Striking—and perhaps instructive for us—are
Learned's personal and professional qualities cited as contributing to the success
of the program. For example, he: (1) was well read and had an excellent memory;
(2) introduced the seminar method "by means of which the students should receive practical training in the preparation of scientific papers" (Shumway, *German-
American Annals* [*GAA*] 19.5/6 [1917]: 152); (3) established the Germanic Association; a monthly meeting of faculty and students at which research papers were read
and discussed; (4) founded the international journal, *Americana Germanica* [*AG*]
(1897–1902; from 1903 to 1919 it continued under the new title *German-American*

Annals); (5) established a monograph series for the publication of seminal studies on German American relations, exercising strict editorial control and ensuring high standards (it is thus not surprising that the *German-American Annals* ceased publication a few short years after his death in 1916); (6) carefully advised students, endeavoring to animate them to achieve their very best (Shumway, *GAA* 19.5/6 [1917]: 152); (7) afer seeing them through their studies, he continued to counsel and encourage his former students (Shumway, *GAA* 19.5/6 [1917]: 153). Moreover, upon his recommendation the University of Pennsylvania (8) established the German Traveling Scholarship which enabled students from various disciplines to study abroad (reported by Rosengarten, *GAA* 19.5/6: 149). Finally, Learned (9) proved singularly successful in placing his students in teaching positions (Shumway, *GAA* 19.5/6: [1917]: 153).

When Learned arrived in Philadelphia there were but one or two students in the graduate program, as Shumway recalls. By the time of his death there were about a dozen, several of them on scholarships. Learned went about his work with such dedication and devotion that David Jayne Hill, former U.S. Ambassador to Germany, could remark: "Not for generations, if ever, will any scholar of American birth, without a trace of German blood, devote himself to the study and teaching of German culture with the disinterestedness, the enthusiasm, and the wholeheartedness that characterized the devotion of Dr. Learned." Little could David Hill know that Daniel B. Shumway, Dr. Learned's former assistant and anointed successor, would in fact compete with Learned's devotion to German culture, although he, like Learned—as Hill put it—was just "an American of the Americans in heredity, in spirit, and in understanding" (*GAA* 19.5/6 [1917]: 160). The phrase is a salient assessment of the man who intuitively realized that Germanics must be cultivated as "an indigenous and not an exotic plant" to ensure survivability.

In recognition of his role as an "interpreter of Germanism to America" Learned was "commended by the Kultusministerium of the German Empire as a worthy recipient of high honor at the hand of the Emperor" (Hill in *GAA* 19.5/6 [1917]: 161). He served as treasurer of the Modern Language Society of America (1893–95), organizer and secretary of the Association of Teachers of German in Pennsylvania (1898), president of the Nationaler Deutsch-Amerikanischer Lehrerbund (1899–1900) and one of the prime organizers (as well as first elected Secretary) of the German-American Historical Society, incorporated in 1901. In 1899 a special fund was established to advance the publication of materials pertinent to German American Studies. For the benefit of this "German Publication Fund of America," the University of Pennsylvania sponsored two German plays, produced by director Heinrich Conried of the Irving Place Theatre in New York.[13]

The "course of instruction" in the graduate program at Penn in the academic year 1897–98 is instructive for its evidence of continuity from the late nineteenth to the late twentieth century. Two professors are listed: Professor Learned and Dr. Shumway. The majors or areas of concentration offered were "Germanic Literature" and "Germanic Philology." Students of Germanics had to take a two-year course in Old Norse, while students of medieval history were expected to take "Sixteenth-Century Drama" (Learned/Shumway) and "Seventeenth-Century Drama" (Shumway). Students of English or Romanic literature had to take six courses selected from among "The Classical Period" (Learned), "The Romantic School" (Learned), "German Literature in America" (Learned), and "America in the German Novel" (Learned). Finally, students of English or Romanic philology were required to take six courses chosen from among "Old Norse" (Learned), "Old High German" (Shumway), "Gothic" (Shumway), "Middle High German" (Shumway), "German Dialects" (Learned), "Germanic Philology" (Shumway), "Comparative German Syntax" (Shumway), and "History of the German Language" (Learned).

Moreover, those students majoring in Germanics who did not have a "satisfactory command of colloquial German" were required to enroll in German Conversation, to participate in the Germanic Association, and to participate in an advanced seminar or "Germanic Seminary." The Germanic Association, still functioning today as a forum for guest speakers at Penn, originated under Learned "as an essential part of the work in German." Faculty and students were expected to present "original papers" in the course of an academic year. That was an innovation at Penn which helped develop the professional skills of the department. Additionally, graduate students in German were required to enroll in at least one advanced seminar during the three-year cycle of offerings. As is still the case today, these specialized seminars were designed for advanced students who had a knowledge of Gothic, Middle High German, High German, New High German, and a general grasp of German literary history. One of the two seminars offered in 1897–98 focused on Goethe's shorter poems, the other on Old High German. The following year the topics were Goethe's Faust and German Minnesong (see *Catalogue* 1897–98: 196–200 and *Catalogue* 1898–99: 195–200).

The designation "The Classical Period" actually referred to the *Sturm und Drang* and *Aufklärung* rather than the period 1787–1805. Moreover, the course on the Romantic Period traced Romantic elements through the earlier eighteenth century as well as stressed its political context by noting its relationship to the "German ideals of 1813–1848" (*Catalogue* 1897–98: 199). Consequently, the research in Romanticism dating from around 1980 to the present which sought to reveal the roots of the Romantic school in the literary feud between Leipzig and Zürich or to underscore the political relevance of the allegedly "esoteric" Romantics was not innovative at all. That double thrust was anticipated by Learned at the outset of Germanics in America.[14]

Moreover, Penn's emphasis on reception studies — German literature in America in the nineteenth century, America in the nineteenth-century German novel — were equally highly innovative, revealing the rootedness of the nascent discipline in native American soil. Learned's course on the German ballad in 1897–98 evinces not only the nationalistic interest in "das Volk," but also an early interest in genre studies. And the several courses offered by Shumway and Learned on Sebastian

Brant, Hans Sachs, Thomas Murner, Ulrich von Hutten, Johannes Fischart, and Martin Luther highlight the Department's interest in the literature and politics of the sixteenth century. They were, of course, in tune with the general thrust of *Germanistik* in Germany, which was widely driven by the search for a German identity.

Finally of interest is a notation in the 1897–98 *Catalogue* that a course in "reading scientific German" was available and was taught by C. W. Prettyman, an assistant in German. The course was open to graduate students in other programs wishing to improve their knowledge of German. That course survives today as German for Reading Knowledge (Jannach), in which texts in the sciences and social sciences dominate the selections. Moreover, the fact that Prettyman, a first-year student, taught the course underscores the forward-looking nature of Learned's conception, for the teaching assistants were stand-alone teachers who were entrusted with more than first- or second-year German.

At the same time that Learned was reorganizing the course of graduate studies in Germanics, he also launched a scholarly journal to carry the thrust of the new program to an audience far beyond the walls of College Hall or the city limits of Philadelphia. That journal, *Americana Germanica,* was first published in 1897 with a distinguished international editorial board which included 33 Germanists from Austro-Hungary, Belgium, England, Germany, and Scotland. While they presumably served more as window dressing given Learned's penchant for tight control of the journal (he made all final decisions), we find among them such luminaries as Konrad Burdach, Max Koch, Jakob Minor, Franz Muncker, Bernhard Seuffert, Oskar Walzel, and Georg Wittkowski. The stated purpose of the journal was "to furnish a distinct medium for the publication of results obtained from the comparative study of the literary, linguistic, and other cultural relations between Germany and America" and to stimulate research on these connections on both sides of the Atlantic. The scope of the journal was intentionally broad, being aimed at reception and translation studies of German literature in America but also of American literature in Germany. Also welcome were dialect studies in the Germanic languages, investigations of "the cultural relations (exclusive of the literary and linguistic) of Germany and America, particularly folklore, manners, customs, industries and arts," and "articles on the general field of Germanics written in America" (*AG* 1.1 [1897]: v). These topics coincided closely with Learned's own research interests.

The inaugural volume offered contributions by leading American Germanists of the day. In addition to Learned and Shumway, who published pieces on "Ferdinand Freiligrath in America," "Pastorius' Bee-Hive" (both by Learned), and "The Verb in Thomas Murner" (Shumway), the volume contained articles by A. B. Faust (Wesleyan) on "Charles Sealsfield's Place in Literature," Kuno Francke on "Cotton Mather and August Hermann Francke," and a critical review of Francke's seminal *Social Forces in German Literature* by Herman Schoenfeld. Articles by G. A. Mulfinger on "Lenau in Amerika," T. S. Baker (Johns Hopkins) on "America as the Political Utopia of Young Germany," and Karl Knortz' "Die Plattdeutsche Litteratur Nordamerika's" rounded out the volume (*AG* 1.1 [1897]).

In the third number of volume one, Learned published an editorial lauding the newly founded *Journal of Germanic Philology (JEGP)* edited by Gustaf E. Karsten (Indiana) in cooperation with Albert S. Cook (Yale), Horatio S. White (Cornell), George A. Hench (Michigan), and George Holz (Leipzig). Of special note for us is Learned's judgment that the initial volumes of the *JEGP* gave "ample evidence that the scientific method has taken root in American soil and will grow as a native plant" (*AG* 1.3 [1897]: 106). In a footnote to that remark, Learned explains that his own journal and Karsten's undertaking complement one another and "augur a new period in the history of Germanic studies in America" (105). While the *Journal of Germanic Philology* takes English and German "in general" as the main goal and solicits contributions from Germany, *Americana Germanica* focuses on the literary, linguistic, and other cultural relations of Germany and America with special emphasis on contributions by American Germanists. Both academic journals aim at a "scientific" (i.e., objective) treatment of issues, publish in English or German, and have an international circulation" (106).

Noteworthy, moreover, is the fact that the journal was published with the generous financial support of German Americans in Indianapolis. Learned expressed the wish that "other Germans in America may well follow this most worthy example of aiding in the extension of German studies in the land of their adoption" (*AG* 1.3 [1897]: 106). Strikingly, the terms "Germanics" and "German studies" are the commonly used phrases to designate the efforts of the early Germanists to establish a native variant of the discipline.

In 1903 the *Americana Germanica* (1897–1902) changed its title to *German-American Annals* (1903–19) and added 15 contributing editors from North America, no doubt to help legitimize further the North American focus: H. C. G. Brandt (Hamilton); W. Carruth (Kansas); Hermann Collitz (Bryn Mawr); Starr W. Cutting (Chicago); Daniel K. Dodge (Illinois); A. B. Faust (Wesleyan); Kuno Francke (Harvard); Adolf Gerber (Earlham College); Julius Goebel (Stanford); George A. Hench (Michigan); W. T. Hewett (Cornell); A. R. Hohlfeld (Wisconsin); H. Schmidt-Wartenberg (Chicago); Hermann Schoenfeld (Columbian University, Washington, D.C.); Calvin Thomas (Columbia); H. S. White (Cornell); Henry Wood (Johns Hopkins).

As noted, Learned also founded a monograph series, utilizing the abandoned journal title for it. The periodicals and the monograph series are valuable sources of information on the nature and contours of Germanics in the early part of this century prior to the founding of the American Association of German Teachers in 1926 with its journals. Equally significant is Learned's American ethnographical survey announced in 1897 in vol. 1, no. 4 of the *Americana Germanica*. It consisted of 25 detailed questions regarding every aspect of ethnographic identification used by Pennsylvanians to characterize themselves or others. The kinds of information requested ranged from dialect, festivals, common racial slurs, and preferred barn structures. Learned requested that the information be reported to him at the University of Pennsylvania. Six years later (*AG* 5) Learned reported on the formal establishment of a group to carry out the "American Ethnographical Survey" in a scientifically rigorous fashion in the Commonwealth of Pennsylvania, notably Lancaster County, then in other German counties of Eastern Pennsylvania, and finally extending to the Western part of the state and into the eastern portion of Ohio (AG 1.4 [1897]: 111–12; AG 5.1 [1903]: 1–7). It had the support of the provost of the University, the governor of the state, the state superintendent of education, and the heads of various societies. Funding was secured and the project begun under Learned's directorship. While these efforts are worthy of closer scrutiny, let it suffice for present purposes to note the areas of inquiry: (1) German industries; (2) German occupations and trades before 1830; (3) German agriculture and rural architecture; (4) Old German domestic life; (5) the literary life of the Germans in colonial Pennsylvania; (6) the religious, social, and political life of the Germans; (7) the speech conditions; (8) old colonial roads; (9) and archeological collections (AG 5 [1903]: 3–6). The results of the survey as well as documents uncovered in the process were later published in the pages of the journal (e.g., *Benjamin Herr's Journal* 1830).

Learned was also instrumental in the founding of the Association of the Teachers of German in Pennsylvania, chairing the organizational meeting on 9 April 1898, in Houston Hall of the University of Pennsylvania. He was subsequently elected its first secretary. Learned delivered the introductory address, "The Teaching of German in Pennsylvania," which covered developments since the colonial period from the pioneer German schoolmaster, Francis Daniel Pastorius onward (AG 2.2 [1898]: 71–92). The meeting was attended by approximately 50 teachers of German from Penn and from various colleges and high schools in the state. It is with some embarrassment that Leaned notes here the fact that the new state of California established an Association of Teachers of German before Pennsylvania did (AG 2.2 [1898]: 75).[15]

Learned lauds in particular three papers presented at the recent meeting of the California Teachers' Association (held in San José, 28–31 Dec. 1897) which succinctly capture the range of concerns among Germanists in the early days of the profession: "The Educational Value of the Study of German" (by Julius Goebel at Stanford), "German in Secondary Education" (by David Starr Jordan of Stanford), and "Methods with German" (by Albin Putzker, California). Learned finds in these papers an innovative thesis and justification for the study of German at all levels of education. He delights in the shift away from the traditional argument of "speech representation" which states that German should be offered in the public schools because so many German speakers have immigrated to America and the needs of their families must be accommodated. Learned specifically objects to that stance when he writes: "If its [the speech-representation argument] cogency were recognized the public schools in our largest American cities would have to provide instruction in half a dozen foreign tongues" (AG 1.3 [1897]: 104).

The real argument for German is the centrality of German culture, not the presence (or absence) of speakers of German. Learning German is a value in its own right, for it opens an avenue to higher learning and is "not merely a tool for business and professional purposes" (*AG* 1.3 [1897]: 104). Putzker's assertion that "Everybody, now-a-days, who claims higher education, must study German either to become acquainted with the great writings stored in that language, or to study its development" (104) is echoed by the other two speakers. Learned took a similar stance himself in July 1898, in an address entitled: "German as a Cultural Element in American Education." He begins his oration with the emphatic assertion: "The study of a foreign language is, in the last analysis, a question of culture and not of race" (3). Learned's conclusion is no less unambiguous, for he claims German culture as a "birthright" even for Anglo-Americans and sees the promise of extraordinary benefit for America from the wedding of this cultural "birthright" with one's own natural birthright as an American (23–24). Note, by the way, that these early Germanists and German teachers "resorted" to the use of English to carry on the business of the profession. The meeting of the California Teachers' Association concluded with the recommendation that German be placed on an equal footing with Latin in the high schools, its chief competitor.

It seemed to Learned that the study of German culture offered a way out of the cultural vacuum he sensed in his own country, which seemed obsessed with money and mass culture. The continuity of his concerns is demonstrated by an admonition from the year 1913 entitled "German in Public Schools." The whole tenor of the piece reveals a crisis mentality on his part. The incidence of German being taught in the schools and the quality of instruction when it is taught were clear causes for concern. While academics today might be inclined to dismiss his argument as reactionary, as deeply indebted to the college mentality of preserving the traditions of the past, his appeal might also be read as an historically revealing document whose significance still obtains. Learned calls upon his colleagues in German to raise the consciousness level of "our school boards and college administrations to the perilous conditions of the educational method, now running riot in American education" (*GAA* 2 [1913]: 100). Consequently, his intent is to sound a warning to educators across the country "against removing the foundations upon which our culture must always rest" (100). The first and fundamental principle of education is and must remain language: mastery of one's own native tongue, but also mastery of a foreign tongue, the language of international culture and research. That language at the turn of the century, to Learned's mind, was German. "German is the key," he wrote, "which unlocks the best sources of literary and scientific knowledge of our age" (102).

In a manner reminiscent of our own day, Learned argues in a two-pronged fashion for the inclusion of German in the school curricula. His first argument is aimed at the value of knowing a foreign language in an age which places increasingly greater demands upon educated individuals; life has become "far more complex" than ever before (101). Intellectual discipline and cultural diversification are necessary tools for success in the modern world. And the study of German provides both: "The first duty of the state is to give the pupil—every boy and girl—the fundamental training necessary to all vocations" (*GAA* 2 [1913]: 103). Foreign languages are part and parcel of this fundamental training. The cultural value of the foreign language should not be calculated according to the number of speakers of the tongue living in the United States—otherwise any number of ethnic groups could claim that their tongue be taught in the schools and a Tower of Babel would arise with German, French, Italian, Swedish, Russian, Polish, Yiddish, Hungarian, and Greek all vying for a place on the curriculum. Rather, the choice must be determined on the basis of which living language is the most essential at present and therefore has the greatest potential value to a vocation-minded public.

It seems clear to Learned that Americans must overcome their "fatal insularism and provincialism" which threatened the English Empire of his day (*GAA* 2 [1913]: 105). Americans are so "notoriously careless in their study of modern languages" that they cut a poor figure next to their European counterparts. The image of the ugly American who is linguistically and culturally limited is already starkly profiled here. Thus Learned recommends that German be taught in the elementary schools and that an "efficiency test" be applied to all language teachers; that is, they must demonstrate mastery of the "pronunciation or idiom" of the languages they teach. The course goal should be to enable pupils "to read and write German." In this way, he would use the primary and secondary schools to teach the fundamentals and allow colleges and universities to concentrate on oral/aural skills as an efficient way of preparing American youth for an increasingly international world. "The movement should be nation-wide and persistent, in order to secure our national prestige in the eyes of the civilized world" (106).

Learned shared the podium in Philadelphia on 8 April 1898 with H. M. Ferren, a teacher at Allegheny High School who spoke on "German in Our Public High Schools" (reprinted in *AG* 2 [1898]: 78–89). While deserving of detailed discussion, especially in light of Learned's praise of the California initiative, I will mention only certain facts bearing on the efforts to establish Germanics as a discipline in the United States around 1900 (and again around 2000). The old dichotomies of high school teacher versus college professor are noted here, as are the need to take the teaching of German seriously by offering it for four consecutive years, and the need for greater coordination between the high schools and the colleges. Especially noteworthy, however, are the statistics Ferren cites. Twice as many girls study German in the schools as do boys. Yet fewer than half of the girls are preparing to go to college: 13 percent of the boys are in college preparatory courses, while only 5.2 percent of the girls are (*AG* 2 [1898]: 82). From replies to 600 letters of inquiry Ferren mailed concerning the study of German in the United States, he learned that "fully one hundred reputable high schools distributed over seventy-four cities had four years of German. In Pennsylvania there are but five of these, Philadelphia being conspicuous for its absence" (83). Of the 250 high schools in Pennsylvania, 69 offered German, and 89 offered four years of another foreign language (84). In other words, 18.4 percent of high school pupils in Pennsylvania took German. This figure compares favorably to the 12 percent average for the nation as a whole, but unfavorably to Maryland where 31 percent took German. By contrast, fully 58 percent of the high school students in Louisiana studied French (88). Ferren concluded his survey with seven proposals for action by the newly constituted Association of German Teachers in Pennsylvania: (1) improve pedagogical methods; (2) introduce German in as many high schools as possible; (3) insist on four years of German; (4) limit the number of subject areas assigned to each teacher; (5) encourage teachers to take postgraduate courses; (6) give German its proper place as an elective in the curriculum [i.e., either Latin or German]; (7) encourage coupling Latin and German [college entrance requirements dictated two languages]; and (8) found a National Association of Teachers of German (*AG* 2 [1898]: 88–89).[16] The latter did not occur until 1926, perhaps a mortal delay.

While he did not pen this report by Ferren, Learned's own work demonstrates that he concurred with Ferren's sense of urgency and frustration over the apathy, even hostility toward German, German accents, and German quirks long before the crisis induced by World War I. Learned utilized every professional (and personal) opportunity, even appearing as Pastorius in period costume, to proselytize for things German. He used the German Department at Penn between 1895 and 1915 as a bridge over the usual gap between town and gown, he orchestrated research topics endemic to a transplanted, nascent discipline, he trained Germanists who were capable of pursuing a wide variety of careers and who were not narrowly focused on higher education but were willing to make high school teaching a career (as advocated by Ferren). He did succeed in placing his academically minded students in institutions such as North Carolina, Illinois, Columbia, Smith, Muhlenberg, Grinnell, as well as in junior colleges and high schools. The German studies training these individuals received in Learned's "workshop" equipped them to be spokespersons for German American and German affairs (as advocated by Ferren). They were trained in the language, in the culture, in the mental habits of Germans. But they were trained from the outside in, not from the inside out. The "Tonangeber" at Penn in this phase were American-born with a deep and abiding, yet not uncritical passion for things German. German at Penn was not yet marked by a view of American culture as the "Negativerfüllung der eigenen [deutschen] Kultur" but rather as "Produkt und Ausdruck einer anderen Geographie, Geschichte und Werthaltung" (Trommler 1989: 254). The goal ultimately was to share in "the formation of a nobler and better type of American for the centuries to come" as Ferren put it (*AG* 2 [1898]: 89).

This line of argument is captured in Learned's exhortation to his audience of Germanists at Columbia University a year later to work toward the goal of establishing a national American literature by adapting the best methods and models of *Germanistik:*

> Es wäre nun die Aufgabe der Germanisten in Amerika nicht nur die Studierenden zu wissenschaftlichen [sic] Forschungen auf einem Spezialgebiet der Germanistik anzuspornen, sondern ihnen und durch sie dem Volke auch eine tiefere Kennt-

nis der deutschen Litteratur und der Beziehungen zwischen der deutschen und amerikanischen Kultur beizubringen und so mit zu arbeiten an der Entwicklung einer wahrhaft nationalen Litteratur in Amerika. ("Germanistik" 13)

With that Learned provides a succinct explanation for his lifelong efforts as teacher and scholar. From the outset he advocated the study of Germanics in the broadest sense of the term as a way of promoting an American culture worthy of association with the great cultures of the world, past and present. His broad vision pierced through the nationalistic parochialism of the early twentieth century, pointing forward to the stance that marks the profession at century's end.

Notes

1 In trying to assess recent interdisciplinary, gendered, and theoretical developments in the profession since the 1980s in the general context of American higher education, Trommler asks whether Germanics functions more as a *Leuchtturm* or as an *Elfenbeinturm* (Trommler 1989: 27). I think we are justified in asking the question about developments around 1900.

2 On the question of American and German academics trained in Germany and their influence on Pennsylvania see Jarausch 1995: 195–211.

3 U.S. Bureau of Education, 1902, which Learned had read in advance sheets when part of Viereck's study was published in the Report of the Commissioner of Education for 1900–1901; that is, just about the time of Learned's Columbia lecture. Viereck details the impact of German culture and educational ideals on American schools and colleges, dividing the history of that influence into three phases: 1700–1825, 1825–76, and 1876–1900. A detailed review of the work (presumably by Learned) appeared in the *German American Annals*, n.s., 1.1 [old series 5.1] (January 1903): 64–67. See also the list of new publications (1.1: 69). A number of similarities exist in Learned's and Viereck's evaluation of developments in the nineteenth century.

4 Striking in this connection is Viereck's study. Meves traces the origins of Germanics as a discipline back to the early nineteenth century when stylistics, rhetoric, and the practical applications of German dominated. His discussion of the developments is differentiated, and he provides useful tables of various kinds of appointments (1994: 115–203, see esp. 148–50 and the tables 201–3). Hermand provides the following dates for the founding of "departments": 1873 in Heidelberg, Leipzig, Strasbourg, and Würzburg; 1874 in Freiburg; 1875 in Halle and Kiel; 1876 in Greifswald und Marburg; 1877 in Breslau, 1878 in Bonn and Jena; 1883 in Erlangen; 1886 in Gießen and Königsberg; 1887 in Berlin; 1889 in Göttingen; 1892 in München; 1895 in Münster (Hermand 1994: 57–58).

5 See the statistics provided in the introduction to the *Catalogue* of the University of Pennsylvania for the years 1843–63.

6   "Regulations of the Collegiate Department," *Catalogue of the Officers and Students of the University of Pennsylvania.* Philadelphia, Feb. 1835, under the heading: "Faculty of Arts (1834–35)."

7   The reorganization of the University was not driven solely by idealism, that is, by a desire to achieve fundamental principles of higher education. Much of the impetus seems to have come from a general malaise in enrollments and in dismal enrollment prospects for the immediate future. Penn was one of 130 or so colleges in the United States at the time, all vying for a stagnant pool of college-bound youth. Recently installed higher standards for high school graduation, the movement at many elite colleges toward the elective system, and the fear that Penn could not compete successfully with the lower costs of colleges located in small towns all informed the Board of Trustees decision to reorganize Penn along the lines of a postcollegiate institution. The model for that reorganization was the German university (and this was 30 years before Gilman's argument). Of particular interest in this regard are two letters penned in response to the Trustees' recommendation. One by Bishop Alonzo Potter is dated 8 July 1852, a second by Professor of Literature Henry Vethake is dated 27 November 1852; these were published as "Miscellaneous Pamphlets of the University of Pennsylvania" (nos. 1: 1–6 and 3: 1–15) for the use of the Board of Trustees. Potter's letter represents a plea to innovate in radical fashion by establishing graduate programs for men in their twenties and to move away from competing with colleges for the 14- to 18-year-old age bracket. Among other suggestions we find one for establishing advanced studies in modern foreign literature. Vethake's letter is a rebuttal to Potter's proposal for establishing Penn as the first and only truly graduate institution in America (a move was underfoot to establish such a university at Albany, N.Y.). Vethake disagrees point by point with Potter, frequently referring to the differences between the German system of higher education and the American one. Central is Vethake's argument that the status of the German professor as a civil servant makes the German system possible because professors are not dependent upon student enrollment as is the case in the United States. Secondly, German universities are organized into four faculties (Theology, Medicine, Law, Philosophy), while U.S. institutions are arranged according to schools and departments. Finally, Vethake believes that American students are too intent upon establishing themselves in their careers during their twenties, not interested in pursuing advanced studies in the humanities, especially as the latter do not prepare one for acquiring wealth and fame. The Trustees went ahead with their plan to reorganize Penn as a graduate institution.

8   That position in Italian was filled in 1852–53, but was again vacant by the 1856–57 session (*Cat.* of University of Pennsylvania, Session 1856–57: 4–5).

9   *Bulletin of the University of Pennsylvania* 1.3 (June 1893) contains an accounting of enrollment figures from 1745–1891. A total attendance of 66,747 is noted in chart form and is accompanied by the notation that "the final total of 66,747 falls considerably below the real figures" since the catalogues prior to 1835 are incomplete "and the attendance in the College during that period is the number of the alumni for the period, and is therefore about one-half of the actual attendance." Of the total 66,747, over 15,000 youths attended the Charity Schools between 1740 and 1876 (5).

10 From 1740 to 1840 the Alumni List alone was used; no *Catalogues* of the college for this early period are at hand. *Bulletin* 1.3 (June 1893): 10.

11 *University of Pennsylvania: The History of a University and its Present Work 1740–1893*
    (n.p, n.d.), 3, 7. The College Department offered 329 courses grouped under 33 head-
    ings and falling roughly into seven divisions: the arts, the sciences, the Wharton School,
    School of American History, Biology, Architecture, Music.

12 A number of "Nachrufe" were included in the *German American Annals* 19.5/6 (1917):
    147–63, detailing Learned's life and work. Here Shumway 1917: 153.

13 See "The German American Historical Society," *Americana Germanica* 7.2 (1902):
    207–13, here 207. Notice of Penn's sponsorship is contained in the University of Penn-
    sylvania *Bulletin* (1900). I have not yet been able to determine which two plays were
    performed.

14 Learned, in turn, was influenced by the early histories of German literature penned in
    the nineteenth century which followed the triadic scheme evident in Hosmer's *Short
    History* and Robertson's later *Outlines*. The most direct influence, however, on the con-
    ceptions of literary periodization was Francke's *Social Forces,* which was reviewed
    favorably in Learned's *Americana Germanica* in 1897. The book was reissued in 1897
    and 1899. All these works reflected the German histories of German literature penned
    after midcentury.

15 Of note in this connection is Learned's report published just the preceding year in
    Americana Germanica (1897) on the teaching of German in the California public
    schools. He sounds a familiar note when he inveighs: "It is the Gold State again which
    attracts attention to the older States of the East to an important problem in American
    culture" (*AG* 1.3 [1897]: 104). The "important problem" is the incidence of German in
    the public schools in California where German was offered in only 35 of the 86 schools
    surveyed and to only 12 percent of the students in the 35 schools where is was an option
    (104).

16 Jedan unknowingly reformulates ideas, procedures, and goals formulated by Learned
    and Ferren around 1900.

Historical Forces, German Departments, and the Curriculum in Small Liberal Arts Colleges in the Midwest

HELMUT ZIEFLE

Much has been written about the current crisis of *Germanistik* or German Studies in the United States. It was a wakeup call when a 1995 enrollment survey of U.S. college students in foreign languages by the MLA showed that enrollment in German had dropped 27.8 percent since 1990 to a new low of 96,263 students (Cage, "Enrollment" A13). If one compares this figure with the 1990 enrollment survey by the MLA it becomes clear that German had already experienced a decline since the 1970s. Enrollment dropped from 202,000 students in 1970 to 133,000 in 1990 (Cage, "Spanish" A15). How did German, which had experienced a growth from 146,000 students to 202,000 in the decade from 1960 to 1970, find itself in such a precarious state in the 1990s? According to Helene Zimmer-Loew, executive director of the American Association of Teachers of German, "there is this constant state of trying to get students and trying to keep students (Cage, "Spanish" A17). According to Cage ("Spanish" A17), relevancy becomes an overriding factor in attracting and retaining students, "if you approach a student about taking French or German, their reaction is, what am I going to do with it?"

While enrollment loss is perhaps the most crucial issue our discipline faces today, it is also important to examine the past and the present in order to find remedies for those losses. Although my focus is the situation of Germanics in small liberal arts colleges in the Midwest, it is, nevertheless, important to look at the national trends as well.

Let us first examine historical developments. According to Victor Lange, history provides us a way of dealing with a rapidly changing outlook: "it is in troubled times like ours, at moments of doubts in the efficacy of our social and intellectual assumptions, under the pressure of changes that challenge and unsettle our self-confidence, that we turn to the consolation of history (Lange, "History" 3). Examining the history of German studies allows us also to make comparisons and identify trends:

> What can the history of the field of study teach us, that has moved, at times irrationally, from near the center of American cultural convictions to a place on the periphery of our educational enterprise; it is an area of interest that was defined at one time by the conviction that the German tradition and its living energy

173

offered exemplary material for our own social potential, but that today appears to many teachers of German in schools and colleges no longer sustained by vigorous interest or strong faith. (Lange, "History" 3)

It is quite clear that "the German tradition and its living energy" are not held in the same esteem in the United States today as they were in the nineteenth century when the German university system was regarded as a model for postsecondary education in the United States. Two world wars and the global leadership role in technology, science, and economics by the United States have diminished the important role Germany once played in the international community. Lange feels that the dependency of German departments in the United States on German scholarship in Germany has been directed "not at the American student, but an audience of German *Germanistik*" (Lange, "History" 10). One factor which has contributed to this situation is that for native-born German professors in the United States it was difficult to relate their culture to Americans:

> Here, then, is another profoundly influential factor in the history of American studies of German life, perhaps another reason why German departments have found themselves in relative isolation: the German native provenance of their members appears to have been valued more highly than their capacity to relate German cultural materials not as superior, slightly arcane abstractions but as comparable social achievements to be understood and judged by Americans. (Lange, "History" 13)

While a national literature such as German literature worked well in a more homogeneous nineteenth-century environment, it is no longer adequate today:

> We can use national literatures only as examples and illustrations of common, transnational literary and cultural efforts. In our enthusiasm for the singular German achievement, we have tended to relate the texts we have offered in the German terrain rather than to issues and problems, whether social and aesthetic, that properly engage the interest of our American students for which, indeed, the German documents should and will supply significant material. (Lange, "History" 13)

Valters Nollendorfs speaks "of the marginalization of the humanities and the fine arts in a modern world dominated by economic and technological thinking" (V. Nollendorfs, "Out of Germanistik" 2). Because of this the role of literature has also declined significantly:

> For the most part, however, we live at the edge of the rapidly evolving present which does not want to be burdened with either the memories or the legacies of the past. In this scheme, literary studies seem to be the most marginalized of all. Not only has the role of literature as we have known it become problematic in the postmodern world of ours; so has literary scholarship, particularly literary history. Even more problematic is that literary scholarship whose object is a foreign literature. (V. Nollendorfs, "Out of Germanistik" 2)

Because of the diminishing role of literature since the 1970s in German Departments curricula have changed. "German Studies, Business German, Film and Media, Women's Literature, German-American Studies, and, above all, recent and current literature have been added to the upper-class curricula" (V. Nollendorfs, "Out of Germanistik" 3). While this student oriented approach has been beneficial, it has not resulted in a large increase in the number of undergraduate German majors (V. Nollendorfs, "Out of Germanistik" 3). According to Joseph McVeigh (58), low enrollments in undergraduate German Departments are largely due to "the perception of the discipline by many undergraduate students who would not be otherwise predisposed to enroll in a German language or culture course, that is, the 'undecideds.' " As a possible remedy Heidi Byrnes emphasizes greater visibility to students: "first and foremost are the students, and that, even for college faculty, includes students at the secondary level and even before who are enrolled in German classes, as well as those great numbers whom we never see in our classrooms" (Byrnes, "How Visible" 50). Acquaintance and articulation with pre-college programs becomes crucial for understanding and addressing the needs of potential students. The emphasis on visibility for students must coincide with visibility to colleagues in other departments and the administration through greater involvement and exposure: "how visible we are is a factor of how visible we make ourselves to be" (Byrnes, "How Visible" 52). Visibility is a crucial factor in our survival and must be addressed in innovative and creative ways.

While these and other trends and challenges have been articulated and analyzed at the national level, the situation at the local level is certainly known to a lesser degree, especially as it relates to German programs at small liberal arts colleges. A study of developments and trends from 1970 to the present would be helpful in articulating the situation of such small colleges to a wide audience in the hope of opening the door to a continuous dialogue with bigger universities and public schools. The survival of a good number of German programs at small liberal arts colleges may depend on their ability to attract students from public schools and to offer them a viable program which will prepare them for meaningful employment opportunities and graduate study. Public Relations and rethinking the curriculum must be vital ingredients in this endeavor.

But what is the situation of German programs at specific small liberal arts colleges in the Midwest? In order to answer this question a questionnaire was sent to a number of institutions in the Midwest, asking for the following publications and/or information: (1) Catalogue copies of the German department or section. (2) Listing of German faculty and courses from 1970 to the present; faculty biographical and professional information, including specialization and subjects taught. How did staffing change over the years? (3) Changes in the curriculum from 1970 to the present. Was there a shift from literature to language acquisition, culture, business? Is there a greater interaction with other disciplines such as "German across the Curriculum" courses? (4) Changes in the role played by German from 1970 to the present. Was it marginalized? (5) Trends in enrollment from the 1970s to the present. Recruitment and outlook for the future? Majors? Minors? (6) Roles of technology in the curriculum from 1970 to the present. (7) Does the institution have its own "Study Abroad Program?" If so, beginning in what year? What is the function in regard to the program of your department? (8) Degrees offered. Any changes since 1970? (9) Major concerns and needs today in regard to staff, curriculum, and enrollment. (10) Should German departments at small liberal arts colleges in the Midwest collaborate with one another in all areas so that they are better prepared than at present to cope with future challenges? The following pages discuss responses from the five institutions surveyed. Replies to the survey are combined below into a general alphabetically arranged overview.

Beloit College

A four-year, independent, liberal arts college on the Wisconsin–Illinois border, Beloit College has enrollments of some 1,250 students per year. During the academic year 1970–71 its German program offered a field of concentration as a departmental unit with eight full courses beyond the elementary level. These included composition and conversation, introduction to literature, and individual courses on German genre as well as *Faust* and contemporary literature. The department also offered five supporting courses related to the major and one term of supervised study spent in a country where German is spoken. Starting in the academic year 1972–73 courses in culture, history of the German language and literary periods were added and the number of genre courses reduced. In 1976–77 German offerings were divided into the following three groups or levels: language acquisition; culture and introductory studies in literature and the contemporary literary scene; and varied topics, ranging from *Faust* to German biography. A course in linguistics was also added to the requirement for a concentration in German. In 1987 the three-level approach was discontinued, replaced by a course on masterpieces of literature with emphasis from 800 to the present. Majors in other fields were encouraged to take German as a second major with a commitment that required courses in the other majors were acceptable as supporting courses towards a major in German. This approach, which is strongly oriented toward literature, has been kept to the present.

In 1970 Beloit College had four full-time faculty members in German. By 1980 that figure had declined to three, and by 1996 two remained. According to Professor Henry Bova, the decline in staffing came after the language requirement was dropped in 1972. German enrollments have been steady over the last decade, and he does not foresee a decline. Beloit has two or three German majors per graduating class, and Professor Bova would like to have an additional staff person in the language. The German program offers a term of study at the University of Hamburg, preceded by a brief period at Schiller College.

Carleton College

Located in Northfield, Minnesota, 40 miles south of Minneapolis–St. Paul, Carleton is a four-year, private, liberal arts institution with an enrollment of 1,754 students. Already in the 1970s this college, unlike Beloit, emphasized courses on literary periods rather than genre. It also had a strong emphasis on conversation and composition courses. In the fall of 1973 a German Foreign Study Program was introduced at Trier. It is a 10-week program that has been offered virtually every year at various locations in Germany and Austria. In 1978 culture and literature in translation courses were introduced. The culture course, which was scheduled for alternate years, was taught until 1992, and the literature course every year to the present. As a matter of fact, in 1989 two literature courses in translation were offered, and in 1991 three. This trend has continued to the present with the exception of academic year 1994–95, when none was offered.

Richard Cantwell, professor emeritus of German at Carleton since 1993, points to a move away from the lockstep approach of the "century courses," which reflects the interests of the staff members (3 May 1996). More courses (often in seminar format) have been offered in such fields as more modern literature, women's literature, "culture," broadly defined—as distinct from a purely literary orientation—for example, a "culture course" using lyric poetry as a springboard, but branching out to include art, history, music history, etc., and the fairy tale, to name only a few. When one compares catalogue copies from the 1990s with those of the 1970s and 1980s, it becomes apparent that this trend has accelerated. Anne Ulmer, chair of the Department of German and Russian at Carleton, sums it up in a letter to me as follows (3 May 1996):

> Since his [Richard Cantwell's] retirement there has been an even greater shift towards "studies" courses, as opposed to strictly literature-based courses—literature in a context, or "culture" courses. We have a number of interdisciplinary courses (Vienna 1900, *Vergangenheitsbewältigung,* The Forest in German Literature, cross-listed Environmental and Technology Studies, a course in German mysticism [team-taught with a member of the religion department], music courses (*Das deutsche Lied,* from Song to Cabaret), film studies, or women's studies courses.

In spite of these significant changes in curriculum and the fact that Carleton has a language requirement of four terms (a term being about 10 weeks), German is not as popular as before. Ulmer writes, "we do have some small enrollments in our upper-level courses—they range in number from about 4 to 10 or 12, especially when taught in German. Film studies and women's studies tend to draw more students than straight 'lit' courses do." The number of graduating majors is normally two to three, but was down to one in 1994 and 1995. In 1979 or 1980 Carleton had six or seven majors, its largest number in history. A minor is not offered, but the deaprtment awards a "Certificate of Advanced Achievement in

Language/Literature Studies," which 15 students earned in 1996. Not unlike other departments in the survey, Carleton would like to have more German majors. Ulmer would also like the reinstatement of a tenure track position, lost upon Professor Cantwell's retirement. She believes strongly that hiring an expert in teaching film courses and "bringing the humanities into our own department" would be a positive step in strengthening the German program at Carleton. The department had 4.5 faculty positions from 1970 to 1996.

Calvin College

A private, comprehensive liberal arts college in the Christian reformed tradition, Calvin College is located in a suburban area of Grand Rapids, Michigan. It enrolls about 4,000 students. Besides the regular language acquisition courses (Elementary German and Intermediate German, which include a course on advanced oral and written composition), Calvin traditionally once had a strong literary component emphasizing mainly literary periods from Classicism to modern German literature. However, this strong emphasis on literature could not be sustained, and in 1972 the second semester of classicism was dropped. In 1973 twentieth-century drama and in 1985 nineteenth-century drama were also eliminated. Other needs had to be met, and in 1971 a course in German civilization was added (primarily for education students). In 1973 a second semester of advanced oral and written composition was also made available, and in 1988 advanced grammar and stylistics. Concerning these changes Wally Bratt of Calvin remarks in a letter to me (4 June 1996): "These additions reflected our awareness that our students needed more work in the language itself." In 1978 Calvin added a course in East German Literature, which used to be very popular but is no longer taught (even though it remains in the catalogue). Only four literature courses are taught today: Introduction to Literature, Classicism, The Nineteenth Century, and The Twentieth Century. The two-semester course in German Civilization has also dropped in popularity and went from an enrollment of 30 to one of 8 or 10.

Bratt notes (4 June 1996) that an important ingredient in the German program at Calvin has been a study experience in Germany entitled the "Interim Abroad," an educational experience that has been in the curriculum since 1970:

> Perhaps the major factor in our retaining students has been our Interim in Germany. We have G 215 (Intermediate Oral and Written Composition) as a prerequisite for the Interim, so that helps *that* enrollment. By the time they come back from the Interim most of them need only two more courses for a minor. So many of them take those two courses. As a result, by May of any given year about 40 percent of our total enrollment in German has been in Germany. We're grateful for that high number.

While these changes in the curriculum and the Interim in Germany program have been helpful, the overall trend in enrollment has, nevertheless, been downward.

According to Bratt, Calvin had 307 students in German in 1987, 214 in 1990, 132 in 1995, and the projection for autumn 1998 was 100. He attributes this decrease not to any deficiency in their program but "to the fact that so little German is offered in high schools any more." He is encouraged that, even though the total number of students has decreased, they still get an enrollment of 12 to 15 students in their Literature courses. In 1996 Calvin graduated a total of 20 majors and minors. Of those 20, seven were majors and 13 were minors. Precise statistics are not available, but regularly a combined total of 18 to 20 majors and minors graduate per year.

The number of people teaching German at Calvin has also declined since 1971. In 1970 there were 7.5 faculty full-time equivalents; in 1982 there were 4; in 1990 there were 4; and the projection for 1997 was 2.5. The overall situation at Calvin is of concern because if enrollments in German continue to decline, it will threaten the existence of the major. As we all know, enrollments and staffing go together, and experience has shown that to sustain a viable major at least two faculty members are required. Bratt notes that the Calvin College administration has been very supportive of German, and it has never been marginalized in its role in the humanities. The program has a strong reputation at Calvin.

Elmhurst College

Elmhurst is a four-year, private liberal-arts institution located ten miles west of Chicago. It has an enrollment of 1,711 students full time; 1,064 attend part time. Like Calvin, the German program at Elmhurst had a heavy emphasis on literary analysis in the 1970s. Changes implemented in 1979 were described as follows by Wally Lagerwey, head of the Department of Foreign Languages and Literatures there:

> In 1979 we added German 452, Special Topics—a course geared to student interest gets offered more and more. This semester, for example, is on contemporary Germany. It is about cultural topics at least as often as literature. The other major change was the addition of German 305, Business German, about 1980. We also abandoned the courses on literatures of specific centuries in the 80's as we moved to more culture courses.

The German program at Elmhurst was challenged when the foreign language requirement there was removed in 1976. Enrollments declined drastically, but the number of German majors stayed fairly consistent, with an average of three graduates per year. Total marginalization was prevented by offering literature courses in translation and introductory linquistics. A note of optimism is that the International Business program at Elmhurst requires a minor in a foreign language. Since quite a number of these students minor in German and then go on to major in German, it is now the single largest source of students for the German program. In addition, it will have internship opportunities in Bonn beginning next year (23 April 96).

Elmhurst's Department of German and Russian joined the languages there as the Department of Foreign Languages and Literatures in 1979. The German program there had four faculty members in 1970, three in 1980, and two in 1996.

Wheaton College

A private, interdenominational Christian liberal arts institution located in Wheaton, twenty five miles west of Chicago, Wheaton has an undergraduate enrollment of about 2,200 students. In 1970 the curriculum of the German program in the Department of Foreign Languages was generally similar to those at the small liberal arts colleges already described—a strong literary component with heavy emphasis on literary periods and also language acquisition. At that time about two sections per academic quarter were offered in Elementary German and three in Conversation and Composition. In 1974 German 54, "Varied Literary Topics," was introduced. The course was designed to make the German program flexible by offering courses of general interest which covered subjects such as a writer or a literary form or theme. The Wheaton College academic summer program began in 1977. Called "Wheaton in Germany," it entailed four weeks of language training at the Eurocenter School in Cologne and three weeks at the Schiller College in Strasbourg. For financial reasons the French and German program at Wheaton shared the same site in France. A year later the entire program took place in Germany and offered courses in Intermediate and Advanced German and German Civilization and Culture, and, since 1982, Varied Topics. The program is still popular and has ranged from about 16 to 24 participants per year over the years. In the summer of 1997 "Wheaton in Germany" was held at the Goethe Institute in Prien, Bavaria. Since its inception this program has been the single most important source for recruiting German majors and minors at Wheaton and for keeping up enrollments in upper division courses.

In 1983 Wheaton added an accelerated elementary course in German, one in which students who had had at least two years of high school German could fulfill the foreign language requirement in two semesters instead of three. While this step was certainly good for language learning, it resulted eventually in decreased elementary German enrollments, to one section per quarter rather than the two sections which had been standard. In 1993 the survey of literature (to 1750) was replaced with "Topics in German Language and Literature," a course which allowed faculty to focus on genre, intellectual history, film, culture, or language, thus enhancing the flexibility and attraction of the German program. This course provided the German program with an opportunity to teach together with the Department of Bible and Theology a "German Across the Curriculum" course on German theologians. The last curricular change was the introduction of a Senior Seminar in 1996, a capstone course open to graduating seniors and advanced juniors.

In 1973–74 229 students were enrolled in German and in 1995–96, 158; this represents a decline of 31 percent. However, the number of majors has increased between 1973–74 and 1995–96 by 41 percent from 7 to 12. Very encouraging is also the fact that the number of minors increased in the last 15 years from an average of 2 to 10 in 1995–96. Wheaton offers a B.A. in German and has had an average of 8.6 majors per year in German since 1973.

From 1970 to 1976 the German section at Wheaton had three full-time faculty members; from 1976 to 1990 two, and from 1990 to the present 1.66. This reduction is largely due to the fact that two sections of elementary German could no longer be sustained. Because of this development German majors depended even more than before on the Wheaton in Germany program to complete the requirements for a major — 32 semester hours above intermediate German.

For the German program at Wheaton it is important that the curriculum be flexible enough to meet the needs of today's students and that enrollments increase across the board. Wheaton would like to have at least 15 to 20 majors within the next two years.

Bova, Lagerwey, and I feel that interinstitutional cooperation between small liberal arts colleges in the Midwest would be beneficial in coping with the challenges of the future. Bova would like still to investigate specifics, but Lagerwey would support and help set up a session for representatives from small liberal arts colleges in the Midwest if it could be arranged through AATG or ICTFL at one of their meetings. It seems to me that such a meeting is essential for articulating our concerns and developing a common strategy. Ulmer, on the other hand, feels that in a climate of diminishing interest in German language and culture, a small consortium within an area where colleagues know one another and their programs, would be better. This idea has merit and should be explored as a follow-up to a larger meeting because of geographical considerations and greater familiarity with German programs at colleges located within the same state or in a particular area of the Midwest. It must be an ongoing process in order to be effective. Bratt, on the other hand (4 June 1996), has some reservations about cooperation: "I don't know what we and Hope, for example, could do together that we can't do separately. We simply have to trust that the administration will continue to support our efforts as long as it is feasible . . . ." While it is true that circumstances vary at each institution and some may not be as critical as in others, it is also true that a unified approach is needed at this critical stage. We need to articulate and share our ideas, express our concerns, examine our programs for relevancy, and develop a common strategy. We need a vision which gives us a common bond to meet the challenges of the future.

In summary, this study has demonstarted that small-college German programs continue to struggle with declining enrollments, updating the curriculum, and retaining faculty. In order to reverse this trend we must offer a curriculum which is attractive and relevant to today's student:

> If the undergraduate German curriculum has a shortcoming that is reflected in the enrollment trends of the last twenty years, it is that the purveyors of this curricu-

lum have been less than stellar in recognizing the forces which have increasingly
determined their share of the enrollment pie. Quite simply, we have neither mar-
keted our curriculum well, nor fine-tuned it sufficiently to appeal to its target constituency: American students. The undergraduate has changed over the last 10–20
years both in his/her preparedness for college in general and his/her perception
of things German in particular. The underlying principle of efforts to reverse the
effects of this trend cannot be structural in nature, i.e. shifting from literature-
based curriculum to inter- or multidisciplinary German Studies. Rather, a core
principle of curricular reform must be: "Know your students and what interests
them." (McVeigh 60–61)

As professors we must make every effort to attract undecided undergraduates who
value foreign language learning but have no preference for one language over the
other. McVeigh sees this as one of the most important tasks facing our profession
today:

> They, like most students who do not have a well-conceived course of study in
> mind upon entering college, need to be seduced into taking a German language
> or literature course. And this is where we will probably find our greatest failing:
> we have not learned to seduce undergraduates to German (Studies), in part be-
> cause what we have to offer is often a curriculum heavy on the "Angst" and light
> on the "Fahrvergnügen"; that is, the image of Germany that we offer our campus
> communities is all too often a somber and uninviting one. (61)

Success or failure in the undergraduate German curriculum can very well depend
on our ability to be visible and accessible on campus and to entice students to study
German. In today's academic climate at undergraduate institutions German professors must reach out to their students outside the classroom and be willing to be
mentors, engage in extracurricular activities such as Stammtisch, German Club,
and other campus and off campus events, and assist them in their professional and
personal development.

Like the curriculum of all areas and departments, German undergraduate offerings must be constantly examined for their value to the student, for what McVeigh
calls the "particular aspects of the college or university enhance the possibility of
success in attracting students (e.g. strong German-oriented offerings in other disciplines such as History, Music, Art History and Political Science). Are there job- or
career-related possibilities that can be better integrated into our curriculum (e.g.
internships)?" (McVeigh 62). This means that undergraduate German professors
not only must relate to their students in new ways, but must also be willing to break
with tradition, go beyond their field and immerse themselves in other disciplines
without formal training. Since many undergraduate students enrolled in German
classes have taken German in high school, it is also important that undergraduate German professors interact with high school teachers and assist them in their
programs.

Thus, it is clear that those programs which historically have been and are most innovative and flexible will have the best chance for survival. On the national and regional levels alike, the strictly literary approach seems no longer sufficient and must be adapted to the needs of today's student. Valters Nollendorfs speaks of a new canon which looks like a flower, "a daisy, with a middle which will hold a more limited amount of basic core materials than is now the case, but still enough to provide selection and choice. The core will include not only literary texts but also important other documents required by the curriculum. Besides maintaining a historical base, it will allow the inclusion of contemporary materials. Its very center will be basically contemporay." Most of the growth will take place in the various petals "which will accommodate various sub-canons, periodical or disciplinary, which maintain contact with the central core. In some respects that is how the canon is arranged now, except that the present core is larger and the petals smaller. The future canon will have larger petals, and they will continue to grow" (V. Nollendorfs, "Out of Germanistik" 9). This model of the future provides a framework and point of departure with its clarity and flexibility for the revision of German programs at undergraduate as well as graduate institutions. May it bring the desired result and blossom as a beautiful flower for all postsecondary German programs.

Finally, we must look at the status of small liberal arts colleges in a given region such as the Midwest and address their relevancy. How do they fit in locally and at the national level, and what is their major contribution? It in fact may be the case that small liberal arts colleges in the Midwest can be a microcosm of the situation in other areas of the United States. It follows that small liberal arts colleges must start an initiative which defines and strengthens their role as an intermediate between secondary schools and larger universities. While most of them do not have large numbers of major and minors, they can serve as an important link in the transition from high school to graduate school. It will certainly be to the advantage of American Germanics to keep and develop this triad.

The National Defense Language Institutes: A Benchmark in the Training of Teachers of German

GERHARD H. WEISS AND WALTER F. W. LOHNES

Background and First-Level Institutes

The National Defense Education Act (NDEA) of 1958, and its various modifications, liberalizations and expansions in subsequent years, was something of a Marshall Plan for education in the United States. It represents one of those rare occasions when the Federal government, with bipartisan support, initiated an educational program that reached from Kindergarten to the postgraduate level. During the first ten years of this legislation alone, the United States government invested over three billion dollars in support of a broad range of educational efforts, ranging from fellowships to language centers and summer institutes. Its main thrust, however, was the improvement of teaching and of teacher preparation, to meet a perceived need that "the strength of the United States depended in large part upon a healthy educational system" (Cohen 2). It was, after all, the height of the Cold War, and the launching of Sputnik in 1957 had raised serious doubts about America's continuing competitiveness in the world arena. Though many of the proponents and supporters of the original NDEA legislation never really thought of the act as a "defense measure," this label nevertheless was politically expedient for its passage through Congress (Cohen 2).

The NDEA's legislative history, brief though it was, does not belong here. Our focus will be directed to the effect which it had on foreign language teaching in the United States—especially on the teaching of German in elementary and secondary schools. Of course, to appreciate fully the breadth of the NDEA's impact on foreign language teaching, one cannot ignore its effect on the postsecondary level. For example, NDEA graduate student fellowships offered generous support for future college teachers. Between 1959 and 1968, 10,000 such fellowships were awarded, covering 90 languages (Rothschild 8). While the number of fellowships in German amounted only to a fraction of the total grants, one can safely say that many of the current generation of college and university German teachers are direct beneficiaries of NDEA. Some might never have entered the profession had it not been for this assistance. The legislative appropriations also provided for Language Centers (primarily for less frequently taught languages), and for library support. This infusion of NDEA funding had an immense impact on the graduate programs in foreign languages at American universities, both qualitatively and quantitatively.

However, of particular significance was the impact on the teaching of languages at the elementary (FLES) and secondary school levels, where language teaching had been a greatly neglected field, desperately needing revitalization. The eight-week summer institutes, which were part of title VI, and later title XI, of the NDEA appropriations, were supposed to remedy this problem.

The goal of the NDEA summer institutes was straightforward: the improvement of language teaching from FLES to Senior High School through the creation of better trained and better qualified teachers. Many teachers lacked adequate familiarity with foreign language teaching methodology; many were unable to speak the target language adequately. In approach, most were strictly oriented to "grammar and translation." Few had had any direct exposure to the country whose language they taught, either through travel or through study abroad. Many textbooks reflected a fairy-tale Germany with scant relationship to postwar realities. In addition, German was not exactly the most popular language after the war, and its teachers often felt marginalized.

These issues were directly addressed by the NDEA. The fact that the federal government was investing considerable sums of money in the improvement of language teaching—funding that one normally expected to go only to the sciences—suddenly gave language teachers a feeling of importance. This feeling was enhanced by the statement that language learning had become a matter of national interest, indeed of national survival. Psychologically, then, the existence of the NDEA gave language teachers a much needed boost in their self-esteem as professionals.

The eight-week NDEA summer institutes offered American teachers of German a total immersion training experience that not only improved their language skills, but also exposed them to new teaching methodologies, new technologies, and the inclusion of everyday culture as part of the language learning process. Indeed, much of what is now considered the "standard language acquisition curriculum," including emphasis on "German Studies," was first introduced to a broader segment of American teachers through these summer seminars.

The curriculum of the institutes was broadly prescribed by the NDEA legislation. Teachers were to be provided with "a full understanding of the areas, regions, or countries in which a language is used" (USOE, *Bulletin* 74). To obtain such understanding, they were to be exposed to "such fields as history, political science, linguistics, economics, sociology, geography, and anthropology .... Literature, art, music, education, religion, philosophy, law and others should also not be ignored. In other words, contributions of both the humanities and social sciences should be considered" (USOE, *Bulletin* 74). The NDEA vigorously promoted the concept that an effective language teacher needed a wide-ranging interdisciplinary background, one that reached beyond merely the acquisition of vocabulary and grammar. The teacher was to be prepared as an interpreter of the target culture in the broadest sense of the word, following Edward Hall's dictum that "culture is communication" (Hall 28). Today, much of this sounds obvious. However, in the late 1950s (and beyond) considerable antagonism and suspicion still existed between the literature-oriented traditionalists on the one hand, and the linguists and cultural anthropologists, on the other. That the two sides could inform and enrich each other was at that time a novel concept. Bringing the hostile camps together was one of the NDEA program's major accomplishments.

The NDEA Summer Institutes for German began in 1959, when 142 teachers attended eight-week programs at Colgate University, the University of Colorado, the University of Maine, and Michigan State University. During the following years, the number of institutes increased to 10 and sometimes even 12, including one or two offering academic-year courses. After 1967, the number was drastically reduced (there were only three in the U.S. in 1968, with two additional ones in Germany), until the institutes were totally phased out by 1970. Each institute targeted a specific teaching level (FLES, Junior High, Senior High) and was graded according to language proficiency, ranging from "4," which required minimal skills, to "1," which called for near-native fluency.

The eight-week intensive summer programs conducted at the University of Minnesota (summers 1961 through 1965) may be considered typical for the German institutes funded each year. It was designated a first-level institute for Elementary and Junior High School teachers of German (with a parallel institute for Spanish), authorized to accept 30 participants in each language. Twenty-eight came from public and two from private schools. Each public school participant received a stipend of $75 per week, plus $15 for each dependent. All tuition costs were carried by the grant. The total government support for the institute each year was approximately $100,000. Since this was an intensive, total-immersion program, participants had to sign a pledge that they would stay in the language dormitories for the duration, even if they lived in the Twin Cities metropolitan area. They had to eat their meals with their language group and, to add to the atmosphere, the staff even prepared special "Speisekarten" and "Zeitungen" for each day. Classes ran from 8:00 o'clock in the morning to almost 5:00 in the afternoon, with evening programs of films, lectures, or language games and songs, as the table opposite shows.

The language competency of many participants was quite low. Some FLES teachers had none at all, but still had been mandated to teach German in their fourth- or fifth-grade classes. They obviously were desperate and most eager to learn. The curriculum was structured in conformity with the NDEA concept. Language instruction and conversational practice played a paramount role. Institute teachers were strict believers in the audio-lingual method and worked extensively through pattern drills. In the culture courses, the anthropological approach was stressed and included heavy emphasis on the small "c" and on the sociological aspects of German culture. In linguistics, participants became acquainted with the basic concepts of the discipline and with the importance of applied linguistics for

University of Minnesota NDEA Summer Institute for Teachers of
German, Daily Schedule

Time	Activity
8:00–8:50	Syntactical Patterns
9:00–9:50	Conversational Practice
10:00–10:30	Coffee Break
10:30–11:20	Civilization Lectures
11:30–12:20	Conversational Practice
12:30–1:30	Lunch
1:30–2:10	Demonstration Classes
2:20–3:00	Practice Teaching
3:15–3:55	M/W/F: Applied Linguistics
	T/Th: Methodology of Teaching
4:05–4:50	Language Laboratory
6:00–6:50	Dinner
7:00–8:30	Mondays: Linguistics, Films, Discussion
	Tuesdays: Special Lectures
	Wednesdays: Film Program
	Thursdays: Games and Songs

language teaching and language learning. The Institute used Belasco's *Applied Linguistics* as well as Kufner's *Grammatical Structures,* Moulton's *Sounds,* and Lado's *Linguistics.* Participants were also introduced to language teaching methodologies for FLES and Junior High. They observed demonstration classes and subsequently became actively engaged in a five-week practice teaching experience for which students were gathered from among children in the Minneapolis–St. Paul area. At the end of each day, all participants spent time in the language laboratory, where they became acquainted with the types and operation of electronic equipment available at the time and the application of the laboratory to language teaching (Stack's *Language Laboratory and Modern Language Teaching* served as background text). After such a rigorous day, participants relaxed by listening to visiting lecturers, such as the linguists Sol Saporta or Robert Lado, historians like Otto Pflanze, methodologists like Emma Birkmaier, or cultural anthropologists such as Robert Spencer. German films (e.g., *Hauptmann von Köpenick; Herrliche Zeiten*), as well as the Henry Lee Smith series of films on language added to their entertainment.

The institutes were quite demanding. However, the stick carried a carrot: those who successfully completed the first level were eligible to apply for the second, the Stanford Institute in Bad Boll, Germany. But even for those who did not continue, the NDEA Institutes were of immeasurable value. A cadre of well-prepared teachers had been created, many of whom passed their institute experience on to their colleagues who had stayed at home. Language instruction in the schools began to improve, and quite a number of the NDEA graduates moved on to positions of leadership. Last but not least, a number of new textbooks and new teaching materials have grown out of the experiences gained in the institutes. The impact of this government sponsored program on the teaching of German in the United States was—and continues to be—enormous.[1]

Second-Level NDEA Institutes in Germany, 1960–1969

In 1958, Stanford University opened its first Overseas Campus in a small town outside Stuttgart, which was attended by 90 students for two quarters each. The success of this enterprise led directly to Stanford's proposal to the U.S. Office of Education to offer a second-level NDEA Institute for teachers who had completed a first-level institute in the United States.

While Stanford appreciated the excellent results of the first-level institutes, such as the one held at the University of Minnesota, it was felt that a summer of intensive training in the country of the target language could expand immeasurably the gains made at an institution at home.

Stanford conducted this institute for 10 years, from 1960 to 1969, for 10 weeks each summer, with about 80 teachers each year. (The number, incidentally, was determined by the seating capacity of Pan Am's DC7C.) Thus, Stanford trained more than 800 teachers over these 10 years, or almost 10 percent of all those who taught German in American primary and secondary schools in the 1960s. For each institute, there were several hundred applications, and the staff was thus able to select those considered most able to profit from exposure to Germany. The majority of participants had never been in Germany. After all, this was before jet travel had become common, and most of the teachers did not have a very good command of the German language. They ranged in age from about 25 to 55 or 60; practically all came from the "old school" of language training, if from any at all. Each participant received a stipend of $750 for the 10 weeks, which at the exchange rate of the time was about DM 3,000 and was sufficient to cover not only meals and housing, but also round-trip transportation between New York and Stuttgart. Other costs, such as salaries and administration, were reimbursed directly by the U.S. Office of Education.

Stanford was fortunate in being able to secure an ideal location for the Institute, the Evangelische Akademie in Bad Boll, about 40 kilometers east of Stuttgart. It was possible to house the participants under one roof, and although the Akademie is not located in an urban center, there was plenty of social interaction with the staff of the Akademie, most of whom were academics who became very much interested in our Institute.

We were equally fortunate in attracting a superb American teaching staff whom we recruited from across the United States, among them Emma Birkmaier (Minnesota), the linguist Madison Beeler (California, Berkeley), William Moulton and Victor Lange (Princeton), Frank Ryder (Indiana), George Scherer (Colorado), Viola

Manderfeld (Chicago), and Gerhard Weiss (Minnesota), who was in Bad Boll in the summer of 1968.

F. W. Strothmann and Walter F. W. Lohnes codirected the Institute. Several members of the Stanford staff were at the Institute, most remarkably, during the first two summers, B. Q. Morgan, a distinguished scholar who was then in his eighties and a master of German folksong. (Morgan had received his doctorate in Leipzig in 1907 and had moved to Stanford from the University of Wisconsin in 1934.) The curriculum was similar to that of the first-level institutes, mandated by the Office of Education.

The teaching methods course built upon the work done at the first-level institutes. The early sixties were the high point of the audio-lingual method, but in the course of the decade that method began to be questioned, and in our last few summers there was a decided shift away from A-LM to more cognitively oriented ways of teaching.

The linguistics course was partly theoretical, to acquaint participants with the then new field of linguistics as opposed to the old historically oriented philology. The practical aspects of the course dealt with German syntax and contrasted German with English. Contrastive linguistics was in its infancy: the only available text was Kufner's *Grammatical Structures,* which had been written, along with Moulton's *Sounds,* expressly for the NDEA Institutes. (Kufner, incidentally, also spent a summer at the Stanford Institute.) Contrastive syntax, of course, was also the backbone of Lohnes and Strothmann, *German: A Structural Approach,* which was developed partly in conjunction with the Bad Boll institutes, and which was later adopted by over 500 colleges and universities.

An innovation was the course in corrective phonetics, required for all participants, which was initially taught by Hans-Heinrich Wängler (Hamburg). A mixture of lectures and small group sessions aimed at eliminating the American accent in most participants' German. In addition to six sections of phonetics, there were also six sections of a conversation and composition course.

One major aspect of the institutes was the extensive field work done by the participants. German was the required language, and through intensive contact with the institute staff, with members of the Akademie and with the population at large, this "German only" requirement was strongly reinforced. From the second summer on, in 1961, we developed an Area Studies Program, for which the participants were divided into six groups, each of which investigated a particular aspect of German society, such as political life, religious life, and housing development. Each group was led by a member of the institute's staff and a member of the Akademie. The logistics of the system were so formidable that from about 1964 on each of the six groups investigated all aspects of one small town in the area. The Area Studies Program resulted in published reports of about 200 pages, which had to be written, edited, and printed before the end of each institute.

The Area Studies Program, like no other aspect of the institute, involved participants in all aspects of German life and thus contributed in a major way to the

U.S. Office of Education mandate that participants be introduced to the entire field of what we now call "German Studies." The program took students into schools, factories, government offices, stores of all sorts, and even into private homes.

A major part of the Area Studies Program was German education. Again, in small groups, students spent two mornings a week, until school closed for the summer, visiting schools from Kindergarten to Gymnasium, rotating from school to school to observe teaching in all fields, including the natural sciences and particularly the teaching of English as a foreign language. Visits to the universities in Stuttgart and Tübingen were also included in the program.

In addition to all these activities, the Institute arranged a number of field trips, some short, some rather extended, taking the participants through the Schwäbische Alb and to Rothenburg and Nördlingen. This latter field trip ended with a private chamber concert at Schloß Leitheim, on a bluff overlooking the Danube.

Major field trips took the participants, at various times, to Nürnberg, Munich, Vienna, and the Bodensee, and every year there was a long weekend trip to Cologne and Bonn, financed in large part by the German government. The government and other institutions like the DAAD and Inter Nationes were very much intrigued by what was being done and at one point seriously contemplated an institute in reverse in the United States for German teachers of English.

The Institute began each summer with a week or 10 days in Berlin. This was the 1960s and the height of the Cold War, and we felt that it was imperative that people should get a sense of what life in that divided city was like. The Berlin Senate and various other organizations supported us both financially and logistically. The participants visited Berlin schools every day in groups of three or four, and many became close friends of their German partners.

The usual sightseeing tours, West Berlin and Wannsee and, after 1961, the Wall, were augmented by visits to East Berlin. There were always complications. Here is just one ludicrous example: The Institute had applied for a group visa, which had to be done via the Swedish travel office in West Berlin. The application came back because it did not have an official stamp. So a staff member went to the toy department of the KaDeWe, West Berlin's leading department store, and bought a kit with individual letters. There were just enough of them for "Stanford University California" in three lines. The application was stamped, and the visa was awarded.

One summer, the Institute decided to charter busses rather than a plane to get from Berlin to Bad Boll. The GDR government extended an invitation to Weimar en route. Upon arrival at the famous hotel Elefant, where lunch was to be served, we found that the manager had not been informed that he had 100 guests for a meal. Nevertheless, half an hour later, a splendid luncheon was on the table. His comment: "This happens all the time, and we are always prepared. Your invitation will get here in a few months."

After the 1962 institute, we felt that we could do even more for the best and the most advanced participants in our earlier institutes. Stanford, therefore, proposed a third-level institute for the summer of 1963, which turned out to be the only one ever offered in any language, because by 1964, funds for such institutes were no longer available.

For this third-level institute, 25 applicants were accepted. Most of them had attended one of the previous Stanford institutes. The rest came from one of the academic-year institutes (there usually were one or two each year, including one at the University of Colorado). Like the summer institutes, these were fully under-written by the Office of Education. Incidentally, one of the Colorado people was Keith Anderson, later president of the AATG from 1994 to 1995.

The 25 people selected were highly proficient in German and had given definite evidence or promise of leadership in the profession. They were also either teach-ing advanced placement courses or were involved in supervisory or curriculum planning activities.

The third-level program reflected these criteria. The methods course, which was jointly taught by George Scherer and Walter Lohnes, dealt with the supervision of elementary and advanced courses and with the teaching of literature in second-ary schools, including the preparation for the College Board Advanced Placement Examination.

The most significant aspect of the third-level institute was a new type of area studies program with the topic of "Germany in Europe." There were a number of one-day field trips in the vicinity of Bad Boll, a visit to the United States Army Headquarters in Stuttgart, and a three-day trip to the Council of Europe in Straß-burg. At the end of the summer, there was a two-week field trip through the Federal Republic, financed and organized in large part by the German government. This area studies program, too, resulted in a 200-page report, which again was published before the end of the institute.[2]

The third level was probably the most effective and far-reaching part of the Bad Boll decade, but it is also fair to say that the entire NDEA enterprise, including the first-level institutes in the United States, was a magnificent "shot in the arm" for the profession that not only boosted morale, but also initiated a new era in the teaching of German. Its impact can be felt to this day.[3]

Notes

1 The preceding section was provided by Gerhard Weiss, instructor and director of the First-Level Institute at the University of Minnesota in Minneapolis, 1961–65.
2 Details on the Stanford and Minnesota Institutes come from the Directors' Final Reports and are available in the archives of both universities.
3 The preceding section was provided by Walter F. W. Lohnes, codirector and instructor of the Stanford NDEA Institute in Bad Boll, Germany.

Control-Alt-Delete:
Reshaping Germanics Publication in
the Age of Electronic Reproduction

JEANNINE BLACKWELL

> The demand of the technicals with us threatens to eliminate all serious study of
> language, even of English, to make room for the encroaching technical courses.
> The same spirit in reality prevails in our professional schools, the lawyer clamors
> for more law, the physician for more medicine, while the liberal arts are passed by
> as unnecessary and—what is to the technical mind far worse—unprofitable—all
> signs not the most promising for a great national culture or for a creative national
> literature.
>
> —M. D. Learned, the MLA President's Address, 1909

The jeremiad sounded by M. D. Learned, professor of German at University of
Pennsylvania and president of the Modern Language Association in 1909, finds
resonance in many foreign language departments today. The "technicals," as he
named them, have not only allegedly stolen our students, their machinery has in-
vaded our very offices and libraries. While many academics welcome the new flexibility of technological document storage and retrieval, many scholars worry about
the impact of the technology revolution on the production and reading of books. I
propose that we use our own critical resources to analyze the confrontation of the
humanities with this revolution. We already have a pattern for such an analysis in
the writings of Walter Benjamin.

In his essay "Das Kunstwerk im Zeitalter seiner technischen Reproduzierbarkeit," Benjamin described the assembly-line speedup of art in the twentieth century as a revolution in ways of viewing the aesthetic. Today the intelligentsia inside
and outside of the university is faced with a later, related intellectual revolution
of similar proportions: the electronic revolution in storing, retrieving, teaching,
and learning information. Benjamin located the traditional value, the "aura" of the
work of art, in its uniqueness and inaccessibility; technologies that rendered art
works quickly and easily reproduced and taken out of their original context dissolve
this aura. "Die Reproduktionstechnik, so ließe es sich allgemein formulieren, löst
das Reproduzierte aus dem Reich der Tradition ab" ("Kunstwerk" 371). Benjamin
maintained that the positive effects of the technical revolution in art also gave birth

to its most cathartic, even traumatic outcome: the liquidation of the traditional work of preserving the cultural heritage. We are witnessing a parallel transformation of knowledge as it has been traditionally preserved and managed within universities, libraries, and archives. Just as the traditional value of the work of art came in great part from its "here and now," its location in a protected, holy, privileged space, so the traditional value (and values) of intellectual production have been determined by the difficulty of access to them and their position in the privileged space of the library, archive, and university. Access to received knowledge, even 20 years ago, was often limited to those who had physical access to university libraries and archives; to those who had mastered research skills developed over several years in elite training programs; and to those who could devote full time to exploration of intellectual questions. The standards for scholarly research were inculcated in its apprentices in part through the years of training and in part through hurdles to be overcome in gaining access—recommendations needed to enter certain archives, letters of recommendation for scholarships, and other keys to the door of the great libraries. Acceptance of one's intellectual labor entailed passing through many gates, by many gatekeepers: thesis committees, major professors, scholarly reviewers, acquisition librarians, and editorial boards.

Today, access to worldwide knowledge, even archival materials, has changed in speed, quantity, and quality, just as access to the work of art changed in the Benjaminian age of reproduction by photography, film, and recording. A simple subscription to an online service offers access to the (online) catalogues of the world's great libraries, where before one had to journey across the sea or have special arrangements and correspondence with archivists and librarians to achieve such access. People with no special training can join discussion groups on literature, language, science, and philosophy. Unfiltered information of all types—thorough, incomplete, inaccurate, scholarly—is now accessible via the worldwide web and internet. Scholarly information from the sciences as well as the humanities, from the American Medical Association to the Vatican, is now available to large numbers of people for whom it was once a distant phenomenon: schoolchildren, the poorly educated, dilettantes, debutantes, and vigilantes. Only by putting up defensive barriers run by gatekeepers, as they are called on the internet, can professionals exclude the dilettantes from this very public debate. On the other hand, scholars whose work was previously known only among a subgroup of the elite now can find themselves "hit on," in the aggressive parlance of the internet, and asked for comments, expertise, and answers. While this can be exhilarating, it is also frightening to those who fled the world of banking, war, industry, and law for a quieter existence. This new very public role of scholarly production has been showcased in particular areas of Germanics where there is controversy or public interest: fascism and National Socialism, feminism, and cultural politics.

The information revolution has, however, been a recurring one. As we teach in our classes on the early modern era, the print revolution of Gutenberg's era also changed the format and accessibility of knowledge as well as its adjacent industries of printing, marketing, and storehousing of books. A second turn in the production and distribution of scholarly work came as the reading public began to expand to new, undereducated literate constituencies: the seventeenth and eighteenth centuries brought encyclopedias, compendia, dictionaries, anthologies, medical, legal, agricultural and cultural handbooks, and selected readings for diverse groups to improve themselves quickly and in a handy fashion.

As the Encyclopedists of the Enlightenment discovered through these projects, speed of access to knowledge changes knowledge itself. And intellectuals in the global marketplace, rather than those solely in universities, will determine access, create new knowledge, and restructure learning in the twenty-first century, for they are the ones who will turn information into knowledge: that is, they will put it in order, explain its significance to outsiders, refute inaccurate information, and teach it to others. The specific role that academicians will play in this brave new world of electronic reproduction of knowledge is not clear; it appears, however, that we have two unequal options. First, we can choose to maintain the traditional tasks of the ivory tower academic, serve the print needs of a small coterie of similarly educated scholars, and teach small groups of white Americans in late puberty. This route will surely be the death of any influence we could have on public policy and mainstream education in America. Or second, we can fashion roles as Encyclopedists, server-managers, and censors for the new audiences. I use the term censors intentionally to show how problematic this role will become when we surrender the cover of the elite institutions which now carry out much of that censorship and selectivity for us. In this second scenario, ever more frequently, we will be called upon to differentiate between false information and reliable; to prune and eliminate superfluous data; and to put ourselves in service to different parts of the population from those of our usual custom. We will be the ones who control, alternate, and delete materials in the body of electronically accessible knowledge.

The phrase "Control-Alt-Delete" refers to the steps necessary to restart your computer while the screen is "frozen" and nothing seems to work. It is, to a great number of academics, a desperate measure to save a bit of text, a program, some communication.

How can we restart our intellectual enterprise while it is still running? How can we switch to a new task of controlling, alternating, and deleting information to produce knowledge, without destroying our own intellectual *raison d'être?* Can we restart and redirect Germanics research while it is still running in the hopes of salvaging the same things: a bit of text, a program, some communication? We must discover ways to communicate our research results in the twenty-first century and control the flow of information in our fields. What should we alternate? What should we delete? And how can we move from being the control-alt-deleters to becoming the interpreters and explainers to the world?

The answers to the questions of our future are written in our recent past, the last 300 years. We can take a page from the book of those who developed the encyclopedias, the compendia, the anthologies of selected literature, the hundreds of translators since the eighteenth century who have unearthed and/or salvaged texts. These positivist hunters and gatherers have showed us how to restructure knowledge in accessible ways for a new reading public: in their case, a reading public not educated in the Classics, in universities, and with access to great libraries. They created encyclopedias, compendia, anthologies, and explanations for target groups of the recently educated, the insufficiently educated, and the monolingual. They, and those after them, enhanced and revised the literary canon and gave a voice to lost and forgotten writers. They show us ways to uncover new knowledge that speaks to the needs of a new public. However, the move to a new audience, and by implication new subject matter, brought its controversies: the battle between the ancients and the moderns. Even those scholars who wholeheartedly supported a shift to the modern age found that they had to change their style: they found they had to use the vernacular, develop new genres, and organize the intellectual enterprise in the sphere of the salon as well as the academy. For the information revolution, we, too, will have to change our style. We can, however, benefit from examples in our past.

Scholars in foreign languages in America have been managing the crisis in text management for more than 100 years, and have shown a startling capacity both to cope with recent adversity and bad market conditions, and to dawdle too long over making changes. An early call came from Horatio White, professor of German at Cornell in 1884, to adapt the German seminar reading system to the American college, yet to make it fit our special national needs:

> [W]hatever the task of the German university, it cannot be precisely the same task as ours, nor are its ways, while admirable, necessarily to be our ways. The German university is largely a nursery for specialists, an invaluable training ground for teachers and investigators . . . . The minor part of our own duty may be to train a limited number of bright minds in progressive and independent work; the major portion of our labors must be consumed in helping large numbers of students to gain such a vantage ground of vision that their sympathies will permanently be enlarged, and the intellectual life possess a generous and catholic range whose influence will touch distant circles which we can never directly reach, but which ought to share whatever diversities of gifts a university may have at its command. (56)

While the move toward an assimilation of the German seminar and the German classics took hold at the university level (Goebel 1884; Francke 1895; Fisher 1984), it took a national resolution of the MLA to bring the discussion to a larger teaching population. The "Committee of Twelve," appointed by the MLA in 1896 to make recommendation on requirements in French and German in college preparatory schools, issued its report to the U.S. Commissioner of Education in 1898 (MLA, Proceedings 1898; MLA, Proceedings 1899; MLA, "Report" 1899). The committee boldly stated that "in our general scheme of secondary education the ability to converse in French or German . . . should not be regarded as a thing of primary importance for its own sake, but as an auxiliary to the higher ends of linguistic scholarship and literary culture" (1395). It did not shy back from suggesting the actual works to be read in elementary, intermediate, and advanced courses in all languages, including German, stressing that the number of sentimental works and fairy tales should be reduced, while more modern prose should be read (MLA, "Report" 1899 1409–21).[1]

The work of this Committee generated much discussion beyond the MLA and began a flurry of proposed reading lists and suggestions for advanced German students in the public schools.[2] Indeed, a decade later (1908) a Committee of Fifteen was constituted to revise and emend the lists from this earlier report, in part driven by "the fact that a number of teachers were strongly opposed to the existing list of textbooks or to any list whatsoever. On the other hand, many others expressed the wish that "the lists recommended by the Committee of Twelve . . . be kept and revised to meet new conditions and include later publications" (xlii). Denying any claim to canonical authority, this Committee returned to the lists many of the previously excluded *Märchen* and *Novellen,* as well as several sentimental texts and love stories. While the recommendations of the Committee of Twelve had been accepted unanimously, there was considerable opposition to the emendations proposed by the Committee of Fifteen (MLA, Proceedings 1910).

Respondents to the Committee of Twelve's work ranged all the way from high school teachers to the president of the MLA. In 1901 Ernst Wolf presented the reading lists for Saginaw High School in Michigan in *Monatshefte,* stressing memorization and conversation about literature (Wolf 1901).[3] M. D. Learned, who was the head of the College Entrance Examining Board which began in 1901, weighed in with a polemic article on "Germanistik und schöne Litteratur in Amerika," in which he identified the "[v]erderbliche Tendenzen" in American culture and the tasks of German Studies at American colleges and universities to reverse these trends (Learned, "Germanistik" 105). Learned described the unfortunate state of American culture in his day: he maintained first that the rapid development of the American economy caused material interests ("Geldmachen") to predominate among students in their choice of studies. Second, he chastised the Anglo-American press for enhancing coarseness in public taste by replacing the fine poets of the past with untalented and superficial modern writers. Third, modern writers were to his mind in the grip of "Novellenwut" to the disadvantage of other genres. Finally, he saw the result of these tendencies as a decline in the literary criticism of his age. Because of this crisis in American literature and culture and because America had itself not experienced a Classical period, Learned maintained, Americans had to seek models in the Classical models of foreign cultures, including modern classics (Learned, "Germanistik" 106). Second, Americans could benefit if they imported the scientific method and literary-historical criticism of *Germanistik;* indeed they had already begun this with their discovery of "Comparative Literature." Third, *Germanistik* would lead Americans to the development of a truly literary cultural history as part of a national heritage, which Learned apparently did not find in America in 1909. Fourth, citing Schiller, Learned claims that *Germani-*

stik would lead Americans to technical facility in using the classical forms, which would finally bring them to inculcate children with an understanding of beauty and hence to the aesthetic education of the whole nation and the development of a national literature.

Other German teachers bristled at the pomposity of this high aesthetic claim by the professors at prestigious "eastern" colleges and universities, and claimed that Germanics in America needed to be more realistic, more modern, more praxis-driven. Already in 1906 Arthur Kiefer, a high school German instructor in Piqua, Ohio, sharply criticized the claim to aesthetic leadership as epitomized by Learned. He uttered the following "ketzerische . . . Gedanken": "Sind nicht viele der ästhe-tischen und rhetorischen Schönheiten, auch in den Klassikern, in Wahrheit nur Werte in den Augen eines oft leben- und weltentfremdeten Schulmannes?" (Kiefer, "Der deutsche Unterricht" 106). Kiefer asserted that the role of the purely aesthetic in literature was overvalued by teachers; it was more important for begin-ning language learners to master the language, most adeptly done by reading short, clear prose pieces. He found that the situations and content of many of the classics were inappropriate for children, not because of his own prudery, but because he believed they had not yet gained enough life experience to appreciate them (107). Students should instead read modern prose with modern themes and fast-moving plots. Kiefer adamantly demanded the removal of all texts featuring exaggerated sentimentality (108). He called for the banishment of all reference to "Schlafrock, Pantoffeln, Zipfelmütze, zerstreute[r] Professor oder ähnlich Großmutterscherzen . . . Dinge mit denen wir Deutsche uns ins eigene Fleisch schneiden" (108).

Two years later Kiefer gave concrete criticisms of and suggestions for the syl-labus: replace the "Idealien" with "Realien." Textbooks, to Kiefer's mind, should begin with interestingly written dialogues, and continue much later with interest-ing historical descriptions. Basing his claims on the Report of the Committee of Twelve, he proposed excluding the following from all high school German courses: all fairy stories and tales; all sentimental stories, even *Immensee;* all stories of chil-dren younger than the students themselves. For advanced courses, Kiefer calls for drama and prose, carefully chosen to avoid explicit sexual content. Finally he calls it folly for the College Entrance Examination papers (and eastern colleges) to be-lieve that a modern spoken language can be acquired in six to eight weeks.

The tension seen here in the early twentieth century between the esteemed president of the MLA, a scholar from a prestigious institution, and the beleaguered high school teacher in Ohio continues in our field today: how and what do we teach, and toward what careers do we aim our students? Do we allow "Geldsachen" to drive our curriculum or not? The tension was expressed again in 1997 by Dorothy James, as she criticizes our "star" system in graduate faculty status, which she sees as undermining our whole academic enterprise:

> It is not . . . enough for the forum leaders of our profession to assert the centrality
> of language learning and teaching in the humanities and social sciences curricu-
> lum. They have to roll up their sleeves alongside the workshop leaders and do

> something about it, throw their individual and collective weight, for example, be-
> hind a serious integrated undergraduate curriculum in all the kinds of colleges
> that exist in the country and simply refuse to accept a curriculum and a faculty
> split, separated, weakened, divided, and ultimately conquered. (James 52)

James perceives modern language studies to be at a crossroads and a crisis: the academic and cultural world has changed on us, and we must restructure our enter-prise to meet new demands. As can be seen from the school curriculum debates of 1898–1914 mentioned above, Germanics has been at such a crossroads before. We have in our history generations of researchers who have had to retool in mid-stream: those who started in German before the 1940s only to see their careers and even their lives devastated by fascism, and who still prevailed as intellectuals; those who were trained after the war in positivism only to be put out to pasture by the New Critics; the New Critics, in turn, who were faced with students demanding social relevance, radical texts, East German literature, and the Frankfurt School; those on the New Left of the 1960s and 1970s who have watched the Frankfurt School become passé as the discussion moved on to phallo-logo-centrism and gen-der performance in the 1980s and 1990s. Yet many of these scholars were able to grow and to develop better theory and practice from the experience. Adaptability to assembly-line speedup is not new to us; the pace and scope of this change to electronic access to information is.

Given these examples of a tradition of tension and flexibility in Germanics in America, we can turn to the problems of the last 30 years to see where our new constituencies will be located — geographically, intellectually, linguistically. Their location will help us determine how we can reshape our information for their use and benefit. How has the profession of Germanics changed since 1968? There has, of course, been the disastrous decline in university study in German and in foreign language requirements at all levels; there has been a decisive turn to theory, cultural texts, film, and popular literature in teaching and research; the graduate student body is now populated preponderantly by women; although interdisciplinarity has increased in many quarters, our connections have not been primarily through com-parative literature programs, but rather through interdisciplinary culture studies, which has entailed the use of English, or at least much translation in many instances of our most interesting work in film, theory, and culture studies. Ever more, we find ourselves including the rubric "Click here for English" in our scholarly work, either because of pressures from publishers or simply because we want our work to find a larger circulation in culture studies. On the other hand, we find our enroll-ments increasing in business German courses, and in professionally driven training settings such as factories and postgraduate management courses. Correspondingly, our student body is changing ever more to a mix of double majors in a variety of professional fields.

These changes, whether they be desperate attempts to pander to a dwindling student public or not, show that Germanics has already been moving toward the global marketplace of ideas even without the prodding of electronic communications. This is not to say that our interdisciplinary work is simply pandering to the public. Germanics journals and individual scholars have had an impact on intellectual life beyond our discipline since 1968, even in the face of a shrinking enrollment and declining university influence. Journals and organizations like *New German Critique,* the Coalition of Women in German, the German Studies Association, Frauen in der Literaturwissenschaft, among many others, and crossover scholars in area studies, film studies, peace studies, and studies of race, nationality, and ethnicity have also been able to make the leap to international recognition beyond *Germanistik* and Germanics, and to influence the work of others in a way that even the early Germanists would have envied. The organizers of the Continuum series, the editors of the *Dictionary of Literary Biography,* and editors at Camden House and University of Nebraska Press have provided important venues for Germanics which reach outside of the discipline, while providing, in the good old-fashioned way, texts and information needed.

This occasion is not, however, one to look fondly back at our methods of coping with adversity. Rather, it provides opportunity to refashion how we transform information into knowledge, and how we present it for others' use.

We must reconsider our audiences. Already virtually all first-year college texts are accompanied by a CD-ROM, and students must have access to this technology to learn. High schools will be using interactive computer learning for foreign languages. Students use the internet to investigate colleges, apply to college, read books, sign up for courses, and get the news. If this is a community of learners we want to influence, we must make ourselves available to them, both through informal networks with their teachers, through online discussion groups, and through presentation of the best materials on the internet. We must grapple with the problems of distance learning via telecommunications: will we lose a valuable audience if we refuse to participate in distance learning? Is the geographically isolated, part-time, "nontraditional" student someone we can ignore? Despite the drawbacks of these audiences—too young, too old, too far away, not sufficiently educated in the Great Tradition—we must simply face, as did the Encyclopedists, that there is a new public out there looking for education in all the wrong places, and it is our task to provide them with the highest quality knowledge possible, gleaned from the sea of information available.

We must regretfully balance our love affair with the printed word on paper with the realistic problems of the print record. Many current problems dictate that print culture will be less frequently our medium for intellectual discourse in the next century: the cost of physical printing and paper, mailing and supply systems (marginally functioning university presses and review organs); the often intangible cost of the lag in time between preparation, publication, marketing, and distribution of print material; the continuing increase in the cost of paper journals and books; and the increasing number of libraries stopping subscriptions to ever more scholarly specialty journals. More libraries will organize cohort-cooperation deals in which they share a pool of books, and thereby purchase fewer books, which will force publishers to raise costs. The paper record of the nineteenth century will continue to deteriorate physically, and many books and journals will be lost forever unless we recover them somehow in electronic form. Soon newsletters of organizations will be on the net, if not on the web, because of prohibitive paper and mailing costs.

Given this grim set of future scenarios, what are we to do as researchers, as journal editors, and as advisers to publishers? We must decide how we will publish, and what the publication expectation is for graduate students, for budding scholars, and for advanced scholars, given the electronic revolution.

Control

Scholars and scholarly organizations must accept, and indeed have done so, the responsibility for electronic reproduction of primary texts. We must also control and manage the evaluation of electronic scholarly production. What has for generations been accomplished by a winnowing process of peer review and editorial decision-making based on quality, word length, and appeal to limited but predictable scholarly audiences will now transpire in an electronic realm. In this new space, size of text does not determine cost and audience is not found in predictable constituencies. We can control both of these tasks — text selection and verification as well as critical evaluation of electronic scholarship — but it will entail reshaping our enterprise.[4]

We can control or at least deeply influence the selection of texts and artifacts available online, because we are the producers and users (although not exclusively so). We need to establish, using our specialty organizations, a to-do list for saving texts in electronic format and, with other national and international organizations, develop protocols for saving them that are both efficient and teachable to the novice scholar. We need to have a more specific protocol for how evaluation of texts and research online will be handled.[5] We need to have something like an AATG or GSA Seal of Approval on electronic materials to indicate that they are complete (primary texts), accurate, and fully described in terms of provenance and bibliography. A protocol for text encoding has been developed by the consortium called the Text Encoding Initiative, based at the University of Illinois at Chicago (http://www.uic.edu:80/orgs/tei/, directed by C. M. Sperberg-McQueen), but we also need to have a layman's critical guide for the use of such texts, for proper use, citation and crediting of electronic research work. Any such venture should be allied with the Center for Electronic Texts in the Humanities at Rutgers and Princeton (http://www.ceth.rutgers.edu/), but we must do the work for this ourselves, because only we know which texts should be included and only we can provide the scholarly apparatus and analysis of their accuracy.

We need to organize a system of readily available electronic texts in German literature, history, culture, and criticism, available on the net or other media. We can take Classics as our example here; two of the first such text-and-image electronic collections are *Perseus,* an anthology of materials from Ancient Greece and Rome (http://www.perseus.tufts.edu/), and *Diotima,* a collection of Classical works dealing with women's culture (http://www.uky.edu/ArtsSciences/Classics/gender. html). A further example is the Women Writers Project, based at Brown University (http://www.wwp.brown.edu/resource.html), which includes English language texts only. This proposed system of accessible German texts should develop ground rules about copyright and access, so that its titles would be clearly legal for academic use. German texts (and their English translations) should be available in one of three formats: as text files which are available for downloading; as an interactive list for ordering/purchasing as CD-ROMs; or as an interactive course packet publication service for the compilation of course materials, delivered either as hard copy or as electronic text. A few online libraries of German texts already exist, but they are necessarily limited in scope: Athena, which has a small number of Swiss and French literary texts (http://un2sgl.unige.ch/www/athena/html/swissaut.html) and *Projekt Gutenberg* (http://gutenberg.informatik.uni-hamburg.de/gutenb/ home.htm), a site for volunteers to place ASCII text files of German literary texts. The *Kassandra Project* (http://www.reed.edu/ccampbel/tkp/), is designed by one individual, limited to a small number of texts by "visionary German women around 1800." Missing from this mix of limited websites are locations with reliable texts in English translation accessible via the Web for classroom use, downloading, and anthologizing.

The advantage of having three types of electronic access (downloadable files, website for ordering course packet, and CD-ROMs for purchase) to all our texts is clear: they would provide fast, efficient access to texts for research or teaching, at a lower cost than expensive book purchase for both students and faculty. Such access to legally available texts in convenient electronic format, particularly for course packets, would eliminate the unfortunate illegal practices of desperate teachers trying to provide custom-designed, contemporary materials at a reasonable cost to students. This would give all of us access to a larger body of materials than is usually available in print media, and would save time and trouble with out-of-print texts.

The disadvantages of such an electronic library are also clear: this system eliminates the publisher as middleman, except in the case of previously available printed books, and thus revolutionizes and perhaps destroys the publisher's very livelihood. It will work best for materials that are already in the public domain, that is, older texts. Since much of our teaching is in twentieth-century topics, the purchase of copyright for electronic reproduction would be steep, and would mandate higher prices to cover these costs. The evaluation, use, and possible abuse of living authors' work is an even more profound issue for such an online library.

One might suggest that the *laissez-faire* approach to the development of such an electronic text marketplace would best be left in the hands of the market; after all, even the Reclam Verlag has begun to offer some of its famous yellow texts as CD-ROMs. I maintain, however, that this service needs to be within the control of academe so that the texts we choose, and not those that the marketplace chooses, are in its library. By doing it ourselves, we avoid the problems of electronic publishers deciding that certain German titles are not profitable enough, or are too controversial. We also provide the crucial service of evaluation of new texts. As a nonprofit, solely academic service, costs would also be lower for researchers and students.

The most profound disadvantage of establishing a German culture electronic library is the impact of electronic publishing on the publishing industry, and by extension, on creative writers who live by the pen. Protecting and nurturing their future texts is also a part of our job, and an all-electronic world of publishing leaves authors without the traditional critical selection and review procedures of print media. For that reason online publishing must be accompanied by online criticism and reviewing, so that excellence can continue to be rewarded.

The research enterprise is profoundly changed by online access. The democratization of research topics via the net means that openly derivative sites by novices and amateurs, some of which are inaccurate or misleading, are just as accessible to our students as are the sites of scholars who have usually produced valid and reliable documents. We must train our students to judge all these documents critically. This challenge to us as teachers will be most serious, for nothing in our training has prepared us for so vast a gate keeping function.

We must also learn to control the rules of evaluation, acceptance, and eventual assessment of electronic publication for people in our fields. In the past we have (more or less) successfully established codes for such activities as multiple submissions, plagiarism, blind submissions and evaluations, and appropriate citation. We must revise and expand that code. The MLA, through its Committee on Computers and Emerging Technologies, has recently issued "Guidelines for Evaluating Computer-Related Work in the Modern Languages," which scholars should know and follow (MLA, "Guidelines" 1996 217–19). We can and must train ourselves, our chairs, and our deans to assess and to value electronic publication of online bibliographies and text editions; video and CD-ROM productions; and the development of distance learning programs. It will become ever more important for those of us who are used frequently as evaluators of research (for tenure and promotion) to be able to comment intelligently on these new media.

Alternate

We can control how we publish or perish only to a limited extent. We can not control the national publishing market, but we can rechannel our business and revise our practices in light of the electronic revolution. Right now we are suffering under long-developing crises in publishing. Since about 1975, new Ph.D.s feel the pressure to publish well before they enter the job market. They feel pressure to give and publish research papers, often before they have done much research. And the whole system of evaluation of work (conference organizing, refereeing of books and articles, and eventually tenure and promotion files) is getting over-loaded in key areas, such as theory, modern women's literature, and race/national identity/ethnicity. The pressure to publish is there, it is real, and it won't go away, even at teaching colleges and what used to be called branch campuses. As the web expands, and the pressures on the shrinking venues for traditional publication continue apace, electronic publishing will become ever more prevalent. Our present task is to revise the way we evaluate scholarship for this new medium and to re-envision the form of scholarly discourse to take advantage of its new possibilities.

Measuring "progress toward tenure," if it still exists in the twenty-first century, will demand new criteria for electronic scholarship. Where before we could rely on such factors as the reputation of a publisher or a given series or the rate of acceptance of submissions to give a quick overview of the importance of a scholarly journal, these indices are less meaningful in the electronic world. Measuring "progress" of a budding scholar in the traditional terms—getting over a certain number of barriers—is also less predictable when this scholar can establish his or her own home page and impact can be measured in the number of anonymous "visits" to the site. We need to develop a means for assessing new electronic scholarship and to devise a rational method for refereeing and reviewing which can serve us as a new standard. A place to begin is the quality of the site's scholarly design; the amount of "pioneer work" necessary for the choice and reclamation of primary materials; the expertise necessary for verification of texts, similar to the preparation of critical editions; the inclusion of recent scholarship for reference points and background when appropriate; creativity in the composition of scholarly juxtapositions and links; and flexibility of the site in presenting information in a differentiated way to various targeted audiences.

Germanists need to help college deans and non-Germanist colleagues to re-think the notion of the book for the tenure file. As many will agree, we have a large number of author-subsidized books out there that have been published prematurely, that will not likely be bought by anybody, not even research institutions, and that are simply used as a hazing mechanism when assistant professors are admitted to the fraternity of the tenured faculty. We should control this situation better. First, we need to convince our deans that innovative electronic research, groundbreaking articles, important translations, and work on the electronic preservation of primary materials are crucial intellectual tasks for our field and should be valued as highly as a dissertation made into book.

Of course, dissertations are our lifeblood, and the best surely need to be made public. We need to establish an refereed online site (a "publisher") for *revised* dissertations. Recent Ph.D.s should not be enticed into spending thousands of dollars to pay publishers to disseminate camera-ready copy for a book that will receive very little publicity and virtually no reviews. Predators do take advantage of the young in this manner. A strongly refereed, online publisher of revised dissertations stored in accessible files, available for access at a small fee or for print-out at a higher fee, is clearly what we need. This service would differ from the highly useful services that *Dissertation Abstracts International* already provides, because these would be revised dissertations—revised first by the recent Ph.D.s and their advisers, and then rewritten after comments have come in from critical readers. Only a fraction of all books reviewed should be accepted for this electronic publication, and the percentage accepted should be posted on the homepage. At the absolute most this should cost $400 per submission, to cover honoraria of evaluators and a processing fee. It should be free of charge, subsidized by sales of the best books in hard copy to research libraries and individuals.

Our graduate programs need to nurture advanced graduate students more effectively than at present to prepare them for the electronic revolution in teaching and research. Graduate mentors should teach them critical evaluation and research skills in both traditional methods and in the emerging technologies. Such training should be part of our graduate programs and testing procedures, and it should be taken into account when candidates are recommended for jobs. We ourselves must learn to evaluate, acknowledge, and use the research produced on line and on the web.

Editors and other scholars need to take a long, critical, and public look at all our specialty journals in Germanics, as well as our scholarly publication in general. As a field we need to know about submission rates, acceptance rates, circulation of journals, numbers of books actually sold. Academic publishers find journals, yearbooks, and anthologies less attractive than monographs, because readers photocopy articles they want instead buying the whole text; they are interested in journals that deliver a stable membership for the subscription list *and* show a potential for growth; some academic publishers are prejudiced against journals which accept articles in a language other than English.[6] A perusal of the 1996 *MLA Guide to Periodicals* reveals some startling facts, self-reported by the journal editors. Of the approximately 55 journals (American and European) dedicated predominantly to German and Germanic literary, linguistics, and cultural studies, more than half (28) have subscriptions in the range of 500 to 1,500, including the most recognized and prominent journals in our field, such as *Euphorion* and *Monatshefte*. The largest, the *German Quarterly* (5,500) and *Neue Rundschau* (7,000), give us the approximate ceiling of subscription possibilities. Those journals with subscription rates below 500 are not likely to be self-supporting ventures, unless their costs are underwritten by association memberships which deliver an automatic number of subscriptions or by presses willing to support the journals for other reasons. Those journals with subscription rates in the range of 300 to 2,000 (63 percent or 35 journals), show the real size of the field of Germanics publication; for many publishers, even this market size is becoming less viable for independent print publication. When we consider the number of people in most of our specialization areas, we see that many of them will be smaller than this minimum market size, and will continue to encounter difficulties in publication.

Although the *MLA Guide to Periodicals* provides scholars with self-reported information on journals, it cannot tell the real story: who reads and uses our research? It would help to know if the Germanics research enterprise in America is populated and used by a very small group of lifelong publishing scholars, plus those in pre-tenure status. Once we know what we publish and how many people are involved, we can better maintain or redirect the research enterprise. Let me stress that the *laissez-faire* model we now follow is working for only a handful of scholars. Since we are now caught in a system of university presses which are ever more reluctant to publish long works, foreign works, and traditionally specialized works, our scholarship will become increasingly marginalized and prohibitively expensive for all but a few libraries if we continue to publish in traditional ways in traditional venues.

One of our most valued venues is the specialty journal, and one of its most appealing characteristics is the juxtaposition of related and mutually enhancing research topics in a handy, portable format. It provides the latest research in an area in such a way that editors can call attention to trends and new information. It provides group identity for the scholars dedicated to the enterprise, and it serves to acknowledge the best work in a field. In the brave new electronic world, we need to maintain these characteristics, but perhaps sacrifice the traditional form. I propose that specialty journals in our field (those with a circulation of less than 500 such as the *GDR Bulletin, Daphnis,* and the graduate student journals) consider becoming exclusively electronic journals for circulation purposes, while retaining hard copy for archival purposes only at selected repositories. Small circulation journals will doubtless fall further into the vicious circle of de-subscription as the number of faculty researchers in our field declines and libraries drop subscriptions. Ever more marginalized, these journals will cease to serve as arbiters of expertise, a function we most definitely need to preserve.

The major interdisciplinary journals with emphasis on Germanics should also become online journals to increase their accessibility to other fields. Particularly, those journals whose cost is now prohibitive for scholars to purchase individually must move to electronic format for their own survival.

Should journals participate in such document delivery systems as UNCOVER or ARTICLEFIRST, by which patrons choose from tables of contents or subject listings which articles they will read? Or should we journal editors boycott this, because it is just an overpriced clipping service, or as one colleague put it, "McJournals on line?" Let us be frank: doing online searches is so convenient and gives scholars such quick and comprehensive access to fields and sources that they will never go back to just flipping through *Monatshefte* and *Colloquia Germanica* and browsing through a dozen other journals in reading rooms. Online searches and delivery services will never replace the tried-and-true methods such as "snowballing," "slash-and-burn," and "calling up experts and asking them." But online searching is inevitably the method of choice for the future. While we still have to train our graduate students to find materials the old-fashioned way, we must also train them to use these new services as well. Germanics must join with other humanities fields, however, in forcing electronic journal services as ARTICLE-

FIRST, CARL and UNCOVER to provide a cut rate for persons ordering the entire issue or getting the whole journal delivered regularly, and to acknowledge the limitations of their service. For example, they should indicate how many journals in a specific field are included in their databases, and indicate whether the run of the journal is historically complete: many such services do not have information on the period before 1980. They should indicate how many and which foreign language journals are included.

The implications for both these electronic phenomena—article delivery services and online publication—are profound for journals. The periodicity of regularly appearing journals (chronologically ordered volumes and issues) has developed because of the need to bundle research in size-limited publications. This necessity disappears in online publications, where ongoing publication is now a reality. Cost is essentially no longer a factor in the "size" a journal could reach: we are thrown back on quality of submission alone for acceptance. Since "size" will be a function of acceptances/rejections over time, we will begin to judge the quality of a journal in a vastly different way. Bundling thematics in special issues will still certainly be part of the journal enterprise, but the links from a special issue to related topics will be much more fluid than before.

The most profound shifts for journal publication are the referee procedure and the place and role of scholarly reviews. Refereeing articles will no doubt transpire much as it has for more than 100 years; however, the revision process will be ongoing and interactive. Authors will be able to change their articles in response to the criticisms of others; dialogues between articles and critics can and should develop. This exciting intellectual prospect could easily get out of the control of the original editors, and it could also make the notion of "review of literature" archaic, for the "seminal articles" will be constantly in flux. We can, of course, insist that original versions be retained, that changes be placed only in links or dated versions, so that the history of critical discourse is preserved. Book reviews, like most other critical-analytical functions, will continue, but the pacing and format of book reviews will no doubt change.

Should we separate out the book reviewing function from the research article function for electronic journals? Academic book reviews should still be associated with their "home" electronic journal or with their specialty organization, for the critical editing function will still be operative. The management function of book reviews should still be handled as a scholarly editorial position, and it should still be handled by academics. Book publishers should still send these books to editors for consideration and circulation. However, reviews might very well appear at a different pace than journal articles, and should be published online as soon as possible. This is only the most logical use of the speed of electronic publication, and it will facilitate the public exposure of new books in Germanics. However, this speedup of the review process will further obfuscate the line between journalistic reviews in newspapers and other popular media and the seasoned and well-considered scholarly assessment of the same material. Editors of online journals will be faced with another issue as well, one which is related to the "size" of the publication: their preselection of books worthy of review will no longer be based on the size limitation of the journal, but rather on a self-imposed control on the basis of pure merit or interest. Editors can then not revert to blaming journal size for exclusions: "I regret to tell you that we will not be able to review your fine monograph in our journal; we are able to review only about 50 of the 300 plus books we receive each year." Instead, there will be either a proliferation and dilution of the book reviewing process, or else a much more explicit and rigorous determination of value up front.

We must alter the way we train students. We must make sure that they receive enough training in both traditional research methods and electronic access to materials. Since they will be among the few experts left who can work with the print record and with manuscripts, it is even more important that we train them in traditional bibliographic and paleographic skills than ever before. We must make sure that our testing procedures for these students examines their fluency in electronics as well as in Germanics. Above all, we must make sure that in their training as teachers they learn how to guide others in the critical use of technology. A good place to start is to make Benjamin's "Kunstwerk" essay required reading in every program.

Delete

It is difficult to predict what will die as the information revolution continues. Certainly the method developed for indexing and citation in scholarly works will be vastly different in the future. Key word searches and word-frequency lists will be more likely tools than traditional indexes as we use search engines for these processes. We must change the traditional form of scholarly citation as well. Citation of scholarly work online should move to using links rather than footnotes or endnotes; these forms have now outlived their usefulness. Using links, readers can actually re-create the research process and directly check on sources; since this is the real purpose of the scholarly citation—the explanation and verification of the research process—links are the more efficient means to the end. Bibliographies as part of a monograph or critical edition will be much more flexible, effective, and efficient if they appear in a searchable text on CD-ROM, rather than simply as 35 more printed pages at the end of the book. Even hard copy books should provide bibliographies and indices in an attached CD-ROM. While we will still need bibliographies, they will take on added importance as they begin to serve as card catalogues for the world.

Librarians have already begun organizing the changes necessary in library access to make texts available to their constituents. Libraries will certainly continue to exist, for they will be the computer connections for those unable to afford the technology necessary to function in this new electronic environment. However, librarians will be working as ringmasters in a capitalist marketplace and will be the purveyors of systems and services for information exchange. As intellectuals we will have to work much more closely with librarians, nonprofit information services, and independent archives to assure open access to as much of the population as possible, so that the modification of information does not become the exclusive preserve of the First World, the affluent, and the entrepreneur.

The enhanced speed and increased access itself has created a new set of problems for new scholars, and for elderly scholars doing new things. And the problems go hand in hand with the accomplishments. An example is the democratization of access. For scholars who have longed to open educational access to more people, it is a delight to have so many using new channels of information. For scholars who already use research tools, it is a great enhancement to have interdisciplinarity almost thrust upon us by search engines, which do not separate out the Germanic from the anthropological or historical. But this same wonderful variety and interdisciplinarity destabilizes the disciplines and the scholarly pecking order. Search engines do not separate out the scholarly from the nonscholarly, the Germanist from the popular culture expert. The crucial sorting services that human catalogers used to perform for us—the *MLA Bibliography* in tidy containers by century, genre, and language, the summaries of all the new work on Fichte, the winnowing out of dubious journals and authors by scholars of, say, witchcraft—are fast dying out, or are simply not available as easily. And so we are inundated with thousands of pieces of information that may enhance our research, or then again might not. New people will get access to us; our enterprise will be much more public, more vulnerable, and less a private club.

A critical problem for virtually every academic journal today is funding and support staff. First, there is the cost of postage and mailing of scores of manuscripts, books, and other correspondence as well as the materials and photocopying to go with it. Many institutions are now refusing to pay, or pay in full for these activities at their universities, or they will do so for only a few years and then stop funding. The scholarly world does not end when one leaves those few universities that are willing to pay. Because of the way the job market has developed (or not developed) in the last 20 years, much of our finest academic talent is NOT at the "top 20 schools." Those younger active scholars are at poorer places or places that refuse to pay for this specialty research task. Are we to cut off our noses to spite our faces and not make it possible for these younger scholars to take on editorial jobs? Certainly not. We must go online, for we need to involve all these "remote sites" in the editorial and critical process.

But if we go online, we may need more, not less staff support for publishing the journals, because of the heavy responsibility of getting the technology and format right. New skills will be needed for these editors and for those who catalogue. Already now we are in the midst of a crisis concerning funding for publishing support. Gone are the days when one of the department secretaries typed up professors' papers for publication—that was long over even before the generation of 1980 entered the profession. Instead, most of us do our own formatting, typing, proofreading, and footnote-checking. And we do it very poorly. At the journals themselves, staff support is a rare luxury. The lucky few have an office assistant; some have a graduate student, but many others do it all themselves: open all the boxes, do all the photocopying, of course do all the proofreading, the databases entries, the retyping on to disk when necessary, and packing up the books and papers to send out for review. Many an office looks like Circuit City, with a scanner and DOS and Mac compatible machines to do all the clerical work in one room. One might be tempted to think that this combination of unalienated und alienating intellectual labor is merely a product of academic assembly line speedup. Yet we read Martin Lowry's depiction of the household of the humanist printer Aldus Manutius in Venice around 1500: Aldus's home is described as "an almost incredible mixture of the sweatshop, the boarding house, and the research institute" (94). Thinking of the electronic workshop in this way aligns us with the Renaissance and the beginning of a textual revolution.

The cost-cutting for journals has to come in the areas of handling, mailing, and photocopying, rather than in staff. But it must really come from separating the journals from the paper publishers. It is no longer a viable enterprise, for journals, for publishers, for libraries, or for the scholarly public. We cannot pay excessive costs that are driven by the high cost of materials and handling and by a corporate publishing structure that demands profits from a non-profit-making enterprise.

This all means we need to have a national organization of research Germanics which we can use to solve many of the pressing problems of publication and graduate training. The American Association of Teachers of German is a wonderful organization for our joint concerns, but the three specific tasks we need to address in research are costly and specific and will stretch the limited resources of the AATG beyond reasonable limits. Those tasks are: to train graduate students in the new technologies as well as to enhance their skills in text restoration; to save texts that are fast deteriorating; and to address issues of electronic publication and evaluation on the national level. The MLA offers some hope in its recent actions, but the actual work of saving the texts and changing our own rules is our job as Germanists.

We have to go electronic, and it will change the way that we think about books. Holding a beautiful and rare book in your hands will still be a moving experience: turning the illustrated pages of a volume of Schedel's *Weltchronik* with clasps and brads intact will still thrill the bibliophile. But we must contrast that joy with holding the only extant copy of a brittle, disintegrating, anonymous fairy tale from the nineteenth century, the call number already fallen off. You may be the last person to hold it before it is gone forever. Those are the texts we have to save somehow, in concert with professional organizations of scholars, librarians, and educators.

What do we control, which patterns should we alternate, what attitudes and activities should we delete? It is not yet clear, but I am convinced that using our own understanding of the works of cultural production and reproduction can give us a guide. Benjamin tells us that the mechanical reproduction of art removed its aura, and emancipated it from dependence on ritual. As we move to the electronic reproduction and organization of knowledge, its aura, too, is removed, and we are deprived of our automatic dependence on the ritual and hierarchy of scholarly access and traditions. Many of those traditions are beloved and beautiful, the "schöne Schein" of our lives in academe. But we have no choice in the matter; one does not, in a revolution. However, there are intellectuals who went before us, who made lemonade from the lemons history gave them. We have to take our cue from the literary historians like Kuno Francke and Christine Touaillon who gathered, anthologized, reprinted, and translated, as we make the paradigm shift from elitist print culture to democratized electronic culture. Elizabeth Eisenstein described the paradigm shift from oral culture to print culture this way: "As learning by reading took on new importance, the role played by mnemonic aids was diminished. Rhyme and cadence were no longer required to preserve certain formulas and recipes. The nature of collective memory was transformed" (34). The mode of production of our collective memory will also be transformed in this next textual revolution and, I hope, democratized in an open and intellectually honest way. But that will happen only if we intellectuals transform ourselves at the same time, without turning the machine off.

Notes

1 The Committee suggests, for instance, that the advanced-level students should read ca. 500 pages of German literature, taken from such writers as: Fulda, Goethe (except *Faust*), Grillparzer, Hauff, Heine's prose, Kleist's *Prinz von Homburg,* Körner, Lessing, Scheffel, Schiller's plays and historical prose, Sudermann, Tieck, and Wildenbruch.
2 See Bahlen 1903; Hänseler 1911; Hohlfeld 1901–2; J. B. E. Jones 1915; Mensel 1914; MLA, Proceedings 1909 and 1910; MLA, Report 1906; Stewart 1914; Winter 1910.
3 For the ninth school year of German, Wolf proposed reading Baumbach; *Bernhardts Novellenbibliothek;* Freytag; *Hoffmanns historische Erzählungen;* Schiller's *Der Neffe als Onkel, Lied von der Glocke,* and ballads. For memorization, poems of Chamisso, Bürger, Müller, Droste-Hülshoff, Rückert, Kerner, Freiligrath, Mosen, Heine, Goethe, and Schiller.
4 See Crane for extensive discussion of this issues of electronic libraries and proposals for their development.
5 For a detailed discussion of the issues of electronic libraries and accessible texts in the humanities, see Hockey.
6 E-mail communication with the editors of the *Women in German Yearbook* 12 February 1989.

Publishing in Germanics: Dissemination, Legitimation, and Validation of Scholarly Communication

MARK W. RECTANUS

> In the concluding paragraph of its mission statement, a major university press presents the following scenario: If the university presses vanished, scholarly communication in the liberal arts, and particularly in the humanities and social sciences, would shrivel; the system for granting academic promotions and tenure would collapse; graduate and upper-level courses would lack texts; and academic libraries would be faced, in many fields, with a sudden shortage of new materials.
>
> (Duke University Press 2)

Despite a heavy dose of hyperbole in this "vision of doom" for scholarly communication, its placement within a mission statement reflects the increasing pressures many university presses encounter in their efforts to maintain fiscal stability and institutional legitimacy. The message to the scholarly audience is clear. Scholarly presses (i.e., both university and independent presses) play a pivotal role in shaping the humanities and, incidentally, therefore, the discipline of Germanics. They publish and promote the books which in turn communicate much of our research and represent significant portions of our careers, both in terms of time and the more intangible "intellectual and cultural capital."

In this sense, scholarly publishing and the book medium perform multiple functions. First, with respect to media use, the book has maintained its historical function within the humanities (particularly in literary scholarship) as a primary *source of text material* (film notwithstanding). Second, books (and journals) remain the main channel for *disseminating scholarly research* (Walker 37), although many Germanists conduct research on texts (in the broader use of the term) in audio-visual or electronic formats. Third, the book is associated with *positive image* factors among academicians in the humanities (L. Freeman 157, 162). Finally, scholarly monographs relate to questions of *institutional validation* (e.g., promotion, tenure, remuneration) and professional status, although they are not the only factors defining these relationships.[1]

While books assume a central position in the representation, legitimation, and validation of professional activities, academicians utilize a diversity of other media

within the contexts of their professional and personal lives. The growing importance of electronic media and communications technologies in our teaching and research continues to shape the process, and in some cases, the products of our work
in both subtle and overt ways. Moreover, "media culture" (Kellner 16) crosses
the artificially delineated boundaries of social interaction between classroom and
living room, teaching and research, or work and leisure. Certainly, media images
of academia and Germany in general, or the humanities and Germanics specifically, influence many of the institutional and social parameters within which Germanics must function. Although much of the research within the profession is
mediated by scholarly books and journals, public perceptions of Germany (and
by association Germanics) are communicated through mass media (television as
well as mass-market magazines and newspapers). However, the media reception of
selected books dealing with Germany (particularly those addressing the Holocaust,
National Socialism, and German Unification) has assumed a greater importance.[2]
In addition to the many other factors shaping Germanics (curricular, disciplinary,
institutional), future configuration(s) of the profession may also depend upon how
effectively Germanists (as authors) and their publishers can bridge the gap between
disciplinary and public discourse, both in terms of fostering an understanding of
the objects and products of our research and garnering interest in, and support for,
the discipline within the context of public policy (e.g., support and funding for
education and the humanities in the United States).

Scholarly presses already perform important functions by mediating the products of scholarly research to readers and publics outside of Germanics. However,
widespread media reception of scholarly works is, obviously, more the exception
than the rule, and a mass-market reception is not necessarily desirable or possible,
given the objectives, parameters, and interests of discourse within academic contexts. Yet there must be a position for books which operate on the boundaries of
disciplinary and public discourses, that is, works that evoke and engage both the
professional and public imagination and discussion while maintaining a critical
dimension.

At least in part, the future of Germanics will depend on how Germanists tra-
verse the distance between these boundaries (e.g., from the social space of the
living room to that of the university) in terms of engaging interpersonal, institutional, multidisciplinary, and public discourses. As Germanists, our classroom
experience at the beginning of each semester reminds us that American undergraduates will "vote with their feet" if the material is not made accessible to them
(Tatlock 33; Bullivant 109). In some respects, this recognition may mirror relations
with the university and the public at large, to the extent that they shape perceptions
of and interest in Germanics. If Germanists do not communicate effectively what
it is they do and how they do it to audiences outside of Germanics, who will?

Scholarly Publishing and the Humanities

In order to approach an assessment of the role of scholarly publishing in shaping Germanics we must identify the contexts which define this relationship. Such an assessment is, in part, based on the assumption that the boundaries, functions, and parameters of Germanics and scholarly publishing are clearly circumscribed or delineated. While many of the systemic characteristics of scholarly communication (e.g., editorial practices, peer-review mechanisms, book and journal marketing) are institutionalized, Germanics and scholarly publishing are marked by processes of reassessment and redefinition which problematize institutional or disciplinary continuity. By questioning disciplinary boundaries or responding to "market forces" Germanists and scholarly publishers are, simultaneously, seizing an opportunity to respond to external and internal forces shaping their respective professions. As a result, they are altering the relations between Germanics and scholarly publishing.

The first step in exploring the intersection of scholarly communication and mass communication is to understand the interrelationships among three areas: (1) the function of scholarly presses in the systems and processes of scholarly communication; (2) factors which structure the environment and process of scholarly publishing; and (3) disciplinary and professional discourses addressing the redefinition of Germanics. The sense of crisis in Germanics and a call to reassess the profession (e.g., Van Cleve & Willson) roughly coincided with concerns in scholarly presses regarding a crisis in the structures and systems of scholarly communication. In an issue of the *Journal of Scholarly Publishing,* Scott Bennett (Librarian, Yale University) and Sanford G. Thatcher (Director, Pennsylvania State University Press) addressed the need to "re-engineer" scholarly communication. In diagnosing the current situation, they revisit a 1979 national report on scholarly communication, which concluded:

> ... the various constituencies involved in scholarly communication—the scholars themselves, the publishers of books and learned journals, the research librarians, the learned societies—are all components of a single system and are thus fundamentally dependent upon each other. Moreover, we found that this single system in all its parts is highly sensitive to influence from two outside factors—the actions of the funding agencies, and the developments of new technologies. Given this interdependence ... it follows that the numerous problems which the system faces can be effectively solved only if the individuals working within one part of the system are fully mindful of the other parts before decisions are taken. (cited in Thatcher 198)[3]

Although recent discussions within scholarly publishing and Germanics have addressed different concerns and remedies, both discourses are situated within the larger interrelationships and dependencies among scholarly presses, authors, and universities, which define scholarly communication. While Germanists have seen the enrollments in many programs stagnate or decrease, their publishers have observed sales and consequently first printings of monographs decline over the past few decades (to under 500 copies in many cases) (L. Freeman 148; Meyer 360; Thatcher 201). Although I do not wish to imply that there is necessarily a causal relation between these two phenomena, I believe they do relate to the types of institutional and structural interdependencies identified in the report on scholarly communication. The manner in which communication within our discipline and about our profession is structured and mediated (e.g., through journals; scholarly and textbook publishing; professional conferences) also relates to the positions and functions of those media and institutions (e.g., universities and professional organizations) within the social context of a larger communications marketplace.[4]

Several publishing industry statistics illustrate the economic and structural characteristics of scholarly publishing. In terms of the number of *titles* produced, scholarly presses make a significant contribution to the publishing industry, accounting in recent years for approximately 17 to 20 percent of total U.S. book production or roughly 8,000 titles per annum (L. Freeman 147; Horowitz & Curtis 304). However, actual *units* sold represent a much smaller proportion of book production because of the relatively low printings of scholarly works. Moreover, income reported by scholarly presses only accounts for about 2 percent of all publishing revenue in the United States. As Freeman observes: "It is this gap between revenue and units [i.e., title production] that is at the heart of the university press publishing enterprise . . ." (148). The gap is also apparent for most independent presses in the humanities, not just university presses.

Academicians are of course not surprised that their publications rarely approach best-seller status, although some titles do account for significant long-term sales as standard works. Yet the potential impact of scholarly titles and communication can be significant, despite the relatively small printings, particularly within disciplinary discourses. In research areas such as political science and economics they may have a considerable impact on public policy issues (Horowitz & Curtis 303). As a group, scholarly books may make quantitative and qualitative contributions to the communications marketplace, in terms of diversity of titles and issues addressed and the rigor and sophistication of their presentation. Still, in attempting to assess the potential reception and impact of books from scholarly presses, we must differentiate between and within disciplines and audiences.

Horowitz and Curtis identify four sectors within scholarly publishing: (1) university presses; (2) professional or academic divisions of major commercial publishers; (3) independent or "niche-market" publishers; and (4) professional societies, trade associations, or institutes (304). I will focus primarily on university presses and independent commercial presses, because they collectively represent a significant proportion of (book) publications and publishing activity in Germanics in the United States.[5] The historical mission of university presses frequently embraced the ideal that they should serve to disseminate forms of scholarly research which were not always commercially profitable. Consequently, they became a major force in humanities and social sciences publishing, beginning in the 1920s.[6]

However, this emphasis on the humanities and social sciences became more problematic as scientific and technical publishing continued its rapid expansion as one of the most profitable sectors in commercial publishing. Particularly during the 1970s and 1980s, scientific and technical publishers contributed to the rise in costs for library journal acquisitions, while university presses were challenged by their institutions to become more profitable.

The second sector (academic divisions of commercial publishers) is less common among U.S. publishers of works in Germanics than it is in Germany, where larger trade publishers also have academic divisions (e.g., Beck, Metzler, or Reclam).[7] To the extent that major commercial publishers in the United States have programs in Germanics, they are primarily within language-teaching pedagogy and language reference rather than monographs or translations. On the other hand, the third sector of publishers (independent or niche-market presses) in Germanics, such as Ariadne Press, Camden House, or Continuum, have performed critical functions by publishing a rather large number of new titles, despite their relatively small size compared to that of many university presses. The "independents" have frequently recognized areas that have been overlooked or underrepresented within university press programs and structured their offerings accordingly (e.g., Ariadne's program in Austrian literature). But they are not simply responding to a market niche. Publishers and editors at independent presses are frequently Germanists or humanists, who possess subject-area expertise combined with a keen sense of reader interests.

Finally, the fourth sector (professional societies and organizations) is particularly involved in publishing scholarly journals, professional newsletters, and reference works in Germanics. The publications of the Modern Language Association (MLA), the American Association of Teachers of German (AATG), and the German Studies Association (GSA) provide a collective barometer or "pulse" of their respective constituencies and memberships through their publishing programs, professional outreach (e.g., AATG regional workshops), and conferences. Book series affiliated with professional journals, for example, the *Monatshefte* Occasional Volumes published by the University of Wisconsin Press, augment communication within Germanics.

Networks and Dynamics of Scholarly Communication

Unlike our roles within the media marketplace—which position us primarily as "spectators" or "consumers" of mass-market electronic and print media—our positions within the academic marketplace of scholarly communication involve us in shifting (and sometimes conflicting) roles as researchers, authors, reviewers/ referees, editors, mediators/distributors, teachers/facilitators, readers—as well as consumers and "spectators" (at conferences). We are intimately involved in the production, mediation, dissemination, and reception of the objects of our research, both as collaborators and competitors. Networks and processes of scholarly communication are characterized by (1) the institutional parameters (e.g., organization, resources, rewards) which define the contexts of our research; (2) how we define the objects of our research; and (3) the extent to which we structure our research in response to institutional (e.g., universities, scholarly journals, presses, funding sources) and disciplinary factors (e.g., the production, mediation, and reception of research).

Many academicians are involved to some degree in all of the major functions of scholarly presses, which Freeman has defined as selection (gatekeeper), refinement (editorial), and marketing and promotion (151).[8] For the scholarly press, selection not only implies a system of peer review, it "includes the much less obvious process of encouraging, commissioning, and influencing what is actually written" (L. Freeman 151). The most visible form of involvement within this process is the position of the series editor, or general editor, who provides a key link between the programmatic development of the press and the dissemination of research on critical issues within the discipline. Leading specialists provide the press validation and legitimation by lending their names to series as editors, and in return they are linked with the positive (or negative) images associated with one or more (un)successful series. Series editors, editorial or advisory boards, and less formally constituted pools of area specialists are instrumental in identifying and suggesting new projects and encouraging colleagues to consider submitting their manuscripts for publication. Editorial boards represent both formal and informal channels of communication within and between disciplines and with scholarly presses.

Although academicians are most extensively involved in the selection function of scholarly communication (both in book and journal publishing), they also participate to some degree in refinement. Series or freelance editors may be involved in the initial stages of editorial refinement, particularly with works that are under contract but have not yet been completed. Pressures to reduce editorial development costs have led some independent and university presses to shift editorial responsibilities to authors and/or freelance editors.[9] While requests from publishers for final manuscript in the form of camera-ready copy has, in some respects, been advantageous to authors and publishers, this process also places greater responsibility and costs (i.e., time and equipment) on authors.[10]

The process of scholarly communications also implicates academicians in marketing and promotion. While publishers perform the most visible functions of advertising, promoting, and selling books to libraries, colleagues, and to the trade, Germanists are also involved in less overt forms of promotion and mediation as a result of their activities within the academic marketplace. Book reviews in leading scholarly journals are one of the most important forms of mediation between authors and readers within and between disciplines. Positive reviews in influential journals or newspapers (*New York Times Book Review,* the *Washington Post Commentary,* and the *New York Review of Books*) are quoted in publishers' advertisements as trade promotion.

Reviews serve multiple functions by facilitating communication and research, providing institutional validation (e.g., citations for promotion and tenure), and simultaneously promoting the image of publishers, series, and authors. Book prizes and conference activities represent additional forms of indirect promotion and institutional validation for publishers and authors within the context of an academic marketplace which Andrew Wernick calls "the promotional university" (168–69).

What can we conclude regarding the functions of scholarly presses and the process of scholarly communication? Because scholarly publishing involves a relatively well-defined audience of both authors and readers who participate (individually and collectively) to varying degrees in the selection, mediation, and reception of their own research production, the notion of the publisher as gatekeeper may be more applicable to trade publishing (which is oriented to book-chain sales and the author's marketability) than scholarly publishing (based on specialized reviews of content). Although scholarly presses have final approval for book contracts, they rely considerably upon the expertise of specialists. Scholarly series directed by leading specialists are granted a high degree of autonomy.[11] However, series editors must work within the thematic and budgetary parameters established for the program area. The series will be financially successful to the extent that series editors and referees can recognize and mediate the research interests of a significant segment of the professional audience and integrate them into the series.

Thus, the relations among authors, editors, book reviewers, and readers on the one hand, and their interaction with scholarly presses on the other, are marked by a high degree of collaboration, but also by a dynamic tension emanating from their mutual dependency within the network of scholarly communication and the academic marketplace. For academicians, this dependency revolves around various forms of institutional validation such as promotion and tenure, grants, or appointments (e.g., endowed chairs) which are inextricably linked to publications in journals and books. For the presses, the dependency relates to *both* the economic validation provided by access to, and the acceptance of, professional audiences. The profession's recognition of a book's contribution to research is translated into market acceptance (book sales). The press translates sales back into a form of cultural validation, which is used to represent its institutional legitimacy to governing boards, politicians, readers, or investors (in the case of commercial publishers). Economic and cultural validation are crucial factors in ensuring the ongoing legitimacy of all scholarly presses, but they are particularly important for university presses in retaining institutional support.

Issues in Scholarly Publishing:
Implications for the Humanities and Germanics

We turn now to key issues defining scholarly publishing and then examine how some interdependencies may affect Germanics as a discipline. In "What Is a University Press," Sheldon Meyer (Oxford University Press) and Leslie Phillabaum (Louisiana State University Press) write:

> The single greatest problem facing university presses is financing. Scholarly publishing is subsidized publishing. Even those few presses that receive no operation subsidies from their parent universities depend heavily on title subsidies to support the publication of individual books. It is simply not possible to publish the kinds of books that university presses exist to publish without financial assistance. Many of the best, most important, and most enduring scholarly books have never sold sufficient copies to pay the cost of their publication. (Meyer & Phillabaum n.p.)

Not surprisingly, economic pressures play a major role in the future both of university presses and of independent scholarly presses which lack the capital support of media conglomerates. Many series in the humanities and Germanics depend upon various levels of support from foundations or other funding sources. The Andrew W. Mellon Foundation, for example, provides support for publications in the University of Nebraska Press's *Modern German Culture and Literature Series* as well as the *Texts and Contexts* series. Independent presses also rely on some subsidies for specialized series. The *German Library* (Continuum Publishing) receives support for translations into English from the following public agencies and corporate sponsors listed in the series catalog: Inter Nationes, Pro Helvetia, Austrian Institute, Stifterverband für die Deutsche Wissenschaft, C. Hueppe Foundation, German Academic Exchange Service, Deutsche Bank, Doenne and Hellwig GmbH and Co KG, Heidelberger Zement AG, Lufthansa, Marie Baier Foundation, Mercedes Benz Foundation of North America, Inc., Robert Bosch Jubiläumsstiftung, Siemens Corporation, and others. Although this number of sponsors for a series in Germanics is quite unusual, in Germany many series, annuals, bibliographies, and *Festschriften* are partially funded through combinations of public and private support, or under the editorship of research institutes.[12]

Publishing costs may also be underwritten more directly by authors, who in turn request subventions from their institutions. Whether institutions are able to fund such requests and at what levels, is another question. While most scholarly presses do not request substantial contributions toward manufacturing costs, a trend toward more and higher subsidies for books that do not reach large markets is apparent. Presses in Germanics that request subventions from authors (and/or their institutions) generally require support within the range of $500 to $2,000, which is consistent with the humanities in general.[13] For monographs with a limited audience, authors must relinquish royalties, or receive them only after their book reaches break-even points. Although few authors expect significant royalties from scholarly monographs, presses will probably respond to economic pressures by shifting their publishing programs to areas that can generate greater sales, rather than requesting higher outright subventions from authors.[14]

Another institutional force shaping scholarly communication and the economics of publishing is the role of the research library. From his perspective as a university librarian, Bennett identifies five structural weaknesses of university presses: (1) the economics of publishing scholarly monographs is becoming untenable; (2)

university presses do not participate in the more lucrative science journals market—leaving it open to commercial publishers—while concentrating primarily on their historical areas of emphasis (the social sciences and humanities), which are less profitable; (3) most university presses are undercapitalized; (4) faculty overlook university presses for networked communication; and (5) presses increasingly operate with lower university subsidies (Bennett, "Repositioning" 243-44).[15]

While most humanists (including Germanists), have experienced the painful process of selectively eliminating journal subscriptions from their library's collection at various times during the past two decades, the link between lower budgets (accompanied by rising journal costs) and lower first printings of scholarly monographs published by scholarly presses has not always been apparent. This nexus was underscored in a *New York Times* article on the state of scholarly publishing in which Thatcher and Walter Lippincott (Director, Princeton University Press) addressed the increasing economic pressures related to publishing monographs (Applebome A14). Lippincott observes that an average library may have spent approximately 70 percent of its budget on monographs and 30 percent on journals in 1975, but by the mid-1990s expenditures were roughly reversed (Applebome A14). Because libraries represent a significant market for first-printings of scholarly monographs, the first printings have been reduced to as low as 300 by many presses (Applebome A14).

With few exceptions, publishers in Germanics identify the decreasing library market as the most significant trend of the past two decades in scholarly publishing. University and independent presses in Germanics indicate that first printings range between 400 and 2,000 copies, averaging 600 to 800 copies depending on the press and sales projections for specific titles. (Those presses with higher first printings also indicated a general decrease in average first print runs during the past decade.) Publishers in Germanics also report that 20 to 90 percent of first printings are sold to libraries; the lower the first printing the higher the percentage sold to libraries. In terms of actual units sold to libraries, these percentages translate to roughly 300 to 600 copies per title.

In order to achieve a greater degree of financial security, publishers have already adopted a variety of survival strategies (while carefully maintaining their image and legitimacy as scholarly presses). William Sisler (Director, Harvard University Press) suggests that scholarly publishers "embrace the opportunities that a continuum of [publication] forms can offer for diffusing their message" (55). Sisler uses Jane Isay's work, *Editors On Editing,* to distinguish editorial strategies among (1) scholarly, (2) midlist, and (3) trade titles. The editorial "mode" selected for each type of book is related to its potential market. Because specialized scholarly manuscripts (such as revised dissertations) are not targeted to wider audiences, publishers' expectations for first printings are adjusted accordingly. Midlist (or midway) titles "can appeal to a broader range of scholars and perhaps somewhat beyond the academy" (Sisler 57).

The market potential for some titles is so great that they will be acquired by leading trade publishers. Daniel Goldhagen's *Hitler's Willing Executioners,* for example, was widely discussed within Germanics (e.g., at the German Studies Association Conference in 1996) and in the mass media. The book also became a hard cover and paperback bestseller for the publisher (Knopf).[16] During the past two decades many larger university presses have made a consistent effort to "re-image" and reposition themselves as "boutique publishers" (Sisler 58) within the new chain super stores (Barnes & Noble, Borders). Commercial scholarly presses such as Routledge (a subsidiary of International Thomson), demonstrated that there was a market for scholarly trade texts within the chains (e.g., for cultural studies, women's studies, and media studies). Routledge has been successful in breaking into the trade market, and that success has included titles by Germanists (e.g., Sander Gilman's *Jew's Body,* Andreas Huyssen's *Twilight Memories,* or Jack Zipes's *Trials and Tribulations of Little Red Riding Hood*). (Scholarly presses have also attempted to enter the market with some success.) The sales and (media) reception of some works within the larger rubric of German Studies demonstrate that scholarly trade books can contribute to public discourse on Germany.

As universities increasingly utilize media promotion (e.g., college rankings in mass-market magazines, faculty in the news) in order to attract students and maintain legitimacy in public and private fundraising, the image and reception of faculty publications becomes an integral part of the system of incentives and rewards within the academic marketplace. Although few scholarly titles are "promotable" within the mass media, they are nonetheless produced, distributed, and received within systems of scholarly communication which cannot be isolated from the "promotional contexts" of the university or the markets for books from scholarly presses (Wernick 175).

Germanics and the Scholarly Press

Although U.S. Germanists publish extensively with presses in Germany as well as in the United Kingdom, I would argue that U.S. scholarly presses perform distinct functions by (1) providing high-profile validation for faculty within U.S. university contexts; (2) facilitating multidisciplinary communication within the humanities; and (3) contributing to public perceptions of faculty in the United States through the presence of their books in university, independent, and in some cases chain bookstore outlets. The image of Germanics and Germanists, both within institutional contexts and in the realm of public policy related to the humanities and language instruction, is shaped for better or for worse largely through the professional activities and publications which are accessible to our colleagues within academe and to various publics (e.g., the market for trade books). With few exceptions, the recognition value, image, distribution, and reception of books published by leading U.S. or U.K. scholarly presses exceeds that of German presses in terms of their potential to communicate with audiences outside of Germanics both within and beyond the university contexts.

The reasons are not just related to publication in English—for many German presses publish series in English or German—they are a result of the inability of most German scholarly publishers to gain a significant base in the U.S. market other than in libraries, especially in the more competitive trade market.[17] The importance of U.S. presses also relates to the increasingly inter- and multidisciplinary orientation of Germanics in the United States and United Kingdom, which has gradually influenced disciplinary discourse within the profession in Germany as well (Bullivant 105–10). As U.S. Germanists collaborate with their colleagues within the humanities and social sciences, both in multidisciplinary research interests and curricular development, they also communicate their research through a variety of publications (journals) and series (books) which address these interests. Discussions in Germanics regarding disciplinary or professional identity are directly linked to the formats and programs within which scholarly communication occurs.

A brief survey of scholarly presses actively engaged in publishing works in Germanics confirms the extent to which U.S. Germanists already publish within multidisciplinary programs, and the integration of these interests into series in Germanics. In the *MLA Directory of Scholarly Presses in Language and Literature,* 37 presses indicate publishing interests in German language, literature, and culture (including Austria) (265, 269). Of the 37 presses, 18 are located within the United States (not including subsidiaries of foreign publishers with U.S. offices). The majority of the other 19 are German presses, although several U.K. and French presses are also listed. While the indexes in the *MLA Directory* provide an indication of presses with ongoing interests in Germanics, the listings are not comprehensive in the sense that many other presses publish works in Germanics, but do not appear in area-related entries because many books are inter- or multidisciplinary in scope. Numerous titles in Germanics are published within general series which are not specific to a particular language or culture (e.g., European literature, film, literary theory). In terms of quantitative production (annual title output) and continuous publishing activity, there are, however, some presses which emerge with program emphases in Germanics:

- Ariadne Press (*Studies in Austrian Literature, Culture, and Thought*)
- Camden House (*Studies in German Literature, Linguistics, and Culture; Literary Criticism in Perspective*)
- Continuum (*The German Library*)[18]
- University of Michigan Press (*Social History, Popular Culture, and Politics in Germany*)
- University of Nebraska Press (*Modern German Culture and Literature Series; Texts and Contexts Series*)
- University of North Carolina Press (*University of North Carolina Studies in the Germanic Languages and Literatures*)
- Wayne State University Press (*Kritik: German Literary Theory and Cultural Studies*)

Among independent scholarly presses, Ariadne (est. 1989) and Camden House (est. 1979) have published significant numbers of monographs during the past decade. Ariadne produces approximately 18 titles annually (Harner 16). Camden House publishes roughly 26 to 30 new titles each year in Germanics and that number has increased significantly during the past decade. Both publishers have contributed to scholarly communication in Germanics through series, which are now well established and widely reviewed in professional journals. Their focus on several core publishing areas (in this case Germanics) is an economic necessity, but also a market advantage. A larger title production for series (compared to university presses) generates a greater market presence which reinforces the series profile. However, university presses have a competitive edge over independent presses in terms of extensive back lists, tax-exempt status, and institutional support, although many have had to become more self-sufficient during the past decade.

Among university publishers, the University of Nebraska Press (est. 1941) has reinforced its significant presence in Germanics with two series, one of which is specifically oriented to Germanics (publishing four to six titles annually). The University of Michigan Press (est. 1930) and Wayne State University Press (est. 1941) have maintained continuous publishing programs in Germanics, but with somewhat lower levels of title production—approximately four titles annually from Michigan and two to three from Wayne State. Although Princeton (est. 1905) does not have a series in Germanics, it publishes roughly five to 15 titles in German Studies. However, it also includes German history in this area, which accounts for the higher number of publications. Publishers with active programs in Germanics indicate that the number of proposals and manuscript submissions in Germanics has increased during the past decade while the number of titles published in Germanics has, for the most part, remained constant. This trend probably reflects increased competition among academicians to publish monographs with leading presses in Germanics and within the humanities.

We can approach a more accurate picture of the breadth and depth of scholarly communication and press production in Germanics if we include inter- and multidisciplinary series and general thematic emphases such as cultural studies, feminist criticism and women's studies, film and media studies, folklore, Jewish Studies and Holocaust Studies, literary theory and criticism, multicultural studies, philosophy and literature, postcolonial studies, and translations of German theory, criticism, and literature. Thus, significant books dealing with issues central to Germanics are also published by the following presses: University of California Press (1893), University of Chicago Press (1891), Columbia University Press (1893), Cornell University Press (1869), Harvard University Press (1913), Indiana University Press (1950), Johns Hopkins University Press (1878), University of Massachusetts Press (1964), Unversity of Minnesota Press (1927), University of Pennsylvania Press (1922), Stanford University Press (1925), State University of New York Press (1965), University of Texas Press (1950), and University of Wisconsin Press (1937).[19] These presses publish up to four books related to Germanics each year, but present them primarily within the contexts of other series (e.g., film, women's studies, theory and criticism). Most indicate that new curricular initiatives in these areas have had a considerable impact in realigning publishing programs and series to meet research and teaching interests.

In general, monographs account for 50 to 85 percent of publishing programs in Germanics, with translations, revised dissertations, anthologies, conference proceedings, anthologies, annuals, and bibliographies composing the remainder, roughly 10 to 15 percent each, depending upon the publisher. Although many of the major scholarly publishers in Germanics include some translations of literature and/or criticism in their programs, several (e.g., Columbia University Press, Continuum, Johns Hopkins University Press, Nebraska University Press, Northwestern University Press) indicate programmatic emphases in this area.

Several U.K. publishers maintain active editorial and distribution operations within the United States, including Berg Publishers, Berghahn Books, and Routledge. Both Berg and Berghahn have series in German Studies with emphases in cultural studies, history, and the social sciences. Within cultural studies, Berg produces the *German Studies Series* and Berghahn publishes *Modern German Studies: A Series of the German Studies Association.* Both programs reflect the integration of scholarship in German Studies from the United States and United Kingdom, where there is a strong tradition of cultural studies, and market it in both regions. Similarly, Routledge is publishing a multidisciplinary *Encyclopedia of Contemporary German Culture* including contributions by scholars in the United Kingdom and United States. These projects seem to be a "win-win" proposition for publishers and Germanists. They provide the basis for a wider recognition (validation for Germanists) and expand the publisher's market in both regions by offering research by "indigenous" scholars.[20]

During the last three decades of the twentieth century, several historical developments within the system of scholarly communication and Germanics have emerged. The most visible force shaping this relationship since the 1970s has been the increasingly prominent role of U.S. and U.K. publishers.[21] Although the majority of publications in Germanics are still produced by German presses, research monographs published by U.S. presses have assumed a central position in shaping U.S. Germanics—particularly with respect to its multidisciplinary orientation. This can be attributed to several factors: (1) the continued programmatic growth and expansion of university presses well into the late 1970s, stimulated in part by the boom in U.S. education during the 1960s; (2) a competitive economic disadvantage for German academic publishers beginning in the early 1980s related to an economic recession in Germany, unfavorable exchange rates for German exports, difficulties accessing U.S. channels of book distribution, and cuts in U.S. library budgets; (3) an increasing awareness among U.S. Germanists of the unique contexts of U.S. Germanics as distinct from German *Germanistik* (McCarthy 6); (4) the reception and integration of multiculturalism and cultural studies into Germanics and German Studies in research and curricula, leading to a competitive edge among U.S. and U.K. presses in these areas; (5) institutional pressures and incentives to increase inter- and multidisciplinary research published by leading university presses, and a wider media reception.[22] In the United States, most of the scholarly presses active in Germanics identified above adjusted their programs and series according to these market and disciplinary shifts. While some presses recognized the expanded markets for multidisciplinary research by embracing the "margins," others, particularly independent presses played an important role in Germanics by disseminating monographs and reference works within the "core" discipline. Finally, Germanics, like other humanities disciplines, reflects the information explosion during the late twentieth century. Scholarly communication of all types, facilitated by presses and journals, is an essential component of the profession's "infrastructure." However, the academic marketplace (e.g., competition for jobs, promotion, and tenure) and demands for institutional or professional validation ("publish or perish") also, incrementally, contribute to the relativization and rapid obsolescence of scholarly communication.

Thus, the impact of scholarly publishing on Germanics has been cumulative. No single press or publication can claim a defining or pivotal position. Indeed, this analysis indicates that Germanics and the institutionalized systems of scholarly communication are inextricably intertwined within complex networks of dependency or "synergy." More important, however, is the degree to which Germanists collectively shape the contents and processes of scholarly communication, functioning as producers, mediators, and consumers of scholarly information. Although we undoubtedly respond, consciously or unconsciously, to the products of and markets for scholarly communication, we also play an essential role in shaping these processes and products. It has become critical to recognize and define our own positions within these complexes. These positions relate to (1) individual and collective dependencies which can be productively engaged through collaborative networks; and (2) the potential to redefine and activate our positions within the systems and institutions of scholarly communication, including but not limited to Germanics, in order to engage publics outside of the discipline.

Transitions

As Germanics enters the twenty-first century, one of the issues that will shape scholarly communication is electronic publishing. As Wolfgang Frühwald has observed, many of the predictions are at present "science fiction" (84–85), but we have considerable evidence that electronic communication has already changed the manner in which we conduct and produce our research. Electronic publishing is an issue occupying much of the professional discourse both in the United States and Germany, among trade and scholarly publishers.[23] Professional organizations (AATG and MLA) are utilizing the internet and World Wide Web (WWW) to communicate with their constituencies, who in turn develop their own web sites and news groups to facilitate communication on areas of research or teaching interest.

Even more essential is our reliance on electronic data retrieval and information processing for conducting research. The issues obviously extend far beyond the parameters of this analysis. What has become clear is the complexity of interrelationships among communication technologies, their mediation, and contexts of use and/or reception.

Scholarly presses agree that various forms of electronic publishing, that is, information/content production, distribution/dissemination, and retrieval, are inevitable, particularly for journals (Hurtado 201–13). For existing professional journals, there will most likely be a gradual evolution to both print and electronic formats.[24] With respect to book publication, the picture is, however, not quite as clear. Presses in Germanics do not foresee electronic dissemination of their scholarly monographs in the near future, with the exception of some text editions on CD-ROM.[25] If and when humanities monographs are published in electronic formats, the change will be incremental. Scholarly publishers also express doubts with regard to the purported cost savings of electronic publishing and suggest that it is more accurate to speak in terms of "cost-shifting" rather than cost savings.[26]

At the outset, I suggested that the book, and by association, the scholarly press, assumed a pivotal position within the humanities. The materiality of the book has retained a privileged position as a medium of scholarly communication and as a form of recognition and validation for professional advancement (Okerson 195–96). Electronic publishing will only be embraced fully by humanists if institutional and professional forms of validation and prestige equivalent to those enjoyed by the book are established. But this process would simultaneously entail a cultural shift among academicians who would grant electronic media equal status with the bound volume of their research on the bookshelf. However, the history of media use suggests a process of "complementarity," whereby media (e.g., multimedia formats) complement each other, rather than substitution or replacement (Saxer 673–85). It is more likely that humanists will research and publish in both electronic and print formats. Within the somewhat nearer future, one of the paradoxes of media use in Germanics will be our use of electronic media to conduct and write research, instruct classes, and communicate within and across disciplines via electronic journals and news groups, while disseminating the results of major research projects via scholarly monographs in book format.

The somewhat paradoxical nature of media use in Germanics and the humanities also relates in a different fashion to the intersection of scholarly communication and mass communication, or how and what we as a profession communicate with/to various publics, audiences, and interest groups. There is increasing consensus within the AATG and MLA that language teachers and scholars must improve public relations efforts, in part by utilizing targeted mass media to communicate information about the profession (Byrnes 253–55; Franklin 5).

Among most segments of the public, the book medium retains a high level of recognition and prestige. Both scholarly and trade books might be used more effectively to "exploit our academic strengths" (Sisler 57) within the media marketplace. While I am not suggesting that it is appropriate or even desirable to instrumentalize our research as public relations vehicles, I propose that we work in collaboration with scholarly presses and professional organizations to promote our own interests, both individually and as a profession. We need to examine the intersection of scholarly communication and mass communication. By seeking suitable formats and venues to present or mediate our books to publics outside of Germanics and academia, we can attempt to more fully engage and participate in public discourses which are dramatically shaping Germanics from outside and, ultimately, from within.[27]

Notes

1   While textbooks play an integral role in the construction and representation of Germanics, the processes of textbook publishing are for the most part structurally and functionally distinct from those of scholarly presses (Rectanus 13–18). These differences may reinforce the "split personality" (McCarthy 6) of Germanists with respect to language teaching and literary research. Although the institutionalized organization of the textbook publishing industry, as well as the distinct manner in which textbooks are written, presents significant barriers to overcoming this dichotomy, a reintegration of these two processes could lead to a productive reformulation of language and culture in both the upper and lower division curricula (Benseler 186–99).

2   Many of the more influential books in terms of media reception are written by journalists and foreign correspondents rather than academicians in German Studies. Three factors regarding publications by journalists are critical: (1) journalists have access to mass-market audiences and reviewing mechanisms (through professional contacts); (2) they frequently utilize styles and formats which are more compatible with mass-market nonfiction and are, therefore, more accessible to readers; and (3) they are attuned to issues which are of interest to readers and are also marketable. One example is the book by Marc Fisher, *After the Wall: Germany, the Germans, and the Burdens of History* (New York: Simon & Schuster, 1995).

3   Thatcher illustrates the lack of a critical understanding of the real interdependencies within scholarly communication by citing efforts by librarians' professional committees to make copyright issues the scapegoat of escalating journals costs in the sciences (198). Nor did task forces representing university research libraries and the universities themselves consider the possible implications of copyright revisions for scholarly presses or scholars in disciplines other than the sciences when they sought cost reductions for science journals through a copyright remedy during 1993–94. Here, Thatcher comments that: "A general myopia seems to pervade the academy these days, as, for example, when scientists take no account of the effect their publishing habits may have on the chances of their humanist colleagues to find publishing outlets" (Thatcher 199).

4   Here I am referring to the internationalization of the publishing industry, integration of textbook and independent publishing into media and communications industries,

and the de-verticalization of the media industry in general (i.e., economic control of production and distribution functions by media conglomerates).

5   Information on scholarly presses publishing in Germanics was gathered from two sources: Harner (*MLA Directory of Scholarly Presses*) and my own informal survey of scholarly presses in Germanics. My survey gathered current statistical information as well as comments on publishing trends from leading presses and editors active in Germanics. Some of the presses participating in the survey included Camden House, University of Michigan Press, University of Nebraska Press, Princeton University Press, and Wayne State University Press. This group also represents many of the scholarly presses with a relatively high annual title production in Germanics.

6   For a historical overview of university presses both in the United States and worldwide see Meyer 354–63, here 357.

7   The differences between the U.S. and German contexts are also obviously related to the positions of German and English as first and second languages, as well as the fact that Germany does not have a network of university presses, although many academic institutes publish research findings, thus fulfilling similar functions of selection and validation.

8   The notion of the gatekeeper, drawn from social sciences and communications studies, has been frequently applied to book research by Coser (esp. 17–25) and Altbach (274–75).

9   L. Freeman notes that this shift has frequently lead to detrimental results in editorial quality (e.g., typographical errors, stylistic inconsistencies) (151).

10   Some publishers have also responded to downsizing or "bottom line" pressures by reducing design costs, with corresponding consequences for the utility and readability of many books. Here, the responsibility lies clearly with the publisher (L. Freeman 151).

11   In some instances, press directors do not know how many manuscripts are actually submitted in Germanics because they are screened directly by series editors who are not "in-house." Of course, directors could determine the number and types of manuscripts submitted if they required this information.

12   Combinations of public (e.g., Alexander von Humboldt-Stiftung, Deutsche Forschungsgemeinschaft) and private funding (e.g., Bosch-Stiftung, Volkswagen-Stiftung) are utilized for publications from university institutes or series from German scholarly presses (e.g., Julius Groos Verlag, Peter Lang Verlag, Georg Olms Verlag, Otto Harrassowitz Verlag, Max Niemeyer Verlag, K. G. Saur Verlag). In the United States, series with a regional or historical focus also are also subsidized at the state and local levels or receive support from professional organizations.

13   Authors in the humanities may pay as much as $4,000 to $5,000 to support publishing costs for books at independent commercial presses, although this is somewhat exceptional. Because much of the research process itself is conducted under the auspices of universities and foundations in the United States and Germany (e.g., grants, sabbaticals, exchanges), authors and presses are directly or indirectly dependent upon external funding for publication.

14   The fact that relatively few U.S. scholarly presses publish dissertations (in contrast to German presses) indicates that this shift has already occurred.

15   Based on statistics from the Association of American University Presses (AAUP), L. Freeman corroborates lower subsidies for university presses. Presses received an average of 7 percent of net sales in 1993. External funding represented 4 percent of

net sales. For small university presses (sales under $1 million) the drop in internal and external funding was more dramatic (162, note 2). However, commercial competitors point out that university presses still enjoy significant economic advantages (e.g., non-taxable income and lower overhead costs) as a result of their nonprofit status within the university administrative structure.

16   Goldhagen's book appeared on the New York Times Best Seller List in May 1996 and on the Paperback Best Seller List during most of 1997. In addition, the book was widely reviewed in media directed to arts and literature audiences (e.g., on the Arts and Entertainment Television Network [A&E]).

17   German media and publishing conglomerates such as the Bertelsmann Group (owner of Bantam, Doubleday, and Dell) or Georg von Holtzbrinck Group (Henry Holt and Co.; Farrar, Straus, & Giroux) are of course involved in trade publishing in the United States.

18   Continuum's program is less relevant to our discussion of scholarly communication, because it is dedicated exclusively to primary literature in translation rather than research monographs. While the *German Library* plays an important role in mediating German literature in translation within the context of humanities courses, its reception within the trade market has been less successful. To the extent that German fiction is available in trade book stores, it is from major trade publishers (e.g., Farrar, Straus & Giroux; Harcourt/HBJ; Henry Holt; Random House/Knopf; Penguin), who are more effective in packaging and promoting fiction for independent book stores.

19   This information is based on book reviews appearing in leading professional journals (the *German Quarterly* and *German Studies Review*), publishers' catalogs and advertisements, and the *MLA International Bibliography*).

20   Many German publishers (e.g., Otto Harrassowitz, Peter Lang, Max Niemeyer, Stauffenburg) have attempted to bridge this gap with international series published in German and/or English. However, none of the major German publishers (including Suhrkamp during the early 1980s) have been able to establish series which successfully combine *all* of the following elements required for the U.S. market: (1) a distinctive and innovative series focus targeted to Germanics and/or German Studies in the United States; (2) strong editorial, marketing, and distribution operations within the United States; and (3) a back list of multidisciplinary titles in English.

21   Some of the data supporting this trend is based on information gathered from book reviews in leading scholarly journals in Germanics appearing during the period 1960–97. (See also note 5.)

22   Both the internationalization of most segments of the publishing industry (including scholarly communication) and the concurrent spread of English as a lingua franca (or *Wissenschaftssprache*) have facilitated international series and programs (Ulmer 99), but make it difficult to define the contours of Germanics based primarily on linguistic difference.

23   Publishing industry trade journals including *Publishers Weekly* and *Börsenblatt für den Deutschen Buchhandel,* as well as the *Journal of Scholarly Publishing,* report regularly on electronic publishing.

24   Some scholarly publishers also envision aggressive expansion into scientific and technical areas or consortia between publishers, libraries, and universities (Bennett, "Repositioning" 245–47; Thatcher 204).

25 Freeman points out that the speed or "front-end" time required to write, select, review, or edit research monographs will not be significantly reduced by electronic publishing and that most of the timesaving advantages of electronic production (on-screen copy editing, coding or correcting author disks, disk-to-film printing) are already being utilized by scholarly presses (155).

26 Some examples of cost-shifting include: authors are given more editorial responsibilities in the production process (thus reducing their time for other tasks); libraries, departments, and universities provide technical support, hardware, and upgrades for publication projects; departments and faculty pay user fees for electronic access and journal subscriptions (L. Freeman 156; Thatcher 202; Walker 41).

27 Rather than respond to external pressures, professional organizations have realized that we must also attempt to participate in, and inform public debate, to the extent possible. We must also be aware that many perceptions of our profession and our objects of inquiry (e.g., Germany and National Socialism) are integral to, and constructed by, media culture. In this sense we cannot avoid participating to some extent in this culture if we wish to communicate and/or mediate our profession.

German Studies as Studies of Cultural Discourses

JANET SWAFFAR

This essay examines current thinking about the future of German taught as a language and as a disciplinary component in college curricula in the United States. It then recasts proposals to reform our task from one of teaching the German language per se to one of designing strategies that identify discourse systems in German texts. The overarching goals of that design would be to help students identify and talk about cultural messages in the structures, signs, and play of texts: the speaker-positioning systems represented in the way those texts present knowledge. In essence, I propose revising our dual and duelling curricular goals of learning language and learning content. In a real sense, then, my alternative introduces the traditional German goal of *Bildung* revised for the American context. I am suggesting we teach German as cultural literacy, as a process of learning register and discourse strategies that are text-specific, not language-specific. Achieving this goal involves setting discrete language tasks and outcomes for the educated student that our current focus on language and content competency does not.

Lack of Consensus and How It Sabotages Students

Current proposals for the future of German stem from different institutional and disciplinary sources. Overarching the field has been a willingness to accept the various dichotomies of foreign language programs in the United States—especially the professional schism between those who teach language and those who teach content, be that in linguistics, literature, German studies, or interdisciplinary courses (Byrnes, "Politics"). Relatively few voices speak for the entire curriculum. In a recent ADFL discussion about the aims of foreign language study, Bernhardt points to the absence of a total spectrum of language and literature scholars from such discussions. The leading figures in literary, cultural, and linguistic studies tend to assume that the identity of a foreign language discipline emerges in work with graduates who already have solid competence with a language rather than in a course sequence that develops literacy skills to be taught undergraduate and graduate students from the outset of their language learning.

Today, then, the job of faculty in most post secondary institutions is divided into several largely unrelated parts. First, we teach largely spoken language in the first year; then we have students practice reading 20 to 40 short texts in the second year; and beyond this stage, taking a very small percentage of students who choose to pursue a language major or studies past an acceptable level of oral proficiency, we present them with classics or examples of discipline-specific prose to be comprehended via sophisticated interpretations. To graduate students we offer, in addition, theory and a variety of topical emphases, often largely written about and discussed (at least by those students) in English.

Responses to the Demographic Dilemma

The dwindling student audience for our current programs has lead to discussion about a change of direction in foreign language instruction in general and in German instruction in particular. In recent decades, numerous collections and special issues of journals have appeared that explore avenues through which to revitalize German departments (e.g., Förster, Neuland & Rupp; Lohnes & Nollendorfs; Lützeler & Peck; Van Cleve & Willson). One avenue that has enjoyed considerable support from NEH, FIPSE, and the American Council on Education (ACE) has been the emergence of interdisciplinary programs that integrate a particular content area with foreign language study (V. Nollendorfs, "Towards Guidelines"). While there are many ways to be interdisciplinary (see Brinton et al.), virtually all programs currently described as interdisciplinary anticipate initial years in which students study language before continuing on in applying that language to study in another discipline be it one in the humanities (Jurasek), engineering (Grandin), or business (Paulsell). The cognitive involvement with a topic that students can experience when using a language to learn becomes a delayed gratification.

Prestigious institutions such as Stanford and Cornell have responded to our disciplinary delay by implementing separate language institutes for the first two years of "rudimentary language instruction," split off from departments in various fields. That response is often dictated by financial considerations, because often smaller departments can be housed under a singled administration. For Spanish, awash with more students than available graduate assistants to teach them in many institutions, that solution barely affects upper division enrollments. Yet, for German with its smaller language departments and limited audiences, such separation has serious perils. Without explicit "bridging" mechanisms available to students completing a requirement outside a department, those students are not motivated to take advanced work in the German department, by definition an unfamiliar language learning environment.

If beginning language is truly taught as a process of acquiring skills of self expression about concrete subjects, students are not prepared and remain largely unmotivated to talk about abstract ideas, to continue work in a language when it shifts to third person reflections about content areas and to emphasize extensive reading and reasoning capabilities. Because it is disappearing from high schools,

German is no longer an option for students in institutions lacking a visible, co-ordinated lower and upper division program that offers appealing options beyond fulfilling the language requirement.

Few voices concerned with the issue "whither Germanics" have challenged the dominant view of our most visible disciplinary identity: that learning German in North America involves study of grammar and vocabulary for beginners and that our advanced students — whether they study literature, linguistics, or German studies — automatically apply such grammar and vocabulary knowledge to read texts of German origin for those features that shed light on the concepts of "Germanness" that can be identified in that text.

Problematics of Curricular Sequence and Cultural Literacy

Concerns about teaching how texts reflect societal consciousness motivate Berman's ("Global Thinking") proposals for a rethinking of the foreign language curriculum around issues of cultural literacy. Most German programs do not focus on courses that sequence consistent strategies for identifying and expressing ways in which texts suggest a particular grouping of German values as well as a particular choice of language. Conventional undergraduate sequences rarely exhibit a recognition that tasks for beginners and advanced learners can share modes of thinking about, for example, dominance, play, or ritual as culture-specific attitudes and behaviors toward social structures common to all cultures. Thus Germanists rarely commence their disciplinary project with an overarching pedagogical theory for teaching students to be culturally literate.

Yet applying theory to cultural texts is precisely what many of the most prominent American Germanists do so well. With the impetus of their insights into, for example, hermeneutics (Hohendahl, *Institution*), reception theory (Holub), post-war German arts and popular culture (Bathrick, "Cultural Studies"; Hermand, *Kultur*), cultural sociology (Ziolkowski, "Was heißt"), New Historical analyses (Trommler, "Resistance") and Germany under National Socialism (Hermand, *Old Dreams*), German scholars research and teach about how reader consciousness is constructed by texts. In linguistic studies, the work on sociolinguistics, historical linguistics, cognitive grammar and syntax and semantics all could, in the sense of Jakobson, inform the enterprise of cultural literacy. Our graduate programs are designed to produce Germanists who engage in precisely such styles of academic analysis. But the idea of making that training the basis for a German department's total curriculum would probably be alien to most of our colleagues in our own as well as other fields.

The pervasive idea that foreign language teachers of undergraduates are transmitters of language rather than guides to how language works in various contexts is reflected in the pedagogical disjunctures that characterize our enterprise. In practice, Germanists teach different languages at different levels of instruction, a fact we rarely acknowledge to our students or even to ourselves. Beginners learn everyday spoken language; intermediates, work with a smorgasbord of different discourses found in short texts; advanced students, engage in sophisticated reading comprehension and the grammar of comparatively long texts, generally those that present the discourses of high culture. Graduate students, trained in this inconsistent discourse sequence, perpetuate it in their curricular enterprise as the only available model for foreign languages learning (Swaffar, "Using FL").

But this upward hierarchy, supposedly well-described in linguistic terms, is fictitious from the standpoint of authorizing students' voices in cultural literacy rather than simply language skills. The purely linguistic hierarchy provides nothing to support discovery of the continuity or the use of context, genre, word choice, sequence and weighting of information that reveals how speakers and writers act as bearers of meaning. Yet early research on vocabulary acquisition called attention to the fact that different authors, genres, and disciplines use widely different words and styles. The effects of different disciplines is far greater. Even a change in topic equates to significant changes in word choice or register. An overlap in word choice and discourse practice will vary most between disciplines, somewhat less between authors, but even a comparison among works of a single author may reveal major differences in vocabulary. What we too often neglect in selecting and arranging texts for our courses is that disciplinary practice and authorial issues determine word choice, not the reverse.

It follows, then, that students in the second year, given textbooks with multiple short texts on different topics, by different authors, often in different genres and on different topics, are unduly burdened when they are not taught the cultural systems on which language differences are, in part, based. With introduction of a reading emphasis in the second year, German programs shift discourse levels from learning about familiar objects and events that are the subject of first-year textbooks to grappling with texts about culturally unfamiliar verbal or conversational systems — diverse literary and nonfiction texts written for native speakers of the language. Students lack the strategies to replicate the schemata of native speakers who, after all, understand not only the language but, just as important, the difference between fiction and history in their own context. With such a quantum cognitive leap, it is no wonder whatsoever that we confound all but the most intrepid or most highly motivated students and encourage their rapid decamping from further pursuit of German.

How Textbooks Perpetrate Culturally Sanitized Reading

I have already anticipated my point for education. To read texts as cultural documents, German students must be able to isolate a text's information or content, its word choice or register, and its rhetorical structure or discourse within a text-internal referential system. Each piece of this text-specific triad can be visualized as corners of a triangle. In the illustrative figure 1, explicitly stated written or spoken facts form the apex, the text-internal norms for the foreign language used. The

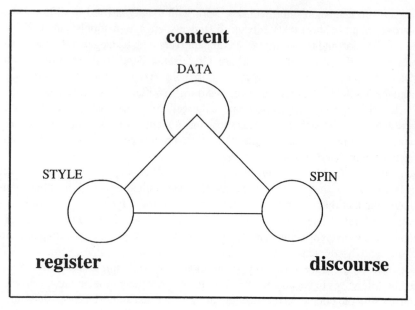

Figure 1. The Triad of Text Meaning

lower left- and right-hand corners represent text-external norms—the words and structures chosen to speak to the intended audience located in the time and place from which the text emerges. Meaning sits squarely in the center and is approached from any angle.

Understanding the words and structures of a language yields little meaning if students fail to see how this triad is at play in a particular text. A textual reference to Caspar David Friedrich's "Vorliebe für leere Landschaften" makes little sense without a grasp of that text's data (we are reading about how a painter depicts nature), its style (references to tiny humans and the mystery of life as themes preferred by the Romantics), or its discourse parameters (high culture for a German audience). Understanding these internal systems is essential for understanding the text's meaning.

Yet, as already noted, most textbooks designed to teach German fail to acknowledge the learner's need to comprehend texts as discourse systems. Our textbooks rarely link cultural and linguistic information as expressions of culture-based value systems, only as reflection of facts. Books for beginners focus on spoken language that refers to actual places, objects, and people. Thus, students have virtually no exposure to written or spoken language as a culturally anchored text, a discourse outside the learner's world, based on unfamiliar objects or mindsets. They have no practice reading a text, video, or web site designed to exert influence over German readers or listeners and to change the way they think about themselves and the world they live in. Generally, that type of text appears only in the second year or advanced phases of instruction.

Small wonder that many German language students are simply confused when the demands of elementary instruction change as the text types do in the second year and above. In the first year, learning German involved weekly chapters devoted to the vocabulary and grammar designed to enable talk about concrete events (vacations or holiday activities) or objects (clothing, home interiors) largely familiar to students. In contrast, in the second year and thereafter, learning German means reading many different texts, literary or nonfiction, with messages and implications embedded in largely unfamiliar cultural frames.

That sequencing necessarily divides language departments and its students into beginners acquiring a "person on the street" style of conversational skills that incorporate features of popular culture, and advanced students (increasingly small in number) taught scholarly approaches to understanding language, literature, and high culture. The first-year experience consists of "active" language use with teachers orchestrating extensive speaking practice in a range of surrogate discourse settings. The subsequent years have generally been marked by increasingly passive classroom interaction and little work on extended oral discourse. Reading is treated as an activity distinct from listening, speaking, and writing, when what it should be is the experience of expanding a linguistic base by understanding and recycling words and phrases that express the cultural base of readings assigned.

Our sequencing results in what Byrnes ("Future" 5) calls the "bifurcation of the curriculum" into language and content. In this way we shortchange our students' cognitive capabilities and deny them the use of German for *Bildung:* learning how to read texts as cultural documents that enhance students' knowledge and consciousness as well as their abilities with words. We have not structured their learning in ways that help students perform central tasks in literacy like locating how a text reveals what is true or untrue, reasonable or fallacious, present or notably absent for its German readers or viewers (Foucault, "Discourse"). In restricting language learning to first person communicative exchanges and the familiarity of everyday life in the first year, we enable students to do little more thereby than react to concrete situations.

Given a set of speaking tasks restricted intellectually to activities such as inquiring about train schedules or ordering meals, students' formal reasoning capability and analytical skills remain largely untapped and unexpressed in German. Inadvertently, then, we are teaching our beginning students that higher order thinking ability is largely irrelevant before one "knows" the language. Thus, we encourage students to think that explicit meanings of words are the basis for comprehending and functioning in the foreign language. Such practice actually deters them from thinking about language meaning as discourse specific—a fundamental precept of linguistic and philosophical study of language since the time of Saussure.

From an institutional standpoint, ignoring that precept is pernicious for language learning and particularly for an expanded view of German studies in this country. First, it sets up two-tier departments, implicitly assigning "pedagogues" and "scholars" to two putatively different camps. We separate "language" as one set of priorities from "content areas" defined here as traditional literary studies. Second, and as a result of the first discrepancy, students who continue beyond introductory language courses often experience serious cognitive dissonance.

The Cognitive Dilemma Posed by Textual Contexts

Let me restate the cognitive problem involved in a more formal way. As beginners, most German students have been instructed in the norms of everyday culture — German language exchanges typical in home, school, and work settings. These exchanges involve only a single use of language in the sense of Wittgenstein — ostensive reference to real-world objects, people, and events. In most textbooks, their task is to engage in speech acts that simulate concrete activities and familiar social intents: requesting a hotel room, engaging in polite pleasantries in social situations, or responding to personal questions. And just when our students start to get good at expressing what they want, think, and feel in foreign words, we introduce a new set norms to intermediate and advanced learners: a register of what Wittgenstein called verbal definitions created in a discourse arising from a consciousness and intentionalities that do not originate with the learner. We suddenly expect our students to apply language that has been used, heretofore, in direct discourse or description to cognitively (as well as linguistically) more complex constructs like planning, manipulating, or arguing a point of information.

When students have not been prepared to understand that the same German language can mean different things in different verbal contexts, this shift confuses. Reading, for example, about *Spuren* in a TV guide for Deutsche Welle does not involve, in any concrete sense, the "tracks" of Caspar David Friedrich (see below). A dictionary defines *Spuren* as visible traces left behind by people or animals: the crumbs we leave on the table, the "signature" of a particular political manipulation, the tracks on the path. When a speaker points to footprints in the snow, unambigious communication results. In the Deutsche Welle text, however, no such ostensive reference is made. We are only figuratively in Caspar David Friederich's tracks.

In that textual reference, redefining *Spuren* involves reading not only the whole phrase *auf den Spuren von* (in the tracks or footsteps of) but also reading additional phrases "Der Film folgt den Spuren Friedrichs: Vom . . . Geburtsort des Malers, geht es auf die Insel Rügen." The verbal system in these phrases turns Spuren from the concrete "track" to the abstract "search." Its interlocking phrases refer to having a viewer or reader "see" what Friedrich saw rather than tracking him in any literal sense. For Americans not familiar with the conventions of nineteenth-century romantic painting, that "seeing" often involves revising their vision of what paintings are all about.

When students have had no prior practice in manipulating such self-contained verbal systems (language systems that mutate across contexts from "track" to "search") in order to see how changing one dimension changes the way language signifies, they can experience a sense of serious linguistic inadequacy. They attribute their comprehension problems to failure to "know the language well enough" when in actuality their problem is cognitive dissonance. Those students have not been taught to read the register differences that emerge when the language of ostensive meanings-in-the-world graduates to language that is verbally (figuratively, conventionally) defined only within a text.

Consequently, the shift from the ostensive references in a factual description of Friedrich's life (one that might be considered appropriate for a beginning textbook), contrasts with the verbally defined language of aesthetic judgments in the Deutsche Welle text. Without practice with comprehension strategies, such discrepancies leave students at a loss. The resulting bemusement will be especially acute for those who know nothing about the high culture attributes of painting. Initial exposure to *Spuren* as "tracks" has not taught them how to substantiate the way language is verbally defined in written texts ("following in the tracks" as "in search of"). They have not learned how to identify resignified language by looking for a passage's internal architecture—its structure, sign, and play, as the title of a familiar article by Derrida ("Structure") has as its title.

A Pedagogy for Cultural Literacy

Such terms could apply to using such a text in a beginning language class in a way that would help reduce cognitive dissonance while teaching the language. Although even intermediate students might not understand many of the words in the German description, the text introduces sociolinguistic and cognitive norms identifiable as *différance* in the sense of Derrida. In other words, the consciousness conveyed by this piece and the longer video text it describes can be read not only for the details of its content, but for what is deferred in the text. In fact, what it tells readers is not as important as what it omits.

Awareness of what is omitted will involve pinpointing how the German text implicitly differs from American counterparts, and in what ways this text is different from them. A pedagogy based on reading discourse systems would focus on each of these in turn: (1) asking students to identify what is "put off" or deferred in the text; (2) what the text's construction implies about its audience (where it "begs to differ" from the opinions of a untaught audience); (3) what is constructed in a fashion that contrasts with treatments of similar topics and genres in their culture. The analysis that follows is based on the German text that reads:

> Caspar David Friedrich (1774–1840) ist der wichtigste deutsche Maler der Romantik. Seine leeren Landschaften, in denen die Menschen klein und unwesentlich erscheinen, sind gefühlsgeladen und geheimnisvoll durch das Undeutliche der Szenerie. Der tiefreligiöse Maler fühlt sich vom unendlichen angezogen; in der

Erhabenheit der Landschaft sucht er das Mysterium des Lebens. Seine Bilder er-
zählen von Sehnsucht und Vergänglichkeit. Er hat seine Zeitgenossen als "Metaphysikus mit dem Pinsel" irritiert und provoziert, er hat durch seine Bilder Diskussionen entfacht und geriet trotzdem noch zu Lebzeiten in Vergessenheit. Erst
mit der großen Jahrhundert-Ausstellung der deutschen Kunst 1906 in Berlin wurde
er wiederentdeckt. Der Film folgt den Spuren Friedrichs: Vom pommerschen
Greifswald, dem Geburtsort des Malers, geht es auf die Insel Rügen. Hier entstand
sein vielleicht bekanntestes Gemälde "Kreidefelsen auf Rügen."

Dresden, wo er viele Jahre zubrachte, ist der Ausgangspunkt für die Wande-
rungen in das bizarre Elbsandsteingebirge und weiter dann ins Riesengebirge.

What is deferred by this text? Given a checklist to choose from, students can
readily establish that text defers mention of the social or political conditions that
contributed to Friedrich's world. Phrases such as "sucht . . . das Mysterium," "als
Metaphysikus, . . . irritiert," "Vorliebe für leere Landschaften" "durch seine Bilder
Diskussionen . . ." all represent sign systems that focus on the relationship between
Friedrich's art and a particular aesthetic idea, not the relationship between his art
and his biographical experience. Naturally, "play" or degrees of flexibility are inherent in such assessments. Friedrich did paint real mountains. Some features of
his biography, such as where he lived and painted, will be mentioned in the text.
The issue is whether readers perceive that mention as focal or peripheral, dominant
or incidental.

Recognizing unfamiliar treatments. Reading for significant features of the text
does not, however, come naturally. Without training, a reader's presuppositions can
readily block perception of main ideas. For example, although biographical docu-
mentaries are a familiar genre on American TV, even PBS prefers distinctly personal accounts of events in an artist's life and paintings that result. Emphasis on a
painter as typical of what Americans consider a part of literary period (*die Roman-
tik*) or as a representative of metaphysical ideas may strike students as a distinctly
unfamiliar approach. Once aware of that emphasis, however, students can explore
its implications for emerging German nationalism after the Napoleonic wars via
a "Germanic" art that rejected the aesthetics of French classical painting—how
nineteenth century German culture differs from North American culture from the
same period.

What does this text's construction imply about its audience? If conducted as a
guided reading in class, even students with minimal linguistic skills can "read"
this passage to assess how the arrangement of information anticipates a particular audience (Swaffar et al.). American biographies feature people and places. Yet
purely in terms of references even a beginner could read, abstraction emerges as a
dominant discourse norm for this text. The first six sentences in this nine-sentence
description have many words with suffixes such as "-lich," "-heit," and "-keit,"
suggesting qualities or generalized concepts rather than concrete objects. By attending to the weighting and sequence of text information, readers can see how
discourse structure alters the import of content—how it argues for a hierarchy that

differs from a contemporary biography written in the United States. Abstract implications characterize the initial five sentences that precede factual observations in concluding sentences seven through nine. The initial focus of a reader is on Friedrich as a signifier for the identity issues that emerged in German consciousness at the time of the *Jahrhundert-Ausstellung* referred to in the sixth sentence.

Thus, if established systematically in individual assignments or class discussion, the text logic identified here might suggest to students that German audiences, at least those addressed by Deutsche Welle, view their artists in terms of artistic movements rather than individual histories. Whereas Americans tend to look at a work of art as a statement about an artist's life, this German audience is presumed to see Friedrich as the epitome of an historical era's idea. The text's discourse, however, argues culturally neutral content (Friedrich as a painter whose landscapes have distant horizons) as a specifically cultural significance (Friedrich the painter providing his German audience with a visions of their landscape as transcendent experience). This cultural literacy requires students to read textual differences not for language skill per se but to see how those differences privilege one point of view over another.

Rethinking the German Curriculum: A Pedagogy of Discourse Analysis

The pedagogy I have just described is not part of the ordinary curriculum. Even most advanced undergraduate German students have rarely approached a foreign language text from the point of view of an alternative audience or practiced sorting the internal coherence and weighting of information in a text—the kind of activity that reveals what those texts set out to accomplish or what a particular text says about its German readers. Even in upper-division courses for majors, students are generally asked only to sample or identify language details—using language to sample content instead of actively negotiating points of view about that content. In other words, because we as Germanists have focused on teaching language or content rather than on how to do things with language, we engage in entrenched curricular and pedagogical practices that sabotage our audience's learning. Learning that ignores the register and discourse of social and discipline-specific language use fails to teach how texts do things with words and how students can use resulting insights to become effective speakers and writers of German (Austin; Searle).

Arguably, current practice in Germanics, understood broadly as spanning the experience of undergraduates as well as graduate students, remains locked within a conceptual sequence that denies our audience's native intelligence and the higher-order grammar necessary to express that intelligence. Stated baldly, we want adults first to learn language as children do, then, magically, to do adult things with it after first or second-year training. To return to the main point: by focusing on language generation in early classes, we inhibit learners' use of prior knowledge and the reasoning processes most adults can draw upon to encode unfamiliar language. By emphasizing content learning thereafter, we inhibit learning the textual portrayal of content as cultural *différance,* as a multiple negotiation between text and audience. Language stays divorced from content and both language and content from the third point of my triangular diagram—from cultural context.

I suggest that our alternative and our challenge for the future is to rethink the German curriculum as *Bildung. Bildung,* after all, rests on the idea that students can use a foreign language to study government, history, social sciences, the natural sciences, art, and music because all such activities stretch the mind. The discourse style of a foreign language, read as a cultural phenomenon, inevitably informs and is informed by other disciplines: the content, register, and social skills of German and the way these contrast with English usage in comparable disciplinary settings.

This approach to integrating language and content learning as cultural literacy has enormous practical appeal for German departments with shrinking enrollments. Courses linking German language materials to aspects of the Holocaust or women's studies appeal to students. In an era when many students come to a college or university with preconceived notions about obtaining credentials in a particular discipline, interdisciplinary approaches provide a bridge to humanist thinking that may have been unfamiliar from secondary curricula. The humanist credo posits that successful problem-solving and creative endeavor arise from integration of many fields. That credo has a pragmatic proving ground if it is related to cultural literacy.

To foster the problem-solving and creativity that makes liberal arts graduates successful in many fields, the undergraduate curriculum in Germanics should be reconceived as providing courses not about the content of a culture but also about how communities within cultures evolve and influence one another: courses in German and European ideas, history, philosophy, architecture, music, and art. Students' choice of a course is no longer the choice of information within a discipline, but the choice of a syllabus that reveals how disciplines inform one another. Only at that nexus can students practice identifying how one content area uses particular structures, signs, and play in its foreign culture discipline or discourses.

In a history course, for instance, students can practice seeing what is not said (and speculate why) and what is different when the German army's participation in NATO is discussed by a German historian and a NATO commander. They can compare the two different disciplinary registers and two different rhetorical strategies dictated by the rapport they seek with an intended audience. To "read" either one, students need to be able to identify the phrases that tag each respective discipline and the structuring of information that reveals their discourse goals (Bourdieu, *Language*).

The Meaning Triad as Curricular Sequence

A German instructor situated in a school with a strong fine arts program might construct a course on "Freud's Vienna," one that offers information about city

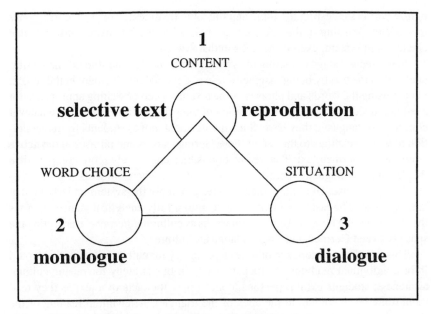

Figure 2. The Triad of Text Complexity—Stages of Student Control

planning, art, history, the emergence of Freudian psychology, and its links to Austrian literature and theater of the day. To be responsive to potential audiences in an institution with a strong architecture college, that same instructor might design a course entitled "City Space as Cultural Space," comparing Vienna and Berlin as great cities of central Europe. Such an approach would focus less on art and particular intellectual movements and more on contrasting public responses to the pressures of population growth and industrialization, thus appealing to students in urban studies, regional and city planners, and architects. The intellectual qualifications necessary to create either course would, nonetheless, be anchored in the instructor's grasp of the German language and culture, and eventually, in the student's mastery of language. A single context can, however, be the basis for multiple discourses and multiple ways of organizing "simple" to "complex" utterances.

Teachers of German literature and culture can forge these links by creating tasks that expand systematically on the triad of content, register, and discourse to incorporate discourse stages sequenced in terms of increasing cognitive complexity as shown in figure 2. The teacher constructing a sequence that will augment cultural and linguistic knowledge simultaneously must respect the alterity of the text's cultural world. Only in appropriate cognitive stages can students graduate successfully to increasing complexity. The cognitively easiest initial stage involves describing features of the text. For this task, readers need do no more than recognize words suggesting the topic and the topic treatment. This task corresponds to ostensive learning in that the student "points" to the linguistic constructs that create a sign system, even if the links in that system are not known.

In the second stage (isolating the style of word choice), the student can be situated within the text by being assigned a role or personal involvement in the subject matter, using the words and phrases of the text in speech or writing appropriate for a cultural insider, adding words and point of view drawn from the text to whatever command of language they have. Such involvement moves students from recognition of word meanings to the use of those German words and phrases in the fictive world of the German text. That realization is thus cognitively more complex than the demand for language reproduction in stage one, where students simply registered language use. Here they must register and apply the system underlying that language use. The last stage makes the leap to a fully analytical stance vis-à-vis the text: assessing how the sign system works as cultural *différance,* transacting the space between German and English language cultures.

This three-stage sequence outlines a pedagogy for cultural literacy that would inform individual readings. As their first step in this strategy for raising cultural awareness, students exhibit personal control over the facts of a text as they read them (they place content at the apex of the triangle). After initial reading of the Caspar David Friedrich text referred to earlier, they might, in class discussion, organize information according to categories such as statements about pictures and statements about actual places. Such a stage is cognitively simple, since it involves recognition only. However, unlike the more typical literal and linear readings that pull individual facts out of the text context into the students' textually removed context, cultural reading praxis encourages students to identify a coherent pattern of information in the text, as reflecting the text's cultural framework, highlighting the way a text organizes information as a key to the world of the text.

In a second stage, focusing on the assigned text's register, teachers might ask students to create monologues about textual facts, but in different fictive voices (as German museum visitors, as art students, as residents of the area in which Caspar David Friedrich painted). For the third stage, the practice of discourse levels and actual use of *différance* to privilege particular points of view, tasks must involve dialogic situation management—active articulation. Two or more fictive *personas* might, for example, negotiate an objective related to a second text or issue—comparing features of a romantic poem with one of Friedrich's paintings, considering whether or not German Romanticism has anything in common with its English counterpart.[1]

Dovetailing English and German Language Curricula: Emphasis on Cultural Literacy

The curricular approaches described in the foregoing, a mix of content, context, and some form of language study, present issues germane to German culture yet provide those interested in other humanistic fields with necessary connections be-tween present-day applications of their discipline and its origins in other times and places. These links can be forged by using texts in German or German texts in En-glish translation. In either case, the focus will be on culturally marked features of information in the sense of *différance* rather than information per se.

Course development from this perspective need look no further than those mo-ments when German *différance* has contributed to American identity. To mention only a few examples: émigrés such as Einstein, Menninger, and von Braun have dramatically changed institutions and research in the United States. Similarly, for the history of military issues and engineering, Germany and Austria-Hungary have had an illustrious tradition of exploration, particularly in Africa and the Antarc-tic (viz. Franz Josephs Land). Syllabi designed around cultural issues encourage students to use their cognitive skills in the service of strategies that unlock the unfamiliar—and to motivate them to learn about how discourse patterns can mani-fest alternative thought systems, whether those systems are expressed in English or German.

I mention these possibilities to illustrate the untapped resources available to those interested in integrating German across the curriculum as content, register, and discourse, not just as places where some texts happen to be written in a for-eign language. The achievements, ideas, and movements I refer to have arisen from interdisciplinary contexts in German. At the same time, they have influenced our own culture in ways that, because those influences have tended to be overlooked, become invisible, or remain largely ignored in sister disciplines. Consequently, the origins, the roots as it were, of much of American culture remain hidden or obscure, but tie into study of German conceptually and discursively.

Despite the rise of German Studies programs and interdisciplinary centers in which German plays a key role (e.g., the language centers at Harvard, George-town, and Berkeley), courses such as those suggested above do not characterize our curricula. "German for Scientists" rarely becomes "Discourses in German Sci-ence." Yet it is precisely course focus on how texts imply values and reflect cultural assumptions that can maximize students' prior knowledge, and reorganize their preexisting sociological and historical understanding. It can, thereby, move them from passively registering to actively interpreting events, individuals, and ideas that characterize a foreign culture. If initially exposed to such course in English, students are prepared to approach German language texts by employing familiar strategies. If, early in their language learning, they use these strategies to read German texts in the German language, we reduce the cognitive dissonance arising when students face new expectations in advanced course work.

Only a curriculum that presents the complexity of content and discourse strate-gies evolving from different disciplines and different voices as case studies in *dif-férance* can bridge the gaps among first, second year, advanced, and graduate stu-dents. Whether we construct our undertaking in introductory courses in English or German, if we fail to provide our audience with the practices of cultural literacy, with the discursive objectives and restrictions conveyed in a culture's texts, we deny our students their most valuable learning strategy: the practice that positions them to understand the unwritten rules of the cultural transactions which the foreign language conveys. Whether we introduce those discourses in English or introductory language courses, our goal must be to recognize that students whose native language is English can still learn to think and be effectively articulate in German contexts.

The Case for Coherence

The curricular project I envision involves a pulling together of the now disparate practitioners of subdisciplines in our field: linguists, literary and German studies scholars, and applied linguists. These specialists have to reconceive themselves as members of the community of scholars within the department and between German departments across the country. Indeed, in several respects such steps are already underway. The AATG and the DAAD have been collecting syllabi and making them available on-line. The AATG has an on-line discussion group addressing curricular issues and has published a major summary of our future needs in a recent newsletter (Byrnes, "Future"). The MLA is encouraging a forum for the voices of major foreign language scholars speaking on behalf of curricular revision (e.g., ADFL 1996). The stage is set for major rethinking of our mission as a discipline in the humanities.

The difference between thinking of German departments as teaching skills and thinking about them as teaching strategies for cultural literacies brings together the strands of diverse suggestions that characterize recent discussions among Germanists and foreign language teachers in general. It addresses what I see as the multiple disjunctures between beginning, intermediate, advanced, and graduate studies. By introducing into the total curriculum the theories about cultural discourse that dominate our research discussions, we enable our students to think about substantive issues in German culture. We help them position themselves in that alternate world. When such positioning starts in the first semester of language study, our graduate teaching assistants can, in their first and second-year language classrooms, apply the theoretical approaches to linguistics and literature they learn in our graduate programs.

If coordinated curricula are designed with these goals in mind, such teaching integrates learning about the language through concrete references to the real world. The same language defined in a concrete frame of reference is, in subsequently used texts, resituated in different verbal frames of reference. The allusions to rooms of the apartment the student lives in can, for example, be resituated by a text that presents "a room of her own" in the sense expressed in Virginia Woolf's essay—a virtual rather than an actual space. The concrete meanings (my study) become verbal (a space that is private, allows for personal creativity).

Such sequencing can also help students learn morphosyntactic features as bearers of meaning. When they learn how the linguistic markers indicating "before and after" dictate the organization of textual ideas (*jetzt/damals, nun/früher*), students are then positioned to identify shifts in tense and syntax that accompany such markers as meaningful. Recent research indicates that students learning grammar as a component of meaning have higher acquisition and retention of those forms than will students who spend commensurate time learning those same features by rote (e.g., VanPatten; VanPatten et al.).

Once they affirm *Bildung* as their project, German departments with undergraduate and graduate programs can rethink the emphases in their curriculum vis-à-vis their institution. To do so, they must recognize that the literary and linguistic theory of those programs must be acknowledged vertically and well as horizontally in our German curricula. What undergraduate students in German need from the outset of instruction is opportunities to develop their cognitive and cultural sophistication. What graduate students in German need to know is how to assist in that development—in themselves and in their undergraduate students. German departments must recognize that our job is to construct coherent programs that spiral learning. We must sequence undergraduate and graduate courses so that students can read and reread texts for content in conjunction with *différance:* readings to be expanded on by other cultural perspectives on the same topic so that students can identify how texts resignify their content through choice of registers and discursive rhetoric.

In essence, this proposal brings into reality the ideas of literary and linguistic theorists such as Bakhtin, Bourdieu, Derrida, Foucault, Jakobson, and Saussure, who state that the binary systems and voices of textual messages must be identified if the social messages of a text are to be understood. Our job as Germanists is to teach students consistent strategies and textually verifiable arguments that reveal how German texts resignify German culture and might reasonably be resignified by various groups, at various points in time, within and outside Germany. The student who can make such arguments in either German or English exhibits cultural literacy. Putting that style of education at their service is the basis for a pedagogy that can revitalize the study of German.

Note

1   A pedagogy of *Bildung* as a pedagogy of cultural literacy should also apply to English language curricula in a German department's interdisciplinary program. A course on the genesis of anthropology in a German context might, for example, introduce these ideas in using the English language but with selected German texts. That syllabus might commence with the travel writings of Alexander von Humbolt, then broaden to Humbolt's

influence on thinkers such as Wilhelm Wundt, Norbert Elias in the social sciences, or Ernst Haeckel in evolutionary biology.

For a humanities course with linguistic content, Wilhelm von Humbolt's work (Alexander's brother) is the basis for the insights of the later Neo-Grammarians, the academicians who documented linguistic change as a cultural phenomenon, the teachers of major twentieth-century linguists such as Saussure (1996).

Editors and Contributors
Bibliography
Index

Editors and Contributors

The Editors

David P. Benseler, Emile B. de Sauzé Professor of German, Case Western Reserve University. Editor, *The Modern Language Journal* (1980–93); *Bundesverdienstkreuz* (1985); Army Commendation Medal for Outstanding Civilian Service (1988). His most recent publication is *A Comprehensive Index to the Modern Language Journal, 1916–1996* (with Suzanne S. Moore, 2000).

Craig W. Nickisch, Professor of Foreign Languages, Idaho State University. Editor, *SELECTA* (1992–). Fulbright scholar. Published three books, two edited, and articles on German literature (Grass, Jünger, Dwinger, Claudius), culture, linguistics, and pedagogy. Author of German fiction and poetry. *Bundesverdienstkreuz*, Legion of Merit, Bronze Star Medal, AATG/Goethe Institut Certificate of Merit.

Cora Lee Nollendorfs, Professor of German, University of Wisconsin–Madison. Lecturer, Sommerschule Wust (Germany). Published Christian Essellen's *Babylon* and articles on topics such as Schiller, Edward Gibbon, Droste, German Studies in America during World War I, and German American *Heimat* literature. Editor, *Monatshefte* (1996–).

The Contributors

Arthur Tilo Alt, Professor emeritus, German and Judaic Studies, Duke University. Author of seven books and editions (Storm, Hebbel, Arnold Zweig), numerous articles on nineteenth- and twentieth-century German literature, Yiddish literature, and German Judaica; NEH panelist, Modern Languages, 1999; Elected Secretary, Academic Council (Faculty Senate), Duke University, 1998– .

Michael Berkowitz, Reader in Modern Jewish History, University College London. His most recent book is *The Jewish Self-Image in the West, 1881–1939*, and he is author of *Western Jewry and the Zionist Project 1914–1933* (1997) and *Zionist Culture and West European Jewry before the First World War* (1993).

Clifford Albrecht Bernd, Professor of German, University of California, Davis. Author of *Poetic Realism in Scandinavia and Central Europe* (1995), *German Poetic Realism* (1981), *Theodor Storm's Craft of Fiction* (1966); editor of *Grillparzer's "Der arme Spielmann": New Directions in Criticism* (1988) and *Theodor Storm–Paul Heyse Briefwechsel*, 3 vols. (1969–74).

Jeannine Blackwell, Associate Professor of German at the University of Kentucky, Lexington. Author of numerous articles and anthologies on German women's literature, fairy tales, autobiographies, and visions. Served on boards, division committees, and councils of the Coalition of Women in German, the German Studies Association, and the Modern Language Association.

David A. Brenner, Assistant Professor of German and Director of Ethnic Heritage and Jewish Studies Programs, Kent State University. Author of *Marketing Identities: The Invention of Jewish Ethnicity in "Ost und West"* (Wayne State University Press, 1998) and numerous articles on German Studies, Jewish Studies, and Holocaust Studies.

Margaretmary Daley, Assistant Professor of German and Comparative Literature, Case Western Reserve University, Cleveland, Ohio. Author of *Women of Letters* (Camden House, 1998) and various articles on German literature of the eighteenth and nineteenth centuries. 1998–99 Glenann Fellow. Two-time recipient of the Mortar Board "Top Prof" teaching award.

Sara Friedrichsmeyer, Professor of German and Head of Department, University of Cincinnati. Author of *The Androgyne in Early German Romanticism,* and coeditor of *The Enlightenment and Its Legacy* and *The Imperialist Imagination;* she coedited *Women in German Yearbook* from 1990 to 1998. Her main research interests are Romanticism and twentieth-century literature and theory.

Jost Hermand, William F. Vilas Research Professor of German Studies, University of Wisconsin–Madison. Published eight books on German cultural history from 1871 to the present. Other publications on Heine, Brecht, the German Jewish symbiosis, the history of literary criticism in Germany and the United States, and the liberal-democratic tradition in literature.

Patricia Herminghouse, Fuchs Professor Emerita, University of Rochester, Rochester, N.Y. Editor or coeditor of volumes on women writers, GDR literature, gender and nation, and German Americana. Articles on nineteenth- and twentieth-century literature and culture, German Studies. Founding member of Women in German; coeditor of *Women in German Yearbook* since 1995.

Gisela Hoecherl-Alden, German Language Program Director and TA-Supervisor, University of Pittsburgh, Pittsburgh, Pennsylvania. Doctoral dissertation on the impact of antifascist refugee intellectuals on American Germanics. Articles on the history of Germanics and language pedagogy. Coauthor of the elementary textbook *Deutsch Heute.*

Peter Uwe Hohendahl, Schurman Professor of German and Comparative Literature and Director, Institute for German Cultural Studies, Cornell University. Author of eight books on German literature and culture from the eighteenth to the twentieth century, with emphasis on literary reception and literary criticism as well as aesthetic and social theory.

Walter F. W. Lohnes, Professor emeritus of German Studies, Stanford. Head, Department of German, Phillips Academy, Andover, Mass., 1951–61. Stanford since 1961; Chairman, German Studies, 1973–79; Director, second-level NDEA Institute (Germany) 1961–69. Coauthor with F. W. Strothmann of *German: A Structural Approach*, 4th ed. 1989.

John A. McCarthy, Professor of German and Comparative Literature, Vanderbilt University. His publications include seven books (three edited) and some sixty articles on eighteenth- and nineteenth-century authors (Lessing, Wieland, Goethe, Schiller, Nietzsche), literary movements, genres, philosophy and literature, law and literature, the institutionalization of literature, and the state of Germanics.

Ellen Manning Nagy, Assistant Director of Career Services, Bowling Green State University (Ohio). She is the author of *Women in Germanics, 1850–1950*. Recent research interests are in the areas of professional preparation of graduate students and foreign language employment trends in higher education.

Susan Lee Pentlin, Professor of Modern Languages, Central Missouri State University. Numerous articles on language teaching and on the Holocaust. Grants from the Fulbright Commission (Germany) and the American Council of Learned Societies. Research Scholar, the College of Arts and Sciences; Appointed Commissioner, Missouri Commission on Human Rights.

Mark W. Rectanus, Associate Professor of German, Iowa State University. Author of four books and numerous articles, including research on the literary marketplace, international literary transfer and reception, popular culture, mass media, cultural politics, museums, and *Kultursponsoring*. Alexander von Humboldt Foundation Research Fellow.

Janet Swaffar, Professor of German, University of Texas at Austin. Wrote articles on teaching, teaching research, literary analysis, and the National Standards for Foreign Language learning. Author of a handbook on German literary magazines; co-translator of a Swedish novel and a German *Novelle*. Coauthor of several textbooks and theoretical works.

Frank Trommler, Professor of German and Comparative Literature, University of Pennsylvania, Philadelphia. Author and editor of books on modern German literature, Weimar culture, German American history and cultural relations, *Germanistik* in the United States, socialist literature, thematics. Director of the Humanities Program at the American Institute for Contemporary German Studies in Washington.

Gerhard H. Weiss, Morse-Alumni Distinguished Teaching Professor of German, University of Minnesota. Published widely on German literature and German Studies; former editor of *Die Unterrichtspraxis*. Past president of AATG and of GSA. *Bundesverdienstkreuz*, Federal Republic of Germany; Nelson Brooks Award for the Teaching of Culture; AATG Outstanding German Educator Award.

Helmut Ziefle, Professor of German, Wheaton College, Wheaton, Illinois. Five books, two edited, and articles on German literature (Hesse, Schwarz), culture, and pedagogy. President of the Northern Illinois Chapter of AATG, 1981–91. AATG/ Goethe Institut Certificate of Merit. Director of summer study program "Wheaton in Germany" 1977–97.

Theodore Ziolkowski, Class of 1900 Professor of German and Comparative Literature, Princeton University. Author of fifteen books on German romanticism, the modern novel, literary genres, and themes from antiquity to present. Past president of MLA and member of academies in the United States and Europe. Received Grimm Prize (DAAD) and other awards.

Bibliography

Adams, Hazard & Leroy Searle. *Critical Theory since 1965.* Tallahassee: University of Florida Press, 1986.

Adelson, Leslie A. "Der, die oder das Holocaust? A Response to Sander L. Gilman's Paper." *German Quarterly* 62 (1989): 205–9.

Adelson, Leslie A. *Making Bodies, Making History: Feminism and German Identity.* Lincoln: University of Nebraska Press, 1993.

Adelson, Leslie A. "There's No Place Like Home: Jeannette Lander and Ronnity Neumann's Utopian Quest for Jewish Identity in the Contemporary West German Context." *New German Critique* 50 (1990): 113–34.

Adorno, Theodor W. *Ästhetische Theorie.* Ed. Gretel Adorno & Rolf Tiedemann. Gesammelte Schriften 7. Frankfurt/M.: Suhrkamp, 1973.

Adorno, Theodor W. "Der Essay als Form." *Noten zur Literatur,* by Theodor W. Adorno. 2nd ed., ed. Rolf Tiedemann. Gesammelte Schriften 11. Frankfurt/M.: Suhrkamp, 1984. 9–33.

Adorno, Theodor W. "Sittlichkeit und Kriminalität." *Noten zur Literatur,* by Theodor W. Adorno. 2nd ed., ed. Rolf Tiedemann. Gesammelte Schriften 11. Frankfurt/M.: Suhrkamp, 1984. 367–87.

Aisenberg, Nadya & Mona Harrington. *Women of Academe: Outsiders in the Sacred Grove.* Amherst: University of Massachusetts Press, 1988.

Albisetti, James. "German Influence on the Higher Education of American Women, 1865–1914." Geitz, Heideking & Herbst 227–44.

Alexis, Joseph E. A. & William K. Pfeiler. *In Deutschland.* Rev. ed. Lincoln: Midwest, 1938.

Altbach, Philip G. "Publishing and the Intellectual System." Altbach & Hohshino 271–78.

Altbach, Philip G. & Edith S. Hohshino, eds. *International Book Publishing: An Encyclopedia.* Garland Reference Library of the Humanities 1562. New York: Garland, 1995.

American Association of Teachers of German. *Constitution and By-Laws.*

American Association of Teachers of German. "Membership Directory." *German Quarterly* (1950).

American Association of Teachers of German. "To the Members of the American Association of Teachers of German." *German Quarterly* 5 (1932): 51–53.

"Americanization as a War Measure." U.S. Bureau of Education. *Bulletin* 18. Washington, D.C.: GPO, 1918.

Angress, Ruth. Letter to the Editor. *German Quarterly* 57 (1984): 361–62.

Anon. Letter. 21 Jan. 1977. WiG Archive. State Historical Soc. of Wisconsin, Madison, Wis.

Applebome, Peter. "Profit Squeeze for Publishers Makes Tenure More Elusive." *New York Times,* 18 November 1996, natl. ed.: A1+.

Arndt, Karl J. R. & May E. Olson. *German-American Newspapers and Periodicals, 1732–1955: History and Bibliography.* Heidelberg: Quelle, 1961.

Aschheim, Steven E. *Brothers and Strangers: The East European Jew in German and German Jewish Consciousness, 1800–1923*. Madison: University of Wisconsin Press, 1982.

Aschheim, Steven E. Rev. of Daniel J. Goldhagen, *Hitler's Willing Executioners. Tikkun* (July 1996): 66+.

Athena. ⟨http://un2sg1.unige.ch/www/athena/html/swissaut.html⟩

Auerbach, Erich. *Mimesis. Dargestellte Wirklichkeit in der abendländischen Kultur*. Berne: Franke, 1988.

Austin, J. L. *How to Do Things with Words*. 2nd ed., ed. J. O. Urmson & M. Sbisa. Cambridge, Mass.: Harvard University Press, 1962.

Babbitt, Irving. *Literature and the American College: Essays in Defense of the Humanities*. Cambridge, Mass.: Riverside, 1908.

Baeck, Leo. "Vernunft, Gerechtigkeit, Vergebung." *Monatshefte* 38 (1946): 114–15.

Baerg, Gerhard. *Deutschland. Kulturlesebuch mit Übungen*. New York: Holt, 1938.

Bagby, Wesley M. *The Road to Normalcy: The Presidential Campaign and the Election of 1920*. Baltimore: Johns Hopkins University Press, 1962.

Bahlsen, Leopold. "Die deutsche Lektüre an den amerikanischen Schulen." *Monatshefte* 4 (1903): 165–76.

Bathrick, David. "Cultural Studies." *Introduction to Scholarship in Modern Languages and Literatures*. Ed. Joseph Gibaldi. New York: MLA, 1992. 320–40.

Bathrick, David. "On Leaving Exile: American *Germanistik* in Its Social Context." Lohnes & Nollendorfs 252–57.

Beall, Florence G. Letter to Susan Pentlin. 6 March 1981.

Beck, Evelyn T. *Kafka and the Yiddish Theater: Its Impact on His Work*. Madison: University of Wisconsin Press, 1971.

Beck, Evelyn T. "The Search for Language, Voice and 'Home.' " Klüger & Merrill 48–53.

Beck, Evelyn T., ed. *Nice Jewish Girls: A Lesbian Anthology*. Rev. ed. Boston: Beacon Press, 1989.

Behrens, Katja. *Salomo und die anderen. Jüdische Geschichten*. Frankfurt/M.: Fischer, 1993.

Belasco, Simon. *Applied Linguistics: German*. New York: Heath, 1961.

Belasco, Simon, ed. *Applied Linguistics: A Guide for Teachers in NDEA Language Institutes*. Boston: Heath, 1961.

Beloit College Catalogues, 1969–97.

Benjamin, Walter. *Illuminationen. Ausgewählte Schriften*. Frankfurt/M.: Suhrkamp, 1977.

Benjamin, Walter. "Das Kunstwerk im Zeitalter seiner technischen Reproduzierbarkeit." *Schriften*. Ed. Theodor Adorno & Gretel Adorno. Vol. 1. Frankfurt/M.: Suhrkamp, 1955. 366–97.

Bennett, Scott. "Re-Engineering Scholarly Communications: Thoughts Addressed to Authors." *Journal of Scholarly Publishing* 27, 4 (1996): 185–96.

Bennett, Scott. "Repositioning Scholarly Presses in Scholarly Communication." *Journal of Scholarly Publishing* 25, 4 (1994): 243–48.

Benseler, David P. "The Upper-Division Curriculum in Foreign Languages and Literatures: Obstacles to the Realization of Promise." *Critical Issues in Foreign Language Instruction*. Ed. Ellen S. Silber. New York: Garland, 1991. 186–99.

Benseler, David P., Walter F. W. Lohnes & Valters Nollendorfs, eds. *Teaching German in America: Prolegomena to a History*. Madison: University of Wisconsin Press, 1988.

Berelson, Bernard. *Graduate Education in the United States*. New York: McGraw-Hill, 1960.

Bergquist, James. "The German-American Press." *The Ethnic Press in the United States: A Historical Analysis and Handbook.* Ed. Sally M. Miller. New York: Greenwood, 1987. 131–59.

Berkowitz, Michael. *Zionist Culture and West European Jewry before the First World War.* Cambridge: Cambridge University Press, 1993.

Berman, Russell A. *Cultural Studies of Modern Germany: History, Representation, and Nationhood.* Madison: University of Wisconsin Press, 1993.

Berman, Russell A. "Global Thinking, Local Teaching: Departments, Curricula, and Culture." *ADFL Bulletin* 26 (1994): 13–15; rpt. *Profession 95* (1995): 89–93.

Bernhardt, Elizabeth. "Response to Claire Kramsch." *ADFL Bulletin* 26 (1995): 13–15.

Bernstein, J. M. *Recovering Ethical Life: Jürgen Habermas and the Future of Critical Theory.* New York: Routledge, 1995.

Bersier, Gabrielle, Yvette Brazell & Robert Holub. "Reappropriation of the Democratic Bourgeois Heritage: Leftist Research in Jacobism, Vormärz, and Naturualism in the Federal Republic of Germany." *Jahrbuch für Internationale Germanistik* 11 (1979): 102–21.

Biller, Maxim. *Land der Väter und Verräter.* Cologne: Kiepenheuer & Witsch, 1994.

Biller, Maxim. *Die Tempojahre.* Munich: Deutscher Taschenbuch, 1991.

Biller, Maxim. *Wenn ich einmal reich und tot bin.* Cologne: Kiepenheuer & Witsch, 1990.

Blackwell, Jeannine. "Domesticating the Revolution: The Kindergarten Movement in Germany and America." Benseler, Lohnes & Nollendorfs 99–119.

Blackwell, Jeannine. "Turf Management, or Why is the Great Tradition Fading?" *Monatshefte* 76 (1985): 271–85.

Bledsoe, Robert, et al., eds. *Rethinking Germanistik: Canon and Culture.* New York: Lang, 1991.

Bledstein, Burton J. *The Culture of Professionalism: The Middle Class and the Development of Higher Education in America.* New York: Norton, 1976–77.

Bloom, Allan. *The Closing of the American Mind.* New York: Simon & Schuster, 1987.

Blum-Dobkin, Toby. "Videotaping Holocaust Interviews: Questions and Answers from an Interviewer." *Jewish Folklore and Ethnology Review* 16 (1994): 50.

Blume, Benhard. *A Life in Two Worlds: An Experiment in Autobiography.* Trans. Hunter Hannum & Hildegard Hannum. Literature and the Sciences of Man 3. New York: Lang, 1992.

Blume, Benhard. *Narziß mit Brille. Kapitel einer Autobiographie.* Ed. Fritz Martini & Egon Schwarz. Veröffentlichungen der Deutschen Akademie für Sprache u. Dichtung 59. Heidelberg: Schneider, 1985.

Borneman, John & Jeffrey M. Peck. *Sojourners: The Return of German Jews and the Question of Identity.* Lincoln: University of Nebraska Press, 1995.

Bosse, Georg von. *Das deutsche Element in den Vereinigten Staaten.* New York: Steiger, 1908.

Bottigheimer, Ruth B. "One Hundred and Fifty Years of German at Princeton: A Descriptive Account." Benseler, Lohnes & Nollendorfs 83–98.

Bourdieu, Pierre. *Homo Academicus.* Paris: Minuit, 1984.

Bourdieu, Pierre. *Language and Symbolic Power.* Trans. Gino Raymond & Matthew Adamson. Ed. John B. Thompson. Cambridge, Mass.: Harvard University Press, 1991.

Bova, Henry. Letter to Helmut Ziefle. 1 May 1996.

Boyarin, Daniel. *Unheroic Conduct: The Rise of Heterosexuality and the Invention of the Jewish Man.* Berkeley: University of California Press. 1997.

Bratt, Wally. Letter to Helmut Ziefle. 4 June 1996.

Braun, Frederick August. *Margaret Fuller and Goethe.* New York: Holt, 1910.

Brenner, David A. *Marketing Identities: The Invention of Jewish Ethnicity.* Detroit: Wayne State University Press, 1998.

Brenner, Michael. *Nach dem Holocaust. Jüdisches Leben in Deutschland seit 1945.* Munich: Beck, 1995.

Brenner, Michael. *The Renaissance of Jewish Culture in Weimar Germany.* New Haven: Yale University Press, 1996.

Breuer, Mordechai. *Modernity within Tradition: The Social History of Orthodox Jewry in Imperial Germany.* Trans. Elizabeth Petuchowski. New York: Columbia University Press, 1992.

Brinten, Donna, Marguerite Ann Snow & Marjorie Bingham Wesche. *Content-Based Second Language Instruction.* New York: Newbury House, 1989.

Brod, Richard & Bettina J. Huber. "Foreign Language Enrollments in United States Institutions of Higher Education, Fall 1990." *ADFL Bulletin* 23 (1992): 6–10.

Bromberger, F. S. "Anton Zech File." George A. Spencer Papers #2466. Western Historical Manuscript Collection, University of Missouri–Columbia, n.d.

Browning, Christopher R. "Human Nature, Culture, and the Holocaust." *Chronicle of Higher Education,* 18 October 1996: A72.

Browning, Christopher R. *Ordinary Men: Reserve Police Battalion 101 and the Final Solution in Poland.* New York: Harper, 1992.

Bruch, Rüdiger vom. *Weltpolitik als Kulturmission. Auswärtige Kulturpolitik und Bildungsbürgertum am Vorabend des ersten Weltkrieges.* Paderborn: Schöningh, 1982.

Bubser, Reinhold K. "Speaking and Teaching German in Iowa during World War I: A Historical Perspective." Benseler, Lohnes & Nollendorfs 206–14.

Buehne, Sheema Z. "Helen Adolf: A Biographical Sketch." *Helen Adolf Festschrift.* Ed. Sheema Z. Buehne, James L. Hodge & Lucille Pinto. New York: Ungar, 1968. 3.

Bullivant, Keith. "The Americanization of German Studies: The Curriculum." McCarthy & Schneider 105–10.

Bullock, Marcus P. "Oblivion's Soldiers: The Postmodern and Poststructuralist Campaign against Images of Totality and History." *Postmodern Pluralism and Concepts of Plurality: The Twenty-Fourth Wisconsin Workshop.* Ed. Jost Hermand. New York: Lang, 1995. 27–53.

Butler, Judith. *Gender Trouble: Feminism and the Subversion of Identity.* New York: Routledge, 1990.

Byrnes, Heidi. "The Future of German in American Education." *AATG Newsletter* 32, 1 (1996): 4–8.

Byrnes, Heidi. "The Future of German in American Education: A Summary Report." *Unterrichtspraxis* 29 (1996): 253–61.

Byrnes, Heidi. "How Visible Are We Now?" McCarthy & Schneider 46–53.

Byrnes, Heidi. "The Politics of Curriculum Instruction: Enter Foreign Languages." Paper, MLA Annual Meeting, Washington, D.C. 28 December 1996.

Cafferty, Helen L. & Jeanette Clausen. "Journal Editing: Issues for Feminists." *Editor's Notes: Bulletin of the Council of Editors of Learned Journals* 9, 2 (1990): 28–32.

Cage, Mary Crystal. "Enrollment in Spanish Shows a Dramatic Increase." *Chronicle of Higher Education,* 18 October 1996: A13.

Cage, Mary Crystal. "Spanish, Si!" *Chronicle of Higher Education,* 12 October 1994: A15–17.

California State Board of Education. *Third Biennial Report 1916–1918.* Sacramento: State
P. O., 1918.

Calvin College Catalogues, 1970–96.

Campbell, T. M. *The Life and Works of Friedrich Hebbel.* Boston: Badger, 1919.

Cantwell, Richard. Letter to Helmut Ziefle. 3 May 1996.

Caplow, T. & R. J. McGee. *The Academic Marketplace.* New York: Basic Books, 1958.

Carleton College Catalogues, 1972–96.

Cattell, Jacques, ed. *Directory of American Scholars.* New York: Center for Electronic Texts
in the Humanities. ‹http://www.ceth.rutgers.edu›

Cernyak-Spatz, Susan E. *German Holocaust Literature.* Rev. ed. American University Studies Ser. 1, Germanic Languages & Literatures 29. New York: Lang, 1989.

Cernyak-Spatz, Susan E. "The Past Revisited." *Language and Culture. A Transcending Bond.*
Ed. Susan E. Cernyak-Spatz & Charles Merrill. New York: Lang, 1993. 103–10.

Chafe, William H. *The Paradox of Change: American Women in the Twentieth Century.* New
York: Oxford University Press, 1991.

Cheyney, Edward P. *History of the University of Pennsylvania, 1740–1940.* Philadelphia:
University of Pennsylvania Press, 1940.

"City to Burn Hun Poison." *Cleveland News,* 5 April 1918.

Clausen, Jeannette. "The Coalition of Women in German: An Interpretive History and Cele-
bration." *Women in German Yearbook* 1 (1985): 1–27.

Clausen, Jeannette. "Women in German." Unpubl. Report to the MLA, 1996.

Clausen, Jeannette & Helen L. Cafferty. "Who's Afraid of Feminist Theory? A Postscript
from the Editors." *Women in German Yearbook* 5 (1989): 131–35.

Clausen, Jeannette & Sara Friedrichsmeyer. "WIG 2000: Feminism and the Future of *Germanistik.*" *Women in German Yearbook* 10 (1995): 267–72.

Cleveland Press, 8 April 1918: 4.

Clifford, Geraldine J. "Introduction." *Lone Voyagers: Academic Women in Coeducational
Universities, 1870–1937.* Ed. Geraldine Joncich Clifford. New York: Feminist, 1989. 1–46.

Clifford, Geraldine J. "Women's Liberation and Women's Professions: Reconsidering the
Past, Present, and Future." *Women in Higher Education in American History.* Ed. John
Mack Faragher & Florence Howe. New York: Norton, 1988. 165–82.

Cohen, Wilbur J. "NDEA: An Idea That Grew." *American Education.* U.S. Department of
Health, Education and Welfare. Office of Education. Washington, D.C.: GPO, September
1968.

Concerns: Newsletter of the Women's Caucus of the Modern Languages 8, 4 (1978): 22–23;
9, 1 (1979): 26–27; 10, 2 (1980): 10–11, 31.

Conway, Jill Ker. *True North.* New York: Knopf, 1994.

Corngold, Stanley. *The Fate of the Self: German Writers and French Theory.* Durham: Duke
University Press, 1994.

Coser, Lewis A. "Publishers as Gatekeepers of Ideas." *Perspectives on Publishing.* Ed. Philip
G. Altbach & Sheila McVey. Lexington, Mass.: Lexington Books, 1976. 17–25.

Cowley, W. H. & Don Williams. *International and Historical Roots of American Higher Education.* New York: Garland, 1991.

Crane, Gregory. "The Perseus Project and Beyond: How Building a Digital Library Challenges the Humanities and Technology." *D-Lib Magazine,* January 1998. (http://www.
dlib.org/dlib/january98/01crane.html).

Creswell, John W. Faculty research performance, lessons from the sciences and the social sciences; prepared by ERIC Clearinghouse on Higher Education, George Washington University. Washington, D.C.: Association for the Study of Higher Education, 1985.

Cronau, Rudolf. *Drei Jahrhunderte deutschen Lebens in Amerika. Ruhmesblätter der Deutschen in Amerika.* Berlin: Reiner (Vohsen), 1909.

Crosby, Donald H. & George C. Schoolfield. "Walter Silz." *Studies in the German Drama: A Festschrift in Honor of Walter Silz.* Ed. Donald H. Crosby & George C. Schoolfield. University of North Carolina Studies in the Germanic Langs. & Lits. 76. Chapel Hill, N.C.: University of North Carolina Press, 1974. i–xxiv.

Curt, Paul. *Lebensbilder aus der deutschen Geschichte.* New York: Harper's, 1939. 1–36.

DAAD Syllabi Data Base. Online. Johns Hopkins University. Available: http://www.jhu.edu/aicgsdoc/daad/syllabi.htm.

Daemmrich, Horst S. "Die Germanistik in den Vereinigten Staaten." *Colloquia Germanica* 25 (1969): 316–32.

Dainat, Holger. "Von der Neueren deutschen Literaturgeschichte zur Literaturwissenschaft: Die Fachentwicklung von 1890–1913/14." Fohrmann & Voßkamp 494–537.

Dane, Gesa. "Melitta Gerhard (1891–1981). Die erste habilitierte Germanistin: 'In bunten Farben schillernder Gast' und 'uniformes Glied der Zunft.' " *Frauen in den Kulturwissenschaften. Von Lou Andreas-Salomé bis Hannah Arendt.* Ed. Barbara Hahn. Munich: Beck, 1994. 219–34.

Danneberg, Lutz & Friedrich Vollhardt, eds. *Wie international ist die Literaturwissenschaft?* Stuttgart: Metzler, 1996.

Davis, Elmer. *History of the New York Times 1851–1921.* New York: New York Times, 1921.

Davis, Todd M., ed. *Open Doors, 1994–95: Report on International Educational Exchange.* New York: IIE, 1995.

Dawidowicz. Lucy S. *From that Place and Time, A Memoir 1938–47.* New York: Norton, 1989.

Deihl, J. D. "Adjusting Instruction in German to Conditions Imposed by the War." *Monatshefte* 17 (1918): 128–34.

Deleuze, Gilles & Félix Guattari. *Kafka: Toward a Minor Literature.* Theory and History of Literature 30. Minneapolis: University of Minnesota Press, 1986.

Derrida, Jacques. "Différance." Adams & Searle 120–36.

Derrida, Jacques. "Structure, Sign and Play in the Discourses of the Human Sciences." Adams & Searle 83–94.

Deutsche auswärtige Kulturpolitik seit 1871: Geschichte und Struktur: Referate und Diskussionen eines interdisziplinären Symposiums. Ed. Kurt Duwell & Werner Link. Beiträge zur Geschichte der Kulturpolitik 1. Cologne: Bohlau, 1981.

Dimension. Ed. A. Leslie Willson. University of Texas at Austin. 1968–95.

Diotima. ⟨http://www.uky.edu/ArtsSciences/Classics/gender.html⟩

Dischereit, Esther. *Joëmis Tisch: Eine jüdische Erzählung.* Frankfurt/M.: Suhrkamp, 1988.

D-Lib Magazine, January 1998. http://www.dlib.org/dlib/january98/01crane.html

Doyle, H[enry] G[rattan]. "Foreign Politics in the Classroom: A Problem for the Modern Language Teacher." *Modern Language Journal* 25 (1941): 91–98.

Draper, Jamie B., ed. "Table I: Foreign Language Enrollments in Public High Schools, 1890–1990." *Foreign Language Enrollments in Public Secondary Schools, Fall 1989–1990.* New York: ACTFL, 1991. 8.

"Dresden 1945: In Memoriam." *GANPAC Brief,* February 1985: 8.

Dührkop, Gisela. "Zur Darstellung des Nationalsozialismus in ausgewählten Lehrwerken: Deutsch als Fremdsprache." M.A. Thesis. University of Hamburg, 1996.

Duke University Press. "A Snapshot of Duke University Press, as of 1996–97. The Press's Mission." Online. (12 December 1996). Available http://www.duke.edu/web/dupress/

Dunlap, Knight. "Value of German Language Assailed." *New York Times,* 2 December 1917: VIII, 9.

Eagleton, Terry. *Literary Theory: An Introduction.* Oxford: Blackwell, 1983.

Efron, John M. *Defenders of the Race: Jewish Doctors and Race Science in Fin-de-siècle Europe.* New Haven: Yale University Press, 1994.

Eisenstein, Elizabeth L. *The Printing Press as an Agent of Change: Communications and Cultural Transformations in Early-Modern Europe.* 2 vols. Cambridge: Cambridge University Press, 1979.

Eisenstein, Elizabeth L. *The Printing Revolution in Early Modern Europe.* Cambridge: Cambridge University Press, 1983.

Elmhurst College Catalogues, 1970–96.

Emerson, Oliver F. "The American Scholar and the Modern Languages." *PMLA* 24 (1909): lxxiii–cii.

Epstein, Cynthia F. *Woman's Place: Options and Limits in Professional Careers.* Berkeley: University of California Press, 1971.

Ernst, A. B. "Stella Hinz." *Monatshefte* 30 (1938): 332–33.

Europa, Europa. Dir. Agnieszka Holland. Artur Brauner/CCC Filmkunst/Margaret Menegoz/Les Films du Losange, 1990–91.

Evans, Marshall & Robert O. Rössler. *Das Rheinland: Easy Readings.* New York: Crofts, 1934.

Faust, Albert B. *The German Element in the United States with Special Reference to Its Political, Moral, Social, and Educational Influence.* 2 vols. 1909; rpt. Baltimore: Clearfield, 1995.

Faust, Albert B. "Teaching German Today." *American-German Review* 5.4 (1939): 2+.

Feise, Ernst. "Report on Referendum." *German Quarterly* 12 (1939): 221–22.

Ferragher, John M. & Florence Howe, eds. *Women and Higher Education in American History.* New York: Norton, 1988.

Ferren, H. M. "German in Our Public High Schools." *American Germanica* 2 (1898): 78–89.

Fife, Robert H. "Nationalism and Scholarship." *PMLA* 59 (1944): 1282–94.

Fife, Robert H. "To the Members of the American Association of Teachers of German." *German Quarterly* 5 (1932): 51–53.

Finkielkraut, Alain. *The Imaginary Jew.* Trans. Kevin O'Neill & David Suchoff. Lincoln: University of Nebraska Press, 1994.

Finney, Gail. "Iphigenie in Germanistik, or the Feminization/Humanization of the Profession." Bledsoe et al. 31–43.

Fischman, Jane V. "Teaching Holocaust Literature in American Universities: A Research Report." *The Holocaust: Progress and Prognosis. Proceedings of the Biennial Conference on Christianity and the Holocaust and the Annual Scholars' Conference on the Holocaust and the German Church Struggle,* 1994. 453–64.

Fisher, John H. "Remembrance and Reflection: *PMLA* 1884–1982." *PMLA* 99 (1984): 398–407.

Flavell, M. Kay. Rev. of *Women in German Yearbook* 4. *Modern Language Journal* 85 (1990): 519–22.

Fohrmann, Jürgen. *Das Projekt der deutschen Literaturgeschichte.* Stuttgart: Metzler, 1989.

Fohrmann, Jürgen. "Von den deutschen Studien zur Literaturwissenschaft." Forhmann & Voßkamp 1–14.

Fohrmann, Jürgen & Wilhem Voßkamp, eds. *Wissenschaftsgeschichte der Germanisktik im 19. Jahrhundert.* Stuttgart: Metzler, 1994.

Follen, Karl. "Die Gründung einer deutsch-amerikanischen Universität. Eine Denkschrift." *Deutsch-Amerikanische Geschichtsblätter* 22/23 (1922–23) / *Jahrbuch der Deutsch-Amerikanischen Historischen Gesellschaft von Illinois 1924:* 56–76.

Foltin, Lore & Hubert Heinen. *Paths to German Poetry.* New York: Dodd, Mead, 1969.

Förder-Hoff, Gabi. "Frauen in der Wissenschaft. Zur Entstehung 'weiblicher Wissenschaft' zu Beginn des 20. Jahrhunderts." *Wissenschaft in Berlin, III: Begleitband zur Ausstellung der Kongreß denkt.* Ed. Tillmann Buddensieg, Kurt Düwell & Klaus-Jürgen Sembach. Berlin: Gebrüder Mann, 1987. 62–69.

Förster, Jürgen, Eva Neuland & Gerhard Rupp, eds. *Wozu noch Germanistik? Wissenschaft, Beruf, Kulturelle Praxis.* Stuttgart: Metzler, 1989.

Foucault, Michel. "The Discourse on Language." Adams & Searle 148–62.

Foucault, Michel. *The History of Sexuality.* Trans. Robert Hurley. Vol. 1. New York: Pantheon, 1978 / New York: Vintage, 1990.

Francke, Kuno. *Deutsche Arbeit in Amerika.* Leipzig: Meiner, 1930.

Francke, Kuno. *The German Classics: Masterpieces of German Literature.* 20 Vols. New York: German Publication Society, 1913ff.

Francke, Kuno. "The Social Aspect of Early German Romanticism." *PMLA* 10 (1895): 83–96.

Francke, Kuno. *Social Forces in German Literature.* New York: Holt, 1896.

Frank, Horst J. *Dichtung, Sprache, Menschenbildung. Geschichte des Deutschunterrichts von den Anfängen bis 1945.* Munich: Hanser, 1973.

Frank, Ted E. "The Dawn of Teaching German in the Public Schools: A Study of *Der amerikanische Leser,* Cincinnati 1854." Benseler, Lohnes & Nollendorfs 120–32.

Franklin, Phyllis. "A Public Relations Assignment." *MLA Newsletter* 29, 1 (1997): 4–5.

Frederick, John. "Reading in War Time." *German Quarterly* 15 (1942): 71–72.

Freeman, Lisa. "The University Press in the Electronic Future." Peek & Newby 147–53.

Freeman, Stephen A. *The Middlebury College Foreign Language Schools, 1915–917: The Story of a Unique Idea.* Middlebury: Middlebury College Press, 1975.

Freundlich, Elisabeth. *Die fahrenden Jahre: Erinnerungen.* Salzburg: Müller, 1992.

Friederich, Werner P. *An Outline History of German Literature.* 1905; rpt. New York: Barnes & Noble, 1948.

Friedrichsmeyer, Sara. "Towards an 'American Germanics'?" *Women in German Yearbook* 12 (1996): 233–39.

Friedrichsmeyer, Sara & Patricia Herminghouse. "The Generational Compact: Graduate Students and Germanics." *Women in German Yearbook* 11 (1995): 223–27.

Frühwald, Wolfgang. "Gesellschaftliche und kulturelle Folgen der Informatations- und Medientechnologie." *Die unendliche Bibliotek: Digitale Information in Wissenschaft, Verlag und Bibliotek.* Ed. Börsenverein des Deutschen Buchhandels, Die Deutsche Bibliotek & Bundesvereinigung Deutscher Bibliotheksverbände. Gesellschaft für das Buch 2. Wiesbaden: Harrassowitz, 1996. 83–91.

Furst, Desider & Lillian R. Furst. *Home Is Somewhere Else: Autobiography in Two Voices.* Albany: State University of New York Press, 1994.

Gadamer, Hans-Georg. *Wahrheit und Methode*. Tübingen: Mohr, 1960.

GANPAC. "Dear Friend, did you hear about this?" Postcard to Susan Pentlin. 24 June 1985.

GANPAC. "Dresden 1945: In Memoriam." *GANPAC Brief,* February 1985: 8.

Gebhardt, Charlotte & Sara Lennox. Letter. 17 September 1976. WiG Archive. State Historical Soc. of Wisconsin, Madison, Wis.

Geitz, Henry. Letter to Susan L. Pentlin. 13 July 1976.

Geitz, Henry, Jürgen Heideking & Jurgen Herbst, eds. *German Influences on Education in the United States to 1917.* Cambridge: Cambridge University Press, 1995.

Gelber, Mark H., ed. *The Jewish Reception of Heinrich Heine.* Tübingen: Niemeyer, 1992.

Gerard, James W. *Face to Face with Kaiserism.* New York: Doran, 1918.

Gerard, James W. *My First Eighty-three Years in America.* Garden City, N.Y.: Doubleday, 1951.

Gerard, James W. *My Four Years in Germany.* New York: Doran, 1917.

Gerhard, Melitta. *Auf dem Wege zur neuer Weltsicht. Aufsätze zum deutschen Schrifttum vom 18. bis 20. Jahrhundert. Melitta Gerhard Festschrift.* Ed. Francke Verlag. Bern: Franke, 1976.

German American Annals. Ed. M[arion] D[exter] Learned. New York: n.p., 1902–19.

"The German American Historical Society." *Americana Germanica* 7 (1902): 207–13.

"German Book, the Enemy." Editorial. *New York Times,* 7 April 1918: E2.

German Quarterly. "Decennial Index." *German Quarterly* 10 (1937): 1–39.

German Quarterly. Vols. 1–71 (1928–1949).

Gilbert, Glenn, ed. *The German Language in America: A Symposium.* Austin: University of Texas Press, 1971.

Gilman, Daniel C. *University Problems in the United States.* New York: Garrett, 1969.

Gilman, Sander L. *Franz Kafka: The Jewish Patient.* New York: Routledge, 1995.

Gilman, Sander L. *Jewish Self-Hatred: Anti-Semitism and the Hidden Agenda of the Jews.* Baltimore: Johns Hopkins University Press, 1986.

Gilman, Sander L. "Why and How I Study German." *German Quarterly* 62 (1989): 192–207.

Gilman, Sander L. & Karen Remmler, eds. *Reemerging Jewish Culture in Germany: Life and Literature since 1989.* New York: New York University Press, 1994.

Gilman, Sander L. & Jack Zipes, eds. *Yale Companion to Jewish Writing and Thought in German Culture, 1096–1996.* New Haven: Yale University Press, 1997.

Gittleman, Sol. "From Junior High School to Graduate Program: The Crisis of Coordination." Lohnes & Nollendorfs 207–10.

Glasscock, Jean, et al., eds. *Wellesley College, 1875–1975: A Century of Women.* Wellesley, Mass.: Wellesley College Press, 1975.

Goebel, Julius. "German Classics as a Means of Education." *PMLA* 1 (1884/85): 156–69.

Goebel, Julius. "Hebbelprobleme." *JEGP* 8 (1909): 445–54.

Goebel, Julius. "Notes on the History and Principles of Hermeneutics." *JEGP* 17 (1918): 602–21.

Goebel, Julius. "Vorbemerkung des Herausgebers." *Deutsch-Amerikanische Geschichtsblätter* 22/23 (1922–23) / *Jahrbuch der Deutsch-Amerikanischen Historischen Gesellschaft von Illinois 1924:* 56.

Goldhagen, Daniel J. *Hitler's Willing Executioners: Ordinary Germans and the Holocaust.* New York: Knopf, 1996.

Goodman, Kay & Ruth H. Sanders. "Introduction." *Women and German Studies: An Interdisciplinary and Comparative Approach. Proceedings of the Second Annual Women in Ger-*

man Symposium. Ed. Kay Goodman & Ruth H. Sanders. Oxford, Ohio: Miami University, 1977. 1–3.

Goodnight, Scott H. *German Literature in American Magazines prior to 1846.* Bulletin of the University of Wisconsin 188. Philology and Literature Series 4, no. 1. Madison: University of Wisconsin, 1907.

Govier, Robert A. "Dear AATG Member." Letter to Susan L. Pentlin. 6 December 1984.

Govier, Robert A. "Letter to AATG Members Who Have Inquired [about the] Ad[vertisement] on Page xv of the Winter 1984 Issue of *German Quarterly."* Letter to Susan L. Pentlin. 5 March 1984.

Govier, Robert A. Letter to Susan L. Pentlin. 21 March 1985.

Graff, Gerald. *Professing Literature: An Institutional History.* Chicago: University of Chicago Press, 1989.

Grandin, John. "The University of Rhode Island's International Engineering Program." *Language and Content: Discipline- and Content-Based Approaches to Language Study.* Ed. Merle Krueger & Frank Ryan. Lexington, Mass.: Heath, 1993. 130–37.

Grimm, Reinhold & Jost Hermand, eds. *High and Low Cultures: German Attempts at Mediation.* Madison: University of Wisconsin Press, 1994.

Grimm, Reinhold & Jost Hermand, eds. *Die Klassik-Legende: Second Wisconsin Workshop.* Frankfurt/M.: Athenänum, 1971.

Grossberg, Lawrence. "The Formations of Cultural Studies: An American in Birmingham." *Relocating Cultural Studies.* Ed. Valda Blundell et al. London: Routledge, 1992. 21–66.

Grossman, Jeffrey A. *The Discourse on Yiddish in Germany from the Enlightenment to the Second Empire.* Columbia, S.C.: Camden House, forthcoming.

Guillory, John. *Cultural Capital: The Problem of Literary Canon Formation.* Chicago: University of Chicago Press, 1993.

Haertel, Martin H. *German Literature in American Magazines, 1846–1880.* Philology and Literature Series 4, no. 2. Madison: University of Wisconsin, 1908.

Hahn, Barbara. "Bertha Badt-Strauss (1885–1970). Die Lust am Unzeitgemäßen." *Frauen in den Kulturwissenschaften. Von Lou Andreas-Salomé bis Hannah Arendt.* Ed. Barbara Hahn. Munich: Beck, 1994. 152–65.

Halbwachs, Maurice. *On Collective Memory.* Ed. & trans. Lewis A. Coser. Chicago: University of Chicago Press, 1992.

Hall, Edward T. *The Silent Language.* 1959; rpt. New York: Doubleday, 1990.

Handschin, Charles. *The Teaching of Modern Languages in the United States.* U.S. Bureau of Education Bulletin 3. Washington, D.C.: GPO, 1913.

Hanlin, Todd C. "DAAD Symposium: A Protocol." McCarthy & Schneider 140–56.

Hänseler, William. "Modern German Literature in the High School." *Monatshefte* 12 (1911): 138–45.

Hansen, Miriam B. "Schindler's List Is Not Shoah: The Second Commandment, Popular Modernism, and Public Memory." *Critical Inquiry* 22 (1996): 292–312.

Harner, James L., ed. *MLA Directory of Scholarly Presses in Language and Literature.* 2nd ed. New York: MLA, 1996.

Hartman, Joan E., et al. "Study III: Women in Modern Language Departments, 1972–73: A Report by the Commission of the Status of Women in the Profession." *PMLA* 91 (1976): 124–36.

Hatfield, Henry C. *Thomas Mann.* Norwalk, Conn.: New Directions, 1951.

Hatfield, Henry C. & Joan Merrick. "Studies of German Literature in the United States, 1939–1946." *Modern Language Review* 43 (1948): 353–92.

Heilbrun, Carolyn. "The Profession and Society, 1958–83." *PMLA* 99 (1984): 408–13.

Heine, Heinrich. "Romantische Schule." *Sämtliche Schriften* 3. Ed. Klaus Briegleb. Munich: Hanser, 1968.

Helbig, Louis F. & Eberhard Reichmann, eds. *Teaching Postwar Germany in America.* Bloomington: Inst. of German Studies, 1972.

Heller, Erich. *The Disinherited Mind: Essays in Modern Thought and Literature.* Cambridge: Bowes, 1952.

Heller, Erich. *The Hazards of Poetry.* London: Bowes, 1953.

Heller, Erich. *In the Age of Prose: Literary and Philosophical Essays.* New York: Cambridge University Press, 1984.

Heller, Erich. *The Ironic German: A Study of Thomas Mann.* New York: Meridian, 1961.

Heller, Erich. "Why Modern Poetry Is Obscure." *Listener* 49 (1953): 437, 439.

Herbst, Jurgen. *The German Historical School in American Scholarship: A Study in the Transfer of Culture.* Ithaca, N.Y.: Cornell University Press, 1965.

Herget, Winfried. "Overcoming the 'Mortifying Distance': American Impressions of German Universities in the Nineteenth and Early Twentieth Centuries." *Transatlantische Partnerschaft. Kulturelle Aspekte der deutsch-amerikanischen Beziehungen.* Ed. Dieter Gutzen, Winfried Herget & Hans Adolf Jacobsen. Bonn: Bouvier, 1992. 195–208.

Hermand, Jost. *Geschichte der Germanistik.* Reinbek: Rowohlt, 1994.

Hermand, Jost. *Judentum und deutsche Kultur. Beispiele einer schmerzhaften Symbiose.* Cologne: Böhlau, 1996.

Hermand, Jost. *Die Kultur der Bundesrepublik Deutschland, 1965–1985.* Munich: Nymphenburger, 1988.

Hermand, Jost. *Kultur im Wiederaufbau. Die Bundesrepublik Deutschland, 1945–65.* Munich: Nymphenburger, 1986.

Hermand, Jost. "Madison, Wisconsin 1959–73. Der Einfluß der deutschen Exilanten auf die Entstehung der Neuen Linken." *Exilforschung. Ein Internationales Jahrbuch* 13 (1995): 52–67.

Hermand, Jost. *Old Dreams of a New Reich: Volkish Utopias and National Socialism.* Trans. Paul Levesque, with Stefan Soldovieri. Bloomington: Indiana University Press, 1992.

Hermand, Jost. "Politics in Poetry: The Search for a Radical German Tradition." *Times Literary Supplement,* 30 April 1971.

Hermand, Jost. "Some Thoughts on the Question: What Is Still 'Political' in German Culture Studies?" *Responsibility and Commitment: Ethische Postulate der Kulturvermittlung. Festschrift für Jost Hermand.* Ed. Klaus L. Berghahn, Robert C. Holub & Klaus R. Scherpe. Frankfurt/M.: Lang, 1996. 283–90.

Hermann, Hans P. "Das Bild der Germanistik zwischen 1945 und 1965 in autobiographischen Selbstreflexionen von Literaturwissenschaftlern." *Zeitenwechsel. Germanistische Literaturwissenschaft vor und nach 1945.* Ed. Wilfred Barner & Christoph König. Frankfurt/M.: Fischer, 1966. 345–60.

Hermann, Matthias. *72 Buchstaben.* Frankfurt/M.: Surhkamp, 1989.

Herminghouse, Patricia. Letter. 3 November 1978. WiG Archive. State Historical Soc. of Wisconsin, Madison, Wis.

Herminghouse, Patricia. Letter. 3 December 1991. WiG Archive. State Historical Soc. of Wisconsin, Madison, Wis.

Hewett, W. T. "The Aims and Methods of Collegiate Instruction in Modern Languages." *PMLA* 1 (1884/85): 25–36.

Hewett-Thayer, Harvey W. *The Modern German Novel.* Boston, Mass.: Marshall Jones, 1924.

Heyl, Matthias. "Education after Auschwitz. Teaching the Holocaust in Germany." *New Perspective on the Holocaust.* Ed. Rochelle L. Millen, Timothy A. Bennett & Jack D. Mann. New York: New York University Press, 1996.

Hilsenrath, Edgar. *Der Nazi und der Friseur.* Cologne: Braun, 1977.

Hobsbawm, Eric J. & Terence O. Ranger, eds. *The Invention of Tradition.* Cambridge: Cambridge University Press, 1983.

Hockey, Susan. "Developing Access to Electronic Texts in the Humanities." *The Evolving Virtual Library: Visions and Case Studies.* Ed. Laverna M. Saunders. Medford, N.J.: Information Today, 1996. 119–33.

Hoecherl-Alden, Gisela. "Germanisten im 'Niemandsland': Die exilierten Akademiker und ihre Wirkung auf die amerikanische Germanistik, 1933–55." Ph.D. diss. University of Wisconsin, 1996.

Hofstaetter, Walther. *Deutschkunde. Ein Buch von deutscher Art und Kunst.* 5th ed. Leipzig: Teubner, 1929.

Hohendahl, Peter U. "Germanistik als Gegenstand der Wissenschaftsgeschichte." *Internationales Archiv für Sozialgeschichte der deutschen Literatur.* Tübingen: Niemeyer, 1996. 143–61.

Hohendahl, Peter U. "Germanistik in den Vereinigten Staaten: Eine Disziplin im Umbruch." *Zeitschrift für Germanistik* 3 (1996): 527–35.

Hohendahl, Peter U. *The Institution of Criticism.* Ithaca, N.Y.: Cornell University Press, 1982.

Hohendahl, Peter U. "Interdisciplinary German Studies: Tentative Conclusions" *German Quarterly* 62 (1989): 227–34.

Hohendahl, Peter U. *Reappraisal: Shifting Alignments in Postwar Critical Theory.* Ithaca, N.Y.: Cornell University Press, 1991.

Hohendahl, Peter U., Herbert Lindenberger & Egon Schwarz, eds. *Essays on European Litereature in Honor of Lieselotte Dieckmann.* St. Louis, Mo.: Washington University Press, 1972.

Hohlfeld, Alexander R. "Address by Professor Alexander R. Hohlfeld, University of Wisconsin, to the Graduating Class of the National Teachers Seminary at Milwaukee on Thursday, 20 June 1918." Ed. Cora Lee Nollendorfs. Benseler, Lohnes & Nollendorfs 197–205.

Hohlfeld, Alexander R. "Der Einfluß deutscher Universitätsideale auf Amerika." *German-American Annals,* n.s., 2 (1904): 242–51.

Hohlfeld, Alexander R. "Der Litteraturbetrieb in der Schule, mit besonderer Rücksicht auf die gegenseitigen Beziehungen der englischen und deutschen Litteratur." [Part 1] *Monatshefte* 3 (1901–2): 46–53, 71–85.

"The 'Holocaust': 120 Questions and Answers." Advertisement. *German Quarterly* 57 (Winter 1984): xv.

Holub, Robert C. "Fragmentary Totalities and Totalized Fragments: On the Politics of Anti-Systemic Thought." *Postmodern Pluralism and Concepts of Plurality: The Twenty-Fourth Wisconsin Workshop.* Ed. Jost Hermand. New York: Lang, 1995. 83–103.

Holub, Robert C. *Reception Theory: A Critical Introduction.* London: Methuen, 1984.

Honigmann, Barbara. *Eine Liebe aus Nichts.* Berlin: Rowohlt, 1991.

Honigmann, Barbara. *Roman von einem Kinde.* Frankfurt/M.: Luchterhand, 1986.

Horkheimer, Max. "Dialektik der Aufklärung." *Max Horkheimer: Gesammelte Schriften,* vol. 5. Ed. Gunzelin S. Noerr. Frankfurt/M.: Fischer, 1987. 144–96.

Horowitz, Irving L. & Mary E. Curtis. "Scholarly Book Publishing in the 1990s." Altbach & Hohshino 303–13.

Hosmer, James K. *Short History of German Literature.* St. Louis, Mo.: Jones, 1879.

Howes, Durward, ed. *American Women.* Teaneck, N.J.: Zephyrus, 1974.

Hubbart, Henry C. "Ohio in the First World War, 1917–1918." *The History of the State of Ohio,* vol. 6. Ed. Carl Wittke, Columbus: Ohio State Archaeological & Historical Society, 1942.

Huber, Bettina. Dir. of Research, MLA. E-mail to Ellen Nagy. 20 October 1996.

Hummer, Patricia M. *The Decade of Elusive Promise: Professional Women in the United States, 1920–33.* Studies in American History and Culture 5. Ann Arbor: University of Michigan Research Press, 1979.

Hurtado, Larry W. "A Consortium for Refereed Electronic Journals." Peek & Newby 201–13.

Huyssen, Andreas. "Postmoderne: Eine amerikanische Internationale?" *Postmoderne: Zeichen eines kulturellen Wandels.* Ed. Andreas Huyssen & Klaus R. Scherpe. Reinbek: Rowohlt, 1986. 13–44.

Huyssen, Andreas, Anson Rabinbach & Jack Czaplicka. "Introduction." *Cultural Studies/ Cultural History.* Special Issue. *New German Critique* 65 (1995).

"IHR Has Links to Proposed University." *B'nai B'rith Messenger,* 13 January 1984: 5.

Indiana University Press. "Marketing and Sales." General Information about Indiana University Press. ⟨http://www.indiana.edu/iupress/⟩ (10 December 1996).

Isay, Jane. *Editors on Editing: What Writers Need to Know about What Editors Do.* New York: Grove, 1993.

Jackson, Eugene. "Foreign Languages: An Instrument for Victory." *High Points* 24 (1942): 69.

Jackson, Eugene & W. D. Pearson. *High Points in German: Two Years.* New York: Coll. Entrance Bk., 1937.

Jakobson, Roman. *Language in Literature.* Cambridge, Mass.: Harvard University Press, 1987.

James, Dorothy. "Bypassing the Traditional Leadership: Who's Minding the Store?" *Profession 1997.* New York: MLA. 41–53.

Jameson, Fredric. *Marxism and Form: Twentieth-Century Dialectical Theories of Literature.* Princeton, N.J.: Princeton University Press, 1972.

Jameson, Fredric. *Postmodernism, or The Cultural Logic of Late Capitalism.* Durham, N.C.: Duke University Press, 1992.

Jancovich, Mark. *The Cultural Politics of the New Criticism.* Cambridge: Cambridge University Press, 1993.

Jarausch, Konrad H. "American Students in Germany, 1815–1914: The Structure of German and U.S. Matriculants at Göttingen University." Geitz, Heideking & Herbst 195–211.

Jay, Martin. *Permanent Exiles: Essays on the Intellectual Migration from Germany to America.* New York: Columbia University Press, 1986.

Jedan, Dieter. "Reshaping the Undergraduate Experience." McCarthy & Schneider 65–90.

Jones, J.B.E. "Richtlinien für die Auswahl des Lesestoffes." *Monatshefte* 16 (1915): 169–76.

Jones, Michael T. "Identity, Critique, Affirmation: A Response to Hinrich C. Seeba's Paper." *German Quarterly* 62 (1989): 155–57.

Jurasek, Richard. "Intermediate-Level Foreign Language Curricula: An Assessment and a New Agenda." *ADFL Bulletin* 27, 2 (1996): 18–27.

Kaes, Anton. "New Historicism and the Study of German Literature." *German Quarterly* 62 (1989): 210–19.

Kansteiner, Wolf. "From Exception to Exemplum: The New Approach to Nazism and the 'Final Solution.' " *History and Theory: Studies in the Philosophy of History* 33 (1994): 145–71.

Kaplan, Marion A. *The Jewish Feminist Movement in Germany.* Westport, Conn.: Greenwood, 1979.

Kaplan, Marion A. *The Making of the Jewish Middle Class: Women, Family, and Identity in Imperial Germany.* Oxford: Oxford University Press, 1991.

Kassandra Project. ‹http://www.reed.edu/ccampbel/tkp/›

Kellner, Douglas. *Media Culture: Cultural Studies, Identity and Politics between the Modern and the Postmodern.* New York: Routledge, 1995.

Kern, Albert J. W. "Geschichtsschreibung: Karl Lamprecht und die 'Neueste Zeit.' " *German-American Annals*, n.s., 4 (1906): 335–44.

Kerrigan, Michael. "No Translations, Please — We're British." *London Times Education Supplement*, 2 April 1993; rpt. *Source* (Fall 1997): 10, 13–15.

Kettelkamp, Gilbert C. "The Adaptation of Headline News to Foreign Language Classwork." *School and Society* 30 (18 November 1939): 661.

Kiefer, A. "Der deutsche Unterricht und der Lesestoff in der Hochschule. — Mit Randbemerkungen." *Monatshefte* 7 (1906): 105–8.

Kiefer, A. "Report on the Present Status of Instruction in German in the High Schools of Ohio." *Monatshefte* 9 (1908): 136–39.

Kimball, Marie Goebel. "Julius Goebel." *Deutsch-Amerikanische Geschichtsblätter* 32 (1932): 529–56.

Kirschbaum, Erik. *The Eradication of German Culture in the* United States, *1917–18.* American-German Studies 2. Stuttgart: Akademischer, 1986.

Klenze, Camillo von. Address before the German University League, New York. 17 March 1915.

Klenze, Camillo von. "The American Association of Teachers of German." *German Quarterly* 1 (1928): 3–6.

Klenze, Camillo von. *Die Zukunft der deutschen Kultur in Amerika.* New York: Stochert, 1915.

Kloosterhuis, Jürgen. *Friedliche Imperialisten: Deutsche Auslandsvereine und auswärtige Kulturpolitik, 1906–18.* Frankfurt/M.: Lang, 1994.

Kloss, Heinz. *Brüder vor den Toren des Reichs.* Berlin: n.p., 1942.

Kloss, Heinz. *Um die Einigung des Deutsch-Amerikanertums.* Berlin: Volk u. Reich, 1937.

Kloss, Heinz. *Das Volksgruppenrecht in den Vereinigten Staaten von Amerika.* Essen: n.p., 1942.

Klüger, Ruth. "The Past Revisited." Klüger & Merrill 103–10.

Klüger, Ruth. *Weiter leben: Eine Jugend.* Munich: DTV, 1994.

Klüger, Ruth & Charles Merrill, eds. *Language and Culture: A Transcending Bond.* New York: Lang, 1993.

Koepke, Wulf. "Germanistik als deutsch-amerikanische Wissenschaft." Trommler, *Germanistik* 46–65.

Koepke, Wulf. "A Reader on Postwar Germany for American Students: Some Preliminary Thoughts." Helbig & Reichmann 151.

Kolbe, Jürgen. *Ansichten einer künftigen Germanistik.* 3rd ed. Munich: Hanser, 1970.

Kolbe, Jürgen. *Neue Ansichten einer künftigen Germanistik.* Munich: Hanser, 1973.

König, Fritz H. "Language and Culture in German Textbooks from the Amana Colonies in Iowa." Benseler, Lohnes & Nollendorfs 144–54.

Kramsch, Claire J. *Context and Culture in Language Teaching.* Oxford: Oxford University Press, 1993.

Kramsch, Claire J. *New Directions in the Teaching of Language and Culture.* Washington, D.C.: NFLC at Johns Hopkins University, 1989.

Kreis, Gabriele. *Frauen im Exil. Dichtung und Wirklichkeit.* Düsseldorf: Claasen, 1984.

Kufner, Herbert. *The Grammatical Structures of English and German: A Constrastive Sketch.* Chicago: University of Chicago Press, 1963.

Kuzniar, Alice. "Cross-Gendered and Cross-Cultural Studies and the German Program." McCarthy & Schneider 122–30.

LaCapra, Dominick. *History and Criticism.* Ithaca, N.Y.: Cornell University Press, 1985.

Lado, Robert. *Linguistics across Cultures: Applied Linguistics for Language Teachers.* Ann Arbor: University of Michigan Press, 1957.

Lagerwey, Wally. Letter to Helmut Ziefle. 23 April 1996.

Lämmert, Eberhard. "Gemanistik: Eine deutsche Wissenschaft." Wiese & Henß 15–36.

Lange, Victor. *The Classical Age of German Literature.* New York: Holmes & Meier, 1982.

Lange, Victor. "The History of German Studies in America: Ends and Means." Benseler, Lohnes & Nollendorfs 3–14.

Lange, Victor. "Thoughts in Season." Lohnes & Nollendorfs 5–16.

Langer, Lawrence L. *Holocaust Testimonies: The Ruins of Memory.* New Haven, Conn.: Yale University Press, 1991.

Langewiesche, Dieter. "Die Universität als Vordenker? Universität und Gesellschaft im 19. und frühen 20. Jahrhundert." *Säculum* 45 (1994): 316–31.

Lauwers-Rech, Magda. *Nazi Germany and the American Germanists: A Study of Periodicals, 1930–46.* New York: Lang, 1995.

Lawton, William C. "A Substitute for Greek." *Atlantic Monthly* 85 (1900): 807–10.

Learned, Marion D. "German as a Cultural Element in American Education." Lecture, National German American Teacher's Association Annual Meeting, Cincinnati, Ohio. 8 July 1898.

Learned, Marion D. "German in the Public Schools." *German-American Annals,* n.s., 2 (1913): 100–106.

Learned, Marion D. "Germanistik und schöne Litteratur in Amerika." Address to the Deutscher Verein der Columbia University, New York. Milwaukee, Wis.: *Pädagogische Monatshefte,* n.d.: 3–13.

Learned, Marion D. "The 'Lehrerbund' and the Teachers of German in America." *Pädagogische Monatshefte* 1 (1899/1900): 10–16.

Learned, Marion D. "The President's Address: Linguistic Study and Literary Creation." *PMLA* 25 (1910): xlvi–lxv.

Learned, Marion D. "The Teaching of German in Pennsylvania." *Americana Germanica* 2 (1898): 71–92.

Learned, Marion D., ed. *Americana Germanica.* 6 vols. New York: n.p., 1897–1902.

Lennox, Sara. "Feminismus und German Studies in den USA." *Zeitschrift für Germanistik,* n.s., 3 (1996): 561–74.

Lennox, Sara. "Feminist Scholarship and Germanistik." *German Quarterly* 62 (1989): 158–70.

Lennox, Sara. Report. *WiG Newsletter* 9 (December 1976): 5–6.

Lennox, Sara. "Some Proposals for Feminist Literary Criticism." *Women in German Yearbook* 7 (1991): 91–97.

Lennox, Sara. "Trends in Literary Theory: The Female Aesthetic and German Women's Writing." *German Quarterly* 54 (1981): 63–75.

Lentricchia, Frank. *After the New Criticism.* Chicago: University of Chicago Press, 1980.

Leopold, Werner. "Realia, Kulturkunde, Nationalism." *Monatshefte* 29 (1937): 23–24.

Leopold, Werner. "Reise durch Deutschland 1935." *Monatshefte* 27 (1935): 299–300.

Levine, Lawrence. *Highbrow, Lowbrow: The Emergence of Cultural Hierarchy in America.* Cambridge, Mass.: Harvard University Press, 1988.

Levy, Richard S. E-mail to David Brenner & Michael Berkowitz. 12 August 1996.

Lewisohn, Ludwig. *Up Stream.* New York: Boni, 1922.

Liebersohn, Harry. "The American Academic Community before the First World War: A Comparison with the German *Bildungsbürgertum.*" *Bildungsbürgertum im 19. Jahrhundert, Teil I: Bildungssystem und Professionalisierung in internationalen Vergleichen.* Ed. Werner Conze & Jürgen Kocka. Stuttgart: Klett-Cotta, 1985. 163–85.

Lindenberger, Herbert. "Reaching Out to the Public." *MLA Newsletter* 29.1 (1997): 3–4.

Liptzin, Sol. "Early History of the A.A.T.G., 1926–31." *German Quarterly* 12 (1939): 20–23.

Literary Digest (30 March 1918): 29+.

Littler, Margaret. Rev. of *Women in German Yearbook* 6. *Modern Language Review* 89 (1994): 533–34.

Lohnes, Walter F. W. & Valters Nollendorfs, eds. *German Studies in the United States: Assessment and Outlook. Monatshefte* Occasional Volumes 1. Madison: University of Wisconsin Press, 1976.

Lohnes, Walter F. W. & F. W. Strothmann. *German: A Structural Approach.* New York: Norton, 1967.

Lorenz, Dagmar C. G. *Verfolgung bis zum Massenmord: Holocaust-Diskurse in deutscher Sprache aus der Sicht der Verfolgten.* New York: Lang, 1992.

Lowenstein, Steven M. *The Berlin Jewish Community: Enlightenment, Family, and Crisis, 1770–1830.* New York: Oxford University Press, 1993.

Lowenstein, Steven M. *Frankfurt on the Hudson: The German-Jewish Community of Washington Heights, 1933–83: Its Structure and Culture.* Detroit: Wayne State University Press, 1989.

Lowry, Martin. *The World of Aldus Marrutius: Business and Scholarship in Renaissance Venice.* Ithaca, N.Y.: Cornell University Press, 1979.

Luebke, Frederick C. *Bonds of Loyalty: German-Americans and World War I.* De Kalb, Ill.: Northern Illinois University Press, 1974.

Lützeler, Paul M. "Letter from the Editor." *German Quarterly* 62 (1989): 139–40.

Lützeler, Paul M. & Jeffrey Peck, eds. *Germanistik as German Studies: Interdisciplinary Theories and Methods.* Special Issue. *German Quarterly* 62 (1989).

Lyotard, Jean-François. *Leçons sur l'analytique du sublime: Kant, Critique de la faculté de juger.* Paris: Galilée, 1991.

Maas, Utz. "Die vom Faschismus verdrängten Sprachwissenschaftler. Repräsentanten einer anderen Sprachwissenschaft?" *Die Künste und die Wissenschaften im Exil, 1933–45.* Ed. Edith Böhne & Wolfgang Motzkau-Valeton. Gerlingen: Lambert Schneider, 1992. 447–52.

Mann, Erika. *Thomas Mann: Briefe, 1889–1936.* Frankfurt/M.: Fischer, 1961.

Mann, Erika. *Thomas Mann: Briefe, 1937–1947.* Frankfurt/M.: Fischer, 1963.

Mann, Thomas. "An die Deutschlehrer Amerikas." Letter. *German Quarterly* 14 (1941): 67–68.

Marsden, George M. *The Soul of the American University: From Protestant Establishment to Established Nonbelief.* New York: Oxford University Press, 1994.

Martin, B. "Zwischenbilanz der feministischen Debatten." Trommler, *Germanistik* 165–95.

Maurer, Heinrich H. "The Earlier German Nationalism in America." *American Journal of Sociology* 22 (1917): 519–43.

McCarthy, John A. "Double Optics: The Americanization of *Germanistik,* the Germanization of Americans." McCarthy & Schneider 1–13.

McCarthy, John A. & Katrin Schneider, eds. *The Future of Germanistik in the USA: Changing Our Prospects.* Nashville, Tenn.: Dept. of Germanic & Slavic Langs., Vanderbilt University, 1996.

McCormick, Charles H. *This Nest of Vipers: McCarthyism and Higher Education in the Mundel Affair, 1951–52.* Urbana, Ill.: University of Illinois Press, 1989.

McVeigh, Joseph. "On the Undergraduate Curriculum: What's Right/Wrong With It?" McCarthy & Schneider 57–64.

Mecklenburg, Norbert & Harro Müller. *Erkenntnisinteresse und Literaturwissenschaft.* Stuttgart: Kohlhammer, 1974.

Menasse, Robert. *Selige Zeiten, brüchige Welt.* Salzburg: Residenz, 1991.

Mencken, H. L. "Die Deutschamerikaner." *Neue Rundschau* 39 (1928): 486–95.

Mensel, Ernst H. "Some Aspects of Modern Language Teaching in This Country." *Monatshefte* 15 (1914): 128–34, 162–68.

Mercer, James K. *Ohio Legislative History.* Columbus, Ohio: Heer, 1920.

Meves, Uwe. "Zum Institutionalisierungsprozeß der Deutschen Philologie: Die Periode der Lehrstuhlunterrichtung (von ca. 1810 bis zum Ende der 60er Jahre des 19. Jahrhunderts)." Fohrmann & Voßkamp 115–203.

Meyer, Sheldon. "University Press Publishing." Altbach & Hohshino 354–63.

Meyer, Sheldon & Leslie Philabaum. "What Is a University Press?" ‹http://www.aaup.pupress.princeton.edu› (27 January 1997).

Mitchell, Breon. "Appreciation." *World Literature Today* (1983): 412.

Mitchell, Breon. E-mail to Ingo Stoehr. 6 February 1997.

Modern Language Association. MLA Committee on Computers and Emerging Technologies in Teaching and Research. "Guidelines for Evaluating Computer-Related Work in the Modern Languages." *Profession 1996.* Ed. Phyllis Franklin. New York: MLA, 1996. 217–19.

Modern Language Association. MLA Committee on Scholarly Editions. "Guidelines for Electronic Scholarly Editions." Ed. Charles B. Faulhaber. http://sunsite.berkeley.edu/MLA/intro.html

Modern Language Association. *MLA Directory of Periodicals: A Guide to Journals and Series in Languages and Literatures.* New York: MLA, 1996.

Modern Language Association. Proceedings for 1898. [On the Committee of Twelve]. *PMLA* 14 (1899): xxiii–xxiv.

Modern Language Association. Proceedings for 1899. [On the Committee of Twelve]. *PMLA* 15 (1900): xxx–xxxi.

Modern Language Association. Proceedings for 1909. [On the Committee of Fifteen]. *PMLA* 25 (1910): xvii–xviii.

Modern Language Association. Proccedings for 1910. [Report of the Committee of Fifteen by L. A. Loiseaux]. *PMLA* 26 (1911): xii–xvii.

Modern Language Association. *Proceedings of the Modern Language Association of America. Supp. to Publications of the Modern Language Association of America.* Baltimore: Furst, 1884–1921; n.p.: Banta, 1922–present.

Modern Language Association. *Publications of the Modern Language Association.* Vols. 1–64 (1884–1949).

Modern Language Association. "Report of the Committee of Twelve of the Modern Language Association of America." *Report of the Commissioner of Education for 1897–98.* Washington, D.C.: U.S. Bureau of Education, 1899. 1391–1433.

Modern Language Association. "Report of the Committee on a Four Years' Course in German for Secondary Schools." *Monatshefte* 7 (1906): 71–76.

Monatshefte. "Personalia, 1943–44." *Monatshefte* 36 (1944): 48–56.

Moore, Wallace H. *The Conflict Concerning the German Language and German Propaganda in the Public Secondary Schools of the United States, 1917–19.* Stanford, Calif.: Stanford University Press, 1937.

Morgan, Bayard Q. "After the War: A Blueprint for Action." *Monatshefte* 36 (1944): 107–9.

Morgan, Bayard Q. "Dear Folks." Letter. 30 March 1939. A. R. Hohlfeld Correspondence Box 14. University of Wisconsin Archives, Memorial Lib., Madison.

Moulakis, Athanasios. *Beyond Utility: Liberal Education for a Technological Age.* Columbia: University of Missouri Press, 1994.

Moulton, William G. *The Sounds of English and German.* Chicago: University of Chicago Press, 1962.

Myers, David N. *Re-inventing the Jewish Past: European Jewish Intellectuals and the Zionist Return to History.* Oxford: Oxford University Press, 1995.

Myers, David N. *Taube und Stern: Roman Hebraica: Eine Spurensuche.* Hünfelden-Gnadenthal: Präsenz, 1994.

Nagy, Ellen M. *Women in Germanics, 1850–1950.* Studies in Modern German Literature 86. New York: Lang, 1997; also "A History of Women in Germanics, 1850–1950." Ph.D. diss. Ohio State University, 1993.

Neumann, Ronnith. *Die Tür.* Frankfurt/M.: Fischer, 1992.

New York Times, 5 April 1918: 24.

New York Times, 2 March 1996: 6.

New York Times, 20 March 1996: B9.

New York Times, 8 April 1996: A15.

Nickisch, Craig W. "German and National Policy: The West Point Experience." Benseler, Lohnes & Nollendorfs 76–82.

Nolden, Thomas. *Junge jüdische Literatur. Konzentrisches Schreiben in der Gegenwart.* Würzburg: Königshausen, 1995.

Noll, [Hans] Chaim. *Leben ohne Deutschland.* Reinbek: Rowohlt, 1995.

Nollendorfs, Cora Lee. "Deutschunterricht in Amerika im Schatten des Ersten Weltkrieges.

Öffentlich-offizielle Verfahrensweisen und gesellschaftliches Gebaren." *Zeitschrift für Kulturaustausch* 35 (1985): 190–99.

Nollendorfs, Cora Lee. "The First World War and the Survival of German Studies: With a Tribute to Alexander R. Hohlfeld." Benseler, Lohnes & Nollendorfs 176–96.

Nollendorfs, Valters. "Eine amerikanische Germanistik. Entwicklungen im amerikanischen Deutschstudium in den 70er und 80er Jahren." *Zeitschrift für Kulturaustausch* 35 (1985): 230–36.

Nollendorfs, Valters. "German Studies: A Pragmatic Look Ahead." Lohnes & Nollendorfs 33–46.

Nollendorfs, Valters. "Out of Germanistik: Thoughts on the Shape of Things to Come." *Unterrichtspraxis* 27 (1994): 1–10.

Nollendorfs, Valters. "Practical Approaches to a History of German Studies in America." *Monatshefte* 75 (1983): 266–70.

Nollendorfs, Valters. "Present Trends and Future Directions of American Germanics." McCarthy & Schneider 53.

Nollendorfs, Valters. "Towards Guidelines for German Studies: A Progress Report." *Monatshefte* 78 (1986): 285–69.

Nollendorfs, Valters & Carol Arness. "Graduate Programs: Looking Toward the 1990s." *Monatshefte* 76 (1984): 311–31.

Oberdorfer, Don. *Princeton University: The First 250 Years.* Princeton, N.J.: Princeton University Press, 1995.

O'Connor, Richard. *The German-Americans.* Boston: Little, 1968.

Okerson, Ann. "University Libraries and Scholarly Communication." Peek & Newby 181–99.

O'Neill, Patrick. *German Literature in English Translation: A Selected Bibliography.* Toronto: University of Toronto Press, 1981.

Organization for Economic Co-Operation and Development. *Higher Education and Employment: The Case of Humanities and Social Sciences.* Paris: Org. for Economic Co-Operation & Dev., 1993.

Oshinsky, David M., Richard P. McCormick & Daniel Horn. *The Case of the Nazi Professor.* New Brunswick, N.J.: Rutgers University Press, 1989.

Paulsell, Patricia R. "A Cultural Rationale for International Business Internships." *Monatshefte* 83 (1991): 243–64.

Pearson, W. D., and Eugene Jackson. *High Points in German: Two Years.* New York: College Entrance Book Co., 1937.

Peck, Jeffrey M. " 'The British Are Coming! The British Are Coming!': Notes for a Comparative Study of Institutions." Benseler, Lohnes & Nollendorfs 271–84.

Peck, Jeffrey M. "Introduction." *German Quarterly* 62 (1989): 141–43.

Peek, Robin P. & Gregory B. Newby, eds. *Scholarly Publishing: The Electronic Frontier.* Cambridge, Mass.: MIT Press, 1996.

Pennsylvania, University of. *Bulletin of the University of Pennsylvania* 1.1 (February 1893); 1.2 (April 1893); 1.3 (June 1893); (1940–41).

Pennsylvania, University of. *Catalogue:* 1850–51, 1856–57, 1857–58, 1868, 1873–74, 1884–85, 1886–87, 1896–97, 1897–98 (pp. 196–200), 1898–99 (pp. 195–200).

Pennsylvania, University of. *Catalogue of the Officers and Students of the University of Pennsylvania.* Philadelphia: University of Pennsylvania, 1835.

Pennsylvania, University of. *Charters and Statutes of the University of Pennsylvania* (1853).

Pennsylvania, University of. "Regulations of the Collegiate Department: Faculty of Arts (1834–35)." *Catalogue of the Officers and Students of the University of Pennsylvania.* Philadelphia: University of Pennsylvania, 1835.

Pennsylvania, University of. *University of Pennsylvania: The History of a University and Its Present Work 1740–1893.* N.p., n.d., 1–14.

Pentlin, Susan L. "Effect of the Third Reich on the Teaching of German in the United States: A Historical Study." Ph.D. diss. University of Kansas, 1977. Ann Arbor, Mich.: UMI, 1982.

Pentlin, Susan L. "German Teachers' Reaction to the Third Reich, 1933–39." Benseler, Lohnes & Nollendorfs 228–52.

Pentlin, Susan L. Personal Notes. Central Missouri State University, College of Arts and Sciences Curriculum Committee Meeting. 21 April 1995.

Pentlin, Susan L. Personal Notes. Central Missouri State University Curriculum Committee Meeting. 28 April 1995.

Peper, Wilhelm. "Deutschkunde als Bildungsgrundgesetz und als Bildungsstoff." *Zeitschrift für den deutschen Unterricht* 6: *Ergänzungsband* 13. *Ergänzungsheft.* Leipzig: Teubner, 1919.

Perseus. ⟨http://www.perseus.tufts.edu/⟩

Pickus, Keith H. *Jewish University Students in Germany and the Construction of a Post-Emancipatory Identity, 1815–1914.* Detroit: Wayne State University Press, forthcoming.

Plant, Richard. *The Pink Triangle: The Nazi War against Homosexuals.* New York: Holt, 1986.

Pochmann, Henry A. *German Culture in America: Philosophical and Literary Influences, 1600–1900.* Madison: University of Wisconsin Press, 1957.

Polenz, Peter von. "Sprachpurismus und Nationalsozialismus." Wiese & Henß 79–112.

Projekt Gutenberg. ⟨http://gutenberg.informatik.uni-hamburg.de/gutenb/home.htm⟩

Rabinbach, Anson & Jack Zipes, eds. *Germans and Jews since the Holocaust: The Changing Situation in West Germany.* New York: Holmes & Meier, 1986.

Radkau, Joachim. *Die deutsche Emigration in den USA. Ihr Einfluß auf die amerikanische Europapolitik, 1933–45.* Düsseldorf: Bertelsmann, 1971.

Rectanus, Mark. "Langenscheidt: Expanding the Socio-Cultural and Technological Contexts of Language Pubishing." *Unterrichtspraxis* 28 (1995): 13–18.

Reichart, Walter A. "Die Germanistik in Amerika." *Germanisch-Romanische Monatshefte* 26 (1938): 373–78.

Reichmann, Eberhard. "German Culture Studies: Pedagogical Considerations." Lohnes & Nollendorfs 59–66.

Reichmann, Eberhard, ed. *The Teaching of German: Problems and Methods.* Bloomington, Ind.: NCSA, 1970.

Reichmann, Eberhard & Ruth M. Reichmann. "German-American Studies: A Research Field in Search of a Classroom." *Monatshefte* 80 (1988): 289–96.

"Release from the Office of Censorship." *Monatshefte* 35 (1943): 95.

Remak, Henry H. H. "Deutsche Emigration und Amerikanische Germanistik." *Modernisierung oder Überfremdung? Zur Wirkung deutscher Exilanten in der Germanistik der Aufnahmeländer.* Ed. Walter Schmitz. Stuttgart: Metzler, 1994. 173–90.

"Report of the Trustees of the University of Pennsylvania." Internal Publ. July 1851.

Reuleaux, Franz. *Briefe aus Philadelphia.* Braunschweig: Vieweg, 1877.

Richter, Werner. "Strömungen und Stimmungen in den Literaturwissenschaften von heute." *Germanic Review* 21 (1946): 81–113.

Ringer, Fritz K. *The Decline of the German Mandarins: The German Academic Community, 1890–1933*. Cambridge, Mass.: Harvard University Press, 1969.

Rippley, La Vern J. "Ameliorated Americanization: The Effect of World War I on German-Americans in the 1920s." Trommler & McVeigh 2: 217–31.

Rippley, La Vern J. *The German-Americans*. Boston: Twayne, 1976.

Robertson, J. G. *Outlines of the History of German Literature*. London: Blackwood, 1911.

Roeber, Anthony Gregg. "The von Mosheim Society and the Preservation of German Education and Culture in the New Republic, 1789–1813." Geitz, Heideking & Herbst 157–76.

Rohr, Martina. Rev. of *Women in German Yearbook* 7. *Women's Studies International Forum* 16 (1993): 306–7.

Roseboom, Eugene & Francis P. Weisenburger. *A History of Ohio*. Columbus: Ohio Historical Soc., 1991.

Rosenberg, Ralph P. "American Doctoral Studies in Germanic Cultures: A Study in German-American Relations, 1873–1949." *Yearbook of Comparative and General Literature* 4 (1955): 30–44.

Rosenberg, Rosalind. "The Limits of Access: The History of Coeducation in America." Ferragher & Howe 107–29.

Roskies, David G. *Against the Apocalypse: Responses to Catastrophe in Modern Jewish Culture*. Cambridge, Mass.: Harvard University Press, 1984.

Roth, Philip. *The Counterlife*. New York: Farrar, 1986.

Roth, Philip. *Operation Shylock: A Confession*. New York: Simon, 1993.

Rothschild, Joyce. "The NDEA Decade." *American Education*. U. S. Department of Health, Education and Welfare. Office of Education. Washington, D.C.: GPO, September 1968.

Salloch, Erika. "Traces of Fascist Ideology in American Professional Journals, 1933–1945." Benseler, Lohnes & Nollendorfs 253–70.

Sammons, Jeffrey. "Die amerikanische Germanistik. Historische Betrachtungen zur gegenwärtigen Situation." *Germanistik International*. Ed. Richard Brinkmann. Tübingen: Niemeyer, 1978. 105–20.

Sammons, Jeffrey. "Germanistik im Niemandsland." Trommler, *Germanistik* 104–20.

Sammons, Jeffrey. "Some Considerations on Our Invisibility." Lohnes & Nollendorfs 17–23.

Sammons, Jeffrey. " 'The Tragicall Historie' of German in the United States." *American Attitudes toward Foreign Languages and Foreign Cultures*. Ed. Peter Heller & Edward Dudley. Bonn: Bouvier, 1983. 23–34.

Sander, Volkmar. "Wohin treibt die Germanistik?" *Germanic Review* (May 1970): 179–87.

Santayana, George. *Egotism in German Philosophy*. New York: Scribner, 1940.

Santner, Eric L. *Stranded Objects: Mourning, Memory, and Film in Postwar Germany*. Ithaca, N.Y.: Cornell University Press, 1990.

Saussure, Ferdinand de. *Course in General Linguistics*. Trans. Wade Baskin. New York: McGraw-Hill, 1966.

Saxer, Ulrich. "Literatur in der Medienkonkurrenz." *Media Perspektiven* 12 (1977): 673–85.

Schieber, Clara E. *The Transformation of American Sentiment toward Germany, 1870–1914*. New York: Russell, 1923.

Schindel, Robert. *Gebürtig*. Frankfurt/M.: Suhrkamp, 1992.

Schindler's List. Dir. Steven Spielberg. Perf. Liam Neeson, Ralph Fiennes, Ben Kingsley, Catherine Goodall, Jonathan Sagalle. Universal Pictures/Amblin Entertainment, 1993.

Schmidt, Hans. "An Open Letter to the American People." *GANPAC Brief,* January 1985.

Schmidt, Henry J. "Interview with Hermann J. Weigand." Benseler, Lohnes & Nollendorfs 285–92.

Schmidt, Henry J. "Policy Statement from the Editor." *German Quarterly* 57 (1984): 362.

Schmidt, Henry J. "Rationales and Sources for a History of German Studies in the United States." *Monatshefte* 75 (1983): 260–65.

Schmidt, Henry J. "The Rhetoric of Survival: The Germanist in America, 1900–1925." Benseler, Lohnes & Nollendorfs 165–75; Trommler & McVeigh 2: 204–16.

Schmidt, Henry J. "What Is Oppositional Criticism? Politics and German Literary Criticism from Fascism to the Cold War." *Monatshefte* 79 (1987): 292–301.

Schmidt, Henry J. "Wissenschaft als Ware. Die institutionellen Grundlagen der amerikanischen Germanistik." Trommler, *Germanistik* 66–83.

Schmidt, Hugo. "A Historical Survey of the Teaching of German in America." *The Teaching of German: Problems and Methods.* Ed. Eberhard Reichmann. Philadelphia: National Carl Schurz Assn., 1970. 3–7.

Schreiber, S. Etta. Letter to Susan L. Pentlin. 26 July 1976.

Schulz, Renate A. "Methods of Teaching German in the United States: A Historical Perspective." Benseler, Lohnes & Valters Nollendorfs 55–57.

Schulz, Renate A. *Options for Undergraduate Foreign Language Programs. Four-Year and Two-Year Colleges.* New York: MLA, 1979.

Schwarz, Egon. *Keine Zeit für Eichendorff. Chronik unfreiwilliger Wanderjahre.* Frankfurt/M.: Gutenberg, 1992.

Schwarz, Egon. "Methodological Approaches." *Monatshefte* 75 (1983): 257–59.

Searle, John R. *Speech Acts: An Essay in the Philosophy of Language.* Cambridge: Cambridge University Press, 1969.

Seeba, Hinrich C. "Critique of Identity Formation: Toward an Intercultural Model of German Studies." *German Quarterly* 62 (1989): 144–54.

Seeba, Hinrich C. "Cultural versus Linguistic Competence? Bilingualism, Language in Exile, and the Future of German Studies." *German Quarterly* 69 (1996): 401–13.

Seligmann, Rafael. *Mit beschränkter Hoffnung. Juden, Deutsche, Israelis.* Hamburg: Hoffmann, 1991.

Seligmann, Rafael. *Rubinsteins Versteigerung.* Frankfurt/M.: Eichborn, 1989.

Sengle, Friedrich. *Biedermeierzeit. Deutsche Literatur im Spannungsfeld zwischen Restauration und Revolution, 1815–1848.* Vol. 3: *Die Dichter.* Stuttgart: Metzler, 1980.

Sengle, Friedrich. *Literaturgeschichtsschreibung ohne Schulungsauftrag.* Tübingen: Niemeyer, 1980.

Seyhan, Azade. "Prospects for Feminist Literary Theory in German Studies: A Response to Sara Lennox's Paper." *German Quarterly* 62 (1989): 171–77.

Shils, Edward. "The Order of Learning in the United States from 1865 to 1920: The Ascendency of the Universities." *Minerva* 16 (1978): 159–95.

Shumway, Daniel B. "Professor Learned as Colleague" *German American Annals* 19, 5/6 (1917): 151–53.

Sichrovsky, Peter. "Das Abendmahl." *Programmbuch* 29. Vienna: Burgtheater, 1988.

Silz, Walter. *Early German Romanticism.* Cambridge, Mass.: Harvard University Press, 1929.

Silz, Walter. *Heinrich von Kleist's Conception of the Tragic.* Baltimore: Johns Hopkins University Press, 1923.

Simons, John, ed. *Who's Who in American Jewry: A Biographical Dictionary of Living Jews in the United States and Canada.* Vol 3. 1938–39. New York: National News Association, 1939.

Simon Wiesenthal Center. "Revisionist Ad in Academic Journal." *Social Action Update* (Spring/Summer 1984): 7.

Sisler, William P. "Defining the Image of the University Press." *Journal of Scholarly Publishing* 28, 1 (1996): 55–59.

Slate, Audrey N. *AGS: A History.* N.p.: Assn. of Graduate Schools in the Assn. of American Universities, 1994.

Smith, Arthur L. *The Deutschtum of Nazi Germany and the United States.* The Hague: Nijhoff, 1965.

Soden, Kristine von. "Zur Geschichte des Frauenstudiums." *70 Jahre Frauenstudium.* Ed. Kristine von Soden & Gaby Zipfel. Cologne: Pahl-Rugenstein, 1979. 9–42.

Solomon, Barbara Miller. *In the Company of Educated Women: A History of Women and Higher Education in America.* New Haven, Conn.: Yale University Press, 1985.

Sorkin, David. *Moses Mendelssohn and the Religious Enlightenment.* Berkeley: University of California Press, 1996.

Sorkin, David. *The Transformation of German Jewry, 1780–1840.* New York: Oxford University Press, 1987.

Spaethling, Robert. "Melitta Gerhard: Zum Gedächtnis, 1891–1981." *German Quarterly* 55 (1982): 630–31.

Spahr, Blake Lee. "The Legacy of Curt von Faber du Faur to the United States." *Colloquia Germanica* 25 (1992): 192–209.

Spiegelman, Art. *Maus.* CD-ROM. New York: Voyager, 1994.

Spitzer, Leo. "Deutsche Literaturforschung in Amerika." *Monatshefte* 37 (1945): 475–80.

Springer, Otto. "Germanic Studies in Germany during the War." *Monatshefte* 38 (1946): 177–86.

Spuler, Richard. "From Genesis to Convention: Literary Criticism as a German-American Institution." Benseler, Lohnes & Nollendorfs 155–64.

Spuler, Richard. *"Germanistik" in America: The Reception of German Classicism, 1870–1905.* Stuttgarter Arbeiten zur Germanistik 115. Stuttgart: Heinz, 1982.

Stack, Edward M. *The Language Laboratory and Modern Language Teaching.* 1960; rpt. New York: Oxford University Press, 1966.

Steinberg, Michael P. "Aby Warburg's Kreuzlingen Lecture: A Reading." *Images from the Region of the Pueblo Indians of North America.* Trans. Michael P. Steinberg. Ed. Aby M. Warburg. Ithaca, N.Y.: Cornell University Press, 1995. 59–114.

Steinberg, Michael P. *The Meaning of the Salzburg Festival: Austria as Theater and Ideology, 1890–1938.* Ithaca, N.Y.: Cornell University Press, 1990.

Stern, Leo. "Griechisch oder Deutsch?" *Pädagogische Monatshefte* 1, 7 (1900): 29f.

Stewart, Caroline T. "The Study of Literature." *Monatshefte* 15 (1914): 347–49.

Stone, George W. "The Beginning, Development, and the Impact of the MLA as a Learned Society." *PMLA* 73 (1958): 23–44.

Stuecher, Dorothea D. *Twice Removed: The Experience of German-American Women Writers in the Nineteenth Century.* New York: Lang, 1990.

Suchoff. David. "Jüdische Kritiker in der amerikanischen Nachkriegsgermanistik." *Weimarer Beiträge* 39 (1993): 393–409.

Swaffar, Janet. "The Competing Paradigm in Adult Language Acquisition." *Modern Language Journal* 73 (1989): 301–14.

Swaffar, Janet. "Using Foreign Language to Learn: Rethinking the College Foreign Language Curriculum." *Reflecting on Proficiency from a Classroom Perspective: Northeast Conference on the Teaching of Foreign Languages.* Ed. June K. Phillips. Lincolnwood, Ill.: National Textbook, 1993. 55–86.

Swaffar, Janet, Katherine Arens & Heidi Byrnes. *Reading for Meaning: An Integrated Approach.* Englewood Cliffs: Prentice Hall, 1991.

Tabori, George. *Meine Kämpfe.* Frankfurt/M.: Fischer, 1991.

Tatlock, Lynne. "Response to Hohendahl." McCarthy & Schneider 29–34.

Taubneck, Steven. "Voices in the Debate: German Studies and Germanistik." *German Quarterly* 62 (1989): 220–26.

Teraoka, Arlene A. "Is Culture to Us What Text Is to Anthropology? A Response to Jeffrey M. Peck's Paper." *German Quarterly* 62 (1989): 188–91.

Text Encoding Initiative. ‹http://www.uic.edu:80/orgs/tei/›

Thatcher, Sanford G. "Re-Engineering Scholarly Communication: A Role for University Presses?" *Journal of Scholarly Publishing* 27 (1996): 197–207.

Thomas, Calvin. *History of German Literature.* New York: Appleton, 1909.

Thomas, Judy. "While Area University Moves to Counter 'Separatist,' Central Missouri State University." *Kansas City Star,* 11 April 1996, Southland edition 2.

Thomas, Ursula. "Mark Twain's German Language Learning Experiences." Benseler, Lohnes & Nollendorfs 133–43.

Tolzmann, Don Heinrich. Pres., Soc. for German-American Studies. Letter to Susan L. Pentlin. 15 March 1985.

Trommler, Frank. "Einleitung." Trommler, *Germanistik* 7–43.

Trommler, Frank. "Inventing the Enemy: German-American Cultural Relations, 1900–1917." *Confrontation and Cooperation: Germany and the United States in the Era of World War I, 1900–1924.* Ed. Jürgen Schröder. Providence/Oxford: Berg, 1993. 99–125.

Trommler, Frank. "Die nachgeholte Resistance. Politik und Gruppenethos im historischen Zusammenhang." *Die Gruppe 47 in der Geschichte der Bundesrepublik.* Ed. Justus Fetscher, Eberhard Lämmert & Jürgen Schutte. Würzburg: Königshausen, 1991. 9–22.

Trommler, Frank. "Über die Lesbarkeit der deutschen Literatur." Trommler, *Germanistik* 222–59.

Trommler, Frank, ed. *Germanistik in den USA. Neue Entwicklungen und Methoden.* Opladen: Westdeutscher, 1989.

Trommler, Frank & Joseph McVeigh, eds. *America and the Germans: An Assessment of a Three-Hundred-Year History.* 2 Vols. Philadelphia: University of Pennsylvania Press, 1985.

Trommler, Frank, Michael Geyer & Jeffrey M. Peck. "Germany as the Other: Towards an American Agenda for German Studies: A Colloquium." *German Studies Review* 13 (1990): 111–38.

"Two Germanys." *New York Times,* 14 September 1939: 22.

Ullmer, Roland. "Die internationalen Buchmärkte." *Börsenblatt für den deutschen Buchhandel* 82 (1996): 99–101.

Ulmer, Anne. Letter to H. Ziefle. 3 May 1996.

"Umschau der Schriftleitung," *Monatshefte* 25 (1933): 242.

United States. Office of Education. "NDEA Language and Area Centers: A Report on the First Five Years." *Bulletin* 41. Washington, D.C.: GPO, 1964.

Useem, Michael. *Liberal Education and the Corporation: The Hiring and Advancement of College Graduates.* New York: de Gruyter, 1989.

Van Cleve, John W. & A. Leslie Willson. *Remarks on the Needed Reform of German Studies in the United States.* Columbia, S.C.: Camden House, 1993.

VanPatten, Bill. "Attending to Form and Content in Input." *Studies in Second Language Acquisition* 12 (1990): 287–301.

VanPatten, Bill, Tricia R. Dvorak & James F. Lee, eds. *Foreign Language Learning: A Research Perspective.* Cambridge, Mass.: Newbury, 1987.

Veysey, Laurence R. *The Emergence of the American University.* Chicago: University of Chicago Press, 1965.

Viereck, Louis. *German Instruction in American Schools,* 1902; rpt. New York: Arno, 1978.

Viëtor, Karl. "Deutsche Literaturgeschichte als Geistesgeschichte." *PMLA* 60 (1945): 899–916.

Viëtor, Karl. *Deutsche Literaturgeschichte als Geistegeschichte.* Bern: Francke, 1967.

Vogt, Silvia M. "Zwischen Demokratie und Anti-intellektualismus. Untersuchungen zur amerikanischen Germanistik, 1933–45." Ph.D. diss. New York University, 1944.

Vonnegut, Kurt, Jr. *Palm Sunday: An Autobiographical Collage.* New York: Delacotre, 1981.

Vowles, Guy R. "Why Study German in 1941?" *Modern Language Journal* 25 (1941): 850.

Walker, Nick. "The University Press in the 21st Century." *Journal of Scholarly Publishing* 27, 1 (1995): 37–42.

Walz, John A. *German Influence in American Education and Culture.* Philadelphia: Carl Schurz Mem. Foundation, 1936.

Warburg, Aby. *Images from the Region of the Pueblo Indians of North America.* Trans. Michael P. Steinberg. Ithaca, N.Y.: Cornell University Press, 1995.

Weber, Charles. "The 'Holocaust': 120 Questions and Answers." Advertisement. *German Quarterly* 57 (1984): xv.

Weber, Charles. Letter to Susan L. Pentlin. 27 June 1988.

Weber, Regina. "Der emigrierte Germanist als 'Führer' zur deutschen Dichtung? Werner Vortriede im Exil." *Exilforschung. Ein internationales Jahrbuch* 13 (1995): 137–65.

Weber, Regina."Zur Emigration des Germanisten Richard Alewyn." *Die Emigration der Wissenschaften nach 1933.* Ed. Herbert A. Strauss et al. Munich: Saur, 1991. 235–56.

Wegmann, Nikolaus. "Was heißt einen 'klassischen Text' lesen? Philologische Selbstreflexion zwischen Wissenschaft und Bildung." Fohrmann & Voßkamp 334–50.

Weigand, Hermann. *Thomas Mann's Novel* Der Zauberberg, 1933; rpt. *The Magic Mountain: A Study of Thomas Mann's Novel* Der Zauberberg. University of North Carolina Studies in Germanic Languaes & Literatures 49. Chapel Hill, N.C.: University of North Carolina Press, 1964.

Weimar, Klaus. *Geschichte der deutschen Literaturwissenschaft.* Munich: Fink, 1989.

Weiner, Marc A. "From the Editor." *German Quarterly* 68 (1995): vii–viii.

Weiner, Marc A. "From the Editor." *German Quarterly* 69 (1996): vi–ix.

Weiner, Marc A. *Richard Wagner and the Anti-Semitic Imagination.* Lincoln: University of Nebraska Press, 1995.

Weiss, Gerhard H. "From New York to Philadelphia: Issues and Concerns of the American Association of Teachers of German between 1926 and 1970." Benseler, Lohnes & Nollendorfs 215–27.

Weiss, Gerhard H. "Teaching Postwar German Culture: An Undisciplined Discipline." Helbig & Reichmann 145.

Wellek, René & Austin Warren. *Theory of Literature.* 1942. New rev. ed. San Diego: Harvest-Harcourt, 1984.

Welles, Elisabeth B., ed. *Graduate Education and Undergraduate Teaching: Juncture and Disjuncture.* Special Issue. *ADFL Bulletin* 27, 3 (1996).

Wernick, Andrew. *Promotional Culture: Advertising, Ideology and Symbolic Expression.* London: Sage, 1991.

Wheaton College Catalogues, 1967–96.

White, Hayden. *Metahistory: The Historical Imagination in Nineteenth-Century Europe.* Baltimore: Johns Hopkins University Press, 1973.

White, Horatio S. "The Teaching of a Foreign Literature in Connection with the Seminary System." *PMLA* 3 (187): 48–57.

Wiehr, Josef. Rev. of *Life and Works of Friedrich Hebbel* by T. M. Campbell. *JEGP* 19 (1920): 290–98.

Wiese, Benno von. "Begrüßungsrede in München am 18. Oktober 1966." Wiese & Henß 248–60.

Wiese, Benno von. Letter, "Dear Folks." 30 March 1939, University of Wisconsin Archives. Memorial Library, Madison, Wis. Box 14. A. R. Hohlfeld Correspondence. University of Wisconsin. College of Letters and Sciences.

Wiese, Benno von & Rudolf Henß, eds. *Nationalismus in Germanistik und Dichtung.* Berlin: Schmidt, 1967.

Wiesenhahn, Gretchen. "The Myth of the Feminization of Germanistik." Bledsoe et al. 27–30.

Wilkinson, Elizabeth M. "Dankesworte der ausländischen Germanisten." Wiese & Henß 362.

Willson, Leslie. "Dimensions of *Dimension.*" Paper, Brücke über den Atlantik Conference, Albuquerque. 1996.

Willson, Leslie. "Perspective: An Encounter with the Group 47 and Its Consequences." *Dimension* 16 (1987): 321.

Willson, Leslie. "Perspective: Novel Beginnings." *Dimension* 17 (1989): 311.

Wilson, W. Daniel. WiG List Discussion. 19 February 1996.

Winter, Joseph. "Der deutsche Unterricht in den New Yorker Schulen." *Monatshefte* 11 (1910): 179–83.

Wittgenstein, Ludwig. *The Blue and Brown Books.* New York: Harper, 1958.

Wittke, Carl. *Against the Current: The Life of Karl Heinzen, 1809–80.* Chicago: University of Chicago Press, 1945.

Wittke, Carl. "Ohio's German-Language Press in the Campaign of 1920." *Proceedings of the Mississippi Valley Historical Association* 10 (1920/21): 468–80.

Wittke, Carl. *Refugees of the Revolution: The German Forty-Eighters in America.* Philadelphia: University of Pennsylvania Press, 1952.

Wolf, Ernst. "Lehrplan für die deutschen Klassen in der Hochschule von Saginaw, E. S., Mich." *Monatshefte* 2 (1901): 206–9.

Women in German. *Coalition of Women in German: Twentieth Annual Conference,* St. Augustine, Fla. 31 October–3 November 1996.

Women in German. "Summary of WiG Business and Planning Meeting, Sunday, 4 September 1978." WiG Archive. State Historical Soc. of Wisconsin, Madison, Wis.

Women in German. *Women in German Newsletter* [News from Women in *Germanistik*]. 1974–present.

Women in German. *Women in German Yearbook*. Lanham: University Press of America, 1985–1991; Lincoln: University of Nebraska Press, 1991–present.

Women in German Archive. State Historical Society of Wisconsin, Madison, Wis. Women Writers Project. ⟨http://www.wwp.brown.edu/resource.html⟩

Wunderlich, Frieda. "Deutsch-Mann über alles." *American Scholar* 7 (1938): 94–105.

Wunderlich, Frieda. Letters to Kurt Pinthus. 10 May 1950, Marbach 71.3746/3 & 4; 27 July 1951, Marbach 71.3746/5.

Wunderlich, Frieda. Letter to Gertrud von le Fort. 19 April 1953. Marbach 74.843/12.

Young, James E. *Writing and Rewriting the Holocaust: Narrative and the Consequences of Interpretation*. Bloomington: Indiana University Press, 1988.

Young, James E., ed. *The Art of Memory: Holocaust Memorials in History*. New York: Prestel, 1994.

Zelle, Carsten. "Vier Überlegungen zum Einfluß der deutschen Emigration auf die amerikanische Literaturwissenschaft." *Modernisierung oder Überfremdung? Zur Wirkung deutscher Exilanten in der Germanistik der Aufnahmeländer*. Ed. Walter Schmitz. Stuttgart: Metzler, 1994. 130–37.

Zerubavel, Yael. "The Death of Memory and the Memory of Death: Masada and the Holocaust as Historical Metaphors." *Representations* 45 (1994): 72–100.

Zerubavel, Yael. *Recovered Roots: Collective Memory and the Making of Israeli National Tradition*. Chicago: University of Chicago Press, 1995.

Zeydel, Edwin H. "Die germanistische Tätigkeit in Amerika, 1918–1926." *Euphorion* 29 (1928): 239–46.

Zeydel, Edwin H. "The Teaching of German in the United States from Colonial Times to the Present." *German Quarterly* 37 (1964): 315–92; rpt. Benseler, Lohnes & Nollendorfs 15–54.

Zimmer-Loew, Helene. Letter to Ellen Nagy. 8 December 1989.

Zimmer-Loew, Helene. Letter to Susan L. Pentlin. 29 September 1987.

Ziolkowski, Theodore. *The Institutions of Romanticism*. Princeton, N.J.: Princeton University Press, 1991.

Ziolkowski, Theodore. "On the Polysyllabification of Learning." *Ideas for the University. Proc. of the Marquette University's Mission Seminar and Conference*. Ed. Ed Block, Jr. Milwaukee, Wis.: Marquette University Press, 1995. 73–89.

Ziolkowski, Theodore. Rev. of *The Rhetoric of Romanticism*, by Paul De Man. *Sewanee Review* 95 (1987): 276–87.

Ziolkowski, Theodore. "Saint Hesse among the Hippies." *American-German Review* 35 (1969): 19–23.

Ziolkowski, Theodore. "Der Text als Feind." *Jahrbuch der deutschen Schillergesellschaft* 39 (1995): 454–59.

Ziolkowski, Theodore. "Was heißt und zu welchem Ende studiert man Germanistik? Oder Schizophrenie als Lebensform." *Germanistische Fachinformation international: Germanistik. Sonderheft*. Ed. Wilfried Barner. Tübingen: Niemeyer, 1990. 9–23.

Index

Note: Books or other literary works are indexed under the author's name. Umlauts are alphabetized with the base letter.

AATF (American Association of Teachers of French), 122
AATG (American Association of Teachers of German), 6, 7, 19, 91, 92, 100, 101, 103, 108, 109, 112, 114, 116, 121–34, 139, 142–44, 173, 181, 200, 209, 215, 224, 225, 244
AATSP (American Association of Teachers of Spanish), 122
Ackerman, Elfriede, 124, 129
ACTFL (Association of College Teachers of Foreign Languages), 101
Adams, Charles Francis, 34
Adams, John Quincy, 19
Adelson, Leslie, 74
Adolf, Helen, 108, 111, 114, 116
Adorno, Theodor W., 13, 72, 77, 79, 85
Age of Goethe, 69, 71, 72
Alewyn, Richard, 51, 113
Alexander, Moses, 59
Alexander von Humboldt-Stiftung, 227
Alexis, Joseph, 139
Allgemeiner Deutscher Sprachverein, 20
Almstedt, Hermann B., 130
Alt, Arthur Tilo, 249
American Association of German Teachers, 165
American Association of Teachers of French. *See* AATF
American Association of Teachers of German. *See* AATG
American Association of Teachers of Spanish. *See* AATSP
American Association of Universities, 55
American Association of University Professors, 133
American Council on Education, 231
Americana Germanica, 24, 161, 164, 165
American Indians, 82
Amish, 16, 19
Anderson, Florence, 129

Anderson, Keith, 191
Andrews, Eleanor Anne Fyfe, 160
Andrew W. Mellon Foundation, 218
Angress, Ruth, 142
Anneke, Franziska, 35
Area Studies Program, 189, 190
Arendt, Hannah, 79
Ariadne Press, 215, 221, 222
Arlt, Gustave O., 129
Army. *See* German Army; United States Army
Army Specialized Training Program. *See* United States Army
Aron, Albert W., 128, 130
ARTICLEFIRST, 205, 206
Aschheim, Steven, 82, 87
Association of American Universities, 45
Association of College Teachers of Foreign Languages. *See* ACTFL
Association of Departments of Foreign Languages, 230, 244
Association of German Teachers in Pennsylvania, 19, 162, 166, 169
Association of Teachers of German, 19
ASTP (Army Specialized Training Program). *See* United States Army
Athena, 201
Atkins, Stuart, 39, 51, 52, 71, 96
Atlantic Monthly, 36
Audio-lingual method, 189
Auschwitz, 76, 85, 145
Austrian Institute, 218
Austrian National Library, 113
Austro-Prussian War, 64

Babbitt, Irving, 45
Baeck, Leo, 23
Baerg, George, 128
Baerg, Gerhard, 137
Bagster-Collins, E. W., 128

Monatshefte Occasional Volumes

Series Editor
Reinhold Grimm
(University of California, Riverside)

Walter F. W. Lohnes and Valters Nollendorfs, editors
German Studies in the United States: Assessment and Outlook

Reinhold Grimm, Peter Spycher, and Richard A. Zipser, editors
From Dada to Kafka to Brecht and Beyond

Volker Dürr, Kathy Harms, and Peter Hayes, editors
Imperial Germany

Reinhold Grimm and Jost Hermand, editors
Blacks and German Culture

Reinhold Grimm and Jost Hermand, editors
Our Faust? *Roots and Ramifications of a Modern German Myth*

Volker Dürr, Reinhold Grimm, and Kathy Harms, editors
Nietzsche: Literature and Values

David P. Benseler, Walter F. W. Lohnes, and Valters Nollendorfs, editors
Teaching German in America: Prolegomena to a History

Reinhold Grimm and Jost Hermand, editors
From Ode to Anthem: Problems of Lyric Poetry

Reinhold Grimm and Jost Hermand, editors
From the Greeks to the Greens: Images of the Simple Life

Kathy Harms, Lutz R. Reuter, and Volker Dürr, editors
Coping with the Past: Germany and Austria after 1945

Reinhold Grimm and Jost Hermand, editors
Laughter Unlimited: Essays on Humor, Satire, and the Comic

Reinhold Grimm and Jost Hermand, editors
1914/1939: German Reflections of the Two World Wars

Reinhold Grimm and Jost Hermand, editors
Re-reading Wagner

Reinhold Grimm and Jost Hermand, editors
High and Low Cultures: German Attempts at Mediation

David P. Benseler, Craig W. Nickisch, and Cora Lee Nollendorfs, editors
Teaching German in Twentieth-Century America